TEXTBOOKS ON IS

Unsettling Colonialism in our Times

The **Unsettling Colonialism in Our Time**s series will publish books at the intersection of settler colonialism studies, decolonisation, and critiques of neoliberalism; illuminating the complex relationship between power and knowledge in the 21st Century.

It encourages research which has previously been studied as 'post-colonial' or as examples of successful 'end of history' processes of modernisation and westernisation to be viewed in light of the struggles for national liberation, democracy and human rights. The series will be a unique meeting point between new and established scholars who will engage with activist intellectual work concerning the welfare and future of the most oppressed communities in the world.

Series Editors

William Gallois, Director of Research at the Institute of Arab and Islamic Studies
Ilan Pappe, Professor of History; and Director of the European Centre for Palestine Studies
Both at University of Exeter, UK

Advisory Board

Lorenzo Veracini, Swinburne University of Technology in Melbourne, Australia
Robert J. C. Young, New York University
Eyal Weizmann, Goldsmiths
Ruba Salih, SOAS
Katsuya Hirano, UCLA
Angela Woollacott, Australian National University

TEXTBOOKS ON ISRAEL-PALESTINE

The Politics of Education and Knowledge in the West

Seyed Hadi Borhani
Assisstant Professor – University of Tehran

I.B. TAURIS
LONDON • NEW YORK • OXFORD • NEW DELHI • SYDNEY

I.B. TAURIS
Bloomsbury Publishing Plc
50 Bedford Square, London, WC1B 3DP, UK
1385 Broadway, New York, NY 10018, USA
29 Earlsfort Terrace, Dublin 2, Ireland

BLOOMSBURY, I.B. TAURIS and the I.B. Tauris logo are trademarks of Bloomsbury Publishing Plc

First published in Great Britain 2022
Paperback edition published 2023

Copyright © Seyed Hadi Borhani, 2022

Seyed Hadi Borhani has asserted his right under the Copyright, Designs and Patents Act, 1988, to be identified as Author of this work.

For legal purposes the Acknowledgements on p. xiii constitute an extension of this copyright page.

Series design by Toby Way
Cover image © Tom Werner/Getty Images

All rights reserved. No part of this publication may be reproduced or transmitted in any form or by any means, electronic or mechanical, including photocopying, recording, or any information storage or retrieval system, without prior permission in writing from the publishers.

Bloomsbury Publishing Plc does not have any control over, or responsibility for, any third-party websites referred to or in this book. All internet addresses given in this book were correct at the time of going to press. The author and publisher regret any inconvenience caused if addresses have changed or sites have ceased to exist, but can accept no responsibility for any such changes.

A catalogue record for this book is available from the British Library.

A catalog record for this book is available from the Library of Congress.

ISBN: HB: 978-1-3502-3308-9
       PB: 978-1-3502-3311-9
       ePDF: 978-1-3502-3309-6
       eBook: 978-1-3502-3310-2

Series: Unsettling Colonialism in our Times

Typeset by RefineCatch Limited, Bungay, Suffolk

To find out more about our authors and books visit www.bloomsbury.com and sign up for our newsletters.

'Those who tell the stories also rule society.'
Plato, *Republic*

CONTENTS

List of Illustrations	viii
Preface: A Personal Story	ix
Foreword by Professor Ilan Pappé	xi
Acknowledgements	xiii
Postscript: From that Thesis to this Book	xv
Prologue: A War on Western Textbooks	xix
INTRODUCTION	1
Chapter 1	
TEXTBOOKS AND THEORY	7
Chapter 2	
WESTERN TEXTBOOKS: PRO- OR ANTI-ISRAELI?	19
Chapter 3	
THE SURVEY OF COLLEGE TEXTBOOKS	47
Chapter 4	
ZIONIST NARRATION OF THE HISTORY	121
Chapter 5	
HOW COLLEGE TEXTBOOKS TREAT THE HISTORY?	131
Chapter 6	
WHO NARRATES THE HISTORY?	187
Conclusion	
WHAT WENT WRONG IN WESTERN TEXTBOOKS	203
References	215
Index	225

ILLUSTRATIONS

Figures

P.1	Palestinian loss of land 1946–2000	xix
4.1	The history as constructed by Zionism	129

Tables

2.1	List of the relevant literature	20
3.1	Frequencies of textbook adoptions on all extracted syllabi	55
3.2	The most adopted textbooks	56
3.3	How most adopted textbooks are taken on in different survey countries	56
3.4	The position of the six selected textbooks in all countries of the survey	57
3.5	All extracted syllabi from British universities	58
3.6	All extracted syllabi from Canadian universities	65
3.7	All extracted syllabi from Australian universities	70
3.8	All extracted syllabi from New Zealand universities	73
3.9	All extracted syllabi from Irish universities	75
3.10	All extracted syllabi from US universities	76
5.1	The framework for the textbook analysis	133
5.2	The results of the textbook analysis	182
6.1	The results of the context analysis	201
C.1	How theories of the history are treated in Western textbooks	209
C.2	The main questions of the thesis and its answers	212

Preface

A PERSONAL STORY

I doubt that my fascination with the Israel-Palestine question can be an accident. I began life the same day that Israel completed its occupation of historical Palestine! I have learnt this from my ID card, where 10 June 1967 is registered as my birth date.

I may have no recollection of that day in the 1960s, but I do remember my childhood in the 1970s when I started to read everything to hand about this question, mostly in newspapers. I was forbidden, then, to read them as my school grades began to decline due to this obsession. The only way to follow this passion was by buying, in secret, the cheap newspapers I could afford, and smuggling them into an isolated corner at home where I could read them far from my parents' watchful eyes.

It was during these days that Iran began its transformation from a pro-Western monarchy to a pro-Palestinian republic; the very first event of this revolution took place only a few metres away from my primary school, Daryush, in Qom. But it was my work in the Ministry of Foreign Affairs, much later in my life, that offered me the first opportunity to engage intellectually with the Israel-Palestine question. Early in my career at the ministry, I saw how everything that happens in the Middle East is affected by this question. Above all, what engaged me to the point of obsession was a perplexing paradox: how Western countries, the same countries that have established the widest and most influential civilization in history in all its post-Renaissance magnificence – its modern education, knowledge, democracy, rule of law and human rights in particular – could at the same time support such injustice in Israel-Palestine – a fundamental source of so much crime and misery in the Middle East.

The first chance to experience, directly, this question occurred when I participated in the 40th Graduate Study Programme (GSP) of the United Nations Office in Geneva in 2002. Many young college graduates came to this programme, most of them from Western countries. The participants had to prepare a report on the main international issues, including human rights, as their assignment in the course. This was an opportunity to raise the Israel-Palestine question. I wrote a statement about the racist aspect of Zionism, in line with the NGOs' position in the Durban Conference to Combat Racism (2001), and followed the drafting procedure from the original version in the team we had on human rights issues up through various levels, to that presented to the plenary session. The statement found its way finally into the concluding report of the programme but the way it was treated showed how the West can be different from what I expected it to be when it comes to Israel.

The same impression struck me when I made a similar contribution to the Fifth Annual Course on Arms Control and National Security (2003) in the Geneva

Centre for Security Policy (GCSP). Several lecturers came to this course to encourage the participants, all of them from Arab countries and Iran, to support a policy of disarmament. The possibly rash comments I made in the closing session about the dangers of such a unilateral policy in the absence of a similar policy in Israel began to look like committing an unforgivable sin. I am not still sure if this is related to the fact that, against all promises made, I have not received the course certificate, but this was, for sure, another event that made me aware of just how a critical view of Israel would be treated in the West, a treatment which seem at odds with the main characteristics of Western civilization.

These experiences, and similar ones, such as that of International Annual Course of the United Nations University in Tokyo (2006), for instance, convinced me that conducting research on this topic, and contributing to dialogue with Western societies about this anomaly might be the best contribution I could make in a better relationship between the West and the Middle East.

One of several attempts to apply for a PhD programme was accepted by the National University of Ireland, Galway (NUIG). I put forward an original proposal to conduct a comparative investigation into EU human rights policy towards some Middle Eastern countries including Iran and Israel, to demonstrate how the West, the EU in this case, ignores its own values and principles when it comes to Israel.

My path to further study didn't go according to expectation, and I had to sacrifice a lot, including my job in the ministry, to save my studies. My studies in Ireland itself didn't go well for different reasons. I learned, however, one significant lesson while struggling with my PhD project; the Western bias towards Israel is not limited to governments and politicians. More importantly, Western knowledge, the most respected part of Western civilization to my mind, is corrupted as well. This became obvious when governing textbooks in Western academia on the Israel-Palestine question were consulted to acquire the essential knowledge needed to inform my academic investigation.

This, I thought, is a much more significant subject for investigation regarding Western pro-Israeli bias. This realization coincided with my first encounter with Professor Ilan Pappé, who came to Dublin to speak about the Israeli invasion of Gaza in 2008-9. A link to this talk – which took place in Trinity College Dublin – had been sent by Tommy Donnellan, a well-known pro-Palestinian activist in Galway on 16 February 2009 at 21:39 when I was alone in the quiet of the PhD room in the NUIG. This email provided an unprecedented moment for me, not because I remained at my desk, on campus, till midnight to watch the video twice, and not for forwarding it to almost all my English-speaking contacts, but for the novel feeling I experienced, embedded in the subject of that forwarded email: 'I can love an Israeli, thank God!'

The days after this encounter were spent reading about this Israeli scholar and his works on the question. In this process of exploration, I found his email address. This address provided me the chance to contact him, express my ideas about the PhD project, and to ask for his supervision. The present research is a product of his welcoming reply and represents the subsequent transformation in my research topic under his guidance.

FOREWORD

By Professor Ilan Pappé

The struggle for peace and justice in historical Palestine is in many ways a struggle over knowledge and cognition. It stems from the very nature of the Zionist project in Palestine and the Palestinian response to it. It is a settler-colonial project that managed to build a settler-colonial state in historical Palestine. Seen from this angle, it is a conflict between settlers and an indigenous population. However, in many places and sites where knowledge is produced, a very different narrative is conveyed about the conflict. There, the dominant version of the narrative portrays the conflict as a process that began out of the blue between two very different national movements struggling for the same piece of land. One national movement, Zionism, is a Western, modern and democratic movement that is struggling against the other movement, a traditional Arab and Muslim national movement. Therefore, the best solution, which has been proffered both by scholarship and Western powers involved in 'the peace process', is to partition the land unevenly between the modern national movement, which will get more of everything including space, and the more primitive one, which will have to be content with less.

There are various ways in which a distorted narrative is being produced and maintained; through education, media, politics and propaganda. Defending such a narrative is also part and parcel of advocacy or lobbying on behalf of those who can benefit from this narrative. The research has so far neglected to investigate the role played by academia in producing a distorted narrative as a basis for a successful advocacy and lobbying campaign. In this respect, academia contributes to a version of historical events that has a huge influence on the lives of people and their well-being. Specifically, in the case of Palestine, this means the continuation of colonization, ethnic cleansing and occupation.

Academia supposedly provides non-biased professional information about the past and presents factual realities about places such as Palestine but, in fact, that is only when it does not contribute in the long run to misconceptions and distortions that are allegedly proven by scientific research.

The academia influences through modules that are based on textbooks. We learn a lot from the textbooks chosen by module conveners about the orientation of their approach to the Palestine question. No neutral approach is possible. There are clearly only two options; one that is based on the validity of the two narratives and one that views the same reality through the prism of a settler-colonial paradigm. The former would be similar to a course or module that would have argued during the heyday of Apartheid South Africa that there was both a legitimate anti-Apartheid narrative and a legitimate Apartheid narrative.

So how dominant is the two legitimate narratives approach or even that which firmly accepts the Zionist narrative over the Palestinian one? Until recently, the answer to these questions had been based on hunches and intuition. The book in front of us answers these questions methodically and systematically by examining major textbooks used in the teaching of modules and courses under titles such as the 'Arab-Israeli conflict'. It also tries to assess whether developments in the academic study of the Palestine question (such as the appearance of the 'new historians' in Israel) has had any influence on the curricula and textbooks in academia.

The results of this examination can be found in this fascinating research. They are important for understanding how much has changed in the way academia frames the situation in historical Palestine and how much has remained the same. What is beyond doubt is that analysing, researching and teaching 'Palestine' in academia is not merely an intellectual exercise taking place in the ivory towers of the scholarly world. That is because, despite its claim to independence and a professional scientific approach, academic works reflect hegemonic discourses and also have a role in changing them.

Since we expect academia and universities to play a critical role in our society (indeed a leading critical role), its rather submissive and at times timid input can be very disappointing. Where it does take the lead, it is surprisingly affecting and transformative.

Seyed Hadi Borhani looks methodically at the changes in the research and their impact on textbooks and curricula, which is the only proper way of assessing the role that academia has played and can play in bringing justice to a place and people that the West has helped to destroy whilst not yet acknowledging its moral responsibility for both the catastrophe and the ways of rectifying it.

ACKNOWLEDGEMENTS

The journey paved for conducting this research was not even and straightforward. Serious difficulties presented themselves which were a severe test of my resilience and fortitude. A happy ending has not been achieved as a result of solitary resistance; much assistance was given to make it possible, for all of which I am very grateful.

First of all, I wish to thank my supervisor, Professor Ilan Pappé, a brave scholar who has devoted his life to providing much-needed knowledge about the criminal occupation of Palestine, and its ethnic cleansing.

Except my supervisor, no one else made a concrete contribution to the content of this thesis. But I should mention three names of people who offered invaluable help for other aspects of completing this piece of work; I am indebted to Dr Marina Williamson for her generous and dedicated support. She kindly edited the whole original thesis. I have also enjoyed the intellectual dialogue I had with my intelligent friend, Dr Barbara Heisserer, when I was developing the first proposal for the thesis. I have had few chances to see and interact with Professor Shlomo Sand but his remarks and his books, *The Invention of the Jewish People* in particular, were a supreme source of information and inspiration for my research.

I was fortunate in having so many generous people around who were ready to help; I should mention and thank Mr Afzal Hasan, Subject Librarian in the Forum Library of Exeter University; Jim Jackson, St Luke's Library Supervisor; and Professor Christopher Lovett in Emporia State University. This is a chance also to thank the staff of several libraries I have visited and used to complete the original thesis: St Luke's Library, the Forum Library, SOAS Library, College Lane Library in the University of Hertfordshire, and Amir Al Momenin Mosque Library in Tehran. I am also thankful to The Open Library for the services I have received online. The staff in the Institute of the Arab and Islamic Studies and SSIS Graduate Research School in Streatham were more than helpful, a kindness which I am thankful for.

I had the privilege of knowing wonderful friends during this journey who were a great source of help in one way or another. I cannot finish this acknowledgement without including their names: Professor Ray Murphy, Seyed Mohsen Nabavi, Dr Siamak Tavakoli, Mohammed Mahdavi Ashraf, Dr Oliver Feeney, Afrasiab Mohammadnejad, Dr Seyed Ali Mahmoudi, Beata Faracik, Ali Mossadegh, Dr Eilis Ward, Dr Mark Haugaard, Haydar Alkhafaji, Professor Chris Curtin, Dr Marilyn Moylan, Dr Brendan Flynn, Mohammad Abutalebi, Zarengiz Karimova, Dr Martina Timmermann, Samantha Borders, Dr Marc Valeri, Dr Mansour Rahmani, Dr Nasrin Mosaffa, Dr Amir Hosein Zamaninia and Dr Lisa Moran. The support I have received came from more friends, indeed. There is no chance to name all of them but I am very grateful for having their friendship and treasured support.

The main support for my efforts to research and write this text came from my family. They were with me before anyone else, and all the way from the beginning to the end, and in the most difficult phases. My father was a main supporter. Without him and his assistance, I could not have completed this research. My loving mother was a fabulous source of support and help. I also owe a huge thank you to my children Yasaman and Amir Salman. I might have been a better and more accessible father had I not been busy with this burdensome research. My special thanks go to a key companion who supported me all the way and through the most difficult times. For her wonderful kindness and the huge sacrifice, she made I dedicate this piece of work to my wife and the true angel of this journey, Aseel.

Postscript

FROM THAT THESIS TO THIS BOOK

This book comes from an academic thesis. The very first idea on transforming that thesis to a publishable monograph has been offered at the viva session by Professor Haim Bresheeth, then a member of the examination board. After passing the exam, a short while was needed to revise the text for completing the PhD project in the European Centre for Palestine Studies at the University of Exeter. Soon after, some measures were taken to follow Haim's idea. A principal step was communicating with those historians whom I dare to analyse in the project. The six textbooks analysed in the dissertation had been scripted by eight prominent historians. The analysis, conducted in the project, not only criticized, seriously if not harshly, their historiography, but scrutinized their background and their personal capacity to produce an unbiased history of the Israel-Palestine question.

An email address was all one need for such communication in the internet era; a search allowed me to have six email addresses out of the eight I was looking for. No email address was located, in that search, for Laqueur and Rubin. A letter has been sent – with 'Analysis of your book in my PhD dissertation' as its subject – to those six historians I was able to contact. It was explained briefly, in that letter, what had been done in the PhD project, expressing my intention to convert the thesis to a publishable book. A request was made in this letter, as well, for any comment they might have about the work.

Four replies were received; none from Smith and Morris. A delivery error was received when Morris was emailed. Having no reply from Smith, however, was a real misfortune since the analysis I have conducted introduces his history as the only, relatively, unbiased one in the whole project. But this misery has been compensated, at least partly, by some positive responses; the most encouraging one came from Professor Mark Tessler, a former president (1989–91) of the Association for Israel Studies in the United States. He described the work, in this reply, as a 'very solid and useful contribution'. His considerate engagement with the work also resulted in uncovering two factual errors; one weakened the study's argument and one strengthened it. When conducting an analysis about the historians' background, I ranked Mark as a Christian historian. He was Jewish! He, himself, corrected this. Based on the same analysis, Smith was a historian with no (good) command of the Arabic language. Tessler corrected the text again: Charles Smith knows Arabic. I know him well. 'There may not be other factual errors, and even if there are a few, this would not reduce the value of the work', he kindly concluded. Other replies were welcoming, polite and professional. I have not felt, from the text of those responses, a serious kind of unhappiness except in one case.

The original thesis, on which this book is based, was presented in 2015. Six years later in 2021, while working through the publication schedule, two main questions are valid to ask before closing this section. First: how relevant is this study – and its results – for a world we live in now, in 2021? And second: what has happened in this specific area of academic knowledge since 2015?

First of all, the centre of the main analysis, in this study, is located in the pre-Zionist era of Israel-Palestine history, mainly ancient Israel. For a time that far off, and a subject so popular to examine, a few years should not bring about a noticeable difference in the relevant knowledge. The only reasonable possibility, for missing something serious in that period, is new editions of the question's history popping up, capable of making a meaningful change in the top-ranked popular textbooks. New history books have been offered, in recent years, in the same area of academic endeavour; indeed, some of them become popular – Rashid Khalidi's book *The Hundred Years' War on Palestine: A History of Settler Colonialism and Resistance*, for instance.

As a result, a quick survey has been conducted to find out if there is any sign of change in the textbook adoption list. The best evidence has been located, in this survey, is a research report published as a working paper by Moshe Dayan Center for Middle Eastern and African Studies in Tel Aviv University (Mueller and Rabi 2017).

This research project involved a survey to explore the most adopted college textbooks in the same area of knowledge, the Israel-Palestine question. The methodology used by this research is very similar to mine; they also extracted syllabi of college courses – about a hundred syllabi from anglophone universities – to determine which textbooks are adopted most. The survey results brought about a list of top textbooks in this area (Mueller and Rabi 2017: 10), as follows:

- *A History of the Arab-Israeli Conflict* by Ian Bickerton and Carla Klausner
- *The Palestinian-Israeli Conflict: A Very Short Introduction* by Martin Bunton
- *The Israel-Palestine Conflict: One Hundred Years of War* by James Gelvin
- *Righteous Victims: A History of the Zionist-Arab Conflict* by Benny Morris
- *A History of Modern Palestine: One Land, Two Peoples* by Ilan Pappé
- *Palestine and the Arab-Israeli Conflict* by Charles Smith
- *A History of the Israeli-Palestinian Conflict* by Mark Tessler.

This list, which comes years later than mine, is very similar to what I already had; the only serious difference is Gelvin's book (*The Israel-Palestine Conflict*). This textbook came up as a popular source in my survey as well but not in the first-six list. Another difference, Bunton's book (*The Palestinian-Israeli Conflict: A Very Short Introduction*) is not an academic textbook, based on the criteria I adopted to recognize such resources. Concerning Pappé's popular textbook (*A History of Modern Palestine*), I have also elaborated in my research, that I have chosen to set aside Pappé's works due to his position as my supervisor, and I affirmed there that Pappé's works are only critical histories of the question that have a chance to be in the top textbooks of the field.

Other pieces of evidence support the idea that the top textbook list produced in my original thesis is still relevant and valid. New editions of these textbooks were published just recently: ninth and tenth editions of Smith's book (*Palestine and the Arab-Israeli Conflict*) were released in 2017 and 2021. Bickerton's book (*A History of the Arab-Israeli Conflict*) came out in its seventh and eighth editions in 2016 and 2017. Laqueur's book (*The Arab-Israeli Reader*) also celebrated its eighth edition in 2016. The first editions of these textbooks were published a long time ago, decades back in some cases. They were quite successful in maintaining their top position as a reference source for many years or decades. This fact supports their solid position, in the top-six list, not only for the present time but also for many years to come.

Their citation rate, also, introduces another piece of evidence. I have recorded each textbook's citation rate in Google Scholar in the original thesis. For the sake of this Postscript, I consulted Google Scholar again; the number of citations for the selected textbooks have almost doubled in this period, from 356 to 797 in the case of Tessler's book, for instance. In conclusion, the evidence and information I have encountered in this brief follow-up survey allow me to claim that the original list of top textbooks is still valid for today's universities in the Western anglophone countries, and all the textbooks I analysed in my thesis are still among the most adopted textbooks for courses related to Israel-Palestine history in Western anglophone universities.

Now we can deal with the second question of this Postscript: what has happened in this specific area of academic knowledge since then? Another survey was been conducted, in late 2020 and early 2021, to explore all academic works that deal with the same subject, i.e. analysing college textbooks that are used for teaching the history of Israel-Palestine question, and only one reference popped up! It is the working paper that I have mentioned already, 'A Critical Survey of Textbooks on The Arab-Israeli and Israeli-Palestinian Conflict' by Moshe Dayan Center for Middle Eastern and African Studies in Tel Aviv University. The centre introduces the project, and articulates its purpose: 'we designed a year-long research project to identify the textbooks that are most commonly used to teach about the Arab-Israeli or Israeli-Palestinian conflict, analyse those textbooks and compare them to a set of criteria designed to assess the quality of history textbooks' (Mueller and Rabi 2017: 6). This study was conducted by a team of three research assistants and interns, authored by Dr Chelsi Mueller (a research fellow in the centre) and Uzi Rabi (the director of the centre), and reviewed by Prof. Asher Susser, professor emeritus of Middle Eastern history at Tel Aviv University.

This research, in its literature review, came to the same conclusion as my thesis in relation to studies conducted in the same area of academic analysis – needless to mention its failure to locate my research, published two years earlier. The authors provide an explanation for this phenomenon:

> Until now, there has been no attempt to compare the relative strengths and weaknesses of textbooks that are used to teach about the Arab-Israeli or Israeli-Palestinian conflict in Anglophone colleges and universities. This lacuna can, to a large extent, be owing to the political minefield surrounding the politics of the conflict. While college level textbooks have not been the subject of dedicated

critique, there has been no dearth of research on textbooks. A brief survey of the relevant literature on textbook research will show that most studies have been conducted on elementary and high school textbooks.

Mueller and Rabi 2017: 6

This academic research, after identifying the most adopted textbooks, conducted a content analysis to examine selected textbooks' contents in relation to the Israel-Palestine question. The results of this analysis are reviewed and reflected in Chapter 5 of this book, where my own textbook analysis takes place. It was quite interesting and surprising that this Israeli-based research, which is taken from a different perspective, supports many results of my own analysis of those textbooks. This idea is elaborated in detail, with related pieces of evidence, in the final part of Chapter 5.

Prologue

A WAR ON WESTERN TEXTBOOKS

Let us start this Prologue with a popular map of Palestine, a map that illustrates the Palestinian loss of land (and, in return, the Zionist gain of land) since Zionist conquest in 1946 (Figure P.1).

This map shows the most basic facts, in the area of land control, since Zionists' interest in Palestine. Simply, if one had four aerial photographs of the area in mentioned dates, i.e. in 1946, 1947, 1967 and 2000, and the photos were capable of recognizing Palestinian land from Jewish/Israeli land, this map (and this fact) would be visible to all eyes. Such photos may not be accessible but there are plenty of

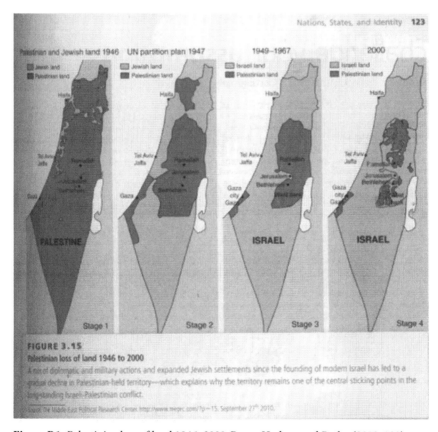

Figure P.1 Palestinian loss of land 1946–2000. Boyer, Hudson and Butler (2013: 123).

documents – Ottoman, British, Palestinian and even Israeli – that can establish this mapping of the area. If one dares to ignore all those documents and pieces of evidence – that can introduce a clear, transparent and factual history of the land about its control – what we have now on the ground is sufficient for establishing those facts, and forming those images; almost every single human-made structure in the land (which is controlled by Israel today), that belongs to pre-Zionist era, is Arab and Palestinian. This includes all buildings, monuments, remaining walls and even old olive trees. Nothing non-Arab could be located on the ground in the whole geography of Palestine (from the river to the sea) and for a long history of a thousand years or more – before Zionist era of the land, of course. Few, less than ten thousand Jews who lived in Palestine before Zionism – who were free to construct their own structure, homes and synagogues for instance – were also Arab and Palestinian, i.e. they spoke Arabic and considered themselves nothing but Palestinian. If there is anything non-Arab on the ground, Roman or Ottoman structures, for instance, they have nothing to do with a presumed historical Jewish domination of the land. This survey of manmade materials, in terms of its Arab (or non-Arab) origins, can establish a pre-Zionist map of Palestine – as an Arabian territory, no less Arab than other Arabian countries, if not more than many. Similar surveys about manmade materials created in other historical periods of the land, in 1946, 1947, and following ones, can establish other relevant maps of the land. This type of mapping, if outlined today, is able to demonstrate the factual quality of the discussed maps.

A Western college-level textbook, *Global Politics: Engaging a Complex World*, risked reproducing this map (Boyer, Hudson and Butler 2013: 123). The textbook, which is used for teaching political science to undergraduate students, is published by McGraw-Hill Education and authored by a team of prominent scholars including Mark Boyer, Professor of Geography at the University of Connecticut; Natalie Hudson, Associate Professor of Political Science at the University of Dayton; and Michael Butler, Associate Professor of Political Science at Clark University. Soon after its publication, pro-Israeli parties attacked the book – and its publishing house – calling it 'anti-Israeli' and 'inaccurate' (Jaschik 2016). The pro-Israeli attack was successful – similar to the case of controlling the land in Palestine – in eradicating the book, and its map, from academia. The real result of this victorious pressure can be seen best in a statement made by a spokesperson for McGraw-Hill Education, Catherine Mathis:

> As soon as we learned about the concerns with it, we placed sales of the book on hold and immediately initiated an academic review. The review determined that the map did not meet our academic standards. We have informed the authors and we are no longer selling the book. All existing inventory will be destroyed. We apologize and will refund payment to anyone who returns the book.
>
> Jaschik 2016

Pro-Israeli campaign against textbooks critical of Israel is not limited to this single case; a war is waged against Western textbooks by these forces. There are numerous instances of such assaults; a Belgian textbook of geography was successfully attacked in 2018, and its anti-Israeli content, a caricature displaying inequality in water distribution between Israelis and Palestinians in the West Bank (an idea supported by international human rights groups including Amnesty International) removed from the book (Eichner 2018).

In another case, Israel condemned a Dutch textbook for its 'anti-Israeli' content after attacking that book by pro-Israeli groups (JTA 2015). The textbook, *Geschiedenis werkplaats [History Workplace]*, published by Noordhoff, is used to teach history to high school students in the Netherlands. Another case is a high school textbook in Tennessee, in the United States. The textbook, *The Cultural Landscape: An Introduction to Human Geography*, is criticized for asking students a challenging question: 'If a Palestinian suicide bomber kills several dozen teenagers in a Jerusalem restaurant, is that an act of terrorism or wartime retaliation against Israeli government policies and army actions?' (Serrie 2013). A British textbook, *English as a Second Language*, is another instance in this respect (Miller 2015).

There are more cases of successful pro-Israeli assaults on history textbooks in Britain: *Understanding History: Britain in the Wider World, Roman Times–Present* a secondary school textbook published in 2019 by a British educational publisher, Hodder Education, was removed from sale after such assault. The Board of Deputies of British Jewry outraged by a question asked in the book, calling it 'dangerous' (JNS 2020). The question is asked in a section on the Israel-Palestine question, and in dealing with 'Muslim mistrust of the West': 'How could it be argued that the creation of Israel was a long-term cause of the 9/11 attacks?' The board's vice-president, Edwin Shuker, justified the attack: 'It invites the students to find a link between the creation of Israel and the 9/11 terrorist attacks, which feeds into a prevalent anti-Semitic conspiracy theory'. After that attack, Hodder Education made a statement asserting: 'We appreciate the phrasing of the question is not as precise as it might have been, and we are very sorry for any offence this has caused. We have removed the book from sale, we will have the content reviewed and will then reissue a revised version' (JNS 2020).

Another attack on Hodder Education publications resulted in the removal of another British history textbook: *Conflict in the Middle East: 1945–95*, a GCSE textbook on Israel-Palestine question, was attacked by a pro-Israeli organization, UK Lawyers for Israel (UKLFI), for 'a number of inaccuracies and a general lack of context within the book, leading overall to a lop-sided presentation of the Arab-Israeli conflict to British school children' (Edmunds 2020). Calling assassination of a British official by Jewish agents as a terrorist act in the textbook, for instance, is criticized in the UKLFI report: 'The judgmental term "terrorism" may be employed in the news industry, but it is misplaced in history lessons. Its meaning – still not clearly defined nowadays – changed through history. It is disputable whether attempts to assassinate the British High Commissioner (a senior figure in an oppressive colonial administration) constitutes an act of terrorism or of violent struggle for national liberation' (Edmunds 2020). This case of pro-Israeli assault on Western textbooks has resulted in another happy ending according to Caroline Turner (UKLFI's director) who cheered Hodder's resolution to pull the book from the market: 'It is very important that children learning about this complex subject are taught in a balanced and accurate manner. We are pleased that another misleading and inaccurate school textbook, purporting to teach about Middle East history, is being withdrawn and reconsidered' (Edmunds 2020).

Another history textbook, *The Middle East: Conflict, Crisis and Change, 1917–2012*, was removed after a similar assault. Pro-Israeli blogger, David Collier, who examined the book, came to a clear conclusion: 'central messages are those that you would find inside an anti-Israel propaganda book' (Chandler 2020). Pearson, the publisher of this GCSE textbook, rejected the allegation of anti-Israeli bias in the book but pulled the book from the market. A spokesman for Pearson explained this decision: 'An independent review of the texts by an educational charity found no overall evidence of anti-Israel bias. It identified some areas where the balance of sources could be improved and we are updating the texts and offering existing customers the option of replacing them for free' (Chandler 2020).

These attacks are not limited to the UK. Other Western countries have also been scenes of such successful attacks. One book, *The Trouble with Textbooks: Distorting History and Religion*, published in the United States, and authored by Gary Tobin, former President of the Institute for Jewish and Community Research in San Francisco, and Dennis R. Ybarra, who analyse numerous American school textbooks, concludes that American textbooks are suffering from anti-Israeli, pro-Arab and pro-Islam bias (Tobin and Ybarra 2008).

The pro-Israeli assault on 'alternative knowledge' – a term I have used in my writing since 2015 (starting with an article titled 'Palestine Studies in Western Academia: Shifting a Paradigm?') to articulate a piece of knowledge that competes with the pro-Israeli one in providing the truth about the Israel-Palestine question – is not limited to textbooks but it includes textbook writers and critical scholars as well. If one opens this dossier of pro-Israeli activities, another long story of successful pro-Israeli assaults on Western academia begins; stories of those scholars, university professors and writers who were attacked by pro-Israeli parties because of their different ideas – different from pro-Israeli ones – of the Israel-Palestine question. Many of these attacks – like those on Western textbooks – have been very successful in silencing them, destroying their positions and even dismissing them from their academic positions. A book, *Out of Bounds: Academic Freedom and the Question of Palestine*, was published by Bloomsbury Academic in 2014 in this regard. The book deals with a few cases of pro-Israeli assault on prominent scholars of the field including Norman Finkelstein, Edward Said and Noam Chomsky (Abraham 2014). It conducts a systemic investigation on how those scholars are pressured, for their ideas about Israel-Palestine questions, by pro-Israeli forces. The author of the book, Matthew Abraham, finds this phenomenon at odds with academic freedom in Western academia (Abraham 2014). The book is a remarkable contribution for raising the question, for the first time, through a systematic investigation but it is not an inclusive source of related cases; it deals only with few (three indeed) in the United States.

Unfortunately, there is no exhaustive investigation that can show the real dimensions of this phenomenon in all Western countries. There are, here and there, news reports about such effective activities by pro-Israeli forces in various Western countries. These successful operations are broadcasted proudly by bodies that support Israel (and attack on its behalf), and a simple search through their online databases can demonstrate that it includes so many cases, probably a record number in attacking academic scholars in the West; I know of no academic subject matter that registers a higher number of such attacks on academics in the Western academia. A PhD study, titled 'Academic Freedom: Costs, Consequences, and Resistance', conducted by Mary E. Husain at the University of California, Davis – presents a noticeable and alarming conclusion on this subject:

> With two exceptions (Juan Cole and Mehrene Larudee) virtually all of the academics I spoke with [altogether she spoke with thirty-two American academics] were attacked based on their work related to Israel/Palestine in one or more of the following categories: publications (academic and/or popular press), public film screenings or talks (including lectures, rallies and/or teach-ins), or classroom teaching. Criticism of Israeli policies, in combination with an insidious racism, was the overarching theme or catalyst driving the attacks which connected the narratives.
>
> Husain 2010: 156

When conducting my PhD project at the University of Exeter (where my supervisor, Professor Ilan Pappé, was receiving death threats from pro-Israeli callers, and had a guard to protect him on the campus) I came across this phenomenon. The information I found on this matter, encouraged me to write an article in this field (titled 'Palestine Studies in Western Academia: Shifting a Paradigm?'). The main argument of this article was about alternative knowledge on the Israel-Palestine question and its successful move to challenge the pro-Israeli one, and its chance to enter the mainstream area in Western academia. The pro-Israeli side needs badly, the article argues, to do something about this development, to keep the pro-Israeli knowledge in its current position, and to force alternative knowledge and its producers away from the mainstream in the Western academic institutions (Borhani 2015). Several policies are advanced by them to get this done. The main part of this article, titled 'Counter Attack' is devoted to investigating the pro-Israeli attacks on alternative knowledge, mainly in the United States. The article finds:

> the vocabulary used by supporters of the pro-Israeli paradigm, for instance, to address the alternative knowledge, if not exceptional, does not represent the conventional language employed for an academic debate; no legitimate place is considered for the alternative knowledge; there is no sign of recognizing the alternative account as another part of the debate; there is no genuine attempt to enter a scholarly dialogue with the other. Almost all terms used to address the alternative knowledge characterise it as an illegitimate/wrong undertaking: 'Propagandistic,' 'dangerous,' 'genocidal,' 'dissemination of hate and violence,' 'serving the enemy' and 'anti-Semitic' are just some instances. The terminology

used suggests that an attempt to destroy the very chance of the alternative knowledge to exist is a key function of pro-Israeli side when dealing with the alternative account.

Borhani 2015: 145

My article mentions other instances of pro-Israeli assaults, recalling a conference held by Israel's foreign ministry – the 4th International Conference of the Global Forum for Combating Antisemitism – that regularly monitors anti-Israel developments:

the serious challenge posed by the alternative knowledge is taken, in the conference, as a 'propaganda' and also 'psychological' war against Israel; 'College campuses, as well as the academic and intellectual environment have ... become the frontline of the propaganda war against Israel and the Jewish people. Israel is increasingly delegitimized and demonized on campus and also within more course curriculum' ('Mission Statements' 2013)

Borhani 2015: 141

There is also a reference, in the conference, to Professor Manfred Gerstenfeld's call 'for the Israeli government to combat delegitimization "as military and cyber wars are fought," with Mossad the "logical candidate" to be assigned as "the focal point to fight this war" … Another contribution in the conference, Small, proposed 'name and shame' to make scholars attacking Israel pay the price' (Borhani 2015: 141–2).

My article also mentions a book published in 2007: *Academics Against Israel and the Jews*. The main message of this publication can be seen in the book's foreword by Nathan Sharansky:

Anti-Semites succeeded in murdering six million Jews only after significant parts of the supposedly enlightened world accepted as a matter of fact that Jews were dangerous and inferior beings. Genocide became legitimate when this attitude permeated universities, the intelligentsia, and other elites.

Against this historical background, the inroads of the anti-Israeli campaign into the Western academic world are extremely worrying. The infrastructure for future crimes or even genocide is being laid by ideologists at universities of the free world.

Gerstenfeld 2007: 13

Students are stimulated, my article adds, to challenge scholars who do not approach the subject matter from the perspective of the pro-Israeli paradigm. They are educated to regard such an approach as 'biased' and 'illegitimate' treatment or a case of misusing academic freedom. 'In this way, they ring fence a narrow area of opinion such as that of legitimate teaching so that a teacher risks being accused of illegitimate conduct such as anti-Semitism, political activism, supporting terrorism or sympathising with Islamism if he just differs from the pro-Israeli paradigm' (Borhani 2015: 135).

Another example, mentioned in the article, is a warning by a pro-Israeli body, the Jewish Civil Rights Group; this group issued a warning to hundreds of university and college presidents around the United States that their schools may be subject to civil and criminal liability over what is called anti-Israel hate on their campuses (IMRA 2011).

These attacks are coordinated by numerous pro-Israeli bodies. The article mentions some of them; some institutes are established whose prime mission is monitoring universities and lecturers to detect what is called anti-Israeli scholarship that includes Campus Watch; Israel Academia Monitor; IsraCampus; Scholars for Peace in the Middle East; Israel Campus Roundtable; The Academic Friends of Israel; Engage; Stand with Us; Israel on Campus Coalition; The David Project; American-Israeli Cooperative Enterprise and Students for Academic Freedom (SAF). But there are other bodies whose prime mission was something different but they are also involved in this endeavour in recent years: AIPAC, CAMERA, the American Jewish Committee, the Anti-Defamation League, the David Project and the B'nai B'rith Hillel Foundation, for instance (Borhani 2015: 128–9). My article's analysis is based on a limited project, mainly in the United States, and does not cover what is really happening in the West in this regard. This might represent only a tip of an iceberg, whose real size is unknown to us today. Unfortunately, there is no independent investigation about the real dimensions of this phenomenon in the West. We only know, via news reports, that there is something serious. We would not be able to grasp the whole story without such a thorough investigation in which the current literature lacks.

The most striking point in this story is the fact that this all is not happening in an isolated corner of the world, is not happening in remote African countries or in my part of the world, the Middle East. It is happening in the heart of the free part of the world! In the West, and right at the centre of academic freedom.

This miserable story about Western knowledge on the Israel-Palestine question has two main sides. One side has just been mentioned: alternative knowledge and non-Zionist scholars are not allowed to enjoy the academic freedom that exists for others in the West. They are removed from mainstream media or formal education. Established facts, simple questions, factual statements about main developments of the question – even those that are taken place just recently in the modern history of the region (within the last few decades), and even those that are established on the abundance of evidence – are prohibited from the debate if they do not match the Zionist narrative of the question.

But this is not the whole story. There is another side, probably a more important one: historical fictions (not facts) about what happened two, three or even four thousand years ago – when the plane alphabet was not at hand for writing historical reports for instance, when a single written document reporting the events was not available, as the world was almost in its prehistorical period – are produced in the mainstream media, in the governing textbooks of academic institutions, as established and undisputed facts. Is there a better title to describe this abnormality than upside-down historiography?

This study is conducted to demonstrate, through a systematic analysis, the second side of the above-mentioned question: how disputed claims or sheer fictions, about the history of the Israel-Palestine question, are introduced as established facts in the most popular history textbooks that are used to teach in Western universities. Based on the results of this analysis, these textbooks are not just biased, pro-Israeli and inaccurate (if not actually lying) but they also utterly mislead college students about the history of the question. They make Western students believe and trust in what is not a trustable and factual history. They pass on such biased and misleading history to justify and legitimize the illegal occupation of Palestine.

A sample of the most popular college-level textbooks on the history of the Israel-Palestine question has been selected, through an extensive survey, to represent relevant Western knowledge. The selected textbooks have been analysed through a method of historical narrative analysis against a pro-Israeli structure of the question's history. The immediate contexts of the histories produced, the relevant historians and their background, are analysed to answer the second part of the key question of the research: How do Western college-level textbooks treat the history of the Israel-Palestine question and why do they treat the question in that way?

The results of the first analysis, a textbook analysis, support the conclusion that textbook knowledge on the question is mainly pro-Israeli in bias. This knowledge is regarded as biased not only for reproducing the main elements of the Zionist historiography but, more importantly, for introducing these contested claims as established facts. In relation to the question *why*, the analysis offers the Jewish pro-Israeli producer as the main factor that can explain that bias in the products.

The textbook analysis I conducted, and its results, may remind one of the pro-Israeli analysis of Western textbooks, mentioned at the beginning of this Prologue – David Collier's analysis of *The Middle East: Conflict, Crisis and Change*, for instance. It is not difficult to imagine if my analysis, like Collier's, was a pro-Israeli work, this book could shake all those who were involved in producing the analysed textbooks, including publishers and writers. If this was a pro-Israeli analysis, soon after its publishing an army of pro-Israeli forces would come to the field, to coordinate a powerful and, probably, successful attack against 'biased textbooks'. The analysed textbooks could be labelled as propaganda books, dangerous narratives of history, misleading historiographies, anti-Israeli or antisemitic versions of history, distorted narratives, a pack of historiographical lies, fundamentalist mythologies, unacademic, non-scientific and so on. Such labels are used, by the pro-Israeli forces, to attack the textbooks, and to blackmail parties complicit in committing an unforgivable crime: producing non-Zionist histories.

In such a situation, things can go in two different directions. If the parties attacked, like the publishers mentioned in this chapter, are aware of pro-Israeli power and its capacity to retaliate and damage, they take a rational position to find a safe side and survive; they take those objections seriously, they order a thorough review of the books, they stop selling the books until the reviews' results are in. The results of such reviews have a known pattern now, thanks to reports of similar cases that have just been mentioned in this Prologue: apology (including for any inconvenience), removing the book from the market or changing its 'inaccurate' or 'imbalanced' content.

But things can go in a different direction as well. If the parties under attack, writers, for instance, ignore the pro-Israeli objections, and stress the Western principle of academic freedom, and the idea that knowledge should be free from the influence of powerful parties, they might end up with a different destiny. There are again a handful of cases of such scholars and academic writers who dare to resist pro-Israeli pressure and who pay the price. The list of those who lost their academic positions or deprived of credits that other academics enjoy in Western academia is not be a short one.

But, thank God, this analysis is not a pro-Israeli analysis! As a result, it is expected that none of those problems and troubles will bother anyone. Peace and calm are guaranteed to continue at its current pace. For the publishers and writers of the analysed biased textbooks, there is nothing to be worried about. This makes it easy for anyone who wishes, to reveal, freely, what they know about the pro-Israeli bias of Western textbooks.

INTRODUCTION

The question of Israel-Palestine, as an issue, occupies a significant position in world politics. For decades now, daily news about this question constitutes a persistent part of the world headlines. No other controversial topic, arguably, has reached such a position. Another important political topic, which should be seen in tandem with this one, is the support Israel has been receiving from the West. Alongside the news about current affairs, which often illustrates the different treatment of Israel by Western countries, the history of the question, also, introduces a wealth of facts that refer to the momentous contribution of the West in helping the realization of Zionist objectives in Palestine, including the establishment of a Jewish state (see for instance Lewan 1975; Bain 1979; Bercuson 1985; Pappé 1988; Mulhall 1995; Mendes 2009).

This important support – which has been described as one of two main factors contributing to the survival of Israel, together with its military superiority to its Arab neighbours (Kermani 2006) – has been analysed by a number of researchers through different academic disciplines including history, international relations, politics, international law, economics, mass media and cinema (see for instance Feldman 1984; Reich 1984; Organski 1990; Ben-Zvi 1993; Bard and Pipes 1997; Chomsky 1999; Allin and Simon 2003; Merkley 2004; Stephens 2004; Gvosdev 2006; Petras 2006; Stephens 2006; Mearsheimer and Walt 2008; Roth 2009; Cronin 2011; Shaheen 2009). Various explanations have emerged from the findings of this body of research, which answer the question of why the West treats the issue in this particular way, by introducing some relevant factors such as national interests, economic interests, security considerations, strategic interests, European guilt over and moral responsibility for a history of Jewish massacres in Europe, or the influence of the Israel lobby in Western capitals.

The relevant literature explored on Western support of Israel, alas, shows no sign of approaching the subject through an empirical analysis on the academic treatment of the Israel-Palestine question. This area, comparable to other areas of the Western treatment of Israel, could be a platform for pro-Israeli parties to bring about a similar bias. If so, is there a legitimate ground for establishing the same idea of Western support for Israel, this time, in how (Western) academic knowledge treats the question? In other words, is the knowledge produced in the West (about the question) influenced by pro-Israeli forces that work, effectively, in other areas?

Trying to deal with that gap in the relevant literature, the main objective of this research, therefore, is to analyse academic knowledge on the Palestine-Israel question in Western academia. This subject seems important for more than one reason: first, it can contribute to advancing a more inclusive notion of the idea of Western support of Israel, and its real dimensions, by highlighting another aspect of Western pro-Israeli bias; second, it addresses a question that can reveal relevant points about the causes of such a tendency in Western policy. This case is related to the influential role that knowledge plays in social and political affairs in Western democracies. Third, Western knowledge on the question is important not only for its impact on Western societies; it can occupy a dominant position, similar to many other bodies of knowledge that come from the West, across a worldwide spectrum. This capacity to inform a much wider audience in the world makes its impact important on a global scale.

There are further characteristics, two at least, that make this subject even more fascinating:

1. It deals with a significant controversy about the Western countries' position on Israel. This position appears as a matter that separates the West from the rest of the world in many areas, specifically in world politics. A quick look at the pattern of the votes of Western countries in the United Nations General Assembly on issues related to Israel-Palestine can illustrate this (Gilman 2000: 15).
2. Another matter that differentiates the West from the rest (of the world) is the Western attitude towards knowledge and scientific research. It is contended that one main element that contributed heavily to establishing the very nature of the West, as a modern civilization, providing it with a chance to present itself as a different and developed part of the world, is rooted in its relatively effective efforts to detach knowledge from non-scientific interruptions, religious and political in particular. Academic treatment of the Israel-Palestine question might appear more momentous if it represents a major failure to respect this Western standard.

This introduction, before ending, deals with two other introductory items; the methodology of the research and the overall structure of the book.

Methodology: The Way this Study Takes to Answer its Main Question

As mentioned earlier, this research is designed to answer a central question; 'How do Western college-level textbooks treat the history of the Israel-Palestine question and why do they treat the question in that way?' The way this study takes to answer that question (the methodological property of the research) including the method used and selection of the sample, is elaborated below.

Method Used

There are various ways that textbooks are analysed. Historical narrative analysis is used as the central method in this research. This method, in comparison to others, has a competitive capacity to capture the key elements of a given history: historical narrative analysis is concerned primarily with how (a given) history is narrated or how the main story (of a given history) is told; how the story begins and where it ends, the sequence of events; what is mentioned; what is omitted; what is emphasized or what is undermined; and other matters that are related to the central elements of the story that a given history is developed for (Pearcy 2011: 60–1). Historical narrative analysis, as a novel approach to examining history, focuses on a given history as a whole rather than on its parts. The central stress, in this analysis, has moved away from the portrayal of distinct historical 'facts' to how the whole history is presented, or how the mega story is structured. It is argued that the meaning of the 'facts' produced in a certain history is dependent on how they are placed in an overall story. The rhetoric is considered ineffective if not reinforced by a structure to support it. It is revealed that such structure comes from the main ideological positions that historians take towards history. There is an emphasis, in this methodology, on the role historians play in constructing historical knowledge (Vanhulle 2009). A shift is advocated in this analysis from focusing on rhetoric and wording to something deeper that underlies the whole history but is not stated as such. What lies here, the structure, can convey the main message of the constructed history, and refer to the main reason a certain history is written (Vanhulle 2009).

Selecting the Sample

A selection procedure is designed to form a list of the most popular textbooks in the field. This is necessary if selected textbooks should have the maximum possible capacity to represent the wider field, that of college-level textbooks on the subject. Textbook analysts have applied different strategies to access required information about textbook popularity. Their experiences suggest that this is not an easy job in general but it appears to be more difficult when it is about college-level textbooks. Publishers, in general, are not willing to reveal the information they have in this regard (Wills 1992: 64). Business considerations, as one influential factor, make them very reluctant to do so. But there are places where some information about this subject can be accessed. The American Textbook Council is one known to many textbook researchers; it provides a list of 'Widely Adopted History Textbooks' in American schools, which can be consulted easily through its website ('Widely Adopted History Textbooks' n.d.).

In relation to college-level textbooks, analysts' statements suggest that there is not such a ready list of popular textbooks (Wills 1992: 65). This research is based on online resources that can provide a novel and an effective chance to access such information. This involved collecting as many cases as possible of 'reading lists' that college lecturers provide to students as recommended sources of knowledge on the history of the Israel-Palestine question. A massive survey was conducted to explore and extract 'reading lists' that are provided by instructors of the relevant modules on college websites for their students. The final stage of the selection procedure started when reading lists were collected; a calculation was needed to determine which books are recommended most often by the subject lecturers. This operation enabled the formation of a list of the most recommended textbooks on the subject. This list, if formed properly, can have the power to represent Western textbooks on the question. That survey and its results are elaborated in Chapter 3.

Limitations of the Study

The following points can draw the major boundaries and limits of this study:

- Knowledge produced in the West on the Israel-Palestine question can be found in almost all the human sciences and disciplines. As covering all sciences and disciplines would be outside the scope of a single piece of research, history has been selected as the academic discipline that is more apt for this analysis. This choice is informed by the idea that the history of the Israel-Palestine question is the principal academic field where pro-Israeli activities can be observed. History, according to the Zionists, gives the Jewish people a right to the land and in this sense, is the main source of the arguments and evidence presented in defence of Israel's occupation of historical Palestine:

  > Supporters of Israel maintain that Jewish rights are derived, in the first instance, from a historical connection with the land of Palestine that was established almost four thousand years ago, when God told Abraham, patriarch of the ancient Hebrews, that he and his descendants would have all of the land of Canaan 'for an everlasting possession' (Genesis, XVII, 8) ... While true believers, Jewish and other, may argue that Palestine should and does belong to the Jews because that is God's will, most supporters of Israel make a different argument. They contend that the facts of Jewish history, regardless of whether or not one believes this history to be Divinely guided, give Jews their legitimate rights. It is a fact, Zionists insist, that the Jews have been involved with Palestine for the whole of their collective history, that even when few Jews lived there they retained a firm conviction that Eretz Yisrael was their country, and that for centuries this conviction guided and inspired Jewish attitudes and behaviour.
  >
  > Tessler 2009: 287–8

- What has been studied in this research, the textbook, is one main fund of knowledge. When knowledge is at stake there are other major sources, encyclopaedia and journal articles in particular, that have not been included in the analysis of this study.
- A limited number of textbooks, six in total, are selected in this study to represent Western textbooks. Analysing a bigger number of dominant

textbooks or all of them can overcome this limitation, but it is beyond the capacity of a thesis of PhD size, on which this book is based.
- Syllabi of the related courses, and their reading lists, are used as the main source of information about textbook adoption but only online syllabi are used, due to practical reasons, for that purpose.
- Countries use their own languages, German or French for instance, as the language of instruction in their universities. English references, however, are used more commonly, in the whole West, for accessing academic knowledge. This allows the research to focus on English-language textbooks. Textbooks in other Western languages, therefore, are not taken into consideration in this study.
- The time limit taken in the survey (2000–13) to find the most popular textbooks of the field represents only contemporary Western universities and not any other periods.

Structure of the Book

The overall structure of this book can be seen best through its table of contents. But providing some details about how the chapter titles on the contents page correspond with the contents of the book might guide readers on how to deal with the book, or how to read it. The main analyses of this study are located in two successive chapters: Chapter 5 and Chapter 6. Chapter 5 is where the main analysis of this book, textbook analysis, takes place. In this chapter, all six selected textbooks are analysed, one by one, through historical narrative analysis. The results of this analysis determine how the six textbooks analysed treat the history of the Israel-Palestine question. Chapter 6 is where context analysis, the second analysis of the study, is located. This analysis is conducted to answer the second part of the main question of the study: 'why do they (biased Western textbooks) treat the question in that way?' The background of all authors of the selected textbooks is analysed with a view to determining their personal capacity to produce a biased version of the question's history. For this purpose, all authors of the selected textbooks, eight authors altogether, and their personal background (about the Israel-Palestine question) are investigated one by one, in alphabetic order. The results of this investigation, summarized in Table 6.1, demonstrate how authors' backgrounds influenced the way their history of the question is constructed. The detailed results of both analyses of this study, and its major implications, can be consulted in the last section of the book, the Conclusion.

Chapters 5 and 6, and the Conclusion are the main locations where the findings of the book will be found. But the book has other chapters and sections to complete its argument, and provide an extensive picture of the question. The Preface offers a personal story of how this research project, from its original idea, came to become a reality. In 'Postscript: From that Thesis to this Book', the measures taken to convert the original PhD thesis to a book, apt for general readers, are presented. This section deals, also, with the relevant developments that are taken place in the related academic field since 2015 when the final version of the thesis was drafted. Reading the next section of the book, 'Prologue: A War on Western Textbooks', is recommended to those readers who have doubts about the idea that there is a fierce war on textbooks that are used to teach Israel-Palestine history in Western academia. This section demonstrates, with numerous cases of pro-Israeli assaults on Western textbooks, that Western academia is under pressure by pro-Israeli forces to deprive it of one side of the debate, the one that criticizes the Zionist version of the question' history.

The first chapter, 'Textbooks and Theory', is interesting only for those readers who care about the scholarly background of the study and can be overlooked by others. The main reason for providing this chapter is, mainly, justifying research choices that are made later, in this study, based on the relevant knowledge or established scholarly treatments of similar questions. Chapter 2, is a converted version of the literature review of the original thesis. This section is focused on other studies that are conducted in the same area of academic knowledge i.e. how Western textbooks treat the question. Relevant studies are reviewed in this section with a view to categorize them into two main categories; works that support the idea that Western textbooks suffer from a pro-Israeli bias as well as those that take an opposite stance i.e. criticize Western textbooks for being anti-Israeli. Again, this section has nothing to do with the main arguments of this study and could be attractive only for those readers who are interested to know more about the background of such studies in the West. Chapter 3 elaborates on one main step in the research, the survey to find the most popular college textbooks (in the field of Israel/Palestine history) and its results. This step was necessary to provide a valid list of Western textbooks that can truly represent the Western textbooks of the field. This list was required for the main analysis of this study i.e. analysis of Western academic knowledge. This chapter could be fascinating for those who are interested to know about how the most popular list (of Western textbooks) are formed and established.

The main discussions of the book are offered in the second half of the book where Chapter 4 starts. This chapter provides an introduction for the main analysis of the book, in Chapter 5. Chapter 5 analyses all selected textbooks to find all cases of pro-Israeli treatment of the question's history. But how can this be done? There is a need, in the first place, to establish what is a pro-Israeli version of the question's history. This is done in Chapter 4 where the main elements of a pro-Israeli version of the history are identified.

Chapter 1

TEXTBOOKS AND THEORY

The textbook in a general sense was present as a main tool of education from the very early past (Venezky 1992: 452). There were certain books that played a central role in teaching and learning in the then educational institutions. *Golestan*, a classic Persian text written by the popular Iranian poet, Sa'adi, could be named as one example in the East. Shakespeare's plays had a similar position in the West (Buckingham 1960: 1517). The Quran and the Bible, as well, could be counted as textbooks in this sense.

The textbook, in the modern sense, started to appear in the 1830s in the West when the name itself was used for such educational materials in English (McCulloch 2004: 78). In this sense, textbooks were materials designed to support teaching and learning in the classrooms of the new schools or colleges (McCulloch 2004: 78). The obvious purpose of the design of the book for the sake of achieving a specific educational goal in a given subject area distinguishes modern textbooks from their old counterparts (Hamilton 1990). *Golestan*, the Quran and the Bible were not designed or written to serve such a purpose.

What is a Textbook?

A textbook is an object easy to perceive for anyone with a school background. At the same time, providing a definition which includes all kinds of textbook and excludes those not in this category does not appear so simple. A prompt reference to a dictionary can provide a proper place to see and define textbooks: 'a book of instruction and study that presents the subject matter of teaching, as prescribed by the curriculum, in a manner appropriate to the subject and to educational principles; this also means that it is in keeping with accepted theories of learning and that, besides providing factual information, it points toward individual learning' (Bamberger 1992: 116). This definition indicates that there are clear elements attached to a textbook that help in recognizing such a medium.

In reality, this does not work in all circumstances. This problem comes from different sources; first of all, the very name of the medium is contested. Another term, 'schoolbook', was used, also, in some places and historical periods (see McCulloch and Crook 2008: 598 for instance). Another source of complexity that is related to the name again comes from the term 'textbook' itself. In some cases, books have this term in their title. *Textbook on International Law* (Dixon 2007) could be mentioned as one example. But this title, itself, does not give a book status as such; if a book with such a title has not been used for such a purpose in educational institutions it might not be regarded as a textbook. At the same time, if a book without such a title plays a role consistent with the roles textbooks are expected to play, enough credit is gained for such a status.

Other efforts in the relevant literature to define the textbook might help further; Buckingham defines it as 'a learning instrument usually employed in schools and colleges to support a program of instruction' (1960: 1517). Lange considers it 'a standard book for any particular branch of study' (Buckingham 1960: 1517). Francis Bacon defines the textbook as 'a book designed for classroom use carefully prepared by experts in the field and equipped with the usual teaching devices' (Buckingham 1960: 1517). All these statements define textbooks, directly or indirectly, as playing a central role in education. But educational systems of different countries are very different and this fact suggests one important, if not the most important, source of complexity in defining the textbook.

From this perspective, educational systems, in different countries, can be delineated by a spectrum of categories with two extremes at the two poles: centralized and decentralized educational systems. Some differences exist between those two polar systems and among others in the middle, but what is related to this discussion is the place they provide for the textbook; in centralized systems, the main decisions, if not all, about textbooks are taken in the centre, mainly by a central national authority. What remains is the use of the books as a teaching tool, which suggests the role of schools and teachers. In this system, the textbook has a very clear and strong position, which is valid and known for all educational institutions nationwide. This enables one to make a clear list of them (McCulloch and Crook 2008: 598–9). On the other hand, in decentralized systems, main decisions are left to local authorities, schools or even teachers. As a result, there is no such solid classification of textbooks. One book could be used as a textbook in one school or even one class but not in the neighbouring one. This implies a textbook status as being relatively weak, with limited validity in time, place or both (McCulloch and Crook 2008: 599).

One more source of complexity comes from the hierarchy of education within an educational system, where education is divided into two main categories: school and higher education. What gives the status to a book as a textbook in higher education mainly comes from an instructor's decision or a relevant council in the university with this authority or a combination of both (Squire 1994: 1416).

With all the problems and complexities that make the job difficult, it is useful to provide a textbook definition that covers the whole range of kinds. Two descriptions that can work are:

1. Objective description: from this perspective textbooks are printed, hardbound, published in good number, and are at hand for students and instructors as a commonplace for educational interaction (Buckingham 1960: 1517),

2. Subjective description: from this view textbooks are related to some main educational concepts: something which is designed to cover a syllabus (McCulloch 2004: 78; Foster and Crawford 2006: xiii); its subject matter is defined by a curriculum (Hudec 2011); it is used as a main source of material to teach, and by students as a main source of learning.

Hence, two main criteria can be offered for recognition of a textbook of any kind, wherever it is:

1. Usage: the wider the usage a book has in educational institutes as the main source of teaching/learning, the greater the chance it has of reaching the status of a textbook (Michael 1990).
2. Authority: textbooks always receive some recognition from the hierarchy in an educational system in order to have such a position. This hierarchy includes national authorities and instructors (Olson 1989).

The Significance of the Textbook

The magnificent civilization humankind enjoys in our time is also called the 'civilization of the book' (Buckingham 1960: 1518). This statement refers to the significance of book, in general, and its role in flourishing contemporary civilization. One might go further to ask: which kind of book is more influential than a textbook in this regard? The importance of the textbook originates in the different categories under which it engages in social life: the first one is related to the textbook's role in education, where the term originally comes from. There are facts everywhere in educational institutes, schools and colleges, classrooms and curricula, and attaching to teachers and students that suggest that the textbook is a player with a central role in education. It is contended that the textbook has been at the centre of education throughout the latter's history (Foster and Crawford 2006: xi). The relevant literature, also, supports the argument that instructors rely on and believe in textbooks as 'the principal source of knowledge' (Foster 2006: 157). Students, who are the main consumers of this medium, commonly regard a textbook's content as 'important' and 'true'. There is evidence that 'students reject what is offered by other sources of knowledge such as family or mass media, if there is an inconsistency with what textbooks provide' (Foster and Crawford 2006: xiii–xiv). The same source argues that what is left out of textbooks is considered 'unimportant'. Textbooks occupy a dominant position in educational activities; one source (Airasian 1994: 793) refers to 'up to 75 percent' as a figure which represents the proportion assumed by the textbook in those activities. Another reference (Tobin and Ybarra 2008: 2) introduce a higher one: 85 to 95 per cent.

In agreement with what has been stated above, about the role of the textbook, many references support its position as 'dominant' and its influence as 'profound' in education (for instance Buckingham 1960: 1518; Foster 2006: 157). According to Woodward, also, many studies confirmed such a result (1994: 6368). The textbook appears closer than any other educational tool to assuming the position of determining what students learn. It contributes significantly in shaping their views about the world (Foster and Crawford 2006: ix). In doing so, textbooks approach the position of a 'holy book'. They place the knowledge presented above suspicion, as religious texts do (Olson 1989).

The role of textbooks as a vehicle that can carry, or infiltrate, ideas, ideologies, values and other social constructions into education and the cognitive area of students' minds opens another chapter in its importance as an effective instrument in social or political processes or projects (Mirkovic and Crawford 2003). There are more justifications, in the remainder of this chapter, that help to establish the significance of textbooks in education and society in our time. This might encourage one to call our civilization a 'civilization of the textbook', if there was any room to refine the concept of 'book' in the definition that began this section – 'civilization of the book'.

History Textbooks

What has been elaborated through the last section might help to establish a link between textbooks and social affairs. That section was, mainly, about textbooks in general, all textbooks in all subjects. But it is difficult to assume that all subjects make the same contribution to that undertaking. Those subjects which are related more to social affairs, civics for instance, play a more important role because they can be the main vehicle for transmitting ideas and values about social and political matters to textbook readers. An interesting case, in this context, is a recommendation by the State Senate Education Committee in Mississippi (United States) prior to desegregation, asserting that it is 'recommended that the civics texts provided for Negro schools contain no references to voting, elections, civic responsibility, or democracy' (Jackson 1992: 445–6).

In this area, different subjects in social sciences have different relevance as well; history is the one that might matter most. Presenting the past through history contributes significantly to controlling the present and shaping the future (Foster and Crawford 2006: 6). What people receive and believe as the past is able to produce huge social energy; it can make people die for a cause or kill for it (Foster and Crawford 2006: 6). A powerful entity, in general, and governments in particular, can use this chance to advance their social and political projects. In reality, there is a fierce battle on writing history. A testimony by late historian Bernard Lewis can support this idea:

> We live in a time when great efforts have been made, and continue to be made, to falsify the record of the past and to make history a tool of propaganda, when governments, religious movements, political parties, and sectional groups of every kind are busy rewriting history as they would wish it to have been, as they would like their followers to believe that it was.
>
> Lewis 1993: 130

Power's Contribution in Textbook Contents

When power and powerful parties, as mentioned above, are operating, biased history is a significant product. Bias has an identified role in undermining some fundamental principles of education and knowledge production in the area of truth and understanding (Bloor and Wood 2006: 21). There are well-known types of bias in textbooks, including racial, national and sexual (Buckingham 1960: 1421). Influenced by these biases, students tend to look at some national values, at national history, racial questions or at the sexes in a way imposed or promoted by biased textbooks. In explaining this phenomenon, why histories are biased or written in particular ways, a number of theories have been suggested: Young (1971) emphasizes the role of power and powerful elites in his theory; 'those in positions of power will attempt to define what is taken as knowledge, how accessible to different groups any knowledge is, and what are accepted relationships between different knowledge areas and between those who have access to them and make them available' (Hartnett 1982: 169). Various studies that have examined history textbooks for such purposes have confirmed that the knowledge provided about the subject works to promote and legitimize the dominant position that the powerful elites occupy in society (Leahey 2007: 38). The knowledge that challenges this position is removed or distorted. One fascinating instance of such treatment is suggested by Christopher R. Leahey, who has observed that no American history textbook (of those he studied) had any mention to Latin American historical giant, Ernesto 'Che' Guevara (Leahey 2007: 38).

As a result, powerful institutions, mainly governments and political systems, tend to use their power to have a history of the past that serves their agenda for the present or future (Foster and Crawford 2006: 6). This could be considered as something common that all do but, at the same time, different governments and political systems treat this matter differently. Some of them are desperate to use history in this way: those whose existence is under threat, those who need a story as a binding tie to create a nation, those who engage to invent or reinvent a national identity. All these reasons put governments in positions that view history and history textbooks through social or political considerations (Foster and Crawford 2006: 6). As a result, some of them use unashamedly ideological and political reasons to tell a particular history. They employ lies and misinform, they distort and manipulate historical information to prove something for the self or deny that for the other (Foster and Crawford 2006: 6–7). Factors that play a role in this area create different countries with different approaches to history; in the worst situations, national histories promote hatred, racism and even ethnic cleansing (Foster and Crawford 2006: 7). Israel is introduced as one main instance by Porat:

> History education is a key tool in the formation of a national identity for the Jews gathered in Israel after its establishment. This population, especially in the early years of the state, came from the four corners of the world. No language, no culture, no belief system united these Jews. Not much united the one million Jews assembled in Israel, including six hundred thousand who came as new

immigrants after the state's establishment in 1948. These Jews spoke more than seventy languages and dialects and came from distinct cultures. Neither did these Jews share one religious orientation. Therefore, history was one potential uniting point and the educational authorities employed it to advance this unity.

Porat 2006: 197

Consequently, the construction of a history for Israel, that legitimizes what Zionists did in the holy land, is a main function when Israeli authorities engage with history, as a subject in education. That is why history occupies a central place in the Israeli curriculum (Porat 2006: 197). In this way, countries and their histories could be defined through different categories. The history textbook is a favourite place to see this. How governments perform in their textbooks also forms a good indicator of their level of tolerance and their capacity to consider others' points of view (Tobin and Ybarra 2008: 153), which is an essential element for a scientific and apolitical approach to history.

Education's Contribution in Textbook Contents

Textbooks are created under the influence of some forces. These forces include economic, political and cultural factors, in a general sense. It is contended that what does generate textbooks is educational priorities, a claim supported mainly by educationalists who are engaged in producing and promoting these books (Farrell and Heyneman 1994: 6365). According to these educationalists, a textbook is an innocent and objective source of knowledge (Romanowski 1993: 68–9). This claim has been undermined repeatedly by a number of scholars who have investigated the relationship between textbooks and social forces. What makes this enterprise possible stems, mainly, from broadening the picture of textbook production where the social context of the schooling can be seen. What knowledge specialists collect about social context, social conflicts and the main forces involved in such processes, power and interests in particular, provides a chance for them to see the root causes of the governing tendencies in textbook knowledge. As a result, social and political factors are considered responsible, mainly or partly, for establishing textbook knowledge (Farrell and Heyneman 1994: 6365; Goodlad 1979: 356). Various empirical studies by prominent scholars in different places support the idea; Pierre Bourdieu, a pioneer who emphasized the role of powerful elites, considered textbook knowledge as the knowledge of the governing elites that was legitimized through education, to secure and maintain the interests of the powerful elites in a given society. This knowledge works as capital, 'symbolic capital' as he named it, for elites, which affects the distribution of capital to economic levels in an unequal way. He regarded school knowledge as an ideology that misrepresents social reality and reproduces existing power relations (Dorliae 1998: 8).

Emile Durkheim, who investigated how the content of French secondary school textbooks developed from the seventeenth century to the early nineteenth, suggested that textbooks represent the interests of the upper class of society, in his case, the Catholic Church (Dorliae 1998: 7–8). Raymond Williams undertook a similar task in the United Kingdom; his investigation of educational materials demonstrated the influence of competing forces in the then British society (Dorliae 1998: 7–8). Studies conducted by Bernstein and Young, also, support the judgement that British school textbooks serve the interests of powerful groups in society (Dorliae 1998: 22). Michael Apple suggested similar ideas about American textbooks. He emphasized, in his analysis, the role that 'form' and 'selection tradition' play in the employment of textbooks by dominant groups (Dorliae 1998: 22). He conceived a novel term, 'official knowledge' (Foster and Crawford 2006: xiii), to refer to the knowledge selected by the power to achieving the status of dominant knowledge at the expense of excluding the competing versions of knowledge from textbooks. All this is discussed nowadays in a topical scholarship, offered by French scholar Michel Foucault, which is known, after him, as the relationship between 'knowledge and power'.

Textbook Production

The actual textbook production, with its key elements including publishers, authors and the market, is a locus where social and political forces operate to shape textbook contents. Publishers play a central role on this level. They design textbooks and take key decisions about authorship and how content should meet the existing expectations in many educational systems. Another factor adds to the importance of the role publishers play; most textbooks are published by few publishers (Tobin and Ybarra 2008: 8). In fact, three mega publishers, Pearson, Education Media and Publishing Group Limited, and McGraw-Hill, control the market of elementary and high school (el-hi) publishing in the United States (Tobin and Ybarra 2008: 8). The number of publishers who have a share in this market has dropped dramatically in recent years (Tobin and Ybarra 2008: 8). This can provide more chances for publishers to control the market, and to be counted as responsible for textbooks and their contents. Publishers, themselves, contend that the main driver for them in designing textbooks is the market and its demand (Jackson 1992: 445). They also tend to consider the content of the textbook as 'neutral knowledge' (Sosniak 1994: 1421). This is, of course, a contested claim (Sosniak 1993: 1421). The market is, of course, one main factor. There is a simple reason for that; tens of millions of dollars are spent on textbooks just in the United States every year, based on one related estimation reported in 1994 (Husén and Postlethwaite 1994: 6369). This huge financial capacity is a powerful force that can affect textbook production. The market is considered to be one factor in this discussion but it could be viewed through several constituting elements which include various factors such as schools, teachers, students, their parents and even pressure groups or lobbies that approach publishers, in the name of a business or similar considerations, to make them incorporate what the lobbyists prefer as textbook content or format.

Authors are also considered responsible for what textbooks provide. This appears natural as they do the actual writing. There is a meaningful difference, at the same time, between authors of school and college textbooks. From this perspective, authors of college textbooks are considered to have greater responsibility in the matter of a textbook and its content while publishers tend to hold this position towards school textbooks (Squire 1994: 1416). College textbooks, formatted, frequently, in the form of a single book, are mainly authored by one or two authors and not more (Squire 1994: 1416).

Textbook as Knowledge

Knowledge, as a cognitive condition, has no apparent realization in the visible or accessible world. There are real objects, however, that have adequate capacity and legitimacy to represent knowledge; encyclopaedia articles, journal articles and textbooks can be regarded as the main ones (Myers 1991). In this sense, they are seen as a 'fund' or 'store' which one can visit or in which one can access knowledge. The textbook, in this relation, is considered as the best such medium; 'by means of books knowledge is accumulated into a permanently available store or fund: and of all books, textbooks are the best instruments for such funding' (Buckingham 1960: 1517). Others offered similar ideas as well: Sharon Traweek, for instance, takes textbooks as an instrument which represents 'constraints on scientific thought' (Myers 1991). Thomas Kuhn, who views the whole of human knowledge through different paradigms, appreciates the textbook as 'the visible form of paradigms' (Myers 1991).

There are reasons for different qualities of representation when different materials are at stake; journal articles tend to represent knowledge in a more temporal and personal sense whereas an encyclopaedia article, in this respect, has a better chance of being judged as a permanent and impersonal representation (Myers 1991). Both of them, however, play a passive role in representing knowledge from one perspective; they are there, like a book on a library shelf, to be consulted if one is willing to. The textbook is different from them in this regard. It has the authority to communicate knowledge to the receiver regardless of his willingness. For this reason, their location in a library in the 'reserve' section, is different from that of other library items. This special position of the textbook is related to its role in education, where educational authorities play a determinative role in what students consult as the 'valid' source of knowledge. That is why Michael Apple, quite reasonably, calls what the textbook represents 'official knowledge' (Foster and Crawford 2006: xiii).

Thomas Kuhn (1970: 165) further contributed to this discussion through his reflection on the knowledge–text relationship, providing a valuable insight into the different roles textbooks play in mediating knowledge in different academic disciplines. He classifies all disciplines in three categories from this standpoint; in one category, mainly graphic arts and music, textbooks play only a secondary role. The first role here is reserved for the artistic product itself, whether it is a painting or a piece of music. At the opposite end of the spectrum, natural sciences assume a very robust position for the textbook on this point. The textbook, here, is the main medium that represents relevant knowledge. The original sources of knowledge, the works of Newton or Einstein, for instance, usually have no significant role to play here.

Another category occupies a place in between. In the social sciences and history, the textbook plays a primary role in transmitting knowledge but it is usually accompanied by some excerpts from original works such as the US Declaration of Independence or *Emile* by Rousseau. These materials are needed as a textbook companion to allow a 'comprehensive' representation of related knowledge (Jackson 1992: 442–3). Here the textbook, comparable to those in the natural sciences, is a prime source of knowledge, but its position is different; here textbook is not the only source. Original works play a role in mediating knowledge, similar to that played by the graphic arts, but not as a primary source.

Textbook Analysis

Analysing the textbook as a systematic investigation started soon after the textbook in its new sense emerged in the nineteenth century. However, textbook analysis is considered an endeavour that took place largely in the twentieth century, since its main progress developed in this period. Now, in the twenty-first century, it is regarded as a popular method of analysis among researchers of different disciplines including education, history and the social sciences. Two main reasons mentioned for this popularity are the established importance of textbooks in educational and social matters and their accessibility. The first reason has been elaborated earlier. The second one is also very relevant to the making of textbook analysis a popular area of research (Sadker and Sadker 1994: 5441). Here textbooks can be seen as a valuable source of a massive amount of data that is ready for use and has a notable potential to represent realities and processes in society that are difficult to apprehend clearly as such (Woodward 1994: 6367; Mirkovic and Crawford 2003).

All the revolutionary achievements that have been made recently in the area of information technology, in general, and text processing, in particular, add another dimension to the important role of textbook analysis and the position it can occupy in the production of knowledge. Tons of monographs and articles, which are based on textbook analysis, can be retrieved by a simple search in relevant sources such as Amazon or Google Scholar. They cover different topics; textbooks published in the United States are the main subject of many academic works. In addition, certain situations where nations have experienced a dramatic change in their political system have attracted a good number of such research enterprises. Germany after the Second World War, Eastern European countries after the Cold War, countries of former Yugoslavia after independence and South Africa after apartheid are the main instances. In all these cases, textbooks that were developed under certain ideological or political conditions became the subject of changes that a new environment made necessary.

Methods of Textbook Analysis

All methods suggested for textbook analysis could be catalogued in three main categories according to Weinbrenner (1992: 21):

- Process-oriented textbook analysis
- Product-oriented textbook analysis
- Reception-oriented textbook analysis

Process-oriented methods of analysis focus on all processes and operations that contribute to the actual production and publication of textbooks. Here regulations and procedures that officially govern the process, as well as forces that shape it through unofficial ways, are taken into consideration. Since the process of textbook production is dissimilar in different countries or educational systems, this process can refer to relatively different matters. But in all cases, this starts with an idea about a particular textbook and finishes when the book has been published. All the processes and activities that are involved could be a subject of analysis (Weinbrenner 1992: 23). The central educational authority, schools and publishers are the main centres of research in this phase. A 1990 PhD thesis by Susan Elizabeth Kerr van de Ven, titled 'State Adoption Policies, Publishing Practices, and Authorship: The Production of Middle East Chapters in World History Textbooks', is one example of process-oriented analysis (van de Ven 1990: v).

In another kind of textbook analysis, the *product-oriented* one, the textbook itself and what it contains is the main subject of research. The *reception-oriented* textbook analysis relates to the last phase when the book is used; how teachers deal with textbooks, and how students receive that teaching is the main concerns of this phase which is not limited, however, to these matters. The reaction of a wider audience in society, including students' parents and social leaders, and the effects made on that audience, are at stake as well (Weinbrenner 1992: 23).

These different kinds of textbook analysis make different contributions: product-oriented analysis is considered a popular model, if not the most popular. Textbook analysis, also, started with this type of research (Weinbrenner 1992: 23). It seems that this type continues to be at the centre of textbook research. What is fascinating about this type of analysis is the provision of easy access to a ready supply of data that can be analysed directly, and also the power this kind of data has to represent social processes.

A text can be analysed in numerous different ways. This is related to the different perspectives and approaches to viewing this text. From one perspective, there are two main categories of analysis: longitudinal and latitudinal (Weinbrenner 1992: 23). The longitudinal refers to those analyses that cover the whole book from one end to another. The latitudinal is research about some parts of the book and not all. From another perspective, textbook analysis is divided into two main general categories: qualitative and quantitative. This division occupies a large part of social research. Quantitative ways of textbook analysis are mainly concerned with the frequencies of using some words in a given text. The space allocated to certain topics could be another criterion for this kind of analysis. This analysis provides a good chance for examining extensive tracts of text (Nicholls 2003). This is facilitated dramatically nowadays by computer programs. Since this type of examination cannot deal with the deep meaning of the text, it has some limitations in some areas of analysis such as the ideological underpinning of the text.

The qualitative method, in contrast, is time-consuming but can provide the chance to analyse deep levels of textual meaning. Meaning is also a point where further divisions take place; if analysis focuses on the manifest meaning of the text, this forms one subcategory which is different from an alternative one, latent analysis, that deals with the hidden meaning (Jackson 1992: 437–8; Franzosi 2008: 184). There are at least two other major categories for different analyses of the 'product'; one is concerned solely with the written text. In the second, other features of a textbook such as pictures, design, diagrams, tables and the like are also taken into consideration.

This is not the end of the ways textbooks are analysed. When one chooses to analyse a textbook through the text there are several possible choices. From one main perspective, the existing ways can start from the level of surface analysis and move towards the deepest one. A brief review of these levels is able to shed some light on different choices available in this area; syntax could be considered as one (Franzosi 2004: 549). The use of passive or active verbs can exert different influences and consequently create different meanings (Hardy and Bryman 2004: 549; Rogers 2004: 21). The varying ways that matters are referred to in a text can be considered as a basis for another kind of analysis. Some personalities, for example, receive positive references all the time in a given text. This pattern of reference can reveal something about the text. The language in which a concept is presented can serve a similar function. The immediate context of a concept is another choice of analysis (Mirkovic and Crawford 2003: 97). When it comes to information or facts presented in a textbook, there are many choices of analysis with the capacity to speak about the book: what is presented in the book's content, and what is omitted from the text, is one (Nicholls 2003); what has been taken as a major matter, and what has been dealt with as a minor one is another choice.

One fundamental question affects the nature of research and its conclusion when a textbook is chosen as a main matter of analysis: it is that of representation. What exactly does a textbook represent in a given analysis? There are two matters, at least, a textbook can represent; it can be viewed as a discrete unit whose purpose is to pass knowledge on, or to transmit facts. In addition, a textbook has a considerable capacity to represent areas broader than itself due to its significant role in forming or being formed by other realities or processes. Education, knowledge and social processes could be considered some areas of investigation that a textbook could be used as a representative to speak for. In this way there is a chance, for instance, to use a textbook as a subject of analysis in order to develop some conclusions about a given educational system.

Everything presented here about the ways textbooks are analysed does not refer to actual methods used for such an enterprise. There are some main methods that are used for textbook analysis, content analysis, discourse analysis, semiotic analysis and narrative analysis could be mentioned, for instance. Textbook analysts either use one of these methods or a mixture of them to conduct a given piece of research. The reader will find soon that the textbook analysis adopted to conduct this study is qualitative, latitudinal and product-oriented. The main method used in this research, historical narrative analysis, is, also, elaborated in the Introduction to this book.

Chapter 2

WESTERN TEXTBOOKS: PRO- OR ANTI-ISRAELI?

How textbooks treat the Israel-Palestine question has been present, as a research problem, in the Western academic circles since 1967 and particularly the 1973 Arab-Israeli war. However, cases of exclusive treatment of the question were not numerous; most relevant works explored in the academic domain deal with the problem under a wider topic such as the Middle East, Muslims or Arabs. A chronological catalogue of such works is listed in Table 2.1.

A thorough review of the related literature can identify the items listed in Table 2.1. Such a review has been conducted, in the original PhD investigation, to explore how the Israel-Palestine question has been treated, both directly and indirectly, in textbooks used in Western educational systems. A detailed report of that extensive review was reflected in the PhD thesis but a selected part, more apt for a general reader, is transferred to this book.

This review produced some outcomes that can contribute to drawing a map of the related literature; it demonstrated that a very limited number of studies have been conducted to exclusively investigate how Western textbooks treat the Israel-Palestine question; only two pieces of research, those done by Michael Walls and Andrea L. Smith, can be classified in this way. These two studies also acknowledged, through their literature review, that they are the first investigations that have focused on such a topic (in their relevant countries, Sweden and the United States respectively; Walls 2010: 24; Smith 2011: 40). Other relevant bodies of research mentioned in this review deal with the question through broader topics such as 'Arabs' or 'Middle East' that might cover, directly or indirectly, the Israel-Palestine question.

The anti-Arab bias explored in the Western textbooks is seen in two different ways; some, like van de Ven (1990), view it as a typical American treatment of a non-Western country or region. But most analysts mentioned in this review consider, explicitly or implicitly, this condition to be at odds with the Western standard of treating such questions.

The common character of pro-Israeli bias explored in the Western textbooks entails presenting the Israeli viewpoint of disputed questions. The Israeli positions on these matters are taken for granted and not questioned in a critical academic manner. In contrast, there is very limited space, if any, for providing students with

Table 2.1 List of the relevant literature

No.	Title	Author	Medium	Publisher	Date
1	Treatment of the Middle East in American High School Textbooks	Glenn Perry	Journal article	*Journal of Palestine Studies*	1975
2	Images of the Arabs in American Social Science Textbooks	Ayad Al-Qazzaz	Chapter	Medina University Press International	1975
3	*The Image of the Middle East in Secondary School Textbooks*	William J. Griswold	Study report	Middle East Studies Association of North America	1975
4	Images of the Arabs in United States Secondary School Social Studies Textbooks	Samir Ahmed Jarrar	PhD thesis	Florida State University	1976
5	Teaching Materials and Sources of Information on the Middle East for Secondary School Teachers	Malcolm Peck	Journal article	*Journal of Social Education*	1976
6	American Images of Middle East Peoples: Impact of the High School	Michael W. Suleiman	Book	Middle East Studies Association of North America	1977
7	Images of the Arabs and of Their Conflict with Israel Held by American Public Secondary School Social Studies Teachers	Yaqub Abdalla Abu-Helu	PhD thesis	Stanford University	1978
8	*The Arab World: A Handbook for Teachers*	Ayad Al-Qazzaz	Book	Women Concerned about the Middle East	1978
9	The Revision of History Textbooks and the Improvement of Teaching Materials: A Way of Contributing to a Better Understanding Between Islam and the West	N/A	Conference report	UN office in Geneva	1979
10	Coverage of the Arab World in American Secondary School World Studies Textbooks	Michel Georges Nabti	PhD thesis	Stanford University	1981
11	Textbooks and Teachers: Conveyors of Knowledge and Agents of Socialization	Ayad Al-Qazzaz	Chapter	University of California Press	1981
12	Teaching the Arab World: Evaluating Textbooks	Deborah Jacobs	Journal article	*The Social Studies*	1981
13	Teaching About the Middle East in Elementary School	Rosanne J. Marek	Journal article	*Indiana Social Studies Quarterly*	1983

No.	Title	Author	Medium	Publisher	Date
14	State Adoption Policies, Publishing Practices, and Authorship: The Production of Middle East Chapters in World History Textbooks	Susan Elizabeth Kerr van de Ven	PhD thesis	Harvard University	1990
15	Rewriting History in Textbooks	Mitchell Bard	Online article	The American-Israeli Cooperative Enterprise	1993
16	Evaluation of Secondary-Level Textbooks for Coverage of the Middle East and North Africa	Elizabeth Barlow	Research report	Center for Middle Eastern and North African Studies	1994
17	Middle East Facts and Fictions	Elizabeth Barlow	Journal article	Journal of the International Institute	1995
18	The Arab-Israeli Conflict as Depicted in Children's and Young Adult Non-Fiction Literature	Marlene Rock	Master thesis	City University of New York	1996
19	A Critical Assessment of Textbooks for Middle Eastern History	Calvin H. Allen	Journal article	Teaching History: A Journal of Methods	1996
20	The Development of a Content Analysis Instrument for Analysing College-Level Textbooks Used in the United States to Teach About the Middle East	Adel Tawfiq Al-Bataineh	PhD thesis	Illinois State University	1998
21	U.S. Global Studies Textbooks' Treatment of Foreign Countries	Alexander Tumanpea	PhD thesis	State University of New York at Buffalo	1998
22	Ethnocentric and Stereotypical Concepts in the Study of Islamic and World History	Joseph G. Rahme	Journal article	History Teacher: A Journal of Methods	1999
23	Evidence of Bias and Censorship in College History Survey Textbooks	James Gregory Goodwin	PhD thesis	University of Houston	1999
24	Blaming the Victims: Spurious Scholarship and the Palestinian Question	Edward Said and Christopher Hitchens	Book	Verso	2001
25	Ancient Israel in Western Civ Textbooks	Jack Cargill	Journal article	*The History Teacher*	2001
26	The Portrayal of the Middle East in School Textbooks from 1880 to the Present	Hani Morgan	PhD thesis	The State University of New Jersey – New Brunswick	2002
27	The Image of Arab and Islam in Introduction to Sociology College Textbooks in the United States	Ayad Al-Qazzaz	Journal article	*Digest of Middle East Studies*	2002
28	The Miseducation of the West: How Schools and the Media Distort Our Understanding of the Islamic World	Joe L Kincheloe and Shirley R Steinberg	Book	Greenwood Publishing Group	2004

(Continued)

No.	Title	Author	Medium	Publisher	Date
29	The Arab and Muslim Image in Public Education Textbooks of the United States of America	Ahmed Al-Banyan	Educational Research	Ministry of Education, Kingdom of Saudi Arabia	2005
30	Studying the Exotic Other in the Classroom: The Portrayal of Arab Americans in Educational Source Materials	David and Ayouby	Journal article	*Multicultural Perspectives*	2005
31	A Novel Reading: Literature and Pedagogy in Modern Middle East History Courses in Canada and the United States	Jane Leeke	MA thesis	McGill University	2005
32	Whose History? Portrayal of Immigrant Groups in U.S. History Textbooks 1800–Present	Stuart J. Foster	Chapter	Information Age Publishing	2006
33	The Portrayal of the Middle East in Secondary School U.S. Textbooks	Elizabeth Marie Brockway	Master thesis	Bowling Green State University	2007
34	The Portrayal of the Middle East in Four Current School Textbooks	Morgan and Walker	Bulletin, Middle East Studies Association	Middle East Studies Association of North America	2008
35	*The Trouble with Textbooks: Distorting History and Religion*	Gary Tobin and Dennis R. Ybarra	Book	Lexington Books	2008
36	American School Textbooks: How They Portrayed the Middle East from 1898 to 1994	Hani Morgan	Journal article	*American Educational History Journal*	2008
37	Framing the Israel/Palestine Conflict in Swedish History School Textbooks	Michael Walls	PhD thesis	University of Gothenburg	2010
38	How the Israel-Palestinian Conflict Is Framed in Swedish History School Textbooks	Michael Walls	Online article	Dissident Voice	2011
39	*The Politics of Teaching Palestine to Americans: Addressing Pedagogical Strategies*	Marcy Jane Knopf-Newman	Book	Palgrave Macmillan	2011
40	How Have Descriptions of the Arab-Israeli Conflict Changed in High School U.S. History Textbooks Since the 1950s?	Andrea L. Smith	MA thesis	Cedarville University	2011

No.	Title	Author	Medium	Publisher	Date
41	Representations of Islam and Arab Societies in Western Secondary Textbooks	Alexander W. Wiseman	Article	*Digest of Middle East Studies*	2014
42	The (Mis) Representation of the Middle East and its People in K-8 Social Studies Textbooks: A Postcolonial Analysis	Rania Camille Salman	PhD thesis	University of North Texas	2014
43	The Post-Ottoman Middle East in Modern World History Textbooks	Gregory Delahanty	PhD thesis	Northern Illinois University	2014
44	Decolonizing World History: Mis-Representations of the Middle East in Secondary Social Studies Textbooks	Amanda Megan Schellhaas	MA thesis	Louisiana State University	2016
45	Re-presenting Muslims and Islam: A Critical Discourse Analysis of Orientalism in High School World History Textbooks	Abdellatif W. Al Sager	PhD thesis	Tennessee Technological University	2016
46	Cultivating an American Worldview: A Comparative Analysis of Perspectives of the Middle East, Arabs, and Muslims in US Public High School 'World History' Curricula	Muhsanah Arefin	MA thesis	University of Toronto	2018
47	Beyond 'Through the Looking Glass' Borders: A Content Analysis of North Africa/Southwest Asia in College-Level World Regional Geography Textbooks	Parisa Meymand	PhD thesis	University of Wisconsin-Milwaukee	2019

the Palestinian perspective of the discussed questions. This treatment leaves no chance for students to understand both sides, and form a balanced view of the question.

A number of methods are adopted for conducting textbook analysis in the studies reviewed in this chapter: content analysis, discourse analysis and comparative analysis are the most applied. Most pieces of research explored in this review are 'product-oriented' investigations but there are cases of 'reception-oriented' and 'process-oriented' analyses as well. Both quantitative and qualitative methods are used to conduct these pieces of research.

Numerous pieces of research have been produced on how Israeli textbooks treat the question. These studies constitute a large part of the existing literature but they have not been mentioned here because this review is designed to cover only textbooks that are used in the area of Western countries, an area that includes European countries, the United States, Canada, Australia and New Zealand.

An evaluation of the current state of the literature can also demonstrate that almost all relevant research explored in this review was conducted by educationalists. Educational considerations dominated, as a result, in these studies. This pushed historical and political considerations to the margin. For instance, the political and divisive nature of the Israel-Palestine question, as an issue that is located at the heart of an existing, long-lasting, confrontational and brutal conflict, and its implications in the research area has been ignored. The aforementioned researchers produced and presented their related research in a way that non-sensitive, non-contentious and neutral topics are presented, where readers can easily trust the researchers and their efforts to find substantial answers to the research questions. Here, strong political tendencies or ideological affiliations that occupy agents of the research, and provide a limited chance for them to act as impartial researchers, are neglected. Educationalists prefer, in general, to pass over such a crucial introduction quickly and jump towards evaluations and conclusions that can be translated into practical results for those who are active in teaching and learning. Hence, they do not seem interested in spending enough time to question the methodological and epistemological aspects of the research where fundamental assumptions of the research are formed or main judgements are made.

The presence of political and ideological motivations should increase the level of scepticism about the nature of the judgements made, where such an intensely political issue interferes in what researchers produce. Clarification, as a solution to such a problem, can shed some considerable light on what such research suggests, giving a chance to readers who are not ready to rely, only, on the writers' personal judgement, and are eager to make their own judgements. This is possible when researchers share useful materials they have with readers, to make such judgement possible; minimizing cases of judgements and maximizing the level of evidence and arguments provision seems like an effective strategy in such a situation. Studies reviewed in this chapter, in general, are short on paying serious attention to such an issue. As a result, they are under-resourced in providing enough material that can make the research clear and repeatable; at the same time, they are too quick and confident in making judgements.

Hence, lack of clarity can form the main flaw in the literature. As mentioned earlier, the special political nature of the question requires the utmost clarity to convince readers about the results of the research and the way it has been produced. This is lacking in the main body of the literature explored in this study. The shortcomings belong, at the same time, to different categories. Some studies are short in making clear how analysed textbooks are selected; many introduce them as the most popular textbooks without explaining how they are ranked as such; and others are short on clarifying the methodological aspect of the research where the reader is not able to realize how this research is conducted or can be repeated. This reduces the chance to convince sceptical readers who see the political aspect of the question as a very effective and powerful factor.

Other results produced by this literature review introduce a significant gap in the literature and justify conducting this research to fill it. There is a clear gap about textbooks used at the college level; only two studies have been found that analyse how college textbooks treat the question; those conducted by Meymand (2019) and Al-Qazzaz (2002). The research conducted by Al-Bataineh in 1998 supports this idea not only for the Israel-Palestine question but also for all pieces of research that are conducted to analyse the textbook treatment of the (whole) Middle East; 'While these studies are useful to a certain degree, they are limited to elementary and secondary levels. This researcher could not find any content analysis studies that were specifically designed to analyse textbooks used at the college level' (Al-Bataineh 1998: 21).

Empirical investigations conducted to investigate the nature of the questioned treatment relied on college textbooks as authoritative sources of relevant knowledge. Their status as true sources of relevant knowledge is taken for granted. Few pieces of research went further and questioned the knowledge that was offered in the college textbooks. One study (by Wiseman in 2014), which appeared later than my original literature review, took a similar approach to the question, and examined textbook bias (on the subject) as a regional, i.e. Western, phenomenon that works beyond individual Western countries, and forms a uniform reality that covers all of them. The political and international role the West plays to support Israel is taken as the real context of the question, and taken as such for the sake of conducting this research. All other relevant works reviewed in this study disregarded the real aspects of the problem and viewed the identified bias as a phenomenon that entails only a single country. No research has been explored that employs historical narrative analysis as a method to analyse the textbook treatment of the question. This method can provide a different opportunity to focus on the historical property of the textbooks being analysed.

This review can show, too, that all relevant pieces of research support the idea that textbooks used to teach the Israel-Palestine question are biased; all of the studies, except two, support the idea that the prevailing bias is a pro-Israeli one. The writers who found an anti-Israeli bias were not academicians, but played an obvious role in promoting Israeli views in the United States. One has acted as president of the Institute for Jewish and Community Research in San Francisco and the other was Executive Director of the American-Israeli Cooperative

Enterprise (AICE). These roles might act as a principal factor in the related manifestation and also can explain best these different positions.

The remainder of this chapter elaborates how the studies take positions on the nature of prevailing bias they located in the analysed textbooks. Two conflicting kinds of bias, explored in these studies, and the arguments that allow such positions, are offered in the following sections of this literature review: pro-Israel and anti-Israel bias.

Pro-Israeli Bias in Western Textbooks

Most studies identified in the course of this literature review support the conclusion that Western textbooks suffer from a pro-Israeli bias. The first published work identified on the subject, 'Treatment of the Middle East in American High School Textbooks' appeared in the *Journal of Palestine Studies* (JPS) in the United States in 1975. The author, Glenn Perry, an Associate Professor of Political Science at Indiana State University, who analysed twenty American junior and senior high school textbooks on history and area studies, focused 'on the extent of coverage and treatment of Islam, the contemporary Arabs, and the Arab-Israeli conflict' (Perry 1975: 46) and suggested some important conclusions about the textbook treatment of the question. According to him, nothing could be found in the Arabs' favour in American textbooks: 'I found no book which could be considered even slightly biased in the Arabs' favour' (Perry 1975: 52–3). He identified the Arab-Israeli conflict as a main area of bias in dealing with the Middle East: 'The result is not only a great deal of misinformation but also – whether from malice or a simple lack of knowledge – biased accounts of certain subjects, especially the Arab-Israeli conflict' (Perry 1975: 57).

He supports his conclusion with several pieces of evidence: 'I might note that even the "basically objective" books strengthen the Zionist case by at least implying that the modern Jews – instead of being a religious group of heterogeneous racial and ethnic backgrounds – are literally the same people as the ancient Israelites' (Perry 1975: 53). In another case he asserts; 'Thus the conception that the Zionist is "returning" to his real "homeland" is uncritically accepted' (Perry 1975: 53). Or 'For instance, the establishment of Israel is briefly described, with a flashback on the history of Palestine which entirely omits the Arab period. The country was thus presumably uninhabited from the dispersion of the Jews until it was "returned to them"' (Perry 1975: 53). He also argues: 'books in a second category are considered biased because they simply neglect to explain why the Palestinians (if they mention that Palestinians exist) and other Arabs might, from their point of view, oppose Zionism and Israel' (Perry 1975: 53).

Perry supports his conclusion by concrete pieces of evidence i.e. biased statements from textbooks he analysed: 'Another book explains the problem as being the result of Israel's "relatively high standard of living, which caused envy and discontent among the Arab peasants"' (Perry 1975: 56–7). There are other cases, according to him, where Palestinian opposition to Israel has been framed in total ignorance of Israeli occupation: 'Part of the [Arab] opposition [to Israel] arose from the reappearance of ancient Moslem hatred of infidels, and part from the fact that, to Moslems, the Jews represented Western power' (Perry 1975: 56). He is successful, as well, to produce other notable instances: 'But the Jews "found a poor, barren, desolate country" until they, with a "tremendous expenditure of labour and money," turned it into "an oasis of Western civilization in the Middle East"' (Perry 1975: 56).

What happened in the United States after the 1973 Arab-Israeli war, and the subsequent oil embargo, might have contributed to the research boom about the Middle East conflict in this era. The Middle East Studies Association of North America published an influential piece of research; in *The Image of the Middle East in Secondary School Textbooks*, William J. Griswold analysed forty-two Canadian and American secondary school books for the way they treated the Middle East.

Griswold is another researcher who supports the idea that there is a pro-Israeli bias where American textbooks treat the Middle East. He takes the Arab-Israeli wars, as one case of analysis, to examine how textbooks treat the Middle East. In relation to the 1948 Arab-Israeli war, he states; 'Few relate the events by which mostly European immigrants established a new state in a land populated predominantly by Arabs. No text parallels the victories of the outnumbered Zionists in 1948 with the agonies suffered by Palestinian Arabs, such as the killing at the village of Deir Yassin' (Griswold 1975: 22). In referring to another fascinating case he mentions the assassination of the United Nations ambassador by Zionists: 'little note is made of the premeditated murder by Zionists of the United Nations ambassador, Count Bernadotte; indeed several authors, using the passive voice, may even lead students to attribute the murder to Palestinians' (Griswold 1975: 22).

Another instance is related to the refugees:

As for the more than one million war refugees, one author views them as a 'problem [which] plagued the new state of Israel' ... Few authors explain the Palestinian refugee question as fundamental to any peace settlement, observing rather, as did a Canadian author, how much wiser the Israelis have been in absorbing Jewish refugees, whereas the Arabs refuse to accept Palestinians.
Griswold 1975: 22

Griswold makes a powerful point here: 'How useful, at this point, would have been an explanation that hearth and home to a displaced Palestinian happens to be the same spot on the earth as that currently occupied by a displaced Jew' (Griswold 1975: 23). In relation to the 1967 war, when Israel invaded neighbouring Arab countries and occupied a considerable part of them, Griswold elaborates how this is treated in the analysed textbooks; 'The Six Day War of June 1967 "broke out" in some texts' (Griswold 1975: 24). He makes clear that 'Most assert the Israeli view that war began when President Nasser ordered out the UNEF [United Nations Emergency Force] troops from Egypt and blockaded the Gulf of Aqaba' (Griswold 1975: 24).

'Women Concerned about the Middle East' published a book, 'The Arab World: A Handbook for Teachers', that supports the idea that there is a pro-Israel bias in American textbooks: 'In American textbooks the indigenous people of Palestine are usually referred to as "Arabs," "refugees," "natives," or "Moslems," as in the media prior to the 1970's, textbooks avoid the word Palestinian' (Al-Qazzaz 1978: 37).

Deborah Jacobs reported the results of her investigation (1981) on textbooks used in metropolitan Washington, DC school systems, sponsored by the National Association of Arab Americans (NAAA), in an article published in *The Social Studies*; 'Teaching the Arab World: Evaluating Textbooks'. This study concentrated on the presentation of the Arab World and Islam in junior and senior high school textbooks used then (1980) in Fairfax County, Virginia, Montgomery County, Maryland, and the District of Columbia. Nineteen textbooks are evaluated against nine subjects: education, economy, political factors, religion, Arab characteristics, ancient history, women, the Arab-Israeli conflict, and geography. Jacobs concludes that five areas of concern have been identified by evaluators of American textbooks. The fourth one is relevant and significant: 'Exposition of the Arab-Israeli conflict often comes out as Arab-equals-bad, Israeli-equals-good' (Jacobs 1981: 151).

A new dimension of textbook treatment of the Middle East has been covered when a PhD thesis was submitted at Harvard University in 1990 titled 'State Adoption Policies, Publishing Practices, and Authorship: The Production of Middle East Chapters in World History Textbooks' (van de Ven 1990). This piece of research, unlike many others that are product-oriented, is process-oriented. The research, identifying the textbook approaches to the Middle East, traces the evolution of the Middle East section of textbooks to evaluate the influence of different factors in textbook production. The author argues, as she puts it, against the popular view that state adoption institutes dictate policy on publishers' agendas (van de Ven 1990: v). She concludes that this is one influential factor, besides others, including publishers' practices and the authorship element (van de Ven 1990: v).

The author acknowledges the bias in textbooks' treatment of the question but she believes that this bias is representative of US textbook treatment of non-Western regions. She mentions the way non-Western nations are described in American textbooks; 'Illiterate Iranians, 'determined Israelis, "warlike and aggressive Turks," and "backward Iraq" simplify the delineation of what Americans view as good and evil, and right and wrong' (van de Ven 1990: 33). Contrary to the researcher's conclusion, the first inference that comes from that instance is about how different Israel, another non-Western country, and its adversaries are depicted in the American textbooks. Other instances, she produces, on the way American textbooks treat Israel raise the same impression:

- 'Macmillan, for example, conveys Israel's moral standing without the use of factual information; "Israel's success story is one of a young, progressive country that continues to honor the time-honored traditions of its people"' (van de Ven 1990: 33).

- 'The Arab-Israeli political controversy is summed up in Globe's description: "Of all the problems faced by this tiny desert nation, the most serious is the hatred shown by its Arab neighbors. 'Tiny' Israel and the 'hatred' of the Arabs suggest a pattern of vulnerability and aggression, without the support of factual information"' (van de Ven 1990: 33–4).

When it comes to Israel's conflict with Middle Eastern countries, the story is portrayed in a biased way as well: 'religious differences are cited as the cause of the Arab-Israeli and Iran-Iraq wars. Repeated referral to the Arab-Israeli conflict as a struggle between Muslim and Jew steers analysis away from the issues of land and political sovereignty' (van de Ven 1990: 38–9). She further explains how this conflict is treated, in the textbooks analysed:

> Factual accounts of the Arab-Israeli conflict are selective, fuelling the mistaken assumption that at the heart of the issue is the loss of land by both sides. Scott Foresman writes that, 'Arabs and Israelis each believed that they had wrongfully lost parts of their lands'... What follows from this contention is the portrayal of the Arabs as historic aggressors ... Indeed, the same text recalls that, 'on the very day Israel become free, six Arab armies attacked it. Since then, Israel's boundaries have changed numerous times as a result of wars with Arab nations'.
>
> van de Ven 1990: 39–40

Van de Ven mentions another textbook with the same treatment: 'Holt pursues the same line of argument. The 1948 Arab invasion of Israel "was only the first of many invasions and raids launched by Israel's neighbors"' (van de Ven 1990: 40). When textbooks are talking about the population in Israel they ignore Arabs or the existing discrimination against them: 'Many people in Israel are Arabs. They have the same rights as Jews. Prentice Hall goes into detail as it focuses upon Israel's ethnic diversity, referring to Ashkenazie and Sephardic Jews, but neglecting to include non-Jews as part of the Country's ethnic make-up' (van de Ven 1990: 41). In relation to Israel's military operations against its adversaries, what is related to Israel is justified but what is about its adversaries is portrayed in a different way:

> The same text pursues its argument for the legitimacy of military action as a means of achieving Israeli interests by stating that 'it took two more wars before the canal was open to Israel.' The rationality of these Middle Eastern wars is thus implied. Finally, Israel's participation in raids against the PLO is legitimized in the context of self-defence, while PLO raiding falls under the label of terrorism. 'The PLO often resorts to raids against Israel. The Israelis fight back to prevent terrorist raids and to retaliate against attacks they cannot prevent.'
>
> van de Ven 1990: 47

The Center for Middle Eastern and North African Studies published another study in 1994 that investigated seventy-five American textbooks for how they treat the Middle East: 'Evaluation of Secondary-level Textbooks for Coverage of the

Middle East and North Africa'. The researcher, Elizabeth Barlow, ranked the studied textbooks in different categories from A to E where A represents the highest quality. Barlow concluded that problems and biases which Griswold identified in 1975 still exist (Morgan 2002: 42). She published an article a year later, in 1995, stressing the results of her investigation:

> The Middle East Studies Association (MESA) and the Middle East Outreach Council (MEOC) have long been concerned with the inadequate and inaccurate portrayal of Middle Eastern history, geography and culture in many pre collegiate texts. In its initial 1974 examination of K–12 textbooks, MESA found them generally disappointing. Although in the last nineteen years, several superior texts have been published, regrettable errors still exist in many other books.
>
> Barlow 1995

She blamed the textbook writers for the disappointing errors she discovered: 'Apparently, when writing about topics that concern the Middle East, American writers do not feel any need to consult world area experts. As a result, several texts offer serious misinformation and frequently only America-centered perspectives' (Barlow 1995).

She concluded that what has been presented about Israel in American textbooks is mainly from the Israeli view (Morgan 2002: 44). She gives instances to support this conclusion: 'mentioning textbook references to the Balfour Declaration as a source of promise for a Jewish homeland but failing to consider the other part of the declaration about the rights of non-Jews in the Holy Land' (Morgan 2002: 44–5). Or in another case, on why Palestinians opposed the establishment of Israel, she argues that many textbooks do not mention how Palestinians' loss of their land is related to the Jewish immigration to the Holy Land. She also refers to the 1967 war that Israel started and refers to textbooks that introduce Egypt as the starter of that war (Morgan 2002: 45). Barlow's research became influential and a principal source of reference for the relevant literature in the years to come.

The first textbook analysis that concentrates specifically on the Arab-Israeli question appeared in 1996. Marlene Rock, through her master's thesis submitted to Queens College, City University of New York, 'The Arab-Israeli Conflict as Depicted in Children's and Young Adult Non-Fiction Literature', tried to fill the gap. She argued that while enough sources exist for adults to get knowledge about the conflict there is not such a chance for schoolchildren. To deal with the problem she identified 103 works about the history of the conflict that can, she claims, help students to access the knowledge of the question (Rock 1996: abstract). The main function of this research is an annotated bibliography of the sources identified, and it does not involve a substantial analysis of the examined textbooks.

Increasing interest in finding unbiased textbooks for teaching the Middle East helped in the development of another academic research exercise in the United States: 'The Development of a Content Analysis Instrument for Analysing College-Level Textbooks Used in the United States to Teach About the Middle East'. The researcher, Adel Tawfig Al-Bataineh, who reviewed the literature on the textbook treatment of the Middle East made three important points: first, most of the relevant works support the conclusion that bias is widespread when it is a matter of textbook treatment of the Middle East; second, no content analysis has been conducted to analyse the problem in college-level textbooks; and third, there is no instrument to use when textbooks are analysed for such a purpose. In his research, he worked to construct such an instrument that can help educators when they are conducting a content analysis of textbooks for their treatment of the Middle East. He used standards and goals suggested by UNESCO and Councils for Social Studies, Geography, and World History on what students should know about a subject, for such a construction (Al-Bataineh 1998: 79).

Hani Morgan in his PhD thesis, 'The Portrayal of the Middle East in School Textbooks from 1880 to the Present' went further to study textbooks' treatment of the Middle East from a different viewpoint where the subject is not seen as a fixed reality but a changing phenomenon. He discussed four different periods in relation to American textbooks' treatment of the Middle East, and came to a notable conclusion:

> Although the later books are in general less biased than the earlier ones and begin to talk about the oppression by Europeans, they often treat other political issues in a biased way. As Chapter 1 suggested, various books from the later period describe the Arab-Israeli conflict in a biased way and leave out important details; thus, readers are led to believe that the Arabs are hostile and responsible for many angles of the conflict that they are not responsible for. Some books also repeatedly make comparisons between the Arab countries and Israel, and emphasize Israel's superiority without stating relevant facts.
>
> Morgan 2002: 174–5

A thesis-length study, 'A Novel Reading: Literature and Pedagogy in Modern Middle East History Courses in Canada and the United States', approached Middle East history from a different angle (Leeke 2005). It focused on course syllabi as the main source for analysing how Middle East history textbooks are treated at the college level: 'The purpose of this study is to explore how the Arabic novel can and does challenge the conventional characterization of what constitutes constructive Middle East historiography. The thesis draws on a case study of undergraduate history course syllabi in order to highlight a number of crucial issues related to Arabic literature and the production of modern Middle East history' (Leeke 2005: abstract). For such a purpose, ninety-three syllabi were collected from introductory or survey undergraduate courses or seminars on the history of the modern Middle East. Sixty-five of them were found fit for the analysis. Two methods were used to collect them: searching relevant keywords in search engines such as Google, and correspondence with lecturers on the Modern Middle East courses through their email addresses (Leeke 2005: 7–8).

The collected syllabi are analysed through text analysis. This analysis is based, theoretically, on David Nunan's study, 'Syllabus Design: Language Teaching: A Scheme for Teacher Education' which states that a syllabus is useful for analysis as it represents a 'statement of content' of a course, and some other materials relevant to syllabus studies (Leeke 2005: 15). Another theoretical assumption that has been borrowed for Leeke's research is related to the role college teachers play in designing a syllabus that includes a section on what students should read (reading list), and the significance of this role in determining the content of the course. Leeke asserts that this role and its affective consequences on what students learn have remained undiscussed:

> Professors make important decisions about how the course subject matter will be taught based on a variety of factors. Unfortunately, as Gregory S. Jay argues, particularly with regard to assigning 'cultural objects' such as novels, many syllabi in the humanities remain 'suspiciously silent about their social and institutional construction: about the choices the syllabus has made, the alternatives it has considered and abandoned, and the external pressures that have shaped it' ... Those decisions, however, are often reflected in the language and structure of the course syllabus. Thus, by examining the selection and description of the 'assigned objects' and 'their place on the syllabus', it is possible to uncover some of the 'process of disciplinary construction that has put them there'.
>
> Leeke 2005: 17

The research allows the researcher to find the most adopted textbooks on the history of the Middle East, and how novels are treated in the course reading lists. William Cleveland's *A History of the Modern Middle East* is introduced as a prime source of course knowledge since it was adopted in forty-two (out of sixty-five) syllabi (Leeke 2005: 33). Lots of points presented in this research can inform and justify what I have done in Chapter 3 to select the most adopted textbooks on the history of the Israel-Palestine question.

Years after American bloody involvements in two Middle Eastern countries, Afghanistan and Iraq, a textbook analysis was developed in 2007 to explore a possible cause of American misperceptions about the Middle East. This research, 'The Portrayal of The Middle East in Secondary School U.S. Textbooks', is grounded on observation of American students, and depict them as those who are walking into college classes on the Middle East / Islam with negative and stereotypical views acquired beforehand (Brockway 2007: 19). For the researcher, Elizabeth Marie Brockway, this is not the most significant problem. She approaches the problem through the influence of a national image of a foreign country/region on American involvement in that area. In this respect, she relies on Holsti's theoretical point on how a belief system affects national decisions: 'The relationship of national images to international conflict is clear: decision-makers act upon their definition of the situation and their images of states – others as well as their own. These images are in turn dependent upon the decision-makers' belief system. And these may or may not be accurate representations of "reality"' (Holsti 1962). American Middle Eastern policy is regarded as problematic in this research, and the solution is seen in what Holsti recommends for such a situation:

Holsti (1962) concluded that in order to resolve international conflict, erroneous images of other countries had to be corrected – leaders' belief systems had to provide a more accurate impression of other people and cultures. In a democracy, leaders must be responsive to the views of their constituents and thus, leaders' belief systems are linked to those of the public. For example: if the people of the United States believe that inhabitants of the Middle East are terrorists, the people will support policies within the U.S. that reflect that, and they will be unlikely to support aid and policies friendly towards the Middle East. Even enlightened leaders will have to respond to these demands or face electoral defeat. Thus the belief systems of ordinary people are crucial to understand.

Brockway 2007: 4

Based on this theoretical foundation the researcher designs a hypothesis for her textbook analysis: 'high school textbooks used in the United States provide an inadequate and negatively biased portrayal of the Middle East' (Brockway 2007: 29). For this investigation, ten world history textbooks from secondary schools are selected for analysis. To represent a wider community, Brockway chooses her selections from the list of 'Widely Adopted Textbooks' that are regularly published by the American Textbook Council (ATC). Quantitative and qualitative methods are used to analyse those textbooks for three kinds of bias: word use, omission of data, and presentation of inadequate information. Six subjects, including the Arab-Israeli conflict, are chosen as the areas of analysis (Brockway 2007: 29–32). The research ends with a conclusion that confirms the original hypothesis of the thesis: 'junior and senior high school textbooks used in the United States provided a negatively biased portrayal of the Middle East through word use, omission, and the presentation of inadequate information' (Brockway 2007: 70). In relation to the Arab-Israeli conflict, the research produces some notable results:

> Some of the textbooks did not allude to the justification of both Israelis and Palestinians to the disputed land, leading students to believe that the land belonged to the Jews (since they do control the land now). The textbooks did not discuss the airlift that the United States provided to Israel that prevented the Arab surprise attack in 1973 from succeeding; thus the books did not adequately explain why OPEC temporarily halted oil shipments to the United States (in response to the airlift). Without understanding that the United States and the West in general have actively been involved in the Middle East, many times without the popular support of the Middle Easterners, students would find it difficult to understand why the region is so hesitant to allow Western influence now.
>
> Brockway 2007: 72

A PhD thesis conducted in the University of Gothenburg, 'Framing the Israel/Palestine Conflict in Swedish History School Textbooks', registered a momentous development in the relevant literature. It might represent, indeed, the only detailed examination of the textbook treatment of the Israel-Palestine question in a Western country. In addition to its topic, it has other significant characteristics that introduce it as a highly important work. The researcher, Michael Walls, identified a problem in Sweden's history textbooks where textbook knowledge about Israel-Palestine shows no sign of a reasonable link with related scholarly knowledge (Walls 2010: 313). He found this at odds with traditional Swedish neutrality that provides an environment for the unbiased treatment of the question (Walls 2010: 13). The different treatment he identified was recognized as a power/knowledge problem (Walls 2010: 13).

Walls analysed twenty lower secondary school history textbooks used in Sweden and thirteen interviews with social science / civics teachers to answer a key question: 'How the Israel/Palestine conflict is framed in Swedish History school textbooks and how it compares to established scholarly debate on the conflict and teacher discourses' (Walls 2010: 13). The answer to this question, according to Walls's analysis, is: 'the linkages between scholarship, textbooks and teachers' statements in general have been very weak and do not provide a platform for a broad critical understanding of the root causes of the conflict on the basis of varying perspectives. Instead, they are far too anchored in ideological assumptions' (Walls 2010: 6).

In his literature review, he mentions cases of relevant research including a piece of research about the subject in Sweden: 'Det är en annan historia ... vilken historia ger vi våra elever?' ['It's a different story ... what story do we give our students?']. This essay, written in Swedish, is designed to examine 'how the history of the Middle East is mediated in teaching aids for History' (Walls 2010: 26) through analysing four Swedish upper secondary textbooks. The review introduced the essay's main argument: 'unfortunately a concentration on concrete problems is absent'; for instance 'why the Palestinians had to pay for the crimes of the Nazis with regard to the crimes against Jews during the Second World War' (Walls 2010: 28).

This doctoral research is based on the results of a pilot study, 'Framing Conflict and War in Lower Secondary School Books: Israel and Palestine' that was conducted earlier through examining four Swedish History textbooks (published between the period of the mid-to late 1990s and early 2000s). The pilot study found that, as Walls put it: 'the historical plight of the Jewish people is highlighted at the beginning of some of the sections I have analysed. However, the plight of the Palestinian Arabs is not highlighted in the same way. Israelis are often presented as benign, victims, retaliatory not aggressive or violent. Arab Palestinians are represented as aggressive, violent and somewhat irrational' (Walls 2010: 17). Walls recognizes the underlying discourse of the textbooks he examined as based on the assumption that 'Palestinians are predisposed to violence, while Israelis merely seek peace' (Walls 2010: 17). He affirms that such a discourse 'creates an impression which misleads and misinforms, fostering prejudice and bias towards both parties' (Walls 2010: 17). This pilot study ends with a significant conclusion:

> I also discovered that certain topics and themes were emphasised more than others in most of the textbook chapters. For example, historical events such as

the Nazi holocaust would very often introduce the history of the conflict as would references to the Jewish people's biblical-historical connection to ancient Israel and their historical suffering. These topics and themes provided a context or framework from which to introduce and study the history of the conflict. An important part of the Palestinian historical narrative, namely, the al-Nakba and the expulsion and flight of the Palestinian Arabs in 1948 also appeared in some of the textbooks somewhere in the middle of a text. Briefly mentioned in the textbooks, this event provided more or less the only back-drop to the plight of the Palestinian-Arabs ... Another finding I made too referred to positive and negative biases in the form of reductive images or one-dimensional roles ascribed to both parties to the conflict. For example, references which reinforced certain stereotypes were the image of Israelis as victims, as reinforced by the references to the Nazi holocaust and historical Jewish suffering, and the Palestinians as aggressors or rejectionists, with references to the Arab rejection of the 1947 Partition Plan and the reaction of the Arab states to the establishment of Israel in 1948.

Walls 2010: 18

Walls compares, then, the findings of his PhD thesis with the results of this pilot study; 'Examination of the History textbook chapters for this thesis has more or less confirmed a repetition of the above with a number of important exceptions' (Walls 2010: 18).

In the first analytical chapter of Walls's thesis (Chapter 4: Making Connections and Constructing Causes), treatment of the root causes and parties to the conflict is examined. This has been done through three sub-chapters (sections):

1. Establishing a Historical Connection to the Holy Land
2. From the Balfour Declaration Onwards
3. Partition, 1948 and the Creation of the Refugee Problem

In the first section, Walls elaborates how Swedish textbooks treat the historical connection of both conflicting parties, Israel and Palestine, to the land:

The opening sections of the textbooks focus on a specific number of topics and themes which, taken together, as Masalha puts it, form 'an unbroken chain of [historical] presence' in the land. These selected topics and themes function to construct a seamless connection between the Jews or Jewish people of ancient Israel to the state of modern Israel and to a lesser extent the Arab Palestinians to ancient Canaan. This is achieved through an interdiscursive mingling of historical, biblical and national topical and thematic references. The most poignant example of this is the reference to modern Israel as the youngest and oldest state in one of the textbooks. Other allusions to nationhood are made when Jerusalem is referred to as the capital city of ancient Israel or Judea or when it is described as the original homeland of the Jews. To strengthen this metahistorical connection further, reference is made to a 3000-year-old presence in the land and to the (national) Jewish remnant following the expulsion of the Jewish people from ancient Jerusalem by the Romans. We also learn that these same Jews were to emigrate to Europe, Africa and America following their exile into Diaspora. Other topics and themes connected to the above are the universally embraced dream of return and the Nazi holocaust. Both of these interact with and are reinforced by the idea of nationhood and biblical mythhistory, to borrow Sand's phrase.

Walls 2010: 152

Walls explains, in the first section of the chapter, how weak or vague historical stories as well as narratives that have no place in history borrowed from national and religious myths to establish a connection between Jews and the land. On the contrary, the obvious facts about the Palestinian connections to the land were located in some twisted historical narratives:

Arab connection to the land is established generally in terms of the invasion of Palestine or their arrival as nomads in Palestine in the Middle Ages. In one textbook, a more metahistorical Arab-Canaanite connection to the land is constructed. In general contrast, however, the Jews of ancient Israel are not portrayed as arriving in Palestine but are always present in the land.

Walls 2010: 152

Swedish textbooks, in line with this strategy, avoided presentation of the obvious fact that the Palestinians were the owners of the land, when the Zionists claimed it, and long before it. This is done, as Walls puts it, to establish a 'natural connection' and for an 'equal claim' to the land; 'However, arguably an "equal" claim to the land is tacitly invoked through the "natural" connections made between history, religion and nation established in the textbooks. That is, through the discourse on Jewish/Arab connection to the land' (Walls 2010: 153). Walls argues that the findings that come from teachers' interviews confirm, also, such a conclusion:

Interestingly too, some of my interview respondents have invoked such a claim. To mention but a few, one respondent claimed that 'the conflict is basically about both parties having a right to the land'. Another intoned that 'both sides are right on that point.' Invoking the connection discourse another teacher added that 'a long time [had] passed' and then 'they [the Jewish people] were able to return.'

Walls 2010: 153

In the next section ('From the Balfour Declaration Onwards'), Walls raised another question: 'How are the issues of Zionism, the Balfour Declaration, Britain's support and broken promises, immigration and increasing tensions treated?' (Walls 2010: 177). The Walls' answer, to this question, is formulated in the following paragraph:

The general discursive framework for understanding these issues consists of a number of interconnected topics and themes introduced throughout the textbook chapters. First of all, in the opening sections, both the construction of a Palestinian and Jewish connection to the land is established in the textbook chapters through, as Andersen puts it, 'the reimagining of an ancient religious community as a nation'. Themes such as religion and nationhood and topics connected to them provide a common-sense framework for understanding and explaining the histories of Jews and Arabs in Palestine. In turn, this supports the emergent and recurrent notion of 'equal' claim to the land. In addition, Jewish (meta) historical identity is constructed around the above topics and themes to seamlessly connect the modern Zionist movement and modern Israel to 'the vast Diasporan centre' and ancient (biblical) Israel. In turn, the purpose of Zionism is not discussed in terms of its political (colonial) or ideological moorings. Instead, it is discussed in terms of a natural connection between Judaism and Zionism and the latter's purpose to provide a safe haven for Jews everywhere under the auspices of Theodor Herzl, following increased anti-Semitism in the late 19th century.

Walls 2010: 177

In relation to Zionism, Walls adds later, 'the role and purpose of the Zionist movement is not placed in any critical light. Instead, it is described as existing to return a persecuted Jewish people to its biblical-historical (and national) homeland to create a haven for all Jews' (Walls 2010: 252). Walls clarifies, also, how Jewish immigration is seen in the context of Jewish suffering:

The theme of historical Jewish suffering introduced in the opening sections of the textbooks (e.g. pogroms, ghettoisation, expulsions etc.) is reintroduced in the historical event of the extermination of six million European Jews during the Nazi holocaust. This event acts as the subsequent backdrop to the topic of Jewish immigration and the explanatory framework for acts of Jewish terror in the wake of the 1939 White Paper along with allusions to British collaboration with the Arabs. In addition, the shifting of the topic of Jewish immigration to the plight of Holocaust survivors pits the latter against the indigenous population and constructs a difficult moral dilemma (e.g. whose plight should the reader adhere to the most).

Walls 2010: 178

As Walls points out, this creates a complicated problem and moral dilemma that locates textbook readers in a difficult position of 'should one support the Holocaust survivors or the Arabs of Palestine?' (Walls 2010: 174)

The last section of Walls's Chapter 4 (Partition, 1948 and the Creation of the Refugee Problem), is guided by a main question: 'How are the topics of the partition proposal, the 1948 war and the creation of the refugee problem treated in the textbooks examined above?' (Walls 2010: 192) The answer, according to Walls, is:

I have already discussed the general framework established in the textbooks in the opening sections of this chapter. Some of these are reinvoked in the treatment of the partition proposal in the textbooks too. For example, the historical event of the extermination of six million European Jews during the Nazi holocaust serves as part of the explanatory frame for understanding the purpose of partition. Partition is understood here to prevent the Holocaust from ever happening again and to provide the Jewish people with a state of their own.

Walls 2010: 192–3

What happened in 1948 constitutes another part of the answer:

The general framework discussed is also present in relation to the topics of the 1948 war or 'War of Independence' and the creation of the refugee problem, including the idea of 'equal' claim to the land. This is mediated through among other things the employment of the term independence to describe Israel's defensive war against the Arab states. As soon as the state of Israel is established and its political independence declared in the textbooks we learn that the Arab states have launched an aggressive attack on it in order to destroy it. The reasons given range from a non-desire to have a Jewish state as a neighbour or a desire to have Palestine continue as an Arabic country. Bringing in the international law discourse, the creation of the refugee problem is also treated in the textbooks. However, no direct connection is made to Israel's own actions but instead 'the war' is ascribed an agentive role in causing either the flight or expulsion of the Palestine Arabs. The issue of Arab flight or expulsion is treated as a contested one in the textbooks. Mention is made of the fact that in defiance of international law the Palestinian refugees are not permitted to return to their homes occupied by Israel in 1949. Mitigating this, it is explained that these homes were needed to accommodate Jewish refugees expelled from Arab countries.

Walls 2010: 193

The next chapter of Walls's thesis (Chapter 5), 'Pivotal Conflicts and Processes of Peace', concentrates on the 'key events of conflict and peace' and examines the textbook treatments of the related matters. In relation to the 1967 war, the results of the textbook examination demonstrate, as Walls puts it: 'First of all, the seminal events or conflict triggers presented in the texts are among other things Egypt's stopping of maritime traffic, the gathering of Egyptian troops along the border and even the claim of an attack launched on Israel' (Walls 2010: 208). One textbook makes a clear statement about this; 'in 1967, Egypt and the other Arab states launched a new attack on Israel' (Walls 2010: 207). Regarding the lands Israel occupied in this war, Walls argues: 'Israel's victory and occupation of the West Bank and Gaza (as well as the Golan Heights and the Sinai) is explained in terms of its security needs or as a defensive act (a "counterattack")' (Walls 2010: 208). Besides this sympathetic position towards Israel, the Palestinian ownership of the land is treated very differently: 'In the next paragraph we learn that "the Palestinians wanted back the land that they felt was theirs". Echoing the framework examined in previous textbook chapters, the nature of Palestinian or local Arab ownership of the land is reduced to a strongly-felt desire or claim' (Walls 2010: 208). In addition, Walls suggests another interesting point about the occupied land when saying: 'Although mentioned from time to time, perhaps one of the least covered contexts presented in the textbooks is that of the Israeli occupation in the post-'67 war period despite the fact that there exists an abundance of information from various sources such as human rights organisations, NGOs etc.' (Walls 2010: 217). As Walls shows, this occupation is justified through other ways in Swedish textbooks:

> 'the Palestinian people still do not have a land of their own'. The reason for this is that Israel 'has refused to return the West Bank and the other areas conquered in 1967'. Following this, an explanation is provided for Israel's refusal which has to do with 'water shortages'. This we learn 'is an important reason for why Israel intends to keep the West Bank' because 'Israel gathers much of its drinking-water from the occupied West Bank'. Previously in the same textbook we learn that the reasons for Israeli occupation have to do with 'security'. Thus the textbook establishes the mitigating hurdles toward ending the occupation as Israeli security and Israeli water shortages but not the occupation itself.
>
> Walls 2010: 221

In relation to the Intifada, Walls found,

> Generally speaking, while the beginning of the first Intifada is connected to Palestinian actions it is only vaguely connected to the Israeli occupation through such slogans as 'humiliation and repression' or a 'desperate situation'. The tendency, then, is to focus on Palestinian violence as the general trigger and Israeli retaliation as the general response. The Israeli occupation itself is not described as a direct cause of conflict or even as a direct act of violence which Palestinians would respond or retaliate to.
>
> Walls 2010: 230

In Walls's Chapter 7, 'Concluding Discussion', the overall results of examining Swedish textbooks are produced. In relation to the fictional history of Jewish redemptionist efforts to return to their 'homeland', Walls concludes, 'Thus, the dream of return is understood in the textbooks and teachers' statements to actually mean the physical, political return of the Jewish people metahistorically connected to the land' (Walls 2010: 298). Walls reveals, also, how textbooks mix different realities to achieve the ideal integrity: 'It is understood throughout the textbook chapters that there is a metahistorical connection between the Zionist settlers, Nazi holocaust survivors and the Jews of ancient biblical times since they are considered one and the same nation-people' (Walls 2010: 301). The point Walls raised about how textbooks treat the Israeli occupation is another interesting case of bias: 'The Israeli role of occupier is never directly referred to and neither is the occupation itself described as a direct cause of the conflict. Nor is the occupation even described as an act of violence which Palestinians would respond or retaliate to or even resist' (Walls 2010: 302).

Walls's thesis started from an initial problem about the gap between textbook narratives on the Palestine-Israel conflict and scholarly sources. One section, 'Comparing Scholarship and the Textbooks' is designed to provide the results of the research in this area:

> Apart from the unique framework the Swedish textbooks proceed from, there is another significant difference between them and the scholarly literature and from time to time the Israeli textbooks themselves. This difference concerns the manner in which the root causes of the conflict are presented. In the Swedish textbooks we learn that the conflict is about two distinctive metahistorical peoples who are struggling over the same piece of land that they share an 'equal' claim to. In contrast, in the scholarly literature, such issues as the political and ideological roots of Zionism are discussed and fought out. And whether 'new historians' or traditional historians agree or not such a discussion appears to be connected to a further one concerning the background causes of the conflict.
>
> Walls 2010: 308

Then the thesis produces a general conclusion in this regard: 'focusing on the textbooks alone, they do not provide the teachers or pupils with a platform for a broad critical-analytical and balanced understanding of the root causes of the conflict on the basis of varying perspectives' (Walls 2010: 313).

A year later, in 2011, Michael Walls published the results of his academic research in an online newsletter, Dissident Voice. In this article, he stressed the Swedish government's neutral policy under Olaf Palme and even under the more pro-Israeli government of Göran Persson that is at odds with how Swedish textbooks frame Israel-Palestine history. Concerning this, he mentions the history of 1948 where new historians brought new perspectives that even find a place in Israeli textbooks: 'For example, since the 1980s and prior to that, discussions between so-called "new historians", traditionalists and anti-traditionalists have touched on topics such as Zionism's political and ideological (and colonial) moorings, the concept of "transfer" and how the Palestinian refugee problem was created. However, such discussions have been continually absent in the Swedish History school textbooks examined' (Walls 2011).

One of the few books explored on the subject, in this literature review, was published in 2011 in the United States: *The Politics of Teaching Palestine to Americans: Addressing Pedagogical Strategies*. This book confirms the existence of a problem in American education when it is about teaching Palestine, stressing the point that teaching Palestine in American schools does not encourage a constructive involvement in the Israel-Palestine question and reinforces the treatment of the question in favour of the powerful side. The book sees indoctrination of American youth with Zionist mythology as a problem and tries to provide ideas for dealing with that (Knopf-Newman 2011). This book does not involve an empirical investigation of American textbooks; it takes Zionist mythology as a problem and goes further to explain its consequences and offer ways to solve such a problem.

The first US study that analysed the textbook treatment of the question appeared in the same year (2011). This analysis, an MA thesis in Cedarville University, focused on how the depiction of the Arab-Israeli conflict has been changed in US history textbooks since the 1950s. No research has been conducted in the United States, prior to this thesis, which focuses exclusively on how American textbooks treat the Arab-Israeli question, the thesis reveals (Smith 2011: 40). To answer the main question of the research, 'how have descriptions of the Arab-Israeli conflict changed in U.S. high school history textbooks since the 1950s' (Smith 2011: 1), the time limitation of the research, from the 1950s to the present (2000s), is divided into six time periods of six succeeding decades. Three textbooks are selected for each decade that belong to three leading textbook publishers. The content analysis, both qualitative and quantitative, is used to examine these books in order to, as the researcher puts it, 'highlight whether there has been more or less emphasis on particular events over time, and to identify major patterns and changes in the Arab-Israeli conflict, and the political, social, and educational implications of those changes' (Smith 2011: iii). For such analysis, an operational concept, key event, has been defined. A key event, according to this research, is an event, term or person related to the conflict 'if more than one textbook made reference to it' (Smith 2011: 44). In this way key events include:

> the British mandate period in Palestine, the Balfour Declaration and establishment of Israel as a nation, the 1956 Suez Canal crisis, the 1967 Six Day War, the 1973 Yom Kippur War, the 1979 Camp David Accords, the 1980s conflict in Lebanon, the 1991–1994 peace talks, and post 9/11 Arab-Israeli conflicts. Key people included Yasir Arafat, Menachem Begin, David Ben-Gurion, Golda Meir, Gamal Abdel Nasser, Yitzhak Rabin, and Anwar Sadat. Key terms included Arab(s), Israel and/or Israeli, Jews and/or Jewish, Palestine, and Palestinian.
>
> Smith 2011: 44

Two categories are designed to evaluate all analysed textbooks. The first allocates a rating from 1 to 3 to three textbooks of each decade. A rating of 3 is awarded to the textbooks that covered the subject more thoroughly and covered, better than others, events that are relevant to the history of the question. A rating of 1, in contrast, is allocated to the one that is less successful in doing that job. All these textbooks, also, are evaluated for pro-Israeli or pro-Palestinian bias. If one textbook shows no sign of such bias it is put in a third category, neutral (Smith 2011: 48). Although a lot of work has been done to elaborate on such a sizeable and innovative topic, some points challenge the way the subject is treated in this research: first, the adopted selection procedure does not seem enough to justify the position of those chosen as the most adopted textbooks in the United States; second, the level of criticality the research involves when dealing with textbooks is quite limited – it takes the dominant college textbook knowledge as the legitimate limits of the related knowledge and then defines 'key events' only in the framework of what textbooks produce. Here, for instance, the possibility of ignoring a key event by the most adopted American textbooks is not taken into consideration.

There is one book that is related, although it does not involve a textbook analysis, to this literature, edited by Edward Said and Christopher Hitchens. *Blaming the Victims: Spurious Scholarship and the Palestinian Question* deals with the related scholarship that is influenced by whoever tries to justify Zionist claims about the Israel-Palestine question. In the editors' words, 'Since the 1948 war which drove them from their homeland, the Palestinian people have consistently been denied the most basic democratic rights. *Blaming the Victims* shows how the historical fate of the Palestinians has been justified by spurious academic attempts to dismiss their claim to a home within the boundaries of historical Palestine and even to deny their very existence' (Said and Hitchens 2001, back cover).

Anti-Israel Bias in Western Textbooks

The majority of studies that analysed the textbook treatment of the Israel-Palestine question in Western countries support the idea that these books suffer from a pro-Israeli bias. But two works are explored that support a contradictory argument. The first one, a research report, 'Rewriting History in Textbooks', was published in 1993. This report might not be considered an academic work, but it is mentioned here as it takes a noticeable position on the textbook treatment of the Israel-Palestine question: '[Jewish] silence has allowed publishers to distribute books that are filled with egregious factual errors and specious analyses. The mistakes invariably are to the detriment of the Jews or Israel, raising questions about the predisposition of authors and publishers' (Bard 1993). The author, Mitchell Bard, the Executive Director of the American-Israeli Cooperative Enterprise (AICE), and the director of the Jewish Virtual Library, examined eighteen American history textbooks, eleven world history and seven American history, concluding that only two of them could be recommended. A list of these eighteen textbooks is provided in the report's bibliography. These books are introduced as 'the most widely used world and American history texts' but nothing is presented to justify this position or how they are selected (Bard 1993). Any discussion of the methods, methodology or theoretical basis that makes such research possible is absent. He claims, in this report, that 'inadequate and inaccurate depictions of Middle East history are the norm' (Bard 1993). In relation to anti-Israeli bias he asserts:

> The anti-Israel bias is usually a result of factual inaccuracy, oversimplification, omission and distortion. Common errors include getting dates of events wrong, blaming Israel for wars that were a result of Arab provocation, perpetuating the myth of Islamic tolerance of Jews, minimizing the Jewish aspect of the Holocaust, apologizing for Arab autocrats, refusing to label violence against civilians as terrorism and suggesting that Israel is the obstacle to peace.
>
> Bard 1993

He sees this situation as a dangerous one due to possible effects it can have on American students and leaders of the future:

> The conclusions students are most likely to draw from these presentations are those held by Israel's detractors; therefore, it should not be surprising if students are easily encouraged to believe the worst about Israel when they reach politicized college campuses. Even more worrisome is the likelihood that future American leaders will have their earliest political attitudes toward Israel shaped by misinformation.
>
> Bard 1993

Bard takes an opposing position against a textbook for mentioning the fact that the land had inhabitants that were forced out when Jewish immigrants came to the land, and consider it as a case of anti-Israeli bias;

> The coverage of the Arab-Israeli conflict is particularly abysmal. Much of the crucial history of Palestine before *1948* is omitted, particularly from the U.S. history books. Those texts that discuss the mandatory period present the Arab version of history; that is, an unrestrained flood of Jewish immigrants invaded a land already inhabited by another people, who were subsequently forced out. The historical Jewish presence in the country is usually ignored.
>
> Bard 1993, original emphasis

Other similar points are made:

> The treatment of the causes and conduct of the Arab-Israeli wars in all the texts was appalling. The complexities of the conflict are usually reduced to the Palestinians wanting independence and Israel resisting. The Arabs' refusal to accept a Jewish state in their midst is softened to an unwillingness to 'recognize' Israel, a subtle difference that suggests passivity rather than an active campaign to destroy Israel.
>
> Bard 1993

The second instance of a work that argues for anti-Israeli bias is a book, *The Trouble with Textbooks: Distorting History and Religion*, which is written, in 2008, by Gary Tobin (former president of the Institute for Jewish and Community Research in San Francisco) and Dennis R. Ybarra. It raises the idea that the bias American textbooks are suffering from is anti-Israeli, pro-Arab and pro-Islam (Tobin and Ybarra 2008). The book is celebrated differently in the American mass media: Fox News channel aired, on 4 September 2009, a one-hour programme, titled 'Do You Know What Textbooks Your Children Are Really Reading?' to raise the points made in this book (Carlson 2009). A website (troublewithtextbooks.org, defunct since 2019), in addition, was dedicated to promoting this book and its results. Other websites, including Family Security

Matters, provided a channel to echo the results of this research (Gies-Chumney 2009).

This book is full of relevant points that might help the readers to become familiar with the concerns of pro-Israeli lobbies about textbook content on the Israel-Palestine question. Furthermore, powerful rhetoric is skilfully used to formulate the results in effective wording but there are some shortcomings in the methodology used. While the main claim of the research rests on 'textbooks', a wide range of other educational resources, under the category 'textbook' or 'supplemental material', are addressed in the research project: principally teachers' editions, advanced placements, DVD, CD, websites, curricula, handouts and teacher training (Tobin and Ybarra 2008: 164). All this material can be a legitimate choice of the investigation if there is a reasonable justification but it does not allow a piece of research to use the related findings for the sake of a claim made for a textbook. Furthermore, there is no time limit for items that are selected for the analysis. Content analysis is introduced as the main method to conduct the research. It is mentioned, as well, that other methods, personal interviews and participant observations, are used. No explanation has been given in the book about why and/or how these methods are used or combined in the research (Tobin and Ybarra 2008: 163–4). Another shortcoming is related to an explanation that clarifies how twenty-eight textbooks are selected for analysis; they are described as the most adopted textbooks but nothing is presented to justify this claim.

The areas of concern in this investigation, according to the book, include four main ones:

1. Jewish history, theology, and religion
2. The relationship between Judaism and Christianity
3. The relationship between Judaism and Islam
4. The history, geography, and politics of the Middle East

Tobin and Ybarra 2008: 164

A number of factors are identified in this research as contributing to the textbook problem. References are made to publishers, writers and interest groups, but considerable effort is made to avoid mentioning a particular party as the main element responsible for the problem. The same approach is noticeable when textbooks are mentioned; no specific textbook is mentioned as worse than any other(s). At odds with this approach to avoid blaming a particular publisher, book or writer for the problems identified, Islamic/Arab interest groups are accused as mainly responsible for wrongdoing in textbook production, for what has been described as 'promoting a particular agenda' (Tobin and Ybarra 2008: 155). The Council on Islamic Education is mentioned repeatedly as a problem, responsible for what went wrong. The authors of the book explicitly suggest that this group should be excluded from the process: 'Both publishers and educators need to be able to better distinguish between advocacy groups that work for historical accuracy such as the American Jewish Committee and the Institute for Curriculum

Services (ICS) on the one hand, and groups promoting a particular agenda such as the Council on Islamic Education (CIE) or Arab World and Islamic Resources (AWAIR) on the other' (Tobin and Ybarra 2008: 156).

A considerable figure, 500, is suggested in the book for the number of problematic statements found in American textbooks. They are classified in different categories; 'Arabs Want Peace – Israel Does not' is one category, for instance. Another one, 'Who Put the Palestinian Refugees in Camps?', blames Arabs for the suffering of Palestinian refugees. The writers argue:

> Some of the textbooks strongly imply that Israel itself placed and kept Palestinian refugees in the camps, in agreement with Palestinian beliefs. This has no defensible logic. The idea that Israel, surrounded by hostile Arab governments and devoid of any influence there, could affect the Arab states' refusal to integrate or resettle the Palestinians seems farfetched. These governments, with the exception of Jordan, carried out a deliberate, cynical, and remarkably inhumane policy of keeping the refugees in squalid camps on their territories so that the refugees would serve as political pawns in world opinion to pressure Israel.
>
> Tobin and Ybarra 2008: 124

In a related category, the authors blamed what is called 'Omission of Jewish Refugees': 'most textbooks make no mention of what essentially became a refugee exchange: hundreds of thousands of Jews, residents of Arab countries for thousands of years, were expelled or chose to flee hostile anti-Semitic societies' (Tobin and Ybarra 2008: 126). Another category, 'Denying the Jewish Connection to the Land of Israel', criticizes textbook statements when they relate the land to Palestinians: 'The coverage of Middle East history and the Arab-Israeli dispute in textbooks and supplemental materials contains significant elements of the Arab narrative, which frames the conflict from Arab and Palestinian points of view' (Tobin and Ybarra 2008: 91). In Chapter 8, 'Terrorism and Internal Conflict', textbooks are criticized for mentioning Zionist terrorism:

> Textbooks do not adequately explain the founding of Israel as a moral redressing from the United Nations for the injustice of the Holocaust and the need to fulfill the national aspirations of the Jewish people. Instead, its founding is reduced to the alleged selection of terrorism as a policy by Israeli forces. Violence occurred but was rejected by most Jews as a strategy, and most historians would agree it was the diplomatic and political efforts of Jewish and Gentile leaders that facilitated the establishment of a Jewish state.
>
> Tobin and Ybarra 2008: 129

This textbook analysis concludes that, 'The history of Israel reflects too many elements of the Arab narrative without respect to historical accuracy' (Tobin and Ybarra 2008: 154). The analysed textbooks are described by the writers as anti-Christian, antisemitic and anti-Israel.

A detailed review of this textbook analysis and others, listed at the beginning of this chapter in Table 2.1, is available in the original PhD research. That review covers the first thirty-eight items of the table. The last seven items, numbered 39–45, have been added after completing the PhD project, and updating the review to 2021 for the purposes of this book.

Chapter 3

THE SURVEY OF COLLEGE TEXTBOOKS

This investigation engaged in a selection procedure to form a sample, a manageable number of relevant textbooks, for its main examination. The ideal is to select certain textbooks that can represent, better than others, a large number of textbook choices that are adopted in Western universities to teach the history of Israel-Palestine question. This level of representation is ideal for the sake of the certain knowledge claim; if our sample of the analysed textbooks can really represent the targeted subject matter – Western academic textbook knowledge in our case – then it is valid to make a general claim about the whole academic knowledge in the area (and not only about the analysed textbooks per se), based on the results of their analysis. This chapter reports on the selection procedure and its results. The main result of this procedure is a list of adopted textbooks that are used most in Western universities to teach the history of the Israel-Palestine question. All details provided in this lengthy chapter work to explain and support the idea that this list can be ranked as the most adopted textbooks in the area of academic knowledge under examination, in Western countries, and consequently can represent the relevant academic knowledge in the West. If someone is not interested in such details and can trust this procedure and its results, they can skip this chapter as this chapter does not deal, in any sense, with the main analysis of this study. The author, however, is keen to provide all related details for the sake of maximum transparency in how those textbooks are selected. The relevant literature, reviewed in Chapter 2, demonstrates that most textbook analyses suffer from a lack of transparency about their choices of popular textbooks; they introduce some textbooks, taken for analysis, as the most popular ones (or among the most popular) without providing any reference that supports such a claim.

It is widely believed, in academic circles, that textbooks that are adopted, as a reference book, more frequently in relevant modules should enjoy a higher degree of representation. For this, it appears necessary to find a way for selecting the most popular/adopted textbooks in Western universities. Several strategies can be considered for such an endeavour:

- Publication figures: the figure that displays the number of volumes of a given published book can refer to 'the book's popularity'. This factor works, in particular, when school textbooks are at stake as they are used, predominantly,

for schooling purposes. This means one can consider the number of published textbooks as a figure very close to that of those actually used in schools as textbooks. On the subject of college-level textbooks, analysts' statements suggest that there is not such a ready list of popular textbooks (Wills 1992: 65). In comparison, textbooks that are used in colleges can be consulted by a large number of interested readers who are not enrolled students. This is quite obvious in history topics, if not so in some other academic disciplines.
- Bestsellers: the figures for bestselling books can also say something notable about the popularity of a book. But this, again, relates to a wider readership as sales are not limited to college students. One good example of such a list is the Amazon bestselling list. Bestselling books on the history of Israel are accessible at www.amazon.com/Best-Sellers-Books-Israel-History/zgbs/books/5001, for instance. The results of the survey, conducted to find the most adopted textbooks, demonstrates that there is a meaningful difference between this list (bestselling books on the history of Israel) and the most used textbooks in colleges.
- The second-hand online textbook market: there are online companies engaged in selling and renting second-hand college textbooks. Valorebooks in the United States is one clear instance. Some information provided on its website (valorebooks.com), the number of used books offered for rent or sale, for example, might indicate the popularity of a book. A place on this website is dedicated to showing the figures for relevant textbooks on Israel (valorebooks.com/new-used-textbooks/history/middle-east/israel). Again here, it is difficult to decide whether or not the figure provides something close to one which can represent the most adopted textbooks. An interest in keeping a useful textbook for probable reference in the future can be one reason for not selling a textbook that has been used for the sake of a given course. Furthermore, these online companies exist only in countries with a huge market for textbooks such as the United States. No similar company has been identified in other Western countries.
- The number of editions: the number of editions can probably indicate a textbook's popularity. At the same time, there are popular books that have not been published in several editions. Textbooks that are published earlier are in a better position if such a criterion is taken for finding the most popular books.
- Other signs can say something meaningful about the popularity of a given book. Citation is one. Databases such as Web of Knowledge or Google Scholar provide figures about how often a given book is cited in other academic works. The number of reviews in main online bookstores such as Amazon can give some idea about the popularity of a book as well.

The syllabus is the main place where a textbook is introduced formally to students of a given module. A textbook introduced in a syllabus has confirmation of its status as an authentic source in a given area of knowledge, granted by an academic hierarchy. Books introduced here should best represent the books students read to access relevant knowledge in a given discipline. As a result, data extracted from syllabi, often located in 'recommended reading' sections, have the capacity to offer an estimation of textbook adoption, and suggest which textbooks represent knowledge in a given academic area. The problem with arriving at such a figure is how to collect the relevant data that are scattered in a seemingly endless number of colleges, universities, courses and classes. Accessing such information poses a challenge that might be dealt with through two main strategies:

1. Communication: through communication, as a medium to reach those who have access to syllabi data, lecturers of the related courses and also others in the university departments or libraries, could be contacted. Communication is easier these days thanks to the provision of email addresses of college staff through university websites. Phone calls and ordinary letters were the main alternatives before the internet era. In either case, using modern or traditional ways of communication, some obstacles might limit the results of such strategy:

   - University lecturers are busy; allocating enough time to provide information for a student in another university/country might not form a priority for them.
   - Due to the controversial nature of the subject and its strong political dimension, lecturers might not feel comfortable disclosing the relevant data when asked by an unknown outsider.
   - The addressees might choose some, and no other, syllabi to send when encountered with a question about readings they suggest to students, for particular professional or political reasons.
   - Communication with a large number of lecturers, hundreds for instance, requires a sizeable amount of time and labour that might not easily be available.

2. Web content mining: as a significant number of universities in the West have started to provide online syllabi, a search engine can be an effective tool to extract syllabi from online sources. This strategy might have a better chance of success if the negative factors of the communication strategy are taken into consideration.

The proliferation of online college syllabi provides a valuable source of information about the 'scholarly impact' of different academic readings in general and textbooks in particular. This has been confirmed through some empirical investigations; 'Assessing the Impact of Disciplinary Research on Teaching: An Automatic Analysis of Online Syllabuses' for instance (Kousha and Thelwall 2008). This study supports the idea that online syllabi provide valuable data for evaluating journal articles in some branches of social sciences including political science, suggesting it as a new source of 'scholarly impact' besides 'journal citation'.

Academic studies have started to use this new source of data; 'By the Book: Assessing the Place of Textbooks in U.S. Survey Courses' is one study that uses online syllabi to find the most adopted textbooks in US colleges for teaching US history (Cohen 2005). The emergence of online syllabi as valuable data encouraged researchers to find more effective techniques to extract the syllabi from online sources. 'The Syllabus Based Web Content Extractor', an article by Saba Hilal and S.A.M. Rizvi, is one piece of work that suggests a technique to make web syllabus mining easier (Hilal and Rizvi 2008). This development, also, encouraged creating databases that store a large number of syllabi. The Syllabus Finder is a source that had collected over a million syllabi between 2002 and 2009 at the time this study was undertaken. This online database, characterized as the largest collection of syllabi ever, according to its founder, has been abandoned, however, due to certain regulations that now govern searching on Google.

Overall Boundaries of the Survey

General guidelines are needed to locate the selection procedure in an exact area that most suits the objectives of the search. Textbooks that are used in Western anglophone universities to teach the history of the Israel-Palestine question are the main target of this search. The following guidelines are designed to focus the search on this exact area:

- Place: all universities that are based in Western countries and can be considered part of Western academia are included in this search in general. The West, or Western countries, is taken as a political concept that is used commonly in a wide range of literature and includes most European countries and those countries outside Europe where a majority of its population have European origins, i.e. the United States, Canada, Australia and New Zealand. There is a language obstacle if all these countries are taken for this textbook analysis, as they speak too many different languages which would require books in numerous languages. Only one language, English, is taken for this analysis as it covers a large part of knowledge production about the subject in the West where the United States, the UK and Canada are taken into account. Other English-speaking countries of the West, such as Ireland, Australia and New Zealand are also included in this survey. There are Western universities that are based in non-Western countries. These cases are not included in this survey due to the fact that their different environment (in non-Western regions) might impact their textbook choices. The American University in Cairo, in which its online syllabi are excluded on this basis, is one instance.
- Time: the research aims to deal with the contemporary West. As a result, it was necessary to put a time limit in the near past to frame a period between then and the date of the study that can be considered as contemporary time. The year 2000 has been chosen for this purpose; all courses that were offered in 2000 or later are counted in the survey. In practice, the search conducted for this survey showed that few online syllabi come from a time before that date. The actual survey took place in several intervals in 2013. As a result, the overall time frame of this survey covers the period 2000 to 2013.
- Reading materials: different kinds of reading materials and resources are introduced in a college syllabus. This includes books, journal articles,

documents, films and so on. For the sake of this research, only the books are recorded. Many books about Israel or the history of the question have been identified while searching online sources. This search excludes all books except those that cover the history of the question in general. Hence books that deal only with some relevant historical events such as 'wars' or the history of Palestine alone, and not Israel, are not calculated. The books chosen through the search are the ones that constitute a survey of the question's history.

- Courses: the main target was courses that deal with the history of Israel or the Arab-Israeli conflict. But other courses such as those on the Middle East or Israel are recorded as well. There are other courses, with no direct relation to the question, that have been used as a source of required data – courses on 'world history', 'peace and conflict' or 'international relations'. The reason for including them is the fact they deal, in one way or another, with the history of Israel, even as a minor part of the syllabus. The main courses that have been removed from the search even though they contained some related data were those that introduced relevant textbooks in a completely different context; Sometimes a syllabus introduces one book just as a general example (of something) regardless of its topic. This was a main case that has not been included in the collected data.

The Survey

Syllabus Finder could have worked as an ideal place to find syllabi that contain required textbooks but its closure deprived researchers of that chance. Other syllabi collections are provided online as well. A small number of academic establishments provide a remarkable number of syllabi in a given discipline. The American Academy of Religion and the American Political Science Association are good instances. Some publishing companies have also established databases that contain information about adopted textbooks. One in the UK, Blackwell's, was successful in building a sizeable database but the data provided is limited and includes only books that they have to sell. No syllabus database was identified, categorically, that provides an adequate number of relevant syllabi.

Websites of university departments can be visited to find course syllabi. There are extensive lists of syllabi for Jewish studies in the UK, the United States and some other Western countries that can be used for such a purpose but many university websites do not have a clear policy on the provision of their syllabi online. The MIT website ocw.mit.edu/courses/ is an exception where all syllabi of the courses offered in the university can be accessed online. Jewish Virtual Libraries was the only source explored that had a good number of syllabi for courses on Israel. Quite a few syllabi of American and Canadian universities, collected in this survey, come from this database.

Alternatively, this study conducted an extensive search on Google to find required data in different Western countries. Searches started with the UK and moved to other countries when the search in one country was exhausted. The last part of a web address i.e. top-level domain, such as 'uk' or 'nz', that identifies the country is used to manage such a search. In some cases, domains that are used only for academic institutions, such as ac.uk for instance, are used to search university websites in a given country. At the first stage, searches are focused on related syllabi and when an extensive list of the textbooks used is formed, textbooks' titles or authors' names can become a main keyword for the search. Some general keywords such as syllabus, course outline, Israel, history, reading list, course code, bibliography, credit, semester, assessment and module proved useful in extracting relevant online syllabi. Advanced Search on Google was also quite helpful; 'File type' was a big help as most of the syllabi found are in PDF format. Others are mainly Microsoft word documents (.doc). A few cases of other files, like HTML, are also explored.

All extracted syllabi have been scanned thoroughly with an aim to find books that deal with the history of the question. All cases of such books are recorded in an independent file for further processing when calculations should be made to determine the most adopted books. Other techniques/considerations that helped to manage the search are as follows:

- Certain syllabi are found more than once in different searches. Only one syllabus is taken for calculation if there was more than one copy on the internet. With all measures to avoid such problems, a final check to find duplication proved necessary. Also, if there was more than one reference to a book on one syllabus, later references were disregarded.
- Books, sometimes, are referred to through their different editions. This difference was overlooked while searching and data collecting was at stake. It was tried, at the analysis phase, to take the last edition of the book, as it can represent, more than older editions, the contemporary condition of the textbook knowledge.
- If there was more than one copy of a syllabus, but they belonged to different academic years/semesters, all copies were taken into account. The fact that different times can refer to different instances of textbook adoption informed this choice.
- Some syllabi referred students to an address on the university intranet, Blackboard for instance, or hand-outs that were distributed in the class, to access reading lists. In such cases where there was no online reading list at all the syllabus was removed from the search. The extracted syllabus is recorded when the whole reading list or part of it is accessible through the internet.
- Books recommended for reading on syllabi were introduced through different channels; some were clearly introduced as textbooks for a course. There were other categories under which these books were introduced: 'Required Texts/Reading/Textbook', 'Principal/Core Texts', 'Mandatory Textbook', 'Suggested/Preliminary Readings', 'Reading Materials' and 'Bibliography' are the main ones. The number of books introduced for reading on a syllabus varied greatly. One book only was introduced in some cases, and in other cases the number might go very high, to constitute tens of books. Sometimes books were introduced as a source for the whole course, and sometimes as a source

for one part/session of the course. All these complexities were discounted when lists of extracted books were formed; a book was recorded if there was a recommendation, in any category, to read the book for the sake of the course.
- Some readings were introduced sometimes without mentioning the book title, by mentioning a writer's name for instance. These general recommendations (to read the writings of a given writer) were also ignored for the sake of simplicity.
- Books written by my primary supervisor, Professor Ilan Pappé, were removed from the search. This was done because analysing books written by one's supervisor might not form a proper subject for an impartial and unbiased investigation. Pappé's writings about the question in general, and *The Israel/Palestine Question: A Reader*, *A History of Modern Palestine: One Land, Two Peoples* and *The Making of the Arab-Israeli Conflict, 1947–51* in particular, were recommended by many syllabi but it was not believed that these books could reach the top adopted textbooks that were selected for this analysis.
- There were a few cases of a syllabus with potential to be counted in this search, but reaching them proved impossible: a message 'page not found' was received every time an enquiry was tried.
- It is quite likely in a few cases that required syllabi were not found due to mistakes that might have occurred in spelling the title of the book or its author in online syllabi; some cases of misspelt titles are explored through other keywords, however.
- All syllabi that were used for this survey came from open online sources. No attempt, whatsoever, has been made to extract or publish syllabi that were designed for the sole use of a certain community.
- Due to the fact that the English language is used in some non-anglophone Western countries such as the Netherlands, Sweden, Switzerland, Finland, Denmark and Norway to teach academic disciplines, a good number of online syllabi from those countries might exist to form a sizeable quantity of data for determining the most adopted textbooks of the field in those countries. In addition, there are courses in these countries that are not taught in English but their syllabus has a reference to English books as reading material. Extending the search to these countries might add something to the results of this survey that is based only on results from six anglophone countries in the West. It is believed that there would be a better chance for such extension in years to come as the numbers of online syllabi are increasing.
- All searches to access extracted syllabi took place in the year 2013; the day and month each syllabus was extracted is given in Tables 3.5–3.10.

The Results of the Survey

Ten tables are developed in this section to report the main results of the survey. Table 3.1 lists all extracted textbooks with their adoption frequencies in all the countries studied. Table 3.2 lists, in order, the textbooks with higher frequencies, to display the top adopted textbooks, and Table 3.3 shows all book frequencies in all countries of the survey. Table 3.4 exhibits the position of the six selected textbooks in all countries of the survey. The remaining tables, 3.5–3.10, record the main information of all extracted syllabi in the six countries of the survey. There are some general points about the results of the survey that come in advance, as follows:

- The search operation conducted for this survey resulted in the extraction of 495 syllabi: 370 syllabi from US universities, 49 from British universities, 41 from Canadian universities, 16 from Australian universities, 11 from New Zealand universities and 8 from Irish universities.
- The position of the six selected textbooks at the top of the list of all adopted textbooks in all six countries of the survey (Table 3.4) supports the idea that a particular pattern of textbook adoption on the history of the Israel-Palestine question governs all six countries of the survey. This significant finding, that one single pattern of textbook adoption is repeated in all six countries of the survey, also proposes the idea that this pattern might govern other Western countries, and the West as a whole.
- There are a few textbooks, six indeed, that have much higher frequencies compared with other textbooks that are recommended through syllabi. The big gap between their frequencies and those belonging to other textbooks narrows any chance of a radical change in the list of the top six textbooks if further searches are conducted. This gives more credit to the top-six list to truly represent the most adopted textbooks.
- Search results in larger countries, the United States, the UK and Canada, which produced more online syllabi, could be more reliable compared with those belonging to smaller countries (Ireland, Australia, New Zealand) that are established on few cases of extracted syllabi.
- The extracted textbooks originate from different courses; some of these courses are designed to teach the history of the Israel-Palestine question or a related subject. Others are focused on other subjects such as those related to the Middle East or world history. A textbook adoption is registered in the survey when the book is mentioned as a source of relevant knowledge on the Israel-Palestine question.
- The selected textbooks are adopted differently in different syllabi; some of them have been introduced as the main textbook for the related courses: *Palestine and the Arab-Israeli Conflict*, *A History of Israel*, *A History of the Israeli-Palestinian Conflict* and *A Concise History of the Arab-Israeli Conflict* are introduced as such in many syllabi. Some others, *Righteous Victims* for instance, have not been regarded as such in most cases. They are provided, mostly, as optional reading for instance.
- Other indications are identified that reinforce the results of the survey; one case can be seen in a popular textbook *A Concise History of the Arab-Israeli Conflict* where almost all books that are 'suggested' for 'further reading' on the 'history of Israel' are the same textbooks that have been explored as 'the most adopted textbooks' in the survey (Bickerton and Klausner 1998: Introduction).

- The list of twenty frequently adopted textbooks on the history of the Israel-Palestine question, shown in Table 3.1, demonstrates that none of them is written by a Palestinian, Arab or Muslim. This survey suggests Professor Ilan Pappé as the only scholar, with a critical view of Zionism, who might have a chance of being included in the list of the top twenty authors of the most adopted textbooks in Western countries, which features in the survey.

Table 3.1 Frequencies of textbook adoptions on all extracted syllabi for the six countries

No.	Textbook title	Author	Countries of the survey					
			UK	IE	CA	NZ	AU	US
1	A Concise History of the Arab-Israeli Conflict	Bickerton and Klausner	5	–	8	–	5	118
2	A History of Israel	Aharon Bregman	3	–	5	–	–	–
3	A History of the Israeli-Palestinian Conflict	Mark Tessler	19	–	13	–	–	61
4	A History of Modern Israel	Colin Shindler	5	–	2	–	–	20
5	A Short History of Israel	Neill Lochery	1	–	–	–	–	–
6	History of Israel: From the Rise of Zionism to Our Time	Howard Sachar	10	1	6	–	4	66
7	Israel: A Concise Political History	Yossi Beilin	4	–	–	–	–	–
8	Israel: A History	Martin Gilbert	7	1	–	–	–	–
9	Israel/Palestine	Alan Dowty	3	–	4	–	–	29
10	Palestine and the Arab-Israeli Conflict: A History with Documents	Charles Smith	16	3	17	4	6	97
11	Righteous Victims: A History of the Zionist-Arab Conflict, 1881–1999	Benny Morris	18	4	15	2	2	82
12	The Arab-Israeli Conflict	Kirsten Schulze	6	1	–	–	–	–
13	The Arab-Israeli Conflict	Thomas Fraser	8	1	1	1	–	8
14	The Arab-Israeli Conflict: A History	David Lesch	2	–	3	–	–	14
15	The Arab-Israeli Conflict: Perspectives	Alvin Rubinstein	–	–	3	–	–	–
16	The Israel-Arab Reader: A Documentary History of the Middle East Conflict	Laqueur and Rubin	7	–	9	2	–	60
17	The Israel-Palestine Conflict: Contested Histories	Neil Caplan	–	–	6	–	–	–
18	The Israel-Palestine Conflict: One Hundred Years of War	James Gelvin	8	1	2	4	–	28
19	The Origins and Evolution of the Arab-Zionist Conflict	Michael Cohen	–	–	–	–	1	–
20	The Siege: The Story of Israel and Zionism	Conor Cruise O'Brien	4	–	–	–	–	–

Table 3.2 The most adopted textbooks and their adoption frequency

No.	Textbook title	Adoption frequency in total	No. of countries of book adoption
1	*Palestine and the Arab-Israeli Conflict: A History with Documents*	143	6
2	*A Concise History of the Arab-Israeli Conflict*	136	4
3	*Righteous Victims: A History of the Zionist-Arab Conflict*	123	6
4	*A History of the Israeli-Palestinian Conflict*	93	3
5	*A History of Israel: From the Rise of Zionism to Our Time*	87	5
6	*The Israel-Arab Reader: A Documentary History of the Middle East Conflict*	78	4

Table 3.3 How most adopted textbooks are taken on in different survey countries

No.	UK	Ireland	Canada	New Zealand	Australia	United States
1	Tessler 19	Morris 4	Smith 17	Smith 4	Smith 6	Bickerton 118
2	Morris 18	Smith 3	Morris 15	Gelvin 4	Bickerton 5	Smith 97
3	Smith 16	Sachar 1	Tessler 13	Laqueur 2	Sachar 4	Morris 82
4	Sachar 10	Fraser 1	Laqueur 9	Morris 2	Morris 2	Sachar 66
5	Gelvin 8	Gilbert 1	Bickerton 8	Fraser 1	Cohen 1	Tessler 61
6	Fraser 8	Schulze 1	Sachar 6			Laqueur 60
7	Laqueur 7	Gelvin 1	Caplan 6			Dowty 29
8	Gilbert 7		Bregman 5			Gelvin 28
9	Schulze 6		Dowty 4			Shindler 20
10	Bickerton 5		Shindler 2			Lesch 14
11	Shindler 5		Lesch 3			Fraser 8

Note:
Every author's name represents a textbook adopted. The figure beside the name gives the adoption frequency of the book in the specified country. Take particular notice of the authors whose names repeat across countries, in the shaded boxes.

Table 3.4 The position of the six selected textbooks in all countries of the survey

No.	UK	Ireland	Canada	New Zealand	Australia	US
1	Tessler 19	Morris 4	Smith 17	Smith 4	Smith 6	Bickerton 118
2	Morris 18	Smith 3	Morris 15	Gelvin 4	Bickerton 5	Smith 97
3	Smith 16	Sachar 1	Tessler 13	Laqueur 2	Sachar 4	Morris 82
4	Sachar 10	Fraser 1	Laqueur 9	Morris 2	Morris 2	Sachar 66
5	Gelvin 8	Gilbert 1	Bickerton 8	Fraser 1	Cohen 1	Tessler 61
6	Fraser 8	Schulze 1	Sachar 6			Laqueur 60
7	Laqueur 7	Gelvin 1	Caplan 6			Dowty 29
8	Gilbert 7		Bregman 5			Gelvin 28
9	Schulze 6		Dowty 4			Shindler 20
10	Bickerton 5		Shindler 2			Lesch 14
11	Shindler 5		Lesch 3			Fraser 8
No of adoption[a]	75	8	68	8	17	484
Ratio of adoption[b]	69%	67%	76%	62%	94%	83%

Notes:
This table demonstrates how six textbooks occupied positions in the most adopted textbooks in all six countries of the survey. The shading reflects the authors highlighted in Table 3.4. The figure beside the author name constitutes the adoption frequency of the book in that country.
[a]This figure reflects how many times the six selected textbooks are adopted, altogether, in each country of the survey.
[b]This figure indicates the ratio of the six textbooks' adoption against the total number of the relevant textbooks' adoption frequency in each country of the survey.

Details of the Survey Extracted Data

In this section, six tables (3.5–3.10) report the detailed results of the survey in all six Western countries. The main information about each extracted syllabus is presented and a link provided to the online syllabus (as it was in 2013). Considerable efforts have been made to provide all related data when a syllabus is presented in a table; this data includes the title of the course, the code of the course, the name of the university/college and the date the course was taught. NA is used in some cases in the table when the related data was not available. With these details at hand, the author is hopeful to provide a chance for others to repeat the same survey, if they are willing to, and if they wish to check the results.

Table 3.5 All extracted syllabi from British universities

No.	College	Course title	Course code	Access date (all 2013)	Date taught	Link
1	SOAS: Department of the Languages and Cultures of the Near and Middle East	Israel, the Arab World and the Palestinians	15PNMC038	5 March	NA	http://www.soas.ac.uk/courseunits/15PNMC038.html
2	SOAS: Department of the Languages and Cultures of the Near and Middle East	Israeli History and the Israel-Palestine Conflict	155901167	5 March	NA	http://www.soas.ac.uk/courseunits/155901167.html
3	UCL: Department of Hebrew and Jewish Studies	The Arab/Israeli Conflict	HEBR7750	5 March	NA	http://www.ucl.ac.uk/hebrew-jewish/students/studentresources/syllabi-details/the-arab-israeli-conflict
4	Brunel University London	Arab-Israeli Conflict	PP3001	5 March	2012&–13	http://readinglists.brunel.ac.uk/lists/7FF1E213-2491-1527-75C7-412C3EF97631.html
5	University of Manchester: Faculty of Humanities	Fundamental Debates in the Study of Israel/Palestine	MEST30722	5 March	NA	http://courses.humanities.manchester.ac.uk/undergraduate/module.html?code=MEST30722
6	SOAS: Department of the Languages and Cultures of the Near and Middle East	History of Zionism	155901168	5 March	NA	http://www.soas.ac.uk/courseunits/155901168.html
7	University of Salford	Arab-Israeli Conflict	HU-L200-20108-13	5 March	NA	http://lasu.salford.ac.uk/displaylist/HU-L200-20108-13
8	University of Edinburgh	The Middle East in International Relations	PGSP 11275	25 April	Semester 2011–12	http://www.sps.ed.ac.uk/__data/assets/pdf_file/0011/74765/Middle_East_in_International_Relations_2011-12_FINAL.pdf

No.	College	Course title	Course code	Access date (all 2013)	Date taught	Link
9	University of Edinburgh	The Arab-Israeli Conflict: Nations in Collision	NA	26 April	2011	http://www.google.co.uk/url?sa=t&rct=j&q=&esrc=s&source=web&cd=1&ved=0CDwQFjAA&url=http%3A%2F%2Fwww.boardofstudies.llc.ed.ac.uk%2F docs%2Fopen%2FThe_Arab-Israeli_Conflict_Nations_in_Collision.doc&ei=fmd6UcfBA8Ly0gWBioDQBg&usg=AFQjCNE74tlFGz769k2Dqhjl8qt7ruCsrA&sig2=ET1yeqvN7d2XQf9i92nLyA&bvm=bv.45645796,d.d2k
10	University of Exeter: IAIS	The History and Historiography of the Palestine Question	ARAM204	6 March	2012	http://socialsciences.exeter.ac.uk/iais/modules/ARAM204/description/
11	University of Leeds	Zionism and the Arab-Israeli Conflict	ARAB2065	6 March	2012/13	http://lib5.leeds.ac.uk/rlists/broker/?bbModuleId=201213_22565_ARAB2065&bbListId=_1765268_1&sess=201213
12	University of Manchester	The Question of Palestine/Israel (1882–1967)	MEST10042	8 March	NA	http://courses.humanities.manchester.ac.uk/undergraduate/module.html?code=MEST10042
13	UCL: Department of Hebrew and Jewish Studies	Anglo-Israeli Relations	HEBRG104	8 March	NA	http://www.ucl.ac.uk/hebrew-jewish/students/studentresources/syllabi-details/anglo-israeli-relations
14	University of Edinburgh	The Arab-Israeli Conflict: Nations in Collision	IMES10072	8 March	2012/2013	http://www.drps.ed.ac.uk/12-13/dpt/cximes10072.htm
15	UCL: Department of Hebrew and Jewish Studies	Graduate Seminar Programme (Graduate Only)	HEBRG035	8 March	NA	http://www.ucl.ac.uk/hebrew-jewish/students/studentresources/syllabi-details/graduate-seminar-programme
16	University of Oxford	Israel: State, Society, Identity	NA	8 March	NA	http://users.ox.ac.uk/~sant1114/MPhilIsrael.pdf

(*Continued*)

No.	College	Course title	Course code	Access date (all 2013)	Date taught	Link
17	University of Southampton	Modern Israel 1948–2007 Part 2	HIST3114	8 March	NA	http://www.southampton.ac.uk/humanities/undergraduate/modules/hist3114_modern_israel_1948-2007_pt2.page
18	University of Southampton	Modern Israel 1948–2007 Part 1	HIST3113	8 March	NA	http://www.southampton.ac.uk/humanities/undergraduate/modules/hist3113_modern_israel_1948-2007_pt1.page
19	University of Glamorgan	Israel, Palestine and the Making of the Modern Middle East	HS2S007	8 March	2009–10	http://www.misterdann.com/syllabusproject/GemieSHIS2S007.pdf
20	University College London	The Arab-Israeli Conflict	HEBR7750 (BA) HEBRG009 (MA)	8 March	2009–10	http://www.misterdann.com/syllabusproject/LocheryNHebr7750.pdf
21	University College London	Israel and the Occupied Territories	HEBR7766 (BA) HEBRG128 (MA)	8 March	NA	http://www.misterdann.com/syllabusproject/RantaRHebr7766.pdf
22	King's College London	A History of the Arab-Israeli Conflict	7AAJM204	8 March	NA	http://www.kcl.ac.uk/artshums/depts/mems/modules/7aajm204.aspx
23	University of Sussex	Peace Processes in Global Order	L2059	9 March	Autumn 2006	http://www.google.co.uk/url?sa=t&rct=j&q=&esrc=s&source=web&cd=1&ved=0CEIQFjAA&url=http%3A%2F%2Fwww.sussex.ac.uk%2FUsers%2Fjs208%2Fpeace_process_in_global_order_2006.doc&ei=Y3h-UYqPOMGN0AXlq4GIDg&usg=AFQjCNHI2F-dzc0zGrL62X2FJMRkxHZhZQ&sig2=G63YIQKfryc_HbxjdPyKaA&bvm=bv.4564579 6,d.d2k

No.	College	Course title	Course code	Access date (all 2013)	Date taught	Link
24	University of Manchester	The Palestine/Israel Question (1882–1967)	Mest10042	12 March	NA	http://community.talisaspire.com/courses/aHR0cDovL3d3dy5yZWFkaW5nbGlzdHMubWFuY2hlc3Rlci5hYy51ay9saXN0Cy8w NDdFNkM3OC03MjdCLU10 QTYtMUZBRS0yRDlBM0NDMDc4REQ=
25	University College London	The Arab-Israeli Conflict	Hebr7750(BA)	18 March	2012–13	http://www.ucl.ac.uk/hebrew-jewish/students/studentresources/syllabi-details/hebr7750-section-information
26	University of Wales, Newport	Imperial Rivalries and Global Conflict in the 20th Century	Hi305	18 March	NA	http://timezone.newport.ac.uk/hi305/hi305bib.htm
27	University of St Andrews	The Arab-Israeli Conflict	Ir 5525	18 March	NA	http://www.st-andrews.ac.uk/intrel/pg/mecass/ir5525/
28	University of Portsmouth	International Politics of the Middle East		18 March	2012–13	http://lists.lib.portsmouth.ac.uk/lists/AC2C4F38-2CCA-9A8B-3B2C-C3252BDABAF4.html
29	Brunel University London	Arab-Israeli Conflict	Pp3001	18 March	2012–13	http://readinglists.brunel.ac.uk/lists/33122C71-EA32-B802-AC04-C520DF542F06.html
30	University of Northampton	Conflict and Diplomacy in the Twentieth Century	His1001	18 March	NA	http://readinglists.northampton.ac.uk/lists/9106E46E-4757-83E8-0E62-B164217A7D70.html
31	University of Birmingham: School of Government and Society	Diplomatic History of the Arab-Israeli Conflict	Pols 339	18 March	NA	http://www.readinglists.bham.ac.uk/readinglist/show/id/10726

(Continued)

No.	College	Course title	Course code	Access date (all 2013)	Date taught	Link
32	University of St Andrews	Conflict in the Middle East	Ir5518	25 April	2012/13, Semester 1	http://resourcelists.st-andrews.ac.uk/lists/3BFDD5BF-386C-7AAA-031C-EB03860D15DC.html
33	University of Exeter	Politics and Economy of the Contemporary Middle East	Ara1010	25 April	2013/4	http://intranet.exeter.ac.uk/socialsciences/moduledescriptions/moduledescription/index.php?code=ARA1010&ayrc=2013/4
34	Durham University	Introduction to Middle East Politics	Poli 1021	25 April	2005–6	http://www.google.co.uk/url?sa=t&rct=j&q=&esrc=s&source=web&cd=13&ved=0CEEQFjACOAo&url=http%3A%2F%2Fwww.thestudentroom.co.uk%2Fattachment.php%3Fattachmentid%3D54443%26d%3D12131880 41&ei=Jmd5UYHIEqie0QWRjYGoAQ&usg=AFQjCNEQOpmO1TCSlkDmTg0ZRtYe_rI7Og&sig2=slZMKTa9Sli6Vrgw3OuTAQ
35	Newcastle University	Politics of the Middle East (S2)	Pol 2012	25 April	2012/2013	https://rlo.ncl.ac.uk/index.php/modules/POL2012/2012
36	University of St Andrews	NA	Ir 3102	25 April	Semester 1, 2012–13	http://www.st-andrews.ac.uk/intrel/ug/readinglistssem1/
37	Harlaxton College	The US in the Middle East. 1919–Present	History 323	25 April	Spring 2010	http://www.ueharlax.ac.uk/academics/curriculum/syllabii/documents/spring2010-HIST323.pdf
38	University of St Andrews	The Arab-Israeli Conflict Past & Present	IR5525	25 April	2011/12 Semester 2	http://resourcelists.st-andrews.ac.uk/lists/2BC191C6-592A-C9AB-2DE5-E7867C6ECE87.html
39	University of Kent	Politics of the Middle East	NA	25 April	2011–2012	http://resourcelists.kent.ac.uk/lists/C9C0A796-6304-454D-1CD2-CBB14DA6161F.html

No.	College	Course title	Course code	Access date (all 2013)	Date taught	Link
40	King's College London	The International Politics of the Middle East	7SSWM191	25 April	2013/14	http://myreadinglists.kcl.ac.uk/lists/28791B59-E6FE-153C-F48F-E7E8D10AF649.html
41	City University London	Contemporary Issues in Global Politics: The Twentieth Century	IP1003	25 April	2012–13	http://readinglists.city.ac.uk/lists/B6926586-7A3C-CCF8-437B-6F4E592BA2E9.html
42	Queens University of Belfast	Middle Eastern Politics	PAI3011	25 April	Autumn 2012–13	http://www.qub.ac.uk/schools/SchoolofPolitics InternationalStudiesandPhilosophy/FileStore/ ModuleGuides2012-13/Filetoupload,338428, en.pdf
43	University of Oxford	The International Relations of the Middle East	NA	25 April	Hilary Term 2008	http://users.ox.ac.uk/~sant1114/MPhilR.pdf
44	University of Oxford	The Development of the International System (2nd Part – From 1950)	NA	25 April	Trinity Term 2003	http://www.sant.ox.ac.uk/people/knicolaidis/ irpost50.pdf
45	University of Edinburgh	Politics of the Middle East	PLIT 10036	25 April	Semester 1, 2012–13	https://www.sps.ed.ac.uk/__data/assets/pdf_ file/0009/91269/POTME_courseguide2012-13. pdf
46	Cardiff Metropolitan University	Politics of the Contemporary Middle East	HUM311	25 April	NA	http://www.uwic.ac.uk/documents/ humanities/Humanities%20modules%20 Level%206%20_third%20year.pdf
47	University College London	Anglo-Israeli Relations 1948–2011	HEBR7761	25 April	2012–13	http://www.ucl.ac.uk/hebrew-jewish/students/ studentresources/ugbib/1213HEBR 7761Anglo_Israeli_Relations_1948-2006.pdf

(Continued)

No.	College	Course title	Course code	Access date (all 2013)	Date taught	Link
48	Queen's University of Belfast	Violence, Terrorism and Security	PAI 7028	25 April	Autumn 2012–13	http://www.qub.ac.uk/schools/SchoolofPoliticsInternationalStudiesandPhilosophy/FileStore/ModuleGuides2012-13/Filetoupload,338429,en.pdf
49	Queen's University of Belfast	Violence, Terrorism and Security	PAI 7028	25 April	Autumn 2011–12	http://www.qub.ac.uk/schools/SchoolofPoliticsInternationalStudiesandPhilosophy/FileStore/ModuleGuides2011-12/Filetoupload,254360,en.pdf

Table 3.6 All extracted syllabi from Canadian universities

No.	College	Course title	Course code	Access date (all 2013)	Taught date	Link
1	Simon Fraser University	The Palestinian-Israeli Conflict	HISTORY 465	13 March	Spring 2012	http://www.sfu.ca/content/dam/sfu/history/Course%20Outlines/2012/spring%202012/H465Sedra.pdf
2	Simon Fraser University	The Palestinian-Israeli Conflict	HISTORY 465	13 March	Fall 2009	http://paulsedra.files.wordpress.com/2013/02/h465syllabusfall2009.pdf
3	Simon Fraser University	The Palestinian-Israeli Conflict	HISTORY 465	13 March	Summer 2010	http://paulsedra.files.wordpress.com/2013/02/h465summer10syllabus.pdf
4	University of Ottawa: Faculty of Social Sciences, School of Public and International Affairs	The Middle East Peace Process	API 6339F	13 March	Winter 2011	http://ssms.socialsciences.uottawa.ca/vfs/.horde/offre_cours/syllabus/00035110807_API6339F.pdf
5	Trent University: Department of History	Apocalypse: Conquest, Revolution, War and Genocide in the Modern World	History 1700	13 March	2010/2011	www.trentu.ca/history/documents/1700Taylorfin.doc
6	University of Toronto	Topics in Middle East History: Palestine and Israel	HIS 304H1-S	13 March	Fall/Winter 2012–13	http://history.utoronto.ca/undergraduate/fw_300level.html
7	Trinity Western University	Politics and Development of the Middle East	POLS 421	13 March	Summer 2011	http://www.twu.ca/academics/fhss/politics/pols-421-syllabus.pdf
8	Acadia University	The Arab-Israeli Conflict	HISTORY 2073 X2	13 March	Winter 2013	http://history.acadiau.ca/tl_files/sites/history/Course%20Outlines%202012-2013/HIST2073%20Winter%202013.pdf

(Continued)

No.	College	Course title	Course code	Access date (all 2013)	Taught date	Link
9	University of Ottawa: Faculty of Social Sciences, School of Public and International Affairs	The Middle East Peace Process	ECH 4350 A	13 March	Winter 2013	http://ssms.socialsciences.uottawa.ca/vfs/.horde/offre_cours/syllabus/00035114062_ECH4350A.pdf
10	University of Manitoba: Department of Political Studies	Selected Topics I – Middle Eastern Politics	Politics 19.314 L01	13 March	2003	http://home.cc.umanitoba.ca/~jacobyta/19_314_L01.pdf
11	Acadia University	The Arab-Israeli Conflict	History 2073 X2	13 March	Winter 2012	http://history.acadiau.ca/tl_files/sites/history/Course%20Outlines%2020112012/HIST2073Jan12.pdf
12	Department of History Trent University	History of the Middle East	HISTY 3650Y	13 March	2011–12	www.trentu.ca/history/.../HIST3650-2011-12Murat.doc
13	University of Fraser Valley: Department of History	Arab-Zionist Relations	HIST 335	13 March	2008–9	http://www.ufv.ca/calendar/CourseOutlines/PDFs/HIST/HIST335-20090522.pdf
14	University of Toronto	Becoming Israel: War, Peace, and the Politics of Israel's Identity	POL 345Y 1 Y	14 March	Fall 2012–Winter 2013	http://politics.utoronto.ca/uploads/syllabus/1213_pol345y1y_l0101.pdf
15	York University: Department of Political Science	War and Peace in the Middle East	AS/POLS 3260 6.0A/AK/POLS 3209J	14 March	2003–4	http://www.arts.yorku.ca/politics/drop_down/courseOutlines/2003/3260A.htm
16	York University: Department of Political Science	War and Peace in the Middle East	AS/POLS 3260 6.0A/AK/POLS 3209J	14 March	2004–5	http://www.arts.yorku.ca/politics/drop_down/courseOutlines/2004/3260.htm

No.	College	Course title	Course code	Access date (all 2013)	Taught date	Link
17	University of Ottawa: Faculty of Social Sciences, School of Public and International Affairs	The Israeli-Palestinian Conflict	API 6339G	14 March	Winter 2010	http://ssms.socialsciences.uottawa.ca/vfs/.horde/offre_cours/syllabus/0003668374_API6339G.pdf
18	University of Toronto	Becoming Israel: War, Peace, and the Politics of Israel's Identity	POL 345H1 (F)	14 March	Fall 2009	http://politics.utoronto.ca/uploads/syllabus/0910_pol345h1f_l0101.pdf
19	University of Toronto	Becoming Israel: War, Peace, and the Politics of Israel's Identity	POL 345 Y Y	14 March	Fall 2011–Winter 2012	http://politics.utoronto.ca/uploads/syllabus/1112_pol345y1y_l0101.pdf
20	University of Ottawa	Conflict and the Peace Process in the Middle East	ECH4350 A	14 March	Winter 2010	http://ssms.socialsciences.uottawa.ca/vfs/.horde/offre_cours/syllabus/0003467742_ECH4350A.pdf
21	University of Toronto	Becoming Israel: War, Peace, and the Politics of Israel's Identity	POL 345 Y Y	14 March	Fall 2010–Winter 2011	http://politics.utoronto.ca/uploads/syllabus/1011_pol345y1y_l0101.pdf
22	University of Ottawa: Faculty of Social Sciences, School of Public and International Affairs	Middle East Peace Process	API 6399 K	14 March	Winter 2012	http://ssms.socialsciences.uottawa.ca/vfs/.horde/offre_cours/syllabus/00036613363_API6399K.pdf
23	McGill University	The Arab-Israeli Conflict, Crisis, War, and Peace	POLI 347	14 March	Fall 2010	http://www.mcgill.ca/files/politicalscience/courseFall2010_poli347.pdf
24	McGill University	Arab-Israeli Conflict, Crisis, War, and Peace	POLI 347	14 March	Fall Term 2007	http://www.mcgill.ca/files/politicalscience/course07_poli347.pdf

(Continued)

No.	College	Course title	Course code	Access date (all 2013)	Taught date	Link
25	Bishops University	Introduction to Middle East Politics	Pol236b	14 March	Winter 2007	http://www.ubishops.ca/fileadmin/bishops_documents/course_outlines/2007/winter/social_science/pol236.pdf
26	McGill University	History of the Arab-Israeli Conflict	HIST 339	14 March	Winter 2011	http://www.mcgill.ca/history/sites/mcgill.ca.history/files/HIST339_Winter2011_Sanagan.pdf
27	McGill University	The Arab-Israeli Conflict, Crisis, War, and Peace	POLI 347	14 March	Fall Term 2009	http://www.mcgill.ca/files/politicalscience/courseFall09_poli347.pdf
28	Simon Fraser University	Politics of the Middle East	315/809	14 March	Fall 2008	http://www.sfu.ca/content/dam/sfu/internationalstudies/documents/outlines/1107/315-809-1107.pdf
29	McGill University	Arab-Israel Conflict, Crisis, Peace	Poli 347	14 March	Fall 2012	http://www.mcgill.ca/politicalscience/sites/mcgill.ca.politicalscience/files/poli_347_fall_2012_0.pdf
30	Western University	Politics of the Middle East	POLITICS 3329F-001	14 March	2012	http://politicalscience.uwo.ca/undergrad/COURSE%20PAGES/COURSES%202012-13/POL%203329F.pdf
31	Carleton University: Department of Political Science	Peace and Conflict in the Middle East	PSCI 3702A	15 March	Winter 2010	http://www1.carleton.ca/polisci/ccms/wp-content/ccms-files/PSCI-3702A-Sucharov-W10.pdf
32	Carleton University: Department of Political Science	Peace and Conflict in the Middle East	PSCI 3702A	15 March	Winter 2011	http://www1.carleton.ca/polisci/ccms/wp-content/ccms-files/PSCI-3702A-Sucharov-W11.pdf
33	McMaster University	The Literature of Israel and Palestine: Peace Studies	4IP3/CL 3MM3	15 March	Fall 2009	http://www.humanities.mcmaster.ca/~english/undergraduate/term_1/Level%204/PDF/English%204IP3%20Bruce%202009-1.pdf

No.	College	Course title	Course code	Access date (all 2013)	Taught date	Link
34	Carleton University: Department of Political Science	Politics and Government in the Middle East	PSCI 3203A	15 March	Fall 2008	http://www1.carleton.ca/polisci/ccms/wp-content/ccms-files/psci-3203a-kirisci-f08.pdf
35	McGill University: Department of Political Science	International Politics and Foreign Policy: The Middle East	Poli 341	15 March	NA	http://www.mcgill.ca/files/politicalscience/course06_poli341.pdf
36	Carleton University: Department of Political Science	Peace and Conflict in the Middle East	PSCI 3702A	15 March	Winter 2007	http://www1.carleton.ca/polisci/ccms/wp-content/ccms-files/3702a-scholey-w07.pdf
37	Bishop's University: Department of History	A History of the Arab-Israeli Conflict	HIS 352A 01	15 March	Fall 2005	http://www.ubishops.ca/fileadmin/bishops_documents/course_outlines/2005/fall/humanities/his352.pdf
38	Carleton University	Peace and Conflict in the Middle East	PSCI 3702	27 April	Fall 2005	http://www.jewishvirtuallibrary.org/jsource/isdf/syl/SucharovMiraIsraeliPalestinianRelations.pdf
39	University of Calgary	The Arab-(Jewish/)Israel Conflict, 1939–Present	Secm 20776	27 April	Fall 2006	http://www.jewishvirtuallibrary.org/jsource/isdf/syl/Arab-IsraeliConflict_DavidTal.pdf
40	University of Calgary	History of the Arab-Israeli Conflict	HTST 390–01	27 April	Fall 2010	https://hist.ucalgary.ca/sites/hist.ucalgary.ca/files/unitis/courses/HTST390.1/F2010/LEC1/HTST390.1-F2010-LEC1-outline.pdf
41	University of Calgary	Issues in Israeli National Security	Hist.593 L03	27 April	Fall 2009	https://hist.ucalgary.ca/sites/hist.ucalgary.ca/files/unitis/courses/HTST593.19/F2009/LEC3/HTST593.19-F2009-LEC3-outline.pdf

Table 3.7 All extracted syllabi from Australian universities

No.	College	Course title	Course code	Access date (all 2013)	Taught date	Link
1	University of Sydney	Approaches to the Arab Israeli Conflict	HSTY2607	19 March	2011	http://register.summer.usyd.edu.au/uos.php?ak=detail&id=3350
2	University of New South Wales: School of Social Sciences	The Middle East and Global Politics	POLS5160	19 March	2012	http://socialsciences.arts.unsw.edu.au/media/File/POLS5160_S2_2012.pdf
3	University of New South Wales: School of Social Sciences	The Middle East and Global Politics	POLS5160	19 March	2011	http://socialsciences.arts.unsw.edu.au/media/File/POLS5160_S2_2011.pdf
4	University of Newcastle Australia: School of Humanities and Social Science	The World in the Twentieth Century	HIST1070	19 March	2007	http://www.newcastle.edu.au/Resources/Divisions/Academic/Library/Cultural%20Collections/pdf/HIST1070_Course_Outline_Sem2_2007.pdf
5	University of Newcastle Australia: School of Humanities and Social Science	Israel and the Middle East: Roots of the Current Conflict	HIST3672	19 March	2009	http://www.newcastle.edu.au/Resources/Divisions/Academic/Library/Cultural%20Collections/pdf/HIST3672_Course_Outline_Sem1_2009.pdf
6	University of Newcastle Australia: School of Humanities & Social Science	Europe and the World	HIST 1080	19 March	2010	http://www.newcastle.edu.au/Resources/Divisions/Academic/Library/Cultural%20Collections/pdf/HIST1080_Course_Outline_Sem2_2010.pdf
7	Macquarie University	International Relations of the Middle East	POL322	19 March	2011	mq.edu.au/pubstatic/public/download.jsp?id=50038
8	Macquarie University	International Relations of the Middle East	IRPG843	19 March	2012	mq.edu.au/pubstatic/public/download.jsp?id=73169

No.	College	Course title	Course code	Access date (all 2013)	Taught date	Link
9	University of New South Wales: School of History & Philosophy	The United States and the Middle East	ARTS 3276	21 March	2011	http://humanities.arts.unsw.edu.au/media/File/ARTS3276_noimages_2011.pdf
10	University of New South Wales: School of History & Philosophy	The United States and the Middle East	ARTS 3288	21 March	2012	http://humanities.arts.unsw.edu.au/media/File/ARTS3288.pdf
11	University of New South Wales: School of Social Sciences	The Middle East & International Law	ARTS3817	21 March	2012	http://socialsciences.arts.unsw.edu.au/media/File/1_ARTS3817_S1_2012.pdf
12	University of New South Wales: School of Social Sciences	The Middle East & International Law	ARTS3813	21 March	2011	http://socialsciences.arts.unsw.edu.au/media/File/ARTS3813_Sem1_2011.pdf
13	Macquarie University	International Relations of the Middle East	POL322	21 March	Semester 2, 2011	http://www.google.co.uk/url?sa=t&rct=j&q=&esrc=s&source=web&cd=111&ved=0CDEQFjAAOG4&url=http%3A%2F%2Fmq.edu.au%2Fpubstatic%2Fpublic%2Fdownload.jsp%3Fid%3D50038&ei=3gx1UfaqHlnZOpLsgZgF8&usg=AFQjCNFmMWzxeYriaDQOLMxAvBIqAmd67Q&sig2=xb47v5uHud4v3efumyYvSQ
14	University of Newcastle: Faculty of Education and Arts, School of Humanities & Social Science	Israel and the Middle East: Roots of the Current Conflict	HIST 3671	21 March	Semester 1, 2007	http://www.newcastle.edu.au/Resources/Divisions/Academic/Library/Cultural%20Collections/pdf/HIST3671_Course_Outline_Sem1_2007.pdf
15	University of Newcastle: Faculty of Education and Arts, School of Humanities & Social Science	The World in the Twentieth Century	HIST1070	21 March	Semester 2, 2007	http://www.newcastle.edu.au/Resources/Divisions/Academic/Library/Cultural%20Collections/pdf/HIST1070_Course_Outline_Sem2_2007.pdf

(*Continued*)

No.	College	Course title	Course code	Access date (all 2013)	Taught date	Link
16	University of New South Wales: School of Social Sciences and International Studies	The Middle East and Global Politics	POLS5160	21 March	Semester 2, 2010	http://www.sprc.unsw.edu.au/media/File/POLS5160_.pdf

Table 3.8 All extracted syllabi from New Zealand universities

No.	College	Course title	Course code	Access date (all 2013)	Taught date	Link
1	Victoria University of Wellington: School of Art History, Classics and Religious Studies	Religion, Law and Politics	RELI 107	19 March	2012	http://www.victoria.ac.nz/fhss/student-admin/course-outlines/2012/trimester-2/reli/RELI107-2012-T2.pdf
2	Victoria University of Wellington: School of History, Philosophy, Political Science and International Relations	Special Topic: Nationalism in World Politics	INTP213	19 March	2008	http://www.victoria.ac.nz/courseoutlines/fhss/2008/Trimester2/INTP/INTP213-2008-T2.pdf
3	University of Wellington: School of History, Philosophy, Political Science and International Relations	Special Topic: Nationalism in World Politics	INTP213	19 March	2009	http://www.victoria.ac.nz/courseoutlines/fhss/2009/Trimester1-FullYear/INTP/INTP213-2009-T1.pdf
4	Massey University	Israel and the Arab World	200.302	19 March	2009	http://www.massey.ac.nz/massey/fms/Colleges/College%20of%20Humanities%20and%20Social%20Sciences/Documents/Outlines/2009/200/200302_0902_PNTH_E.pdf
5	Massey University	Israel and the Arab World	200.302	19 March	2008	http://www.massey.ac.nz/massey/fms/Colleges/College%20of%20Humanities%20and%20Social%20Sciences/Documents/Outlines/2008/200/200302_0802_PNTH_E.pdf
6	Massey University	Israel and the Arab World	200.302	19 March	2011	http://www.allanwilsoncentre.ac.nz/massey/fms/Colleges/College%20of%20Humanities%20and%20Social%20Sciences/Documents/Outlines/2011/200/200302_1101_PNTH_I.pdf

(*Continued*)

No.	College	Course title	Course code	Access date (all 2013)	Taught date	Link
7	Massey University	Israel/Palestine and the Arab World	200.302	19 March	2013	https://www.massey.ac.nz/massey/learning/departments/school-people-environment-planning/study/subjects/paper.cfm?paper_code=200302&paper_offering_id=1193109&study_year=2013
8	Victoria University of Wellington: School of History, Philosophy, Political Science and International Relations	Prelude to Peace: Displaced Persons and Refugees in Postwar Europe	CRN 18772	19 March	2011	http://www.victoria.ac.nz/fhss/student-admin/course-outlines/2011/trimester2/hist/hist338-2011-t2.pdf
9	Victoria University of Wellington: School of History, Philosophy, Political Science and International Relations	Prelude to Peace: Displaced Persons and Refugees in Postwar Europe	CRN 18772	19 March	2012	http://www.victoria.ac.nz/fhss/student-admin/course-outlines/2012/trimester1-fullyear/hist/HIST338-2012-T1.pdf
10	Victoria University of Wellington	Advanced Studies in Religion and Politics Part I: Political Thought in the Middle East	RELI 422	19 March	2011	http://www.victoria.ac.nz/fhss/student-admin/course-outlines/2011/trimester1-fullyear/reli/reli422-2011-t1.pdf
11	University of Canterbury: School of Social and Political Sciences	Introduction to International Relations	POLS 104	19 March	2009	http://www.saps.canterbury.ac.nz/docs/course-outlines/pols_104_S2_09.pdf

Table 3.9 All extracted syllabi from Irish universities

No.	College	Course title	Course code	Access date (all 2013)	Taught date	Link
1	Dublin City University: School of Law & Government	The Politics of the Arab-Israeli Conflict	LG563	12 March	2010–11	http://www.dcu.ie/registry/module_contents_archive_years.php?subcode=LG563&function=2&module_archive_year=2011
2	Trinity College Dublin	Conflicts Zones: Case Studies	SO7017	12 March	NA	http://www.tcd.ie/sociology/ethnicracialstudies/about/modules/conflict-casestudies.php
3	Dublin City University: School of Law & Government	The Politics of the Arab-Israeli Conflict	LG563A	12 March	2009–10	http://www.dcu.ie/registry/module_contents_archive_years.php?subcode=LG563A&function=2&module_archive_year=2010
4	Dublin City University: School of Law and Government	The Politics of the Arab-Israeli Conflict	MA-LG 563	12March	2005–6	www.dcu.ie/~cavatorf/arabisrael/Course%20Outline.doc
5	National University of Ireland, Galway: School of Law	Conflict-Post Conflict	NA	12 March	2009–10; 2012/13; 2008–9	www.nuigalway.ie/human_rights/.../conflicttemplate.doc
6	University College Dublin	The Israeli- Palestinian Conflict and the 'Arab Spring'	TN110	12 March	2012–13	http://www.ucd.ie/adulted/coursesbycode/tn110/
7	Dublin City University	The World Since 1945	HIST 103	26 April	2011–12	http://www.spd.dcu.ie/MAIN/academic/history/documents/FirstYearBA201112.pdf
8	National University of Ireland, Galway	International Law and Conflict	NA	26 April	2012/13	http://www.google.co.uk/url?sa=t&rct=j&q=&esrc=s&source=web&cd=3&ved=0CD4QFjAC&url=http%3A%2F%2Fwww.nuigalway.ie%2Fhuman_rights%2Fdocuments%2Fconflictpc201213.doc&ei=kZ96UYOtJ6SW0AWuBA&usg=AFQjCNHfHNFXwxCUOFWyfU1lAwS0o2oP8Q&sig2=ZBScZeDAuK0vPB7fl1GuuQ

Table 3.10 All extracted syllabi from US universities

No.	College	Course title	Course code	Access date (all 2013)	Taught date	Link
1	University of Texas at Austin	Re-forming the 20th Century Arab East	HIS 364G; MES 322K	22 March	Spring 2011	http://www.google.co.uk/url?sa=t&rct=j&q=&esrc=s&source=web&cd=2&ved=0CDoQFjAB&url=http%3A%2F%2Fwww.utexas.edu%2Fcola%2Ffiles%2F1022375&ei=qwN4UZrUPLL50gXl6YHwAQ&usg=AFQjCNHc_O_E0HB1N6JQkXgAJBlzixfmwg&sig2=tljkDlrEZPBGdCk3gcNv1w&bvm=bv.45580626,d.d2k and http://www.google.co.uk/url?sa=t&rct=j&q=&esrc=s&source=web&cd=2&ved=0CDoQFjAB&url=http%3A%2F%2Fwww.utexas.edu%2Fcola%2Ffiles%2F1022375&ei=0_B3Ub-PAqnM0QWhqoGYCw&usg=AFQjCNHc_O_E0HB1N6JQkXgAJBlzixfmwg&sig2=QjEZElVLlFuUe0hP0oc-gQ
2	University of Wisconsin	The Arab-Israeli Conflict	Political Science 333	22 March	Spring 2009	http://www.google.co.uk/url?sa=t&rct=j&q=&esrc=s&source=web&cd=4&ved=0CEcQFjAD&url=http%3A%2F%2Fde pt.polisci.wisc.edu%2Fsyllabi%2F1094%2FPS%252033%2520The%2520Arab-Israeli%2520Conflict.doc&ei=MWhMUfXnLMi00QXEiIHQCg&usg=AFQjCNG5Mo_zi9ILzmPA9tovJgZ6r6JocA&sig2=K_-XkBkfQOd-v830qEdDGg
3	University of Puget Sound	War and Peace in the Middle East	IPE 180	22 March	Fall 2009	http://www.google.co.uk/url?sa=t&rct=j&q=&esrc=s&source=web&cd=7&ved=0CF0QFjAG&url=http%3A%2F%2Fwebspace.pugetsound.edu%2Ffacultypages%2Fbdillman%2F1 syllabus180Fall2009.doc&ei=MWhMUfXnLMi00QXEiIHQCg&usg=AFQjCNGiQMsYHJmSVcemgXHaLTEuUlgb1Q&sig2=WEGNzv0ZKIW1VwTAShP8rQ
4	University of Alabama	A Multi-Ethnic Israel	Core 174C	22 March	2011	http://daniel,j.levine.people.ua.edu/uploads/1/3/4/9/13498793/syllabus_-_multi-ethnic_israel_-_3_feb_2011.pdf

No.	College	Course title	Course code	Access date (all 2013)	Taught date	Link
5	Syracuse University	The Israeli⊠Palestinian Conflict: Religion, International Relations, and the Media	PSC 600.001; MES 600.001	22 March	Spring 2011	http://faculty.maxwell.syr.edu/melman/pdfs/Elman%20M%20PSC%20600,%20Israeli-Palestinian%20Conflict,%20Spring%202011.pdf
6	University of Utah	Introduction to the History of the Middle East from 1750 to the Present	HIST 1460; MID E 1545; UGS 1460	22 March	Spring 2012	https://www.humis.utah.edu/humis/docs/organization_298_1326237497.pdf
7	University of Virginia	Government and Politics of the Middle East	PLCP 3410	22 March	Summer 2012	http://www.ise.virginia.edu/syllabi/A12/Barghothi_PLCP3410_GovtandPolitics.pdf
8	University of California, San Diego	Representations of the Israeli/Palestinian Conflict	COSF 188	22 March	Spring 2011	http://communication.ucsd.edu/courses/cosf-188/cosf-188-s-11.html
9	University of Florida	The Israeli-Palestinian Conflict	NA	22 March	Fall 2009	http://www.google.co.uk/url?sa=t&rct=j&q=&esrc=s&source=web&cd=14&ved=0CF4QFjADOAo&url=http%3A%2F%2Fplaza.ufl.edu%2Ftsorek%2Farticles%2FSyllabus%2520IP%2520fall%252009.doc&ei=V3hMUa_nGOnX0QXHkoDoBg&usg=AFQjCNE7JNJUV175nlg2iqEfuM9LAhF_sw&sig2=_os_4oVsjlmbJ7gLdVCR4Q
10	University of Florida	Israelis and Palestinians	Jewish Studies 16740000	22 March	Fall 2012	http://fora.aa.ufl.edu/docs/47//21Feb12//UCC_21Feb12_JST3XXX.pdf
11	University of Notre Dame	Comparative Conflict Regulation: Israel/Palestine, Northern Ireland and Sri Lanka	POLS 34557	22 March	Fall 2011	http://www3.nd.edu/~ndlondon/ug/FA11_syllabi_web/Syllabus_FA11_POLS34557.pdf

(Continued)

No.	College	Course title	Course code	Access date (all 2013)	Taught date	Link
12	University of Utah	Introduction to the History of the Middle East from 1750 to the Present	HIST 1460; MIDE 1545; UGS 1460	22 March	Spring 2010	http://www.humis.utah.edu/humis/syllabi/Syllabus1257176544.pdf
13	University of Wisconsin	The Arab-Israeli Conflict	Political Science 631	22 March	Spring 2013	http://jewishstudies.wisc.edu/jewishstudies/wp-content/uploads/2011/07/Political-Science-631-The-Arab-Israeli-Conflict1.pdf
14	Brandeis University	Sociology of the Israeli-Palestinian Confrontation	Sociology 157a	22 March	Spring 2007	http://www.brandeis.edu/departments/sociology/syllabi/Spring2007/Soc157aSyllabus-Spring2007.pdf
15	San Francisco State University	International Political Economy	IR/PS312	22 March	2010	http://userwww.sfsu.edu/aymouke/syllabi/ir-312.htm
16	Columbia College Chicago	Middle Eastern History and Culture	49-1504-01/MW	22 March	Spring 2008	https://www.google.co.uk/url?sa=t&rct=j&q=&esrc=s&source=web&cd=21&ved=0CDwQFjAAOBQ&url=https%3A%2F%2Foasis.colum.edu%2Fics%2FPortlets%2FICS%2FHandoutportlet%2Fviewhandler.ashx%3Fhandout_id%3D11eb46e1-4bc1-473c-8ffc-eff4c8107437&ei=LIxMUc_IOMir0AWdjYHIDg&usg=AFQjCNESS_UaIUGBU1RszeN-liRUHVRgZg&sig2=CqyKIkpFsHlfNO4avtbfg&cad=rja
17	University of Wisconsin	The Arab-Israeli Conflict	Political Science 631	22 March	Spring 2011	http://dept.polisci.wisc.edu/syllabi/1114/PS%20631%20Arab-Israeli%20Conflict%20Spring.pdf
18	University of Wisconsin	The Arab-Israeli Conflict	Political Science 333	22 March	Spring 2008	http://dept.polisci.wisc.edu/syllabi/1084/333.pdf
19	University of Florida	Israelis and Palestinians	NA	22 March	Spring 2013	http://plaza.ufl.edu/tsorek/articles/IPconflict.pdf

No.	College	Course title	Course code	Access date (all 2013)	Taught date	Link
20	University of Florida	Ethnic Conflicts in Comparative Perspective	SYA7933, section 1370 POS 6933, section 04H1	22 March	Fall 2011	http://plaza.ufl.edu/tsorek/articles/ethnic.pdf
21	Portland State University	Introduction to the Arab-Israeli Conflict and Peace Process	PS 362U	22 March	Winter 2010	http://www.pdx.edu/sites/www.pdx.edu.sociologyofislam/files/Lindsay%20Benstead%20Arab%20Israeli%20Conflict%20362.pdf
22	University of Mary Washington	The History of the Arab-Israeli Conflict	HIST-385-13654	22 March	Spring 2012	http://www.academia.edu/1749233/Arab-Israeli_Conflict_Syllabus_Spring_2012
23	Georgia State University	Through the Looking Glass: Perceptions and Misconceptions of Israeli-Arab Relations	PERS2001	22 March	2011 Spring	http://www.academia.edu/1788849/Syllabus_Through_the_Looking_Glass_Perceptions_and_Misconceptions_of_Arab-Israeli_Relations
24	Brigham Young University	International Conflict Bargaining and Management	B140 JFSB	22 March	NA	https://politicalscience.byu.edu/Syllabi/Sp08/Blimes_379R_Sp08.pdf
25	University of Southern California	International Relations of the Contemporary Middle East	IR 362	22 March	Spring 2011	http://www.wrigley.usc.edu/assets/sites/32/docs/362_Spring_2011.pdf
26	University of Wisconsin-Whitewater	Arab-Israeli Conflict, 1900–Present	HIST 338	22 March	Fall 2007	http://www.google.co.uk/url?sa=t&rct=j&q=&esrc=s&source=web&cd=15&ved=0CGAQFjAEOAo&url=http%3A%2F%2Facadaff.uww.edu%2FUCC%2F2006-07%2F012607%2FHISTRY338.doc&ei=MihPUabFAeS40QWlhYH4CA&usg=AFQjCNFbaAXEgAHuadyNtPYeZcvx2ELjiA&sig2=Vk_i6f7VLUJut-1wzRRl4g
27	College of Wooster	Modern Middle East	Hist 227	22 March	Fall 2011	http://middleeast.voices.wooster.edu/syllabus/

(Continued)

No.	College	Course title	Course code	Access date (all 2013)	Taught date	Link
28	University of South Carolina	The History of Zionism and the State of Israel	NA	22 March	Fall 2009	http://artsandsciences.sc.edu/jstp/courses/Kerenji.HIST492H.Fall.2009.pdf
29	University of Northern Colorado	Conflict in the Middle East	PSCI 325-001	22 March	Spring 2012	http://www.unco.edu/PSCI/current/sp12_syllabi/PSCI%20sp12%20syl%20pdfs/PSCI_325_reading_list_blair_sp12.pdf
30	Nazareth College	Conflict and Crisis in the Middle East	HIS/PSC 309G PII	22 March	Fall 2007	http://www-pub.naz.edu:9000/~psc309/index.htm
31	University of San Francisco	International Relations of the Middle East	Politics 354	22 March	Spring 2006	http://www.google.co.uk/url?sa=t&rct=j&q=&esrc=s&source=web&cd=27&ved=0CGsQFjAGOBQ&url=http%3A%2F%2Fisanet.ccit.arizona.edu%2Fsections%2Ffpa%2Fsyllabi%2FNew_2009%2FIRME_2006.doc&ei=djNPUYqsKu-m0wXciYGwDw&usg=AFQjCNGSC0GRtkfS9pCJF1E9ZF_hG5z3g&sig2=6fQj058X8gBmT7BxviUlvQ
32	Southern Connecticut State University	Narrating the Israeli-Palestinian Conflict	JST 110	22 March	NA	http://www.academia.edu/1748524/Narrating_the_Israeli-Palestinian_Conflict
33	Oberlin College	Emergence of the Modern Middle East	Hist-122	22 March	2012	http://new.oberlin.edu/dotAsset/3867199.pdf
34	University of Colorado Boulder	International Behavior: Conflict Bargaining and Management	PSCI 3193	22 March	Fall 2006	http://sobek.colorado.edu/~blimes/3193.pdf
35	University of Wyoming	Historical Methods: Israeli-Palestinian Conflict	History 3020-1	22 March	Spring 2011	http://www.uwyo.edu/history/_files/documents/syllabi/kampsyllabushist3020spr2011.pdf

No.	College	Course title	Course code	Access date (all 2013)	Taught date	Link
36	Swarthmore College: Department of History	History of the Modern Middle East from the Ottomans to the Iraq War	History 6b	22 March	Fall 2009	http://www.swarthmore.edu/Documents/academics/history/F09%2206b%20Syllabus.pdf
37	Clark College	Geopolitics of the Middle East	GEOG/POSC 220	22 March	Spring 2011	http://www.google.co.uk/url?sa=t&rct=j&q=&esrc=s&source=web&cd=34&ved=0CFMQFjADOB4&url=http%3A%2F%2Fweb.clark.edu%2Fpcole%2Fsyllabi%2FGEOG%2FSp11%2FGEOGPOLS220_1DL_Kheirabadi_Sp11_syl.docx&ei=dT1PUeakCsup0AXMkIA4&usg=AFQjCNFJ2s4rL_1iOxcnluoUac2P1MZIBg&sig2=D8f_sKLEHRBoLGyXlsHDNw
38	Columbia University	Civil Wars and Peace Settlements	INAF U8869	22 March	Fall 2008	http://www.columbia.edu/~sa435/SevCW08.pdf
39	University of Nevada, Las Vegas: Department of Political Science	International Relations of the Middle East and North Africa	Political Science 405K	22 March	Fall 2009	http://liberalarts.unlv.edu/Political_Science/Syllabi/Fall%202009/PSC%20405KTamadonfar.pdf
40	Penn State University	Introduction to the Middle East	HIST 181, Section 1	22 March	24 August 2009	http://wwwaltoona.psu.edu/upload/syllabi/fa09_hist181001.pdf
41	California State University, Northridge	Israel's History and Peoples	JS 427	22 March	Fall 2013	http://www.google.co.uk/url?sa=t&rct=j&q=&esrc=s&source=web&cd=43&ved=0CF4QFjACOCg&url=http%3A%2F%2Fwww.csun.edu%2F~cohumcur%2FJS%2FNC_JS_427_11_29_11.doc&ei=uU1PUfrMN4PD0QXwnoCYAQ&usg=AFQjCNGCMotpYLS0XgN6Zr0ZafIktwz2xQ&sig2=0KBFnj2vffPJKluj_bAzfA
42	Wofford College	Modern Middle East	HIS 391	22 March	2008	http://webs.wofford.edu/whisnantcj/his391/bibliography.htm
43	Clark College	Geopolitics of the Middle East	GEOG/POSC 220	22 March	Winter 2012	http://web.clark.edu/pcole/syllabi/GEOG/W12/GEOG_POLS_220_1DL_Kheirabadi_W12_syl.pdf

(Continued)

No.	College	Course title	Course code	Access date (all 2013)	Taught date	Link
44	University of California, Berkeley	History of the Middle East from the 18th Century: From Ottoman Rule to the Arab Spring	History 109C	22 March	Fall 2012	http://history.berkeley.edu/sites/default/files/syllabus/109C%20Syllabus%20T%20W%20Hill%20Final.pdf
45	Lincoln Memorial University (LMU)	Middle Eastern Civilizations	HIST 495	22 March	Spring 2006	http://www.google.co.uk/url?sa=t&rct=j&q=&esrc=s&source=web&cd=49&ved=0CIwBEBYwCDgo&url=http%3A%2F%2Fwww.lmunet.edu%2Ffactools%2Fbb%2Farchives%2FSPRING2006%2FARTS_SCIENCES%2FHUMN_FA%2Fsyllabi%2FHIST495.doc&ei=uU1PUfrMN4PD0QXwnoCYAQ&usg=AFQjCNHYZQ2FqAix3oycBK_rFMprsD5QKg&sig2=FhM2lY-mRbrd3QFfDH0FQ
46	Columbia University: Department of Political Science	Politics of the Middle East and North Africa	W4445x	22 March	Fall 2011	http://polisci.barnard.edu/sites/default/files/inline/ps_4445me2011.pdf
47	University of California, San Diego	Middle East in the Twentieth Century	HINE 118	22 March	Spring 2011	http://history.ucsd.edu/Syllabi/Spring%202011/HINE%20118-SP11-Gheissari.pdf
48	California Lutheran University	The History and Politics of the Modern Middle East	History/ Political Science 384	22 March	Fall 2008	http://www.callutheran.edu/admission/undergraduate/cal_lu/2009_spring/academics/professorial_pastimes/documents/384f08sy.pdf
49	Brigham Young University	International Conflict Bargaining and Management	Pl Sc 379r	22 March	NA	https://politicalscience.byu.edu/Syllabi/W09/Blimes_379R_W09.pdf
50	Ithaca College	Seminar: Law, Nation and Occupation: Israel and Palestine	310-40100-03	22 March	2005	http://www.ithaca.edu/hs/depts/politics/coursess2005/coursesf05/

No.	College	Course title	Course code	Access date (all 2013)	Taught date	Link
51	The University of Georgia	The Arab–Israeli Conflict	HIST 4580	22 March	Fall 2012	http://history.uga.edu/_syllabi/HIST4580_walde_0812.pdf
52	Kent State University	Oil, Suicide Bombers, & the Veil: Demystifying the Politics of the Middle East	POL 40591-001	22 March	Fall 2009	http://www.personal.kent.edu/~jstacher/docs/FINAL.MEPoliticsSyllabus.Fall2009.pdf
53	Brown University	History of the State of Israel – 1948 to the Present	JUDS1981Q	10 April	Fall 2012	http://www.brown.edu/Courses/uploads/JUDS%3A1981Q%3A2012-Fall%3AS01.pdf
54	Boston University	The History of Israel	CAS. HI. 392	10 April	Spring 2012	http://www.bu.edu/history/files/2012/02/392Sprg12.pdf
55	New York University	World Cultures: Modern Israel	MAP V55.0537	10 April	Fall 2009	http://map.cas.nyu.edu/docs/CP/2248/0537zweig093.pdf
56	Loyola Marymount University	Modern Israel	JWST 398 / POLS 495	10 April	Spring 2012	http://bellarmine2.lmu.edu/cds/Spring%202012/JWST/JWST%20398%2001%20SS%20Modern%20Israel-Soomekh.pdf
57	University of California, San Diego	The Middle East in the Twentieth Century	HINE 118	10 April	Winter 2013	http://history.ucsd.edu/Syllabi/Winter%202013/HINE%20118-WI13-Kayali.pdf
58	University of California, San Diego	The Middle East in the Twentieth Century	HINE 118	10 April	Spring 2009	http://history.ucsd.edu/Syllabi/Spring%202009/HINE%20118-SP09-Kayal%C4%B1.pdf
59	Emory University	Viewing Israel: Current Issues	MESAS 190-002	10 April	Fall 2011	http://college.emory.edu/home/academic/course/schedules/2011/fall/section/regular/middle_eastern_south_asian/MESAS190-002.html
60	University of California, San Diego	The Middle East in the Twentieth Century	HINE 118	10 April	Spring 2010	http://history.ucsd.edu/Syllabi/Spring%202010/HINE%20118-SP10-Kayali.pdf

(Continued)

No.	College	Course title	Course code	Access date (all 2013)	Taught date	Link
61	Portland State University	Sociology of the Middle East	INT/SOC 483U	10 April	Fall 2009	http://www.pdx.edu/sites/www.pdx.edu.sociologyofislam/files/Sociology%20of%20Middle%20East%20Fall%202009%20Tugrul.pdf
62	University of Utah	The Middle East Since 1914: Imperialism, Nationalism, Revolution and War	History 3400/6920; MIDE 3540/5540	10 April	Spring 2013	https://www.humis.utah.edu/humis/docs/organization_298_1357334033.pdf
63	New York University	War and Peace in Israel and Palestine in the 20th Century	NA	10 April	NA	http://www.nyu.edu/content/dam/nyu/globalPrgms/documents/florence/academics/syllabi/HBRJD-UA9800_Simoni.pdf
64	Loyola Marymount University	Modern Israel	Pols 398/Jewish Studies 398	10 April	Fall 2012	http://bellarmine2.lmu.edu/cds/Fall%202012/POLS/POLS%20398%20&%20JWST%20398%20Modern%20Israel%20%28Soomekh%20F12%29.pdf
65	San Diego State University: Department of History	Modern Jewish History	HIST 488	10 April	Fall 2012	http://sdsu-dspace.calstate.edu/bitstream/handle/10211.10/2805/488%20%20Modern%20Jewish%20Hist%20%20Naor.pdf?sequence=1
66	Loyola Marymount University	Israel and its Historical Perspectives	Jewish Studies 3xx	10 April	9/13/2012	http://www.lmu.edu/Assets/Centers+$!2b+Institutes/Center+for+Teaching+Excellence/Levitsky-Syllabus.pdf
67	Fordham University	History of Modern Israel	HSRG 3675-001	10 April	Spring 2009	http://www.google.co.uk/url?sa=t&rct=j&q=&esrc=s&source=web&cd=2&ved=0CDkQFjAB&url=http%3A%2F%2Fwww.fordham.edu%2Fimages%2Fundergraduate%2Fspecial_programs%2Fstudyab%2Fhistory%2520of%2520modern%2520israel%2520-%2520syllabus.doc&ei=GpRIUYmhEcKSOPiHgKA1&usg=AFQjCNGW6Z6rD0I-WrNdhsN7micitPQN4Q&sig2=me5LZFuXUQUFDWr8LehQ2A&bvm=bv.44990110,d.d2k

No.	College	Course title	Course code	Access date (all 2013)	Taught date	Link
68	University of Texas at Arlington: Department of Political Science	Israel Identity and the Arab-Israeli Conflict	5381	10 April	Fall 2009	http://wweb.uta.edu/faculty/bsasley/5381%20syllabus.pdf
69	University of Texas At Arlington: Department of Political Science	Israeli Identity and the Arab-Israeli Conflict	5339-001	10 April	Fall 2012	https://www.uta.edu/ra//real/syllabi/20816_1934_5339_syllabus.pdf
70	The University of Texas At Austin	Israel: Politics, Society, Foreign Relations	GOV 365N	10 April	Spring 2010	http://www.utexas.edu/cola/depts/government/courses/archive/27629
71	University of California, San Diego	Zionism and Post Zionism	NA	10 April	Summer 2012	http://icenter.ucsd.edu/_files/pao/global-seminars/jerusalem/Course2.pdf
72	George Washington University	History of Modern Israel	History 101.17	10 April	Spring 2008	http://www.google.co.uk/url?sa=t&rct=j&q=&esrc=s&source=web&cd=3&ved=0CD8QFjAC&url=http%3A%2F%2Fwww.gwu.edu%2F~history%2Fdocs%2FSchwartz_hist101.doc&ei=Rp9lUbr0HceLONiVgZAO&usg=AFQjCNGFY9brBQZbYe8FnZU1aQhtn3P_kQ&sig2=S-AbEKyBGFyHpxzC6l6Rsw
73	University of Wisconsin	The Arab-Israeli Conflict	Political Science 631	10 April	Spring 2010	http://www.google.co.uk/url?sa=t&rct=j&q=&esrc=s&source=web&cd=4&ved=0CEcQFjAD&url=http%3A%2F%2Fdept.polisci.wisc.edu%2Fsyllabi%2F11104%2FPS%2520631%2520The%2520Arab-Israeli%2520Conflict.doc&ei=Rp9lUbr0HceLONiVgZAO&usg=AFQjCNFf7Ld86a6oDqWVHgMULOaqnkvHA&sig2=Gh0ShzkGwmlhf7-w7oet0g

(Continued)

No.	College	Course title	Course code	Access date (all 2013)	Taught date	Link
74	University of Wisconsin	The Arab-Israeli Conflict	Political Science 631	10 April	Spring 2012	http://jewishstudies.wisc.edu/jewishstudies/wp-content/uploads/2011/08/Political-Science-631-The-Arab-Israeli-Conflict.pdf
75	Brandeis University	Arab-Israeli Conflict	NA	10 April	Summer 2011	http://www.brandeis.edu/summer/courses/coursesyllabi/2011/nejs189a.pdf
76	Oral Roberts University	The Rise of Modern Israel	HIS 473	10 April	Spring 2010	http://www.google.co.uk/url?sa=t&rct=j&q=&esrc=s&source=web&cd=7&ved=0CFwQFjAG&url=http%3A%2F%2Fsyllabi.oru.edu%2F%3Fid%3D32769&ei=Rp9lUbr0HceLONiVgZAO&usg=AFQjCNEJdBE0wGHTBb1PvwZOkMgBnf6hKg&sig2=SBla7iFl40ItNQOsyvm2kA
77	Oral Roberts University	The Rise of Modern Israel	HIS 473	10 April	Spring 2002	http://www.google.co.uk/url?sa=t&rct=j&q=&esrc=s&source=web&cd=8&ved=0CGMQFjAH&url=http%3A%2F%2Fsyllabi.oru.edu%2F%3Fid%3D62868&ei=Rp9lUbr0HceLONiVgZAO&usg=AFQjCNG_UWWBviirnifTlnvN3mw2CFrTZg&sig2=uiOyyOb5qKpExSJxFXAuMQ
78	University of California, Los Angeles	The Arab-Israeli Conflict	POL 129	10 April	Fall 2006	http://www.sscnet.ucla.edu/polisci/faculty/trachtenberg/syllabi.lists/120b/arab-israeli/maoz1.pdf
79	University of Memphis	Political History of Israel	JDST 4820; POLS 4820	10 April	Fall 2010	https://www.memphis.edu/jdst/pdf/JDST_4820-001_Abosch.pdf
80	University of Alabama	Special Topics in Political Science: The Israel-Palestine Conflict	Psc 321-003	10 April	Fall 2012	http://daniel.j.levine.people.ua.edu/uploads/1/3/4/9/13498793/ip_conflict_-_poli_sci_revise_version_-_fall_2012.pdf
81	State University of New Jersey	Advanced Topics in Middle Eastern Politics: Arab Israeli Conflict	790 and 685:452	10 April	Spring 2010	http://polisci.rutgers.edu/dmdocuments/PS452%20Abdel-Jaber%20syllabus%20S%2010a.pdf

No.	College	Course title	Course code	Access date (all 2013)	Taught date	Link
82	University of Wisconsin-Whitewater	Arab-Israeli Conflict, 1900–Present	HIST 338	10 April	Fall 2007	http://www.google.co.uk/url?sa=t&rct=j&q=&esrc=s&source=web&cd=13&ved=0CD4QFjACOAo&url=http%3A%2F%2Facadaff.uww.edu%2FUCC%2F2006-07%2F012607%2FHISTRY338.doc&ei=latlUaPzO9Cr0AWJ14DoAQ&usg=AFQjCNFbaAXEgAHuadyNtPYeZcvx2ElJiA&sig2=viAV0pWHdNCfphavj5FTEg
83	New York University	Modern Israel	MAP V55.0537	10 April	Spring 2006	http://map.cas.nyu.edu/docs/CP/2252/zweigspring2006.pdf
84	George Washington University	History of Modern Israel	History 3820	10 April	Fall 2010	http://www.google.co.uk/url?sa=t&rct=j&q=&esrc=s&source=web&cd=17&ved=0CFwQFjAGOAo&url=http%3A%2F%2Fdepartments.columbian.gwu.edu%2Fhistory%2Fsites%2Fdefault%2Ffiles%2Fu9%2FHist%25203820%2520syllabus%2520FA%252010%2520.doc&ei=latlUaPzO9Cr0AWJ14DoAQ&usg=AFQjCNGqZGLxnDHOvY9eMFO4TwplwsfKVQ&sig2=gdkBxYpsKdyKBoNe94-H5w
85	Liberty University	History of the Jewish People (From Ca. 2000 B.C.E. to the Present)	BIBL 497-371 / HIEU 497-371	10 April	2011	http://www.liberty.edu/media/1144/pdf/History%20of%20the%20Jewish%20People%20INTENSIVE%20-%20UNDERGRADUATE%20Syllabus.pdf
86	American Jewish University, Los Angeles	Israel: Socio-Political History and Analysis	NA	10 April	NA	http://currentstudents.ajula.edu/assets/0/68/76/104/856/9e9a064b-ad72-4da6-afc7-6f4d913becc7.pdf
87	University of Maryland	Israel: Politics and Society	JWST 419X	10 April	Winter/Spring 2009	http://www.bsos.umd.edu/gvpt/courses/spring2009/399lasensky.pdf
88	University of California, Davis	Arab-Israeli Relations	POL 136 and 198	10 April	2010	http://summer-abroad.ucdavis.edu/programs/syllabus/Arab-Israeli%20Relations-2010.pdf
89	University of Wisconsin, Madison	Israeli Politics and Society	Political Science 665	10 April	Fall 2007	http://dept.polisci.wisc.edu/syllabi/1082/665.pdf

(Continued)

No.	College	Course title	Course code	Access date (all 2013)	Taught date	Link
90	University of California, Los Angeles	History of the Yishuv and Israel, 1917–1948	191L	12 April	Spring 2008	http://www.google.co.uk/url?sa=t&rct=j&q=&esrc=s&source=web&cd=1&ved=0CDEQFjAA&url=http%3A%2F%2Fwww.international.ucla.edu%2Ffiles%2FLavsky-UCLA-yishuv.doc&ei=Lg5oUb2THeKy0QWayoCgDQ&usg=AFQjCNGoUKw0XiGSJac4L8BmTVZFq-5oDg&sig2=UOsqgC9Q0UhHlqwOuDcvew&bvm=bv.45175338,d.d2k
91	University of California, San Diego	Modern Jewish Societies and Israeli Societies	Sociology 188F	12 April	Fall 2006	http://www.academia.edu/1731687/Modern_Jewish_Societies_and_Israeli_Society
92	Oral Roberts University	The Rise of Modern Israel	HIS 473	12 April	Spring 2012	http://www.google.co.uk/url?sa=t&rct=j&q=&esrc=s&source=web&cd=13&ved=0CEIQFjACOAo&url=http%3A%2F%2Fsyllabi.oru.edu%2F%3Fid%3D36179&ei=YhNoUbi7DKO70QWY3IC4AQ&usg=AFQjCNFgqL1ygAJtZJKi50as3Jc4QMga3g&sig2=KzWZRlMxDO4Qh2R3EtYBCw&bvm=bv.45175338,d.d2k
93	American Jewish University: Department of Political Science	Israeli Politics	POL 251	12 April	Fall 2007	http://www.ajula.edu/Media/Images/SCM/ContentUnit/fall07/POL_251.pdf
94	University of Chicago	Seminar on Zionism and Palestine	Political Science 28500	12 April	Spring 2011	http://mearsheimer.uchicago.edu/pdfs/S0013.pdf
95	Northwestern University	Historical Background to Establishment of Israel	847/467-3896	12 April	Fall 2012	http://www.northwestern.edu/class-descriptions/4480/WCAS/HISTORY/300-0/12312.html
96	State University of New Jersey	Advanced Topics in Middle Eastern Politics: Arab Israeli Conflict	790-452 and 685:452	12 April	Spring 2011	http://polisci.rutgers.edu/dmdocuments/PS%20452_01%20Abdeljaber%20sp11.pdf

No.	College	Course title	Course code	Access date (all 2013)	Taught date	Link
97	Wesleyan University	Political Thought and Politics of Israel	GOVT 394	12 April	Spring 2013	https://iasext.wesleyan.edu/regprod/!wesmaps_page.html?crse=013459&term=1131
98	Oral Roberts University	The Rise of Modern Israel	HIS 473	12 April	Spring 2006	http://www.google.co.uk/url?sa=t&rct=j&q=&esrc=s&source=web&cd=65&ved=0CEwQFjAEODw&url=http%3A%2F%2Fsyllabi.oru.edu%2F%3Fid%3D19290&ei=CCNoUcmzDa6o0AXftYCQBg&usg=AFQjCNGLVl5Um5QixCHnnuaTPHXf7IfVDw&sig2=4FNWVhoQu5FrnQqPSW0B0Q
99	Brandeis University	History of the State of Israel	NEJS 145a	12 April	Fall 2008	http://www.google.co.uk/url?sa=t&rct=j&q=&esrc=s&source=web&cd=71&ved=0CDAQFjAAOEY&url=http%3A%2F%2Fwww.brandeis.edu%2Fdepartments%2Fnejs%2Fsyllabi%2Fdocs%2F2008fall%2FNEJS145aFall2008.doc&ei=wyRoUYW_OOiY0AXg8IDgCw&usg=AFQjCNGjl_-V6-cqk_9AoQ5PtBYCFEu8og&sig2=uLF0KfxjzuGgBx2Z08WHgg
100	Brandeis University	History of the State of Israel	NEJS 145a	12 April	Fall 2004	http://www.brandeis.edu/departments/nejs/syllabi/docs/2004/NEJS145aFall2004.pdf
101	Brandeis University	History of the State of Israel	NEJS 145a	12 April	Fall 2006	http://www.brandeis.edu/departments/nejs/syllabi/docs/2006/njes145a-f2006.pdf
102	Brandeis University	History of the State of Israel	NEJS 145a	12 April	Fall 2005	http://www.brandeis.edu/departments/nejs/syllabi/docs/2005/nejs145a-f2005.pdf
103	Brandeis University	Arab–Israeli Conflict	NEJS 189a	12 April	2012	http://www.brandeis.edu/summer/courses/coursesyllabi/2012/nejs189a.pdf
104	Brandeis University	History of the State of Israel	NEJS 145a	12 April	Fall 2007	http://www.brandeis.edu/hornstein/pdfs/syllabi/nejs145a_syllabus.pdf

(Continued)

No.	College	Course title	Course code	Access date (all 2013)	Taught date	Link
105	American Jewish University	Israeli Politics	POL 270	12 April	Spring 2009	http://www.google.co.uk/url?sa=t&rct=j&q=&esrc=s&source=web&cd=88&ved=0CGkQFjAHOFA&url=http%3A%2F%2Fcurrentstudents.ajula.edu%2FWorkArea%2FDownloadAsset.aspx%3Fid%3D2443&ei=pCloUdrO1-nJ0QXt4ICgCQ&usg=AFQjCNEt_3Og0U9DXo8sIPNHJ_YPXb40eg&sig2=Unz8ctczKhGGL31o5zuntQ
106	Emory University	History of Modern Israel	HIST 370-000	12 April	Spring 2010	http://college.emory.edu/home/academic/course/schedules/2010/spring/section/regular/history/HIST370-000.html
107	University of California, Davis	The Arab-Israeli Conflict	POL 136	12 April	Spring 2011	http://psfaculty.ucdavis.edu/zmaoz/A-I%20Conflict/Spring%202011/a-i-syllabus2011.pdf
108	Northwestern University	Historical Background to Establishment of Israel	847/467-3896	12 April	2011	http://www.northwestern.edu/class-descriptions/4360/WCAS/HISTORY/300-0/22980.html
109	University of California, Davis	The Arab-Israeli Conflict	POL 136	12 April	Winter 2012	http://psfaculty.ucdavis.edu/zmaoz/A-I%20Conflict/Winter%202012/a-i-syllabus2012.pdf
110	University of California, San Diego	Government and Politics of the Middle East	Pol. Sci. 121	12 April	Winter 2010	http://courses.ucsd.edu/syllabi/WI10/671728.pdf
111	Amherst College	A History of the Israeli/Palestinian Conflict	FYSE-118	12 April	Fall 2011	https://www.amherst.edu/academiclife/departments/courses/1112F/FYSE/FYSE-118-1112F
112	New York University: Department of Politics	Israeli National Security Strategy, Policy and Decision Making	G53.1732.001	12 April	Spring 2008	http://politics.as.nyu.edu/docs/IO/6106/freilich_1732_sp08_syllabus_final.pdf

No.	College	Course title	Course code	Access date (all 2013)	Taught date	Link
113	University of Wisconsin	The Arab-Israeli Conflict	Political Science 333	12 April	Spring 2009	http://www.google.co.uk/url?sa=t&rct=j&q=&esrc=s&source=web&cd=143&ved=0CEEQFjACOIwB&url=http%3A%2F%2Fdept.polisci.wisc.edu%2Fsyllabi%2F1094%2FPS%2520333%2520The%2520Arab-Israeli%2520Conflict.doc&ei=eD5oUe6vGqSZ0QX_mYGoCg&usg=AFQjCNG5Mo_zi9LzmPA9tovJgZ6r6JocA&sig2=AbikU1VkFmIVStQwwjnXUA
114	New York University	Cultures and Contexts: Modern Israel	MAP V55.0537	12 April	Fall 2010	http://cas.nyu.edu/docs/CP/3878/0537zweig103.pdf
115	University of California, Davis	The Arab-Israeli Conflict	POL 136	12 April	Winter 2010	http://www.google.co.uk/url?sa=t&rct=j&q=&esrc=s&source=web&cd=164&ved=0CEYQFjADOKAB&url=http%3A%2F%2Fmesa.ucdavis.edu%2Ffiles%2Fdocuments%2Flink-documents%2Fa-i-syllabus-w-2010.pdf%2Fat_download%2Ffile&ei=XEFoUe_KKseO0AWW-oCwBQ&usg=AFQjCNGO_WWkmlyYtMakyo7_fe110eud9A&sig2=9y7ED_wQeFmM6_YFUqoZ6A
116	New York University	Cultures and Contexts: Modern Israel	MAP_UA 513	12 April	Spring 2013	http://map.cas.nyu.edu/docs/IO/24191/537ZweigS13.pdf
117	University of Wisconsin–Madison	Israeli Politics and Society	Political Science 665	12 April	Spring 2007	http://dept.polisci.wisc.edu/syllabi/1074/665.pdf
118	George Mason University	Israel and Palestine: Conflict Resolution: Peace Building and Development	NA	12 April	January 2009	http://globaled.gmu.edu/docs/Israe-Palest-syll-09.pdf
119	California State University, Northridge (CSUN)	Israel's History and Peoples	Hist/JS 496ih	12 April	Spring 2012	http://www.csun.edu/faculty/jody.myers/documents/HistJS496ihsyllabus2.17.12.pdf

(Continued)

No.	College	Course title	Course code	Access date (all 2013)	Taught date	Link
120	University of California, San Diego	Modern Jewish Societies and Israeli Society	Sociology 188F	12 April	Spring 2009	http://sociology.ucsd.edu/undergraduates/documents/SOCD188FSP09SHAFIR.pdf
121	New York University	Cultures and Contexts: Modern Israel	MAP UA 513	12 April	Spring 2012	http://map.cas.nyu.edu/docs/IO/20434/537zweig121b.pdf
122	New York University	MAP World Cultures: Modern Israel	MAP V55.0537	12 April	Spring 2008	http://map.cas.nyu.edu/docs/CP/2250/zweigspring2008.pdf
123	Oakland University	The Modern Middle East	History 356	12 April	Fall 2005	http://www2.oakland.edu/sehs/mde2/syllabi/socialstudies/sylHST356.pdf
124	Liberty Christian University	History of the Jewish People	OBST 597-371	12 April	2011	http://www.liberty.edu/media/1144/pdf/History%20of%20the%20Jewish%20People%20INTENSIVE%20-%20GRADUATE%20syllabus.pdf
125	College of Charleston	Modern Jewish History	History 359	12 April	Fall 2004	http://knees.people.cofc.edu/pdfs/knee_359_f04.pdf?referrer=webcluster&
126	American Jewish University	Modern Jewish History	HIS 460.01	12 April	NA	http://currentstudents.ajula.edu/assets/0/68/76/104/918/84249f63-3360-40a0-b532-1d34efe20cd4.pdf
127	California State University, Northridge	Israel's History and Peoples	Hist/JS 496ih	12 April	Fall 2009	http://www.google.co.uk/url?sa=t&rct=j&q=&esrc=s&source=web&cd=12&ved=0CDcQFjABOAo&url=http%3A%2F%2Fwww.csun.edu%2Ffaculty%2Fjody.myers%2Fdocuments%2FHist-JS496ihsyllabus8.25.09.doc&ei=7mFoUaq2NuSW0AXPv4HQBw&usg=AFQjCNFsyf6dzbFh1oOE8YPQ_WZrBr1U8w&sig2=trNA3yTQnttadBDfUvhFeQ
128	New York University	The Arab-Israeli Conflict: Can It Ever Be Solved?	GA.1733.001	14 April	Spring 2013	http://politics.as.nyu.edu/docs/IO/27054/Arab_Israeli_conflict_NYU_spring_2013.pdf

No.	College	Course title	Course code	Access date (all 2013)	Taught date	Link
129	University of Colorado	Israel, Its Neighbors and the Great Powers: War and Peace in the Middle East in A Comparative Perspective	NA	14 April	Fall 2007	http://www.colorado.edu/IAFS/Files/077_IAFS3000-002_syl.pdf
130	Boston University	The War for the Greater Middle East	KHC HI 101	14 April	Fall 2011	http://www.bu.edu/cas/files/2011/12/KHC-HI101-F11-The-War-for-the-Greater-Middle-East.pdf
131	University of North Carolina at Asheville	150 Years Ongoing Conflict: Israel-Palestine	NA	14 April	Spring 2013	http://nccr.unca.edu/sites/nccr.unca.edu/files/Instructor_Handouts/Amara/Amara_Ahmad-150_Years_of_Conflict-Course_Content_and_Schedule.pdf
132	University of California, Berkeley	Israel and the Palestinian Economy in the West Bank and Gaza: Perceptions and Realities, 1967–2007	Middle Eastern Studies 130	14 April	Spring 2008	http://emlab.berkeley.edu/users/webfac/arnon/e190_s08/syllabus.pdf
133	Harvard University: Kennedy School of Government	Sixty Odd Years of Middle Eastern Diplomacy	IGA330M	14 April	Fall 2008	http://ksgnotes1.harvard.edu/degreeprog/Syllabus.nsf/0/DF15627DEF13F43B852574BF005FD549/$FILE/syllabus.pdf
134	University of Colorado	History of the Arab-Israeli Conflict	IAFS/JWST 3650	14 April	Spring 2013	http://www.colorado.edu/history/chester/IAFS3650Syllabus.pdf
135	University of Rochester	The Arab-Israeli Conflict	PSC 276, REL 284, JST 276	14 April	Spring 2006	http://www.rochester.edu/College/PSC/syllabi/gluckman/PSC276.pdf
136	Harvard University: Kennedy School of Government	Sixty Years of Middle Eastern Diplomacy	ISP 335M	14 April	Fall 2007	http://ksgnotes1.harvard.edu/degreeprog/Syllabus.nsf/0/6908f520ba857112852573 4e00579e15/$FILE/ISP%20335M%20Syllabus%20Fall%202007.pdf

(*Continued*)

No.	College	Course title	Course code	Access date (all 2013)	Taught date	Link
137	American University, Washington DC	Israel: A Mosaic of Cultures, Identities and Landscapes	SIS-303-N03 N04 & SIS-603-N03/N04	14 April	NA	http://www.american.edu/sis/faculty/upload/2011SU-SIS-603-N03-4.pdf
138	University of Utah	The History of the Middle East from 1945 to the Present	HIST 3420/5420, MID E 3542/5542	14 April	Spring 2008	http://www.humis.utah.edu/humis/syllabi/Syllabus1199724460.pdf
139	University of Alabama	Religions, Politics and Cultures of the Middle East	REL 372.001	14 April	Fall 2008	http://www.as.ua.edu/rel/pdf/REL372jacobsSyllabusFall2008.pdf
140	Boston University	The War for the Greater Middle East	NA	14 April	Fall 2010	http://www.bu.edu/khc/files/2010/09/UHC-H1-101-Fall-2010.pdf
141	University of Colorado	Borderlands of Empire	History 4339	14 April	NA	http://www.colorado.edu/history/chester/HIST4339Syll.pdf
142	University of Texas At Arlington	International Relations of the Middle East	4370-001	14 April	Spring 2010	https://www.uta.edu/ra/real/syllabi/13092_1934_4370_syllabus.pdf
143	University of Utah	The Middle East Since 1914: Imperialism, Nationalism, Revolution and War	History 3400/6920: MID E 3540/5540	14 April	Fall 2011	https://www.humis.utah.edu/humis/docs/organization_298_1309900467.pdf
144	University of Texas At Arlington	International Relations of the Middle East	4370-001	14 April	Spring 2012	https://www.uta.edu/ra/real/syllabi/17172_1934_4370_syllabus.pdf
145	University of Washington	The Arab-Israeli Conflict	Political Science 325A	14 April	Summer 2009	http://www.polisci.washington.edu/Undergraduate/Undergrad_Courses/UndergradSummerQtr2009.pdf
146	Wesleyan University	Cold War International Relations	GOVT120	14 April	Autumn 2011	https://wesfiles.wesleyan.edu/courses/syllabi/1119-mjwilliams-013317-361.pdf

No.	College	Course title	Course code	Access date (all 2013)	Taught date	Link
147	New York University	Revolution and Continuity: Comparative National Security Strategies of the Countries of the Middle East	NA	14 April	Spring 2012	http://politics.as.nyu.edu/docs/IO/22034/ME_NS2012.pdf
148	University of Missouri – Kansas City	Politics of the Middle East	NA	14 April	NA	http://www.google.co.uk/url?sa=t&rct=j&q=&esrc=s&source=web&cd=4&ved=0CEoQFjAD&url=http%3A%2F%2Fh.web.umkc.edu%2Fhafezm%2Fcourses%2Fpmeg.doc&ei=dRhrUY_HEcTeOuXpgYgF&usg=AFQjCNHd1fiDjEM5lf7b9jEcUt]3cCQSEw&sig2=hF4xPth5GxR3xvUskq_i_g
149	University of Wisconsin-Whitewater	Special Topics in Peace and Social Justice	PAX 488	14 April	Fall 2011	http://www.google.co.uk/url?sa=t&rct=j&q=&esrc=s&source=web&cd=58&ved=0CFEQFjAE&url=http%3A%2F%2Fwww.uww.edu%2Facadaff%2Fucc%2F2010-11%2F090310%2FPAX488.doc&ei=dRhrUY_HEcTeOuXpgYgF&usg=AFQjCNEy5KliTi-pWwkK4-Um06nY2eQG4Q&sig2=j8_1JdrbmeuxwMEm_RIX7g
150	Western Illinois University	The Modern Middle East and the Arab-Israeli Conflict	H344	14 April	2013 Spring	http://www.google.co.uk/url?sa=t&rct=j&q=&esrc=s&source=web&cd=7&ved=0CGAQFjAG&url=http%3A%2F%2Fwww.wiu.edu%2Fcas%2Fhistory%2F344%2520pring%25202013.doc&ei=dRhrUY_HEcTeOuXpgYgF&usg=AFQjCNGIU2yuER1zA_b1KG8Zcd6EVugp9Q&sig2=gOasnwnnGoMROJcyqaqgqg
151	University of Utah	The Middle East Since 1914: Imperialism, Nationalism, Revolution and War	History 3400/6920: MID E 3540/5540	14 April	Fall 2009	https://www.google.co.uk/url?sa=t&rct=j&q=&esrc=s&source=web&cd=1&ved=0CDUQFjAA&url=https%3A%2F%2Fevals.ugs.utah.edu%2FuploadedFiles%2FMID%2520E%25203540%2520(since%25201914)%2520Fall%25202009.doc&ei=YvN3UfPrIYWe0QWu1oC4Dg&usg=AFQjCNFHcSBGdh6ahVHJMI3dcO2N1rTXeg&sig2=_gg_DAj4qd78tFjQamS6YQ&bvm=bv.45580626,d.d2k&cad=rja

(*Continued*)

No.	College	Course title	Course code	Access date (all 2013)	Taught date	Link
152	Harvard Extension School	Comparative National Security of Middle Eastern Countries	GOVT E-1961	14 April	Spring 2011	http://www.google.co.uk/url?sa=t&rct=j&q=&esrc=s&source=web&cd=19&ved=0CGoQFjAIOAo&url=http%3A%2F%2Fisites.harvard.edu%2Ffs%2Fdocs%2Ficb.topic864784.files%2Fext%2520school%2520-%2520ME%2520NS%2520spring%25202011.doc&ei=ZB1rUY2uI4mCOOKQgJAO&usg=AFQjCNGdIjYeHFuzh_PqAPut-HEBQgh2pQ&sig2=5Zqndpoy2ROyPmTV3QM3Ow
153	University of Pennsylvania	The Arab-Israeli Conflict Through Literature and Film	History 166	15 April	NA	http://www.history.upenn.edu/courses/syllabi/hist166/powell.pdf
154	University of Colorado At Boulder	The Arab-Israeli Conflict	IAFS 3000-001	15 April	Spring 2010	http://iafs.colorado.edu/sites/default/files/files/Syllabi/101_3000_Levey-syllabus.pdf
155	University of Michigan	The Arab-Israeli Conflict	NA	15 April	NA	http://sitemaker.umich.edu/kirschner/files/kirschner_arab_israeli_syllabus.pdf
156	University of Colorado at Boulder	The Arab-Israeli Conflict	IAFS 3000-001	15 April	Spring 2011	http://iafs.colorado.edu/sites/default/files/files/Syllabi/2111_3000_Levey-syllabus.pdf
157	University of California, San Diego	The Israeli-Palestinian Conflict	INTL190	15 April	Spring 2012	http://isp.ucsd.edu/_files/Syllabi/190_SP12_Shafir_Syllabus.pdf
158	University of Hawaii at Manoa	Topics in Comparative Politics – ME's Contemporary Issues	POLS 307F	15 April	Summer 2013	http://www.politicalscience.hawaii.edu/courses/syllabi/sum13/pols307f_plassecouture_sum13.pdf
159	Wayne State University	The Arab⊠Israeli Conflict	CRN 28447	15 April	2012–13 Semester1	http://studyabroad.wayne.edu/salford_modules/modulebooklet_politics.pdf
160	University of Pennsylvania	Arab-Israeli Relations	Political Science 398	15 April	Fall 2004	http://www.sscnet.ucla.edu/polisci/faculty/trachtenberg/syllabi.lists/120b/arab-israeli/lustick.pdf

No.	College	Course title	Course code	Access date (all 2013)	Taught date	Link
161	University of Maryland	Comparative Study of Foreign Policy	GVPT 450	15 April	Summer 2006	http://www.bsos.umd.edu/gvpt/courses/Summer2006/GVPT450_SU06.pdf
162	Brigham Young University	The Arab-Israeli Conflict	PL SC 474	15 April	Winter 2013	https://politicalscience.byu.edu/Syllabi/W13/Gubler_474_W13.pdf
163	Rhodes College	An Introduction to Selected Nationalisms and Islamist Ideologies of the Middle East	INTS 244-1 CRN 10315	15 April	Fall 2009	http://dlynx.rhodes.edu/jspui/bitstream/10267/4983/1/INTS%20244-01.pdf
164	Wayne State University	Arab-Israeli Conflict	CRN 28447	15 April	2009–10 Semester2	http://studyabroad.wayne.edu/mis-documents/10_salford_level_2_module_booklet.pdf
165	American University, Washington DC	U.S. Foreign Policy toward the Middle East	SIS-496.003; SIS-653.012	15 April	NA	http://www.american.edu/sis/usfp/upload/653-012-USFP-Towards-the-ME-Ziv.pdf
166	Brigham Young University	Arab-Israeli-Palestinian Conflict	Political Science 474-001	15 April	Fall 2003	https://politicalscience.byu.edu/Syllabi/F03/Bowen_474_F03.pdf
167	Brigham Young University	NA	Political Science 474	15 April	Fall 2010	https://politicalscience.byu.edu/Syllabi/F10/Gubler_474_F10.pdf
168	Skidmore College	The Middle East	GO 239	15 April	Fall 2010	http://cms.skidmore.edu/government/syllabus/upload/GO239sylFall2010.pdf
169	Brigham Young University	Political Systems of the Middle East	Political Science 357-001	15 April	Winter 2012	https://politicalscience.byu.edu/Syllabi/W12/Bowen_357_W12.pdf
170	Brigham Young University	Political Systems of the Middle East	Political Science 357-001	15 April	Fall 2012	https://politicalscience.byu.edu/Syllabi/F12/Bowen_357_F12.pdf
171	New York University	The Arab-Israeli Conflict: Can It Ever Be Solved?	NA	15 April	Spring 2012	http://politics.as.nyu.edu/docs/IO/22034/Arab_Israeli_conflict2012.pdf

(Continued)

No.	College	Course title	Course code	Access date (all 2013)	Taught date	Link
172	University of California, Davis	Diplomacy and Negotiation	Political Science 190	15 April	Winter 2005	http://psfaculty.ucdavis.edu/zmaoz/diplomacy2005syl.pdf
173	Portland State University	Introduction to Middle East Politics	PS 361U	15 April	Fall 2012	http://www.pdx.edu/hatfieldschool/sites/www.pdx.edu.hatfieldschool/files/PS%20361U.pdf
174	University of Florida	Arab–Israeli Conflict: Analysis	CPO 4401 (7384); JST 4905 (7440)	15 April	Fall 2007	http://www.clas.ufl.edu/users/pjwoods/aicfall2007.pdf
175	New York University	International Politics of the Middle East	V53.0760	15 April	Fall 2010	http://politics.as.nyu.edu/docs/IO/15214/IPMEFall2010FirstVersion.pdf
176	American University: School of International Service	Peace Building in Divided Societies: The Case of Israel and Palestine	SIS 516.001; HURST 208	15 April	Fall 2009	http://www.american.edu/sis/ipcr/upload/sis-516_abunimer_pb-in-divided-societies-f09.pdf
177	Portland State University	Politics and Policy of the Middle East	PS 507; PAP 607	15 April	Fall 2012	http://www.pdx.edu/hatfieldschool/sites/www.pdx.edu.hatfieldschool/files/PS%20507-003.pdf
178	University of Georgia	Comparative Politics of the Middle East	INTL 8315	15 April	Fall 2008	http://intl.uga.edu/lowrance8315fa08.pdf
179	New York University	International Politics of the Middle East	V53.0760	15 April	Summer 2007	http://politics.as.nyu.edu/docs/IO/5397/v53.0760_erbal_sum07.pdf
180	Massachusetts Institute of Technology (MIT)	The Causes and Prevention of War	/17/sp11/17.42/	15 April	Spring 2011	http://web.mit.edu/ssp/people/vanevera/1742syllabus-2011.pdf
181	Rutgers University	Contemporary Politics of the Middle East	790/685:351	15 April	Summer 2012	http://polisci.rutgers.edu/dmdocuments/PS351-B6%20Sum%202012%20Weirich%20Syllabus.pdf
182	University of Nevada, Las Vegas	Middle East and North Africa	Political Science 760.1	15 April	Fall 2008	http://liberalarts.unlv.edu/Political_Science/Syllabi/Fall%202008/760-001Tamadonfar.pdf

No.	College	Course title	Course code	Access date (all 2013)	Taught date	Link
183	George Washington University	The Arab-Israeli Conflict	PSc2476	15 April	Spring 2013	http://www.google.co.uk/url?sa=t&rct=j&q=&esrc=s&source=web&cd=3&ved=0CEIQFjAC&url=http%3A%2F%2Fdepartments.columbian.gwu.edu%2Fpoliticalscience%2Fsites%2Fdefault%2Ffiles%2Fu43%2FPSC%25202476_Stern_Spring%2520213.doc&ei=JTZsUYOIGuLG0QWG91GwDQ&usg=AFQjCNE9ZXv66Sffyz4VpDtkstO-O20PoQ&sig2=LMN9ZNSp3STcK-I8lUNuoA&bvm=bv.45175338,d.d2k
184	Emory University	Politics of the Middle East	Pols 338	15 April	Fall 2004	http://www.google.co.uk/url?sa=t&rct=j&q=&esrc=s&source=web&cd=19&ved=0CHsQFjAIOAo&url=http%3A%2F%2Fhumanrights.emory.edu%2Fdownload%2FPOLS%2520338%2520-%2520Politics%2520of%2520the%2520Middle%2520East.doc&ei=fzhsUZT11ob80QW-uICgDQ&usg=AFQjCNEKZYCm6h86r7tSfS_UZiToiM7hkA&sig2=p-fNMn2hsmDDTMz4ewgS5A&bvm=bv.45175338,d.d2k
185	University of Michigan	International Security Affairs	SPP 673	15 April	Winter 2012	http://www.google.co.uk/url?sa=t&rct=j&q=&esrc=s&source=web&cd=28&ved=0CGYQFjAHOBQ&url=http%3A%2F%2Fwww-personal.umich.edu%2F~axe%2FSyllabus%2BSPP%2B673%2BW%2B12.doc&ei=1ztsUfrIGo3Y0QWvjIHoDQ&usg=AFQjCNFHQImgEZYE03k3pygvlzM3UQq4zw&sig2=EAX6OZNQFTodlhRBOudEPw&bvm=bv.45175338,d.d2k
186	University of Texas At Austin	Arab-Israeli Politics	Government 320L/MES 323K	15 April	Fall 2008	http://cherry.webhost.utexas.edu/aip/syl.html
187	University of California, San Diego	Representations of the Israel/Palestinian Conflict	COSF 188	15 April	Spring 2010	http://communication.ucsd.edu/courses/cosf-188/cosf-188-s-10.html

(*Continued*)

No.	College	Course title	Course code	Access date (all 2013)	Taught date	Link
188	University of Delaware	History of the Arab-Israeli Conflict	SHL 116	15 April	Spring 2009	http://www.udel.edu/History/matthee/ARIS380-09.html
189	University of Michigan	The Arab-Israeli Conflict	POLSCI 353	15 April	Winter 2002	http://www.lsa.umich.edu/saa/publications/courseguide/winter/archive/w02final/450.html
190	University of Michigan	The Arab-Israeli Conflict	POLSCI 353	15 April	Winter 2001	http://www.lsa.umich.edu/saa/publications/courseguide/winter/archive/winter01cg/450.html
191	College of Charleston	Politics of the Middle East	POLS 324-001	15 April	Fall 2006	http://sacsarchive.oiep.cofc.edu/documents/syllabi-fall/s067_POLS324001_Creed_J.pdf
192	American University	Peace Building in Divided Societies: The Case of Israel and Palestine	SIS 516.001	16 April	Fall 2011	http://www.american.edu/sis/ipcr/upload/SIS_516_001_PeacebuildingInDividedSocieties_AbuNimer_F11.pdf
193	University of California, San Diego	Introduction to Contemporary Israeli Society and Culture	NA	16 April	Summer 2012	http://icenter.ucsd.edu/_files/pao/global-seminars/jerusalem/Course1.pdf
194	Johns Hopkins University	The History and Dynamics of the Arab-Israeli Conflict	NA	16 April	Fall 2009	http://krieger.jhu.edu/internationalstudies/PDF/191.335_Fall_2009.pdf
195	Emory University	History of Israeli Politics: Institutions and Society	NA	16 April	Fall 2007	http://ismi.emory.edu/home/assets/syllabi/H385004HistIsrlPol.pdf
196	Oberlin College	Zionism and the Arab-Israeli Conflict	Hist-290	16 April	NA	http://new.oberlin.edu/dotAsset/3867227.pdf
197	Texas A&M University	U.S. History from 1865 to Present	History 1302.01E	16 April	Fall 2010	http://www.tamuc.edu/academics/cvSyllabi/syllabi/201080/82858.pdf
198	Texas A&M University	U.S. History from 1865 to Present	History 1302.01W	16 April	Fall 2010	http://www.tamuc.edu/academics/cvSyllabi/syllabi/201080/82859.pdf
199	University at Albany	Political Violence	TPOS 260	16 April	Fall 2012	http://www.albany.edu/rockefeller/syllabi/fall2012/Fall%202012/TPOS%20260%20Asal%20fall%202012.pdf

No.	College	Course title	Course code	Access date (all 2013)	Taught date	Link
200	American Public University System	Arab-Israeli Conflict: Contemporary Politics & Diplomacy	MILH 669	16 April	NA	http://www.amu.apus.edu/sebin/w/w/MILH669-Arab-Israeli%20Conflict%20Contemporary%20Politics%20and%20Diplomacy.pdf
201	American Public University System	Arab-Israeli Conflict: Contemporary Politics & Diplomacy	IRLS463	16 April	NA	http://www.apu.apus.edu/sebin/g/y/IRLS463%20Arab-Israeli%20Conflict%20Contemp%20Politics%20and%20Dip.pdf
202	Mount Holyoke College	The Arab-Israeli Conflict	IR 318	16 April	Fall 2003	http://www.jewishvirtuallibrary.org/jsource/isdf/syl/Lasensky.pdf
203	University of California, Davis	The Arab-Israeli Conflict	NA	16 April	Winter 2008	http://www.jewishvirtuallibrary.org/jsource/isdf/syl/arabisraeliconflict_benporat.pdf
204	Brown University	The Arab-Israeli Conflict	JS110; PS 182; Sec 27	16 April	Spring 2006	http://www.jewishvirtuallibrary.org/jsource/isdf/syl/SteinKennethArabIsraeliConflictSeminar.pdf
205	Tulane University	The Arab-Israeli Conflict	JWST 322-01; HISM 322-01	16 April	Spring 2009	http://www.jewishvirtuallibrary.org/jsource/isdf/syl/conflict_Naor.pdf
206	Indiana University	The Arab-Israeli Conflict	JSTU-J 204	16 April	NA	http://www.jewishvirtuallibrary.org/jsource/isdf/syl/arabisraeliconflict_Tsimhoni.pdf
207	University of Colorado at Boulder	The Arab-Israeli Conflict	PSCI 2028-705	16 April	NA	http://www.jewishvirtuallibrary.org/jsource/isdf/syl/arabisraeliconflict_levey.pdf
208	Rutgers University	The Arab-Israeli Conflict	Middle Eastern Studies 685:352; Jewish Studies: 563:383; Political Science 790:352	16 April	Fall 2009	http://www.jewishvirtuallibrary.org/jsource/isdf/syl/conflict_Peleg.pdf
209	San Diego State University	Arab-Israeli Relations, Past and Present	HIST 574	16 April	Spring 2011	http://www.jewishvirtuallibrary.org/jsource/isdf/syl/Relations_Meyers.pdf

(Continued)

No.	College	Course title	Course code	Access date (all 2013)	Taught date	Link
210	University of Colorado at Boulder	History of Israel	HIST-343	16 April	Spring 2007	http://www.jewishvirtuallibrary.org/jsource/isdf/syl/NaomiGalehistoryofIsraelsyllabi.pdf
211	American University, Washington, DC	History of Israel	His 343-001	16 April	Spring 2009	http://www.jewishvirtuallibrary.org/jsource/isdf/syl/history_Peri.pdf
212	University of Illinois	A History of Israel	HIST 396	16 April	Fall 2011	http://www.jewishvirtuallibrary.org/jsource/isdf/syl/historyofisrael_seidelman.pdf
213	University of Texas at Austin	History of Israel: Politics, Society, Foreign Relations	40350; 38940; 42260	16 April	Spring 2010	http://www.jewishvirtuallibrary.org/jsource/isdf/syl/historyisrael_Nevo.pdf
214	University of California, Davis	History of Modern Israel	His 113	16 April	Spring 2009	http://www.jewishvirtuallibrary.org/jsource/isdf/syl/historymodernisrael_benporat.pdf
215	Emory University	History, Politics, and Diplomacy of the Arab-Israeli Conflict	History 169; Political Science 169; Jewish Studies 169	16 April	Fall 2000	http://www.jewishvirtuallibrary.org/jsource/isdf/syl/Steinhispol.pdf
216	University of Virginia	Intro to Israel Studies	RELG 3559	16 April	Spring 2012	http://www.jewishvirtuallibrary.org/jsource/isdf/syl/introtoisraelstudies_shelleg.pdf
217	University of California, Los Angeles	Major Debates in Israeli Historiography	History 191L-2	16 April	Fall 2009	http://www.jewishvirtuallibrary.org/jsource/isdf/syl/majordebates_likhovski.pdf
218	University of Arizona	Modern Israel	JUS377	16 April	Fall 2009	http://www.jewishvirtuallibrary.org/jsource/isdf/syl/modernisrael_talshir.pdf
219	University of Arizona	Modern Israel	JUS/NES/HIST/POL 377	16 April	Spring 2008	http://www.jewishvirtuallibrary.org/jsource/isdf/syl/modernisrael_Aronson.pdf
220	University of Texas at Austin	The Origins of the Arab-Jewish Conflict in Palestine	NA	17 April	Spring 2007	http://www.jewishvirtuallibrary.org/jsource/isdf/syl/OriginsoftheArab-JewishConflict_YoavGelber.pdf

No.	College	Course title	Course code	Access date (all 2013)	Taught date	Link
221	United States Naval Academy	The Roots of the Arab-Israeli Conflict	NA	17 April	Spring 2013	http://www.jewishvirtuallibrary.org/jsource/isdf/ZisenwineConflict.pdf
222	Brandeis University	Sociology of the Israeli-Palestinian Confrontation	Sociology 157a	17 April	Spring 2005	http://www.jewishvirtuallibrary.org/jsource/isdf/syl/llmanGordonSociologyoftheIsraeliPalestinianConfrontation.pdf
223	Brown University	Zionism, Anti-Zionism and Post-Zionism: Israel – Past, Present, Future	JUDS 0980O	17 April	Fall 2008	http://www.jewishvirtuallibrary.org/jsource/isdf/syl/zionism_Lehman-Wilzig.pdf
224	University of Southern California	Zionism, Israel and the Modern World	JS 214	17 April	NA	http://www.jewishvirtuallibrary.org/jsource/isdf/syl/zionismisrael_mendelsson.pdf
225	University of California, Davis	The Arab-Israeli Conflict	POL 129	17 April	Fall 2006	http://www.sscnet.ucla.edu/polisci/faculty/trachtenberg/syllabi.lists/120b/arab-israeli/maoz1.pdf
226	Massachusetts Institute of Technology	The Middle East in 20th Century	21H.615	17 April	Spring 2003	http://ocw.mit.edu/courses/history/21h-615-the-middle-east-in-20th-century-spring-2003/
227	Massachusetts Institute of Technology	Seminar on Politics and Conflict in the Middle East	17.405 / 17.406	17 April	Fall 2003	http://ocw.mit.edu/courses/political-science/17-405-seminar-on-politics-and-conflict-in-the-middle-east-fall-2003/
228	Massachusetts Institute of Technology	Israel: History, Politics, Culture, and Identity	17.565	17 April	Spring 2011	http://ocw.mit.edu/courses/political-science/17-565-israel-history-politics-culture-and-identity-spring-2011/
229	University of Texas at Arlington	Politics and Foreign Policy of Israel	4371-001	17 April	Spring 2013	https://www.uta.edu/ra/real/syllabi/24981_1934_4371_syllabus.pdf
230	University of Wisconsin, Eau Claire	Arab-Israeli Conflict	Political Science 336/536	17 April	Winter 2006	http://www.google.co.uk/url?sa=t&rct=j&q=&esrc=s&source=web&cd=8&ved=0CGUQFjAH&url=http%3A%2F%2Fpeople.uwec.edu%2Fabootaar%2Fcoursesyllabi%2FSYL1336%2520WINTERIM%25202006.pdf&ei=PtRuUauBLJCc0wXi9ID4CA&usg=AFQjCNFwPOO5Fc4g3EKpdaS5jr9yC2dd0Q&sig2=CFhGBZU7rcbFflSEmfPKmg

(*Continued*)

No.	College	Course title	Course code	Access date (all 2013)	Taught date	Link
231	Ohio State University	Politics of the Middle East	Political Science 546	17 April	Winter 2001	http://polisci.osu.edu/sites/polisci.osu.edu/files/PS%20 546.%202001_0.pdf
232	California State University, Northridge	Israel's History and Peoples	JS 427	17 April	Spring 2013	http://www.csun.edu/~cohumcur/JS/NC_JS427_71612.pdf
233	City University of New York (CUNY)	Transformational Moments in the Arab/Israeli Conflict	History 255	17 April	Spring 2012	https://senate.qc.cuny.edu/Curriculum/Syllabi/HIST-255_2012-10-26.pdf
234	Northwestern University	The Israeli-Palestinian Conflict	Political Science 395	17 April	Winter 2012	http://faculty.wcas.northwestern.edu/wendy-pearlman/documents/SyllabusPolisci395Israeli.PalestinianConflictWinter2012.pdf
235	Rutgers University	Israeli Politics	Political Science 790:352	17 April	Fall 2012	http://polisci.rutgers.edu/dmdocuments/PS352%20Peleg%20syllabus%20F%202012.pdf
236	University of Alaska, Fairbanks	Isaac Versus Ishmael: The Israeli-Palestinian Conflict	RELG F193 CRN 35734	17 April	Spring 2011	http://www.uaf.edu/files/uafgov/99-UNC_RELG-F110-IPC-revised-syllabus.pdf
237	Georgetown University	The Arab-Israeli Conflict	LSHV-490-01	17 April	Spring 2010	http://info.scs.georgetown.edu/pf/12/webfiles/LS%20Syllabi/LS%20Spring%202010/LSHV-490_Spring_2010_Syllabus.pdf
238	Penn State University	Society and Cultures in Modern Israel	JST/PL SC/SOC 060.001	17 April	Fall 2009	http://www.la1.psu.edu/online/courses/syllabus/jst060syllabus.pdf
239	University of Colorado, Boulder	Cultures of Israel and Palestine	JWST 4050/ANTH 4050/5050	17 April	Fall 2011	http://www.colorado.edu/anthropology/courses/documents/Fall2011CulturesofIsraelandPalestineSyllabus.pdf
240	Georgetown University	The Arab-Israeli Conflict	LSHV-490-01	17 April	Spring 2011	http://info.scs.georgetown.edu/pf/12/webfiles/LS%20Syllabi/Graduate%20Spring%202011/LSHV-490_Spring_2011_Syllabus.pdf

No.	College	Course title	Course code	Access date (all 2013)	Taught date	Link
241	Tufts University	The Israeli Political System: A Guide to the Perplexed	PS 13808	17 April	Fall 2010	http://ase.tufts.edu/polsci/curriculum/syllabi/Spring2011/ps138-08_Blander.pdf
242	George Washington University	Israeli Politics and Foreign Policy	PSC 2379	17 April	Spring 2013	http://departments.columbian.gwu.edu/politicalscience/sites/default/files/u43/PSC%202379_Rynhold_Spring%202013.pdf
243	Syracuse University	Religion and Politics in the Israeli-Palestinian Conflict	PSC/MES/REL/JSP 300	17 April	Fall 2009	http://faculty.maxwell.syr.edu/melman/pdfs/PSC%20300%20Elman%20Fall%202009%20syllabus.pdf
244	Emory University	History of Modern Israel	HIST190-02P/JS190-02P/MES190-01P	17 April	Spring 2006	http://ismi.emory.edu/home/assets/syllabi/H190ModernIsrael.pdf
245	Michigan State University	Regional Politics, Cooperation, and Conflict in the Middle East	MC324a	17 April	Spring 2011	http://jmc.msu.edu/syllabus/2.pdf
246	University of Southern California	Third World Negotiations	IR 383	18 April	Spring2011	http://dornsife.usc.edu/assets/sites/32/docs/383_Spring_2011.pdf
247	University of Wisconsin–Madison	Israeli Politics and Society	Political Science 665	18 April	Fall 2012	http://jewishstudies.wisc.edu/jewishstudies/wp-content/uploads/2012/09/Israeli-Politics-and-Society.pdf
248	University of California, Santa Barbara	Israeli Politics	POLS 149	18 April	Spring 2012	http://www.polsci.ucsb.edu/faculty/hstoll/classes/polisci149/syllabus.pdf
249	Kansas State University	Seminar: International Politics of Middle East	POLSC 799	18 April	Spring 2009	http://www.k-state.edu/polsci/faculty/sciftci/Syllabus_POLSC%20799_Final.pdf
250	Ohio State University	History of Zionism and Modern Israel	History 334	18 April	NA	http://crmtview.asc.ohio-state.edu/currofc/docs/1613/History%20334%20Syllabus.pdf

(Continued)

No.	College	Course title	Course code	Access date (all 2013)	Taught date	Link
251	New York University	Israeli Politics and Society	V53.0540	18 April	Spring 2005	http://politics.as.nyu.edu/docs/IO/5397/v53.0540_zubida_s06.pdf
252	University of Kentucky	Middle Eastern Politics and Diplomacy	DIP-755	18 April	Fall 2010	http://www.google.co.uk/url?sa=t&rct=j&q=&esrc=s&source=web&cd=2&ved=0CDsQFjAB&url=http%3A%2F%2Fwww.uky.edu%2F~stempel%2FDIP755SyllabusFall2010.doc&ei=eeJvUd-9N6nL0QW004C4Bg&usg=AFQjCNEylizprdMNfyuHS7JdxBLpuTEqhA&sig2=MEHL9ZdT5PS0-mPGTJgVUQ
253	University of Wyoming	Modern Middle East	RELI 3220-40 HIST 3220-40	18 April	Spring 2011	http://www.google.co.uk/url?sa=t&rct=j&q=&esrc=s&source=web&cd=5&ved=0CFAQFjAE&url=http%3A%2F%2Fwww.uwyo.edu%2Fsward%2Fspring2011%2Fmme-reli4500-hist3220.htm-online-uw.doc&ei=eeJvUd-9N6nL0QW004C4Bg&usg=AFQjCNEFZSm8Wrcx87YvwMh-fSmcyFJvjg&sig2=uTP7If5Zk7SCkSl9B80CyQ
254	Brown University	History of Zionism and the Birth of Israel	JUDS 0650	18 April	Fall 2011	http://www.google.co.uk/url?sa=t&rct=j&q=&esrc=s&source=web&cd=10&ved=0CHUQFjAJ&url=http%3A%2F%2Fww.brown.edu%2FCourses%2Fuploads%2FJUDS%253A0650%253A2011-Fall%253AS01.doc&ei=eeJvUd-9N6nL0QW004C4Bg&usg=AFQjCNHUrtAFX7L_5ySSch-MG8ZIyIhhzg&sig2=lHYwMlw4lT5h5SDd_kGWdg
255	Brown University	History of Zionism and the Birth of Israel	JUDS 0650	18 April	Fall 2009	http://www.google.co.uk/url?sa=t&rct=j&q=&esrc=s&source=web&cd=11&ved=0CDMQFjAAOAo&url=http%3A%2F%2Fwww.brown.edu%2FCourses%2Fuploads%2FJUDS%3A0650%3A2009-Fall%3AS01.doc&ei=BuhvUemEA-uX0QWz4oCwCA&usg=AFQjCNFwkz6tjpi_tk7ZDXWnYr143eoBpA&sig2=hWs-erRrfbojfbsSD8XpJQ
256	University of Kentucky	Middle Eastern Politics and Diplomacy	DIP-755; PS 711-003	18 April	Fall 2008	http://www.google.co.uk/url?sa=t&rct=j&q=&esrc=s&source=web&cd=14&ved=0CEsQFjADOAo&url=http%3A%2F%2Fwww.uky.edu%2F~stempel%2FWelcome_files%2FMIDEAST08.doc&ei=BuhvUemEA-uX0QWz4oCwCA&usg=AFQjCNH7lbDrtmnDCuN2JrdkRWuzoVlsMA&sig2=dZYONrNjoQ1LH0g91IyhkQ

No.	College	Course title	Course code	Access date (all 2013)	Taught date	Link
257	Boston University	The Great Powers and the Eastern Mediterranean	CAS IR 325 / HI 229	19 April	Fall 2012	http://www.bu.edu/ir/files/2012/09/Syllabi_Fall2012_IR325_Goldstein.pdf
258	Truman State University	US Relations with the Islamic World	History XXX	19 April	Spring 2007	http://provost.truman.edu/facsenate/archive/2006-2007/April_2006/SB4905.pdf
259	University of Kansas	Sociology of the Middle East	SOC532	19 April	Fall 2010	http://people.ku.edu/~andac/Sociology%20532-fall10.pdf
260	University of Utah	Senior Seminar: The Arabs and Israel; An Endless Conflict	History 4990-003	19 April	Spring 2008	http://www.humis.utah.edu/humis/syllabi/Syllabus119972457.pdf
261	University of Utah	The History of the Middle East 1914–1948	History 3410/5410, MID E 3541/5541	19 April	Fall 2007	http://www.humis.utah.edu/humis/syllabi/Syllabus118736152.pdf
262	University of Utah	The Contemporary Middle East: Crises and Revolutions	History 4450/6450: MID E 4546/6546	19 April	NA	https://www.google.co.uk/url?sa=t&rct=j&q=&esrc=s&source=web&cd=3&ved=0CEQQFjAC&url=https%3A%2F%2Fevals.ugs.utah.edu%2FuploadedFiles%2FHIST%25204450%2520revamped%25202010.doc&ei=gX1xUbD8O8av0QWN94GYAw&usg=AFQjCNFpNFmvBoDEK20vBQuHrnH9yXS5QQ&sig2=Nt9YAwvNiRG3SmCnsVCPCw&cad=rja
263	City University of New York	The Modern Middle East	Political Science / History 3086	20 April	Spring 2010	http://www.google.co.uk/url?sa=t&rct=j&q=&esrc=s&source=web&cd=14&ved=0CFQQFjADOAo&url=http%3A%2F%2Fwww.baruch.cuny.edu%2Fwsas%2Facademics%2Fpolitical_science%2Fdocuments%2FSyllabusSpring2010.doc&ei=3oNyUaaqNpCk0AXAlYHoCw&usg=AFQjCNFr_P2G9aKpNKvea68Ar9BOOBjcsg&sig2=HMVNOzN9AHMz-0OnQ45mHA

(Continued)

No.	College	Course title	Course code	Access date (all 2013)	Taught date	Link
264	State University of New Jersey, Rutgers	Jews in the Islamic World	Jewish Studies 563:308:01 / History 508:391:01 / Middle Eastern Studies 685:395:03	20 April	Fall 2011	http://www.google.co.uk/url?sa=t&rct=j&q=&esrc=s&source=web&cd=19&ved=0CHkQFjAIOAo&url=http%3A%2F%2Fhistory.rutgers.edu%2Fcomponent%2Fdocman%2Fdoc_download%2F429-508391gribetz&ei=3oNyUaaqNpCk0AXAlYHoCw&usg=AFQjCNG9xO49JncjVxpWPCDqIldT1cm-oA&sig2=CavcCDMuVHaFHAmYumUg
265	Roosevelt University	International Relations of the Middle East	POS 358	20 April	Fall 2011	http://www.google.co.uk/url?sa=t&rct=j&q=&esrc=s&source=web&cd=20&ved=0CIABEBYwCTgK&url=http%3A%2F%2Fsites.roosevelt.edu%2F2Fdfaris%2Ffiles%2F2011%2F11%2FFall2011IRMiddleEast.docx&ei=3oNyUaaqNpCk0AXAlYHoCw&usg=AFQjCNFogxuO14qJ4E4If79S5754ZAldjw&sig2=G0l_FgR2HjuR7zBS9WG1QA
266	Rhodes College	Government and Politics of the Middle East	INTS 243-1 CRN 19539	20 April	Fall 2008	http://dlynx.rhodes.edu/jspui/bitstream/10267/15596/1/INTS%20243-1.pdf
267	University of California, Davis	Topics in Judaism: Israel-Palestinian Encounter	Religious Studies 124	20 April	Spring 2010	http://religions.ucdavis.edu/archived-course-schedules/spring-2010?destination=node/76
268	University of California, Davis	Palestinian/Israel Film	Religious Studies 124	20 April	Spring 2009	http://religions.ucdavis.edu/archived-course-schedules/spring-2009
269	St. Lawrence University	Palestine and the Arab-Israeli Conflict	HIS 368A	20 April	Spring 2012	http://www.stlawu.edu/academics/sites/stlawu.edu.academics/files/368_eissenstat.pdf
270	University of California, San Diego	Contemporary Conflicts in the Modern Middle East	HINE 119	20 April	Fall 2008	http://history.ucsd.edu/Syllabi/Fall%202008/HINE119-FA08-Provence.pdf
271	Oberlin College	Palestine-Israel Conflict	Politics 122	20 April	Na	http://new.oberlin.edu/dotAsset/2705356.pdf

No.	College	Course title	Course code	Access date (all 2013)	Taught date	Link
272	Massachusetts Institute of Technology	Seminar on Politics & Conflict in the Middle East	17.405/17.406	20 April	Fall 2011	http://web.mit.edu/polisci/people/faculty/syllabus/Choucri.17.405-406_Fall%202011.Updated%20October%2024.pdf
273	College of Charleston	International Relations of the Middle East	POLS 379-001	20 April	Spring 2012	http://polisci.cofc.edu/pv_obj_cache/pv_obj_id_88AC94F5E739067D5163C4D89C6B089C8ACC0100/filename/379creed-s12-1.pdf
274	University of California, Los Angeles	International Politics in the Middle East	Government 1968	20 April	Fall 2003	http://www.sscnet.ucla.edu/polisci/faculty/trachtenberg/syllabi.lists/120b/arab-israeli/saivetz.pdf
275	College of the Holy Cross	Politics of the Middle East	Political Science 272	20 April	Fall 2007	http://www.google.co.uk/url?sa=t&rct=j&q=&esrc=s&source=web&cd=6&ved=0CFkQFjAF&url=http%3A%2F%2Fcollege.holycross.edu%2Ffaculty%2Fvlangohr%2FME%2520Pol%2520F07%2520syllabus.doc&ei=86dyUevsO62g0wXt4YHoBA&usg=AFQjCNFkDhLJIJixpmynoRTli2gYmvmQOQ&sig2=kq_bSYE87LdRjp9aH_542A
276	University of North Carolina at Chapel Hill	Israeli Society and the Palestinians: Social and Political Perspectives	GPOL 6016	20 April	Spring 2006	http://www.google.co.uk/url?sa=t&rct=j&q=&esrc=s&source=web&cd=7&ved=0CGAQFjAG&url=http%3A%2F%2Fwww.unc.edu%2F~kurzman%2FMideastSociology%2FRam_Syllabus_2006.doc&ei=86dyUevsO62g0wXt4YHoBA&usg=AFQjCNFZi7WzSA3sytoxqVu9EgfcoEKb-Q&sig2=rzkxi0HTj3AqHUECJWiFBw
277	Columbia University	Islam and Politics	POS S 4429-D	20 April	Summer 2000	http://www.columbia.edu/~ljb34/islam_and_pol/summer.html
278	Emory University	The Arab-Israeli Conflict	HIST 383-000	20 April	Fall 2011	http://college.emory.edu/home/academic/course/schedules/2011/fall/section/regular/history/HIST383-000.html
279	Heidelberg University	The CIA Declassified: The 1973 Arab-Israeli War	HNR 103-20	20 April	Spring 2013	http://people.heidelberg.edu/~moreilly/syllabus-403.pdf

(Continued)

No.	College	Course title	Course code	Access date (all 2013)	Taught date	Link
280	Oakland University	The Arab-Israeli Conflict	History 357/557	20 April	Winter 2008	http://www2.oakland.edu/sehs/mde/syllabi/Secon.%20Social%20Studies/HST%20357%20Syllabus%20W08.pdf
281	Rowan University	The Arab-Israeli Conflict	NA	20 April	Spring 2011	http://www.rowan.edu/colleges/chss/departments/history/current/syllabi-sp11/AIsys11.pdf
282	Brandeis University	The Arab-Israeli Conflict	NEJS 189a	20 April	Fall 2005	http://www.brandeis.edu/departments/nejs/syllabi/docs/2005/nejs189a-f2005.pdf
283	Emory University	Israeli Society and Politics	HIST 385	20 April	Spring 2012	http://ismi.emory.edu/home/assets/syllabi/Israeli%20Society%20and%20Politics%20Ayalon.pdf
284	University of Wisconsin-Whitewater	The Arab-Israeli Conflict	History 338	20 April	Spring 2011	http://courses.uww.edu/Files/2111/HISTRY/HISTRY338Patterson01.pdf
285	University of West Georgia	Arab Israeli Conflict	POLS4985/5985	20 April	Summer 2012	http://www.westga.edu/~gdixon/courses_c/pols4985/pols4985_aris_pack_su2012.pdf
286	DePaul University	Global Connections of the Arab-Israeli Conflict	INT 150	20 April	Fall 2012	http://las.depaul.edu/int/docs/CourseSyllabi/INT150Fall2012Kamin.pdf
287	Haverford College	Modern Mediterranean History	H117B	20 April	Spring 2009	http://www.haverford.edu/history/kitroeff/courses/Modern%20Med%20Syllabus%20Spring%202009.pdf
288	American University	U.S. Foreign Policy in the Middle East	SIS-419-048	20 April	Spring 2013	http://www.american.edu/sis/usfp/upload/USFP-Middle-East-Spring-2013.pdf
289	New York University	World Cultures: Nations and Nationalism: Islam, Jews, and the West	NA	20 April	Spring 2006	http://www.google.co.uk/url?sa=t&rct=j&q=&esrc=s&source=web&cd=3&ved=0CEQQFjAC&url=http%3A%2F%2Fhistory.fas.nyu.edu%2Fdocs%2FIO%2F5943%2FMapBerenson.doc&ei=mNRyUdiDG8PG0QXep4HACA&usg=AFQjCNGQd2LaNPC9mnKqDUAHRthK7UcjNQ&sig2=FcKuGNHKQZzbNCSGm8Pogw

No.	College	Course title	Course code	Access date (all 2013)	Taught date	Link
290	Brown University	The Israeli-Palestinian Conflict: Contested Narratives	University Course 0980	20 April	Spring 2011	http://www.google.co.uk/url?sa=t&rct=j&q=&esrc=s&source=web&cd=4&ved=0CEwQFjAD&url=http%3A%2F%2Fwww.brown.edu%2FCourses%2Fuploads%2FUNIV%253A0980%253A2012-Spring%253AS01.doc&ei=mNRyUdiDG8PG0QXep4HACA&usg=AFQjCNEpJpkX-2yTJATW1lBUz2FNh_rHgg&sig2=AKmTb6xHSGtQtwnEoXX3aA
291	American University, Washington DC	Seminar: The Israeli-Palestinian Conflict: Law and Policy	NA	20 April	NA	http://www.google.co.uk/url?sa=t&rct=j&q=&esrc=s&source=web&cd=7&ved=0CGQQFjAG&url=http%3A%2F%2Fwww.wcl.american.edu%2Fregistrar%2Fcoursesapp%2Fsyll%2Fspring_2011_LAW-795-003.doc&ei=mNRyUdiDG8PG0QXep4HACA&usg=AFQjCNHH2VZEO1-1Rd8dqyliL744aAea3w&sig2=62EZ5aF1voTi8RbaN5-HGA
292	Bryn Mawr College	Case Studies of Ethnopolitical Conflict	NA	20 April	2005 Summer	http://www.brynmawr.edu/aschcenter/asch908/si99-05/05syllabus.html
293	University of Michigan	Modern Middle East History	History 443; AAPTIS 487	20 April	Winter 2001	http://www.lsa.umich.edu/saa/publications/courseguide/grad/winter/archive/W01/390.html
294	University of Colorado Boulder	Cultures of Israel and Palestine	JWST 4050 / ANTH 4050/5050	22 April	Fall 2010	http://www.colorado.edu/anthropology/courses/documents/08.06.10FinalSyllabuFall2010CulturesofIsraelandPalestine.docx.pdf
295	Boston University	Israel: History, Politics, Culture, Identity	HI 393	22 April	Fall 2012	http://www.bu.edu/history/files/2012/10/393Fall12.pdf
296	University of South Carolina	Jews & Race	RELG 388	22 April	NA	http://people.cas.sc.edu/vehlowk/relg388.pdf
297	Georgia State University	Israeli & Palestinian Peace mongers	NA	22 April	Fall 2010	http://www.academia.edu/1788848/Syllabus_Israeli_and_Palestinian_Peacemongers_GSU_

(*Continued*)

No.	College	Course title	Course code	Access date (all 2013)	Taught date	Link
298	George Washington University	Israeli Politics and Society	PSC 3192	22 April	Spring 2013	http://www.google.co.uk/url?sa=t&rct=j&q=&esrc=s&source=web&cd=46&ved=0CFcQFjAFOCg&url=http%3A%2F%2Fdepartments.columbian.gwu.edu%2Fpoliticalscience%2Fsites%2Fdefault%2Ffiles%2Fu43%2FPSC%2520319_2W_Finkel%2520%28Israel%29_Spring%25202013.docx&ei=Q1V1Ub2eaaLB0gXD11CwAQ&usg=AFQjCNENP_Gc4YhrWLeZSB1-IzA5Fj_cwg&sig2=d3R2jM-WusLMGVFHulOJVw
299	Duke University	War and Middle East Security	POLSCI-199D.01	22 April	Fall 2003	http://people.duke.edu/~roshan/PS199.htm
300	University of Oklahoma	The Modern Middle East	Hist. 3953 Sec. 001	22 April	Spring 2004	http://www.google.co.uk/url?sa=t&rct=j&q=&esrc=s&source=web&cd=11&ved=0CD8QFjAAOAo&url=http%3A%2F%2Ffaculty-staff.ou.edu%2FL%2FJoshua.M.Landis-1%2FMod_Mid_East_2004.doc&ei=72p1UaSgBqbB0QXjs4DoCg&usg=AFQjCNF5V1gdOfwAhjmOCSLqHhIS80ACGg&sig2=wgscDviDFFnb5SarnhMtzg
301	Wartburg College	Modern History and Culture of the Middle East	HI 224	22 April	May 2011	http://faculty.wartburg.edu/walther/courses/hi224/h224_syl%20m11.htm
302	Gustavus Adolphus College	Israel and Palestine	REL-256	22 April	J-Term 2003	http://homepages.gac.edu/~wolfe/J-term/israel-2003/
303	Bryant University	The Middle East in War and Peace	POLS365	22 April	Fall 2003	http://www.google.co.uk/url?sa=t&rct=j&q=&esrc=s&source=web&cd=28&ved=0CGYQFjAHOBQ&url=http%3A%2F%2Fweb.bryant.edu%2F~marshapp%2FPS365syl.doc&ei=pmx1UZyOKYKcoWS21HgDQ&usg=AFQjCNFPEcFLfeOczwqYzxx_VNwlVObjTA&sig2=ake-VKUjDWX43i0aUEznqg

No.	College	Course title	Course code	Access date (all 2013)	Taught date	Link
304	University of Memphis	The Arab-Israeli Conflict	UNHP 1100-303	22 April	NA	https://umdrive.memphis.edu/jjudaken/public/Arab-Israel.html
305	Emory University	The Arab-Israeli Conflict	JS 169	22 April	Fall 2002	http://www.js.emory.edu/undergrad/Fall2002ug.htm
306	Tufts University	U.S. Foreign Policy in the Middle East	PS 162	22 April	Spring 2003	http://ase.tufts.edu/polsci/curriculum/syllabi/ps162.pdf
307	Hobart and William Smith Colleges	Introduction to International Relations	Political Science 180	22 April	Spring 2001	http://people.hws.edu/beckman/pol180/syllabuspol180.html
308	Emory University	The Arab-Israeli Conflict	HIST 383-000	22 April	Fall 2010	http://college.emory.edu/home/academic/course/schedules/2010/fall/section/regular/history/HIST383-000.html
309	Juniata College	Introduction to International Politics	PS102	22 April	Spring 2008	http://jcsites.juniata.edu/faculty/nagengast/PS102Spring08.html
310	Juniata College	Introduction to International Politics	PS102	22 April	Spring 2011	http://jcsites.juniata.edu/faculty/nagengast/PS102spring11syll.html
311	Juniata College	Introduction to International Politics	PS102	22 April	Spring 2007	http://jcsites.juniata.edu/faculty/nagengast/PS102Spring07.htm
312	University of Illinois	Psychology of Ethnic Conflict	PSY450	22 April	Spring 2004	http://internal.psychology.illinois.edu/~lyubansk/Conflict/syllabus.pdf
313	Emory University	The Arab-Israeli Conflict	JS 169-000/001/002	22 April	Fall 2000	http://www.js.emory.edu/undergrad/Fall2000ug.htm
314	Juniata College	Introduction to International Politics	PS102	22 April	NA	http://jcsites.juniata.edu/faculty/nagengast/intro_ip.htm
315	Juniata College	Introduction to International Politics	PS102	22 April	Fall 2006	http://jcsites.juniata.edu/faculty/nagengast/PS102Fall2006.htm
316	Emory University	The Arab-Israeli Conflict	JS 169-000/001/002	22 April	Fall 2006	http://www.js.emory.edu/undergrad/Fall2006ug.htm

(Continued)

No.	College	Course title	Course code	Access date (all 2013)	Taught date	Link
317	University of Colorado at Boulder	Political Economy of the Middle East	Econ 4999	22 April	Spring 2004	http://www.colorado.edu/Economics/Syllabi/spring04-syllabi/spring04-4999-006syllabus.htm
318	University of Oklahoma	The Modern Middle East	Hist. 3953 Sec. 001	22 April	Spring 2002	http://faculty-staff.ou.edu/L/Joshua.M.Landis-1/modmideast2002.htm
319	New York University	Arab-Israeli Conflict	G53.1735.001	22 April	Spring 2010	http://politics.as.nyu.edu/docs/IO/12734/freilich_sp10_syllabus_1735.pdf
320	University of Oklahoma	The US in the Middle East	IAS 5940-001	22 April	Fall 2004	http://faculty-staff.ou.edu/L/Joshua.M.Landis-1/IR_grad_2004.htm
321	Wartburg College	Modern History and Culture of the Middle East	HI 224	22 April	Fall 2003	http://faculty.wartburg.edu/walther/Courses/HI224/hi224syl_f03.html
322	Massachusetts Institute of Technology	Causes and Prevention of War	17.42	22 April	Spring 2009	http://ocw.mit.edu/courses/political-science/17-42-causes-and-prevention-of-war-spring-2009/readings/furthr_reading/
323	George Washington University	Economics of the Middle East	Economics 295.13	23 April	Spring 2008	http://www.gwu.edu/~iiep/assets/docs/syllabi/economics_of_middle_east_spring_2008.pdf
324	University of Missouri	Arab-Israeli Conflict	NA	23 April	Na	http://www.google.co.uk/url?sa=t&rct=j&q=&esrc=s&source=web&cd=1&ved=0CDIQFjAA&url=http%3A%2F%2Fh.web.umkc.edu%2Fhafezm%2Fcourses%2Faic.doc&ei=zW12UYkvHMqG0AWw8oH4CQ&usg=AFQjCNGdFVqDUQ361GfF2kQcm0PTyvBC3g&sig2=vl3ji1fhNbJ0s24Pbr5nyw
325	Brigham Young University	History of the Arab-Israeli Conflict	Political Science 474	23 April	Winter 2011	https://politicalscience.byu.edu/Syllabi/W11/Gubler_474_W11.pdf
326	University of California, Berkeley	Social and Revolutionary Movements in the Middle East	Political Science 149Z	23 April	Spring 2012	http://polisci.berkeley.edu/research/courses/syllabi/2012/spring/PS149Z-SP12.pdf

No.	College	Course title	Course code	Access date (all 2013)	Taught date	Link
327	University of California, San Diego	The Arab-Israeli Conflict: A Rashomon of Perspectives	138D	23 April	Fall 2006	http://weber.ucsd.edu/~dformanb/138D.pdf
328	University of Vermont	International Politics of the Middle East	Political Science 157	23 April	Spring 2013	http://www2.uvm.edu/~polisci/syllabi/Spring%2013%20Syllabi/POLS%20157A%20-%20International%20Politics%20of%20the%20Middle%20East%20-%20Gause%20-%20S13.pdf
329	University of Vermont	International Politics of the Middle East	Political Science 157	23 April	Spring 2011	https://www2.uvm.edu/~polisci/syllabi/Spring%2011%20Syllabi/POLS%20157A%20-%20Intern%20Pols%20of%20Middle%20East%20-%20Gause%20-%20S11.pdf
330	Brandeis University	The Making of the Modern Middle East	NEJS 185b	23 April	Spring 2005	http://www.brandeis.edu/departments/nejs/syllabi/docs/2005/nejs185b-s2005.pdf
331	University of Nevada, Reno	Middle East in World Affairs	Political science 407p/607p	23 April	Fall 2009	http://www.unr.edu/cla/polisci/documents/PSC407pFall2009.pdf
332	University of Nevada, Reno	Middle East in World Affairs	Political Science 407p/607p	23 April	Fall 2008	http://www.unr.edu/cla/polisci/documents/PSC407PFall2008.pdf
333	Lehman College of the City University of New York	The Arab-Israeli Conflict	HIW 305	23 April	NA	http://www.lehman.edu/lehman/about/senate/reports/history_march06a.pdf
334	University of South Florida	Conflict in The World	INR 4083 602	23 April	Spring 2005	http://dspace.nelson.usf.edu/xmlui/bitstream/handle/10806/6289/INR4083_Ravid_2005Spring.pdf?sequence=1
335	University of Oklahoma	Relations – Mid East	IAS 3433 001	23 April	Fall 2007	http://www.ou.edu/honors/curriculum/newsletters/fall07.pdf
336	Mount St. Mary's College	History of the Middle East	SOC 192	23 April	Fall 2003	http://www.msmc.la.edu/PDFFiles/WCsyllabiarchive/Fall2003/his124fa03.pdf

(Continued)

No.	College	Course title	Course code	Access date (all 2013)	Taught date	Link
337	Tufts University	US Foreign Policy War, Peace and Security in the Middle East	PS 165	23 April	Spring 2007	http://ase.tufts.edu/polsci/curriculum/syllabi/ps165.pdf
338	East Carolina University		POLS 6425	23 April	2008	http://www.google.co.uk/url?sa=t&rct=j&q=&esrc=s&source=web&cd=88&ved=0CGQQFjAH&url=http%3A%2F%2Fwww.ecu.edu%2Fcs-acad%2Fgcc%2Fupload%2F10_15_08_POLS_6425_Course_Proposal_Form.doc&ei=9YF2UZDGIMis0QXZo4DgBw&usg=AFQjCNGW7QNPKtBX_s_A8_ZqRSjOzTUHNg&sig2=Mcn8CltSos54uG7B7cgW-A
339	Brandeis University	The US and the Middle East	NA	23 April	Spring 2005	http://www.google.co.uk/url?sa=t&rct=j&q=&esrc=s&source=web&cd=10&ved=0CHIQFjAJ&url=http%3A%2F%2Fpeople.brandeis.edu%2F-hoffmann%2FPapers%2FReadings%2520Class%2520US%2520Middle%2520East%2520Spring%252005%2FUS-Middle%2520East%2520Bibliography%2520Feb10.doc&ei=9YF2UZDGIMis0QXZo4DgBw&usg=AFQjCNGOOOKa2RL2dSF86MA00z55_C4dMA&sig2=2hVVpXFyBC_7Msew9fb2ug
340	Harvard Extension School	Comparative National Security of Middle Eastern Countries	GOVT E-1961	23 April	Spring 2010	http://www.google.co.uk/url?sa=t&rct=j&q=&esrc=s&source=web&cd=12&ved=0CDgQFjABOAo&url=http%3A%2F%2Fisites.harvard.edu%2Ffs%2Fdocs%2Ficb.topic698875.files%2FHarvard%2520extenstion%2520-%2520ME%2520NS%2520biblio%2520spring%25202010.doc&ei=MYV2UdSgB8jQ0QWahYDoCA&usg=AFQjCNF41glerQkQHLq3lQWVzD9TkVDEYg&sig2=aOq9MM3OblL6w0LAb9bZjw
341	Juniata College	Introduction to International Politics	PS102	23 April	Fall 2010	http://jcsites.juniata.edu/faculty/nagengast/PS102Fall10syll.html
342	Wartburg College	Modern History and Culture of the Middle East	HI 224	23 April	May 2009	http://faculty.wartburg.edu/walther/Courses/Hi224/h224_syl%20m09.html

No.	College	Course title	Course code	Access date (all 2013)	Taught date	Link
343	Texas A&M University System	International Relations of the Middle East	Political Science 586	23 April	Summer 2010	http://www2.ct.tamus.edu/jeffreydixon//online/mideast.html
344	University of Colorado Boulder	Political Economy of the Middle East	Econ 4999-004	23 April	Fall 2006	http://www.colorado.edu/Economics/Syllabi/fall06-syllabi/fall06-4999-004syllabus.html
345	Fairfield University	Islamic Societies and Cultures	NA	23 April	Fall 2006	http://www.faculty.fairfield.edu/dcrawford/06f_islam.html
346	Emory University	The Arab-Israeli Conflict	HIST383-000	23 April	2013	http://atlas.college.emory.edu/fall2013/section/HIST/HIST383-000.html
347	Emory University	Arab-Israeli Conflict	POLS 383	23 April	Fall 2009	http://polisci.emory.edu/home/undergraduate/schedules/2009fall.html
348	Washington University	Israeli Politics in Broad Perspective	L32 3781 Pol Sci	23 April	Spring 2010	http://costa.wustl.edu/IsrPol/syllabus.pdf
349	Brigham Young University	History of the Arab-Israeli Conflict	Political Science 474	23 April	Summer 2011	https://syllabus.byu.edu/view/tNpNDmnUxbhk.html
350	Emory University	History of the Near East, 1914 to the Present	MESAS 370	23 April	Fall 2007	http://mesas.emory.edu/home/undergraduate/schedules/fall07.html
351	Emory University	Land of Israel 1882–1948: Sources, Narratives, Perspectives	MESAS 370SWR	23 April	Fall 2007	http://mesas.emory.edu/home/undergraduate/schedules/fall07.html
352	San Diego State University	Arab-Israeli Relations, Past and Present	HIST 574	23 April	Fall 2012	http://sdsu-dspace.calstate.edu/bitstream/handle/10211.10/2811/574%20Arab-Israeli%20Relations%20Naor.pdf?sequence=1
353	Washington University	Israeli Politics and the Arab Spring	L32 3781 Pol Sci	23 April	Spring 2013	http://polisci.wustl.edu/files/polisci/imce/l32_3781.pdf
354	Brigham Young University	International Relations of the Middle East	Pl Sc 381	23 April	Summer 2010	https://politicalscience.byu.edu/Syllabi/Su10/Nelson_381_Su10.pdf

(Continued)

No.	College	Course title	Course code	Access date (all 2013)	Taught date	Link
355	Brigham Young University	Arab-Israeli Conflict	Political Science 474	23 April	Winter 2012	https://politicalscience.byu.edu/Syllabi/W12/Gubler_474_W12.pdf
356	Millsaps College	The Twice-Promised Land	H.3500	23 April	Na	http://www.millsaps.edu/_resources/author_files/peace_studies_history_syllabus.pdf
357	Tufts University	U.S. Foreign Policy in the Middle East	PS 172	23 April	Fall 2011	http://ase.tufts.edu/polsci/curriculum/syllabi/Fall2011/ps172.pdf
358	Tufts University	Israeli Foreign Policy and National Security	PS80	23 April	Fall 2006	http://ase.tufts.edu/polsci/curriculum/syllabi/ps80.pdf
359	College of the Holy Cross	Politics of the Middle East	Political Science 272	23 April	Spring 2009	http://college.holycross.edu/faculty/vlangohr/ME%20Pol%20F09%20Syllabus.pdf
360	College of the Holy Cross	Political and Social Life in the Muslim World	NA	23 April	Spring 2010	http://college.holycross.edu/faculty/vlangohr/honors_syllabus.pdf
361	Western Illinois University	The Modern Middle East and the Arab-Israeli Conflict	H344	23 April	Fall 2011	http://www.wiu.edu/cas/history/pdf/History344Fall2011.pdf
362	Oberlin College	Middle East and North Africa History: From 1800 to Present	HIST-122,	23 April	Spring 2010	http://new.oberlin.edu/dotAsset/1688613.pdf
363	Harvard University	International Relations of the Middle East	IGA-340	23 April	Fall 2009	http://ksgnotes1.harvard.edu/degreeprog/Syllabus.nsf/0/517C281E44F25626852576080056 81C6/$FILE/iga-340-syl-2009.pdf
364	University of South Florida	Comparative Governments / Politics of the Middle East	CPO 4930 601	23 April	Fall 2005	http://dspace.nelson.usf.edu/xmlui/bitstream/handle/10806/5809/CPO4930_Ravid_2005Fall.pdf?sequence=1
365	University of South Florida	Comparative Governments / Politics of the Middle East	CPO 4930 601	23 April	Fall 2006	http://dspace.nelson.usf.edu/xmlui/bitstream/handle/10806/6228/CPO4930_Ravid_2006Fall.pdf?sequence=1

No.	College	Course title	Course code	Access date (all 2013)	Taught date	Link
366	Harvard University	Middle Eastern Politics and Policy	IGA 207	23 April	Spring 2009	http://ksgnotes1.harvard.edu/degreeprog/Syllabus.nsf/0/4932767B6FB4AEC8525756 2007CF842/$FILE/syllabus.pdf
367	University of South Florida	Comparative Governments / Politics of the Middle East	CPO 4930 601	23 April	Spring 2005	http://dspace.nelson.usf.edu/xmlui/bitstream/handle/10806/6290/CPO4930_Ravid_2005Spring.pdf?sequence=1
368	San Diego State University	Arab-Israeli Relations, Past and Present	HIST 574	23 April	Spring 2013	http://www.google.co.uk/url?sa=t&rct=j&q=&esrc=s&source=web&cd=1&ved=0CDIQFjAA&url=http%3A%2F%2Fsdsu-dspace.calstate.edu%2Fbitstream%2Fhandle%2F10211.10%2F3612%2FHistory%2520574%2520Naor.doc%3Fsequence%3D1&ei=w792UbjmM6uQ0QWqxICoBA&usg=AFQjCNHTJTbrBZYD2QGLb0YoefiD4VVADg&sig2=X3OAaIy2dzAK9NW0dkUVng
369	Tarleton State University	International Relations of the Middle East	Political Science 586	23 April	Fall 2008	http://www.google.co.uk/url?sa=t&rct=j&q=&esrc=s&source=web&cd=7&ved=0CF8QFjAG&url=http%3A%2F%2Fww2.ct.tamus.edu%2Fjeffreydixon%2F%2FMiddleEastSyllabus.doc&ei=w792UbjmM6uQ0QWqxICoBA&usg=AFQjCNFH-EEIG6ptKU2bBhyX7Co7HuxLPg&sig2=N6n9VNWFoJxdKyYNPx7urA
370	University of West Georgia	History of Modern Israel	History 4485-25H	24 April	Spring 2005	http://www.westga.edu/~history/FacultyUpdated/Goldstein/IsraelsyllabusSUWG2005.htm

Chapter 4

ZIONIST NARRATION OF THE HISTORY

Prior to arriving at actual analysis of the selected textbooks (Chapter 5), the main characteristics of the Zionist, or pro-Israeli, historiography of the question is introduced in this short chapter, to make one able to recognize such a version of history in the relevant literature.

Writing on the history of 'Israel' is a recent phenomenon; it started when Zionism arose in Europe on the eve of the twentieth century (Sand 2008a). Aged history of the land, however, plays a crucial role in how that history is being narrated, and written, by Zionist historiography. The controversial nature of the Zionist claim to the land, and widespread rejection of this claim by non-Zionists contributed to such a state of affairs. The Ancient Time is taken, by Zionist historiographers, as a principal source for the production of some evidence in supporting the legitimacy of the Zionist claim to the land. This enterprise has been directed by a critical need to justify occupying a land thousands of kilometres away from where the first Zionist Jews belonged, in Europe, and one which was populated and owned, already, by other people i.e. Palestinians. This was not possible without a long journey, thousands of years back in history, to a time when a 'Jewish domination of the land' can be imagined. From here the Zionist historiography came to function as a main producer of 'history' about the Jewish presence in the land, to demonstrate 'the right of Jews' to establish a 'Jewish state' in Palestine. As a result, a Zionist history of Israel has been constructed that can establish a link between modern Israel and the history of the land. The main elements of this history can be outlined as follows:

- 'The Holy Land' was the birthplace of the 'Jewish people', where their 'national identity' was formed.
- In this land 'Jewish people' established their own statehood. Zion (Jerusalem) is introduced as the centre of this ancient 'Jewish state'.
- Palestine was populated by 'Jewish people' before a forced expulsion by Romans that drove them out.
- All Jews in different corners of the world are descended from the same ancestors, those who were expelled from Palestine. Thus, there is a Jewish ethnos.

- Wherever they settled outside Palestine, after the 'expulsion', they kept the hope to return to 'their land', and establish their 'national home' and strove to achieve their dream.

These elements that are produced, in one way or another, in different versions of Zionist histories of the land, are the same elements that introduce Israel's history in 'Israel's Declaration of Independence' (to justify the Zionist mission in Palestine):

> The Land of Israel was the birthplace of the Jewish people. Here their spiritual, religious and national identity was formed. Here they achieved independence and created a culture of national and universal significance. Here they wrote and gave the Bible to the world. Exiled from the Land of Israel the Jewish people remained faithful to it in all the countries of their dispersion, never ceasing to pray and hope for their return and the restoration of their national freedom. Impelled by this historic association, Jews strove throughout the centuries to go back to the land of their fathers and regain their statehood.
> Laqueur and Rubin 2008: 81

Escorting the establishment of this mega narrative about the land's 'Jewishness' there are two complementary lines of historiography that function to complete that narrative, however, in two different ways: the first one undermines any major Jewish collective experience in other lands except those that function as a reminder of the Jewish dispersion. In this way, thousands of years of the presence of Jewish communities in other lands, Iran and Iraq for instance, are discounted. Jewish achievements in establishing states, the Himyarite kingdom and the kingdom of Adiabene, for instance, and even an empire, the Khazarian Empire, outside the Holy Land are seen as outside the mainframe of Jewish historical experience. There are reports, from Israel, about how the Israeli educational system treats such unwelcome cases; 'Thus the chapter about the Judaizing Himyarites was abandoned by the historiographical roadside in Israel's educational system, and secondary school graduates know nothing about it. It is the sad fate of this mighty Jewish kingdom, which dominated its region, that its descendants are not proud of it and that many others fear to mention its very existence' (Sand 2009: 199). It is added in the same report that this treatment, of the Himyarite case, is not an exception but the norm; other Jewish domains outside Palestine, in North Africa and near the Caspian Sea, are similarly suppressed: 'From 1951 to the present moment, not a single historical work about the Khazars has appeared in Hebrew.... The Israeli academic world has been mute on this topic, and no significant research has taken place' (Sand 2009: 235–6).

In a different but related historiographical line, all that has been experienced in the history of the land after the Jews' supposed expulsion is overlooked. As a result, there is a clear tendency in Zionist historiography to ignore the Arab history of the land; all that happened in this long period, almost two thousand years, is considered as something temporary, minor, foreign or irrelevant. It is not difficult to see how these two complementary lines of historiography can contribute to forming a single picture of the land as a place originally belonging to the Jews who were deprived, at one stage, of being present in it, but managed later to regain their right to the homeland. These two lines of historiography are developed, indeed, to safeguard the Zionist mega narrative (about the land's Jewishness) from contradictory features of the Jewish history; it thus undermines the history of Jews in other lands to break any Jewish link to other territories other than Palestine. Based on the finest Zionist mega narrative, Palestine is the only place where Jews belong; the only place where a Jewish state has been established; the only motherland of all Jews; the only place where establishing a Jewish state is possible and legitimate. From this perspective, all Jewish states of history including Himyarite in Yemen, Adiabene in Kurdistan, Khazarian on the shores of the Caspian Sea are harmful to the Zionist mega narrative, and accordingly, should be suppressed. These features undermine the supposed centrality of Palestine in the 'Jewish national history', and its position as the only place where Jews had their own statehood, and can have their own again.

Based on the Zionist mega narrative, there are only two Jewish states in the course of history: one ancient (Israel), and one modern (Israel) that comes to revive the ancient one; both states take place only in one location i.e. Palestine where supposedly is the sole Jews' motherland. This narrative is desperate, in the face of a world that opposes the illegal occupation, to provide a justification for occupying Palestine. Establishing Jewish states in other territories, other than Palestine, damages such a narrative that is designed to demonstrate Palestine as the only perceived Jewish state. Establishing those Jewish states, outside Palestine, also demonstrates that the 'expelled Jews' ignored Zionist historiographers' view of Palestine as the sole place that a Jewish state can be established. Moreover, mighty Jewish states of history, Adiabene for instance, had shown no interest in reviving a Jewish state in the supposed Jews' motherland when they had the power to realize such a goal. No report is mentioned, in history, of any attempt by those mighty Jewish states to 'liberate' that motherland, or fostering a Jewish Aliyah to where they were expelled from, and belonged to.

This (Zionist) image of the land's history is not necessarily factual, representing what really happened. It was constructed at a certain historical stage when the Zionist movement needed to justify its claim to the land. This point has been articulated by a number of historians, including Israeli historian Shlomo Sand. He clarifies, in his works, how the Zionist history has no precedent in the pre-Zionist era of Jewish history and was invented later by Jewish nationalists in Europe in the nineteenth and twentieth centuries:

> At a certain stage in the 19th century intellectuals of Jewish origin in Germany, influenced by the folk character of German nationalism, took upon themselves the task of inventing a people 'retrospectively,' out of a thirst to create a modern Jewish people. From historian Heinrich Graetz on, Jewish historians began to draw the history of Judaism as the history of a nation that had been a kingdom, became a wandering people and ultimately turned around and went back to its birthplace.
>
> Sand 2008a

This Zionist mega narrative is criticized by other historians, including Norman Finkelstein, American Political Scientist, and Ilan Pappé, chair of the Emil Tuma Institute for Palestine Studies in Haifa (2000–6), who have contributed to the formation of a significant body of critical literature on the subject. Shlomo Sand summarized the related critique, and added to it, mainly through his book, *The Invention of the Jewish People*. This summary can highlight some problems of this mega narrative; the first case is related to the ancient time when a 'united Jewish kingdom' under David and Solomon was established: 'The central myths about the primeval origin of a marvelous nation that emerged from the desert, conquered a spacious land and built a glorious kingdom were a boon for rising Jewish nationalism and Zionist colonization. For a century they provided textual fuel of canonical quality that energized a complex politics of identity and territorial expansion demanding self-justification and considerable sacrifice' (Sand 2009: 122). Sand brings up the new archaeological discoveries to reveal how the myths of a united Jewish kingdom and the ancient Jewish state are advanced for ideological and political reasons. He refers to the fact that no 'trace of memory' has been found of the 'glorious kingdoms of David and Solomon'. The significance of this development is reflected in Sand's own words:

> The next biblical story to lose its scientific historicity as a result of new archaeological discoveries was the jewel in the crown of the long national memory. Ever since Graetz, through Dinur and the Israeli historians who followed, the united national kingdom of David and Solomon was the glorious golden age in Jewish history ... It was not possible to dig under the Haram al-Sharif, but explorations at all the other sites that were opened up around it failed to find any traces of an important tenth-century kingdom, the presumed time of David and Solomon. No vestige was ever found of monumental structures, walls or grand palaces, and the pottery found there was scanty and quite simple.
>
> Sand 2009: 120

Sand concludes that these archaeological discoveries do not allow for the recognition of a political entity bigger than a 'small tribal kingdom' at the time of the presumed Jewish kingdom, if such an entity ever existed (Sand 2009: 121). He offers a general conclusion on the united Jewish kingdom that is supported, according to him, by most recent archaeologists:

> The conclusion accepted by a majority of the new archaeologists and Bible scholars was that there never was a great united monarchy and that King Solomon never had grand palaces in which he housed his 700 wives and 300 concubines. The fact that the Bible does not name this large empire strengthens this conclusion. It was later writers who invented and glorified a mighty united kingdom, established by the grace of the single deity.
>
> Sand 2009: 122

In relation to another Zionist historiographical construction, Jewish expulsion from the Holy Land when conquered by the Romans, Sand argues that no historical document of what the Romans did in the Holy Land supports a mass expulsion of Jews: 'Nowhere in the abundant Roman documentation is there any mention of a deportation from Judea. Nor have any traces been found of large refugee populations around the borders of Judea after the uprising, as there would have been if a mass flight had taken place' (Sand 2009: 131). He puts this case in a wider context of how Romans treated others in the region; this allows an affirmative conclusion: 'the Romans never exiled any nation from anywhere on the eastern seaboard of the Mediterranean' (Sand 2008b). Sand argues, further, that the Romans did not possess the necessary means for such large-scale dispossession of a large population even if they had been willing to undertake such an enterprise:

> Roman rulers could be utterly ruthless in suppressing rebellious subject populations: they executed fighters, took captives and sold them into slavery, and sometimes exiled kings and princes. But they definitely did not deport whole populations in the countries they conquered in the East, nor did they have the means to do so – none of the trucks, trains or great ships available in the modern world.
>
> Sand 2009: 130

A Christian myth is processed, according to Sand, to construct the story of exile. This Christian myth is used to explain the disappearance of Jews from the Holy Land, through a religious tradition that relates it to punishment by God for committing a grave crime, killing the Christ (Sand 2009: 134). He elaborates how this Christian belief, once it was incorporated in the Jewish tradition, could be taken as a useful account that could make a link between Jews in other places, Europe for instance, and Palestine (Sand 2009: 134). This influential invention succeeded in becoming a dominant historical account in the West and was exhibited as a historical fact. Sand emphasizes the extraordinary Zionist success in establishing this narrative as a true history of the ancient Jews with no evidence to support it:

> The myth that recounted the expulsion of the 'Jewish people' by the Romans became the supreme justification for claiming historical rights over a Palestine that Zionist rhetoric transformed into the 'land of Israel.' We have here a particularly astonishing example of the molding of a collective memory. Thus, even though all specialists in ancient Jewish history know that the Romans did not deport the population of Judea (there is not even the slightest work of historical research on this subject), other, less qualified individuals have been, and largely remain, convinced that the ancient 'People of Israel' were forcibly uprooted from their homeland, as is solemnly stated in the Declaration of Independence of the State of Israel.
>
> Sand 2009: 317

The Arab-Israeli Conflict (published under Oxford History series for GCSE), perhaps the most adopted textbook in the British schooling system on the subject, can be given as an instance where this Zionist construction is taken as an undisputed fact; 'The Jews were driven out of Palestine by the Romans after two revolts in AD 70 and AD 135' (Rea and Wright 1997: 4). Sand also deals with why such an invention took place. Without that, he argues, the Zionist claim to Palestine was incomplete: 'The ultra-paradigm of deportation was essential for the construction of a long-term memory wherein an imaginary, exiled people-race could be described as the direct descendants of the former "people of the Bible"' (Sand 2009: 130). The invention of exile, according to him, was a necessary construction for justifying the Zionist claim of the people without a land to the land without a people, as well;

> National mythology determined that the Jews – banished, deported or fugitive emigrants – were driven into a long and dolorous exile, causing them to wander over lands and seas to the far corners of the earth until the advent of Zionism prompted them to turn around and return en masse to their orphaned homeland. This homeland had never belonged to the Arab conquerors, hence the claim of the people without a land to the land without a people.
>
> Sand 2009: 188

Sand refers to the 'Jewish people', and the 'Jewish nation' in its modern sense, as another case of Zionist historiographical invention that took place to complete the claim's justification; 'Only this myth of Hebrew ancestors could justify the right that they claimed over Palestine. Many people are still convinced of this today. Everyone knows that, in the modern world, membership of a religious community does not provide ownership rights to a territory whereas an "ethnic" people always have a land they can claim as their ancestral heritage' (Sand 2009: 316). He elaborates how Jews before this invention saw themselves as people who shared a religious belief and not a common ethnic background. He argues, subsequently, that there was not such a thing as a Jewish people in history: 'With the exception of Eastern Europe, where the demographic weight and uniquely distinctive structure of Jewish life nurtured a specific form of popular culture and vernacular language, no Jewish people – as a single, cohesive entity – ever appeared' (Sand 2009: 322). He names a volume by Heinrich Graetz, *History of the Jews from the Oldest Times to the Present*, published in the 1850s, as a pioneering work in that invention (Sand 2009: 73). The story of expulsion from the land, and also 'the myth of the Jewish ethnos' (Sand 2009: 308) is manipulated to construct a Jewish people. It is argued in this Zionist narrative that Jews who were expelled from the land did not try to convert other people to Judaism, so that all the Jews who live in other lands are real descendants of the Jews who were forced to leave Palestine. Sand rejects this claim and mentions a number of major cases in history where the Jews succeeded in the mass conversion of other people: Arabs in Arabia, Berbers in North Africa and Khazars in Europe, for instance (Sand 2009: Ch. 4). He puts a notable emphasis on the Khazarian Empire that was converted to Judaism in the eighth century. The importance of this case, for him, lies in the fact that Khazar descendants are the Jews who spread later into the eastern and central European countries, and formed major Jewish populations in these areas. He refers to the fascinating irony that these Jews, known now as Ashkenazi Jews, are those who started the call for a return to the ancestral land in Zion, and constituted the main part of Jewish immigrants in early Israel, and still form the main part of the population and power in this country (Sand 2009: Ch. 4).

Sand also deconstructs the Zionist myth of Jewish redemptionist efforts to return to the homeland where Zionist historians insist on the idea that there have been continuous Jewish efforts to return to the Holy Land, introducing the Zionist movement as the last, and the only successful one in accomplishing that long-tried project:

> Over the centuries, Jews ardently longed for Zion, their holy city, but it never occurred to them, not even to those living close by, to go and settle there in their earthly life. It is certainly hard to live at the heart of a holy place, all the more so when the small minority who did live there were well aware how they continued to live in exile: only the coming of the Messiah would allow them to reach the metaphysical Jerusalem – along with all the dead, we should not forget.
>
> Sand 2009: 317

He explained later in this account that this longing had no national or physical meaning, but it was a religious mythology based on waiting for the coming of the saviour, the Messiah, in Zion where all the dead would rise to join the event. To support this idea, he further refers to the chances provided in some historical periods for Jews in the 'diaspora' to return but no interest was shown by them for such a Zionist enterprise. Babylonia is mentioned as the first instance: 'Therefore, when the Jewish cultural centers in Babylonia declined, the Jews migrated to Baghdad, not to Jerusalem, although both cities were ruled by the same caliphate' (Sand 2009: 136). Another main chance became available when the Jews were expelled from Andalusia, Spain: 'The Jewish deportees from Spain migrated to cities all around the Mediterranean, but only a few chose to go to Zion. In the modern age, with its ferocious pogroms and the rise of aggressive nationalism in Eastern Europe, masses of the Yiddish people migrated Westward, mainly to the United States' (Sand 2009: 136). The migration to Palestine, according to him, found momentum only when the American borders became closed to Jews: 'Only when the American borders closed in the 1920s, and again after the horrendous Nazi massacres, did significant numbers migrate to Mandatory Palestine, part of which became the State of Israel' (Sand 2009: 136). Sand concludes in this regard: 'The Jews were not forcibly deported from their "homeland," and there was no voluntary "return" to it' (Sand 2009: 136).

Deconstruction of the Zionist history of the pre-Zionist era, by Sand and other historians, has contributed to providing other relevant points which can be summarized as follows:

- The Old Testament is the main source for the Zionist history of ancient times. There is no legitimate ground for considering this book of religious Jewish tradition as a reliable source of historical facts. Sand elaborates how some secular historians, Zionists, take a different approach to the religious tradition, in this case, and why:

> This is why, in the eyes of the first Zionist historians, the Bible ceased to be an impressive theological text and became a book of secular history, whose teaching is still dispensed to all Jewish Israeli pupils in specially designated lessons, from the first year of elementary school to graduation from high school. According to this teaching, the people of Israel were no longer made up of those chosen by God, but became a nation issuing from the seed of Abraham. And so when modern archaeology began to show that there had not been an Exodus from Egypt, and that the great, unified monarchy of David and Solomon never existed, it met with a bitter and embarrassed reaction from the secular Israeli public; some people did not even flinch from accusing the 'new archaeologists' of 'Bible denial'.
>
> Sand 2009: 316

- Other relevant historical evidence, archaeological or textual, does not have the power to support the Zionist history of ancient times as factual; it may in fact be seen to reject it.
- A large part of what is represented in Zionist history as 'historical facts' has no chance, whatsoever, of being established as such due to two main reasons: many of the events reported occurred a very long time ago, thousands of years in the past, for instance, and this makes them too remote, from the viewpoint of historical investigation, to be verified as historically accurate. They are, in fact, close to the prehistoric era, seen from this perspective. The second reason refers to a substantial shortage of written reports that have survived from that time.
- Without any doubt, it is a historical fact that Arabs were populating the land when Zionist settlers came in. This Arab settlement can be seen, through a wealth of evidence and documents, not only for that time but also for most of the land's 'certain history' (a history that is documented by enough reliable proof) if not all.

The aforementioned review of the Zionist historiography of the Israel-Palestine question of the pre-Zionist era, discussed already in this chapter, can reveal a certain functioning structure of this historiography:

- It has a certain beginning: the history of the land starts with the Jews' presence in the land, ignoring others who possessed the land before them, or alongside their presence.
- The supposed Jewish time of the land, that of Ancient Israel, is constructed as the principal history of the land in the pre-Zionist era: it is narrated, also, in a way to provide the essentials of a perceived Jewish state, such as 'Jewish people', 'Jewish kingdom' and 'Jewish independence'.

- This 'glorious Jewish time' has a certain ending; the forced mass expulsion of the Jews from the land, by the Romans, is articulated as the ending of the 'Jewish domination', and the main event responsible for the absence of the Jews in the land for the last two millennia.
- The main bulk of the land's history, the last two thousand years, that constitute almost the whole documented history of the land is not taken as a significant piece of the land's history; the main history of this time, according to the Zionist historiography, is located outside Palestine where Jews lived, who regarded, supposedly, Palestine as their homeland. Their history is summarized simply as their efforts to keep the link with the 'mother land', their hoping to return to it, and their striving to realize that hope.

Accordingly, the land's history is structured in a way that starts with the Jews, and ends with them, and leaves no space, in between, in the land's thousands of years of history that might be filled by others' history. This structure secures a history-long Jewishness of the land, providing a safe historiographical place for the 'Jews' where they are not bothered by others' presence, history and rights. This constructed history can be exposed through a cyclic graph as seen in Figure 4.1.

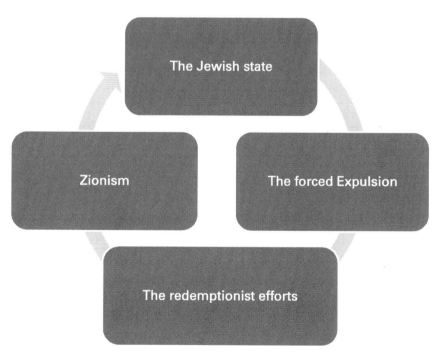

Figure 4.1 The history as constructed by Zionism.

Chapter 5

HOW COLLEGE TEXTBOOKS TREAT THE HISTORY?

This chapter reports the results of the main analysis of this study, in which all selected textbooks are examined, one by one, through historical narrative analysis to find out how the history of the Israel-Palestine question is treated.

Before turning to report the outcomes of this analysis, an introduction is offered here on the procedure used in this study to analyse those books. As mentioned in the Introduction, 'history' is a principal discipline in which Zionist activities to support the legitimacy of 'modern Israel', in the area of knowledge production, can be observed and recognized. Pioneering Zionists employed Jewish history, in general, and 'Ancient Israel', in particular, to invent what their project badly needed: 'Jewish people' and its 'motherland'. Later on, other justifications, from modern history, are added to legitimize Israel (the Balfour Declaration and the Holocaust for instance), but the history of the pre-Zionist era remained as the core of this enterprise. Hence it is taken, in this study, as the focal area of its textbook analysis. This choice was informed by an assumption that the legitimization of Israel's right to the land of Palestine has no real chance to be convincing without a reference to the land's pre-Zionist history. As a result, other phases of the question's history are not analysed in this analysis; the narrative analysis is limited only to one phase, the pre-Zionist history of the question. This phase has, arguably, the best capacity to reveal how the history of the question is treated. No Zionist historiography of the question can dare, I believe, to ignore Zionist elements of this phase's history for their vital role in establishing a convincing argument to support the Zionist claim of the land. An analysis of the selected histories (history textbooks in this research) on how the main elements of the Zionist historiography of the pre-Zionist history of the land are treated can provide a opportunity to distinguish biased (pro-Israeli) histories from others – whether it takes those elements as established and undisputed facts, or exercises enough scholarly scrutiny when dealing with them.

A history is classified as pro-Israeli, in this analysis, when it passes on, without any serious challenge or scientific scepticism, the main elements of the Zionist historiography (of the pre-Zionist era). Such history typically starts the history of the land with the Jews, stressing their peoplehood and statehood that concluded with a foreign – Roman – intervention that led to their forced expulsion from the land. According to this history, Jews outside Palestine had no more important business, for about two thousand years, than returning to the homeland, experiencing in the interim an interruption to their collective life. At the same time the land, in its turn, was brought to a sudden standstill, waiting to see the return of its real owners, with no authentic intervening experience of the local population, people, civilization or any character that might demonstrate that the land had any owner other than Jews. This history, which is called 'mythistory' due to its mythical foundations (Sand 2009: Ch. 2), pays no serious attention to the problems and challenges of this story, and represents it as historical fact. In this way, any case of such treatment of the question, where those Zionist claims are presented as historical facts, is taken as one instance of pro-Israeli bias in this analysis. Textbooks that function as such are considered, accordingly, pro-Israeli histories. It is very important to clarify that any mention of main elements of pre-Zionist Jewish history in the analysed histories, Jewish redemptionist efforts, for instance, is not regarded as a case of pro-Israeli bias. A case is classed as biased only if these controversial elements are taken as 'established facts' ignoring all problems that challenge that status.

It worth mentioning here, before moving to the actual analysis of the textbooks, that the focus is not on criticizing or challenging the pro-Israeli accounts that are offered in the selected textbooks; the main point of this analysis lies in examining the influence of the Zionist historiography on textbooks that are used, in Western academia, as authoritative sources of knowledge on this subject.

The remainder of this chapter reports an analysis of the six selected textbooks. The report starts with the most popular textbook in the top-six list, and proceeds in descending order. Table 5.1 helps visualize the main concepts of this analysis; all six textbooks in the table are analysed to examine how they treat the main elements of the pro-Israeli history of Israel-Palestine question in the pre-Zionism era. These seven elements are given in the rightmost columns of the table. Each question mark in the lower rows of the table represents a related question: how a given textbook treats a certain element of the Zionist history. The results of the analysis in this chapter determine the answers, revealing how a given textbook treats a certain element of Zionist historiography. The completed version of the table appears towards the end of this chapter (Table 5.2), where the main results of this textbook analysis are concluded.

Palestine and the Arab-Israeli Conflict

This book is written by an American scholar, Charles Duryea Smith, who used to be a lecturer, now retired, in the University of Arizona in the United States. The book, supplemented by almost sixty primary documents, sixty maps and many photographs, is structured in clear chapters, each containing its own conclusion and chronology, and also some 'questions for consideration'. The textbook has a website companion, to guide students and provide them with some information or images they might need for their course. The first edition was published in 1988 and the eighth, the most recent at the time of the survey, was published in 2013.

Table 5.1 The framework for the textbook analysis

Textbook title	How selected textbooks treat the 'main elements of Zionist historiography'						
	History of the land starts with …	Ancient Israel	How Jews disappeared in Palestine?	Jewish redemptionist efforts to return	Position on Jewish ethnos	Arab history of the land	Jewish polity in other lands[a]
Palestine and the Arab-Israeli Conflict	?	?	?	?	?	?	?
A Concise History of the Arab-Israeli Conflict	?	?	?	?	?	?	?
Righteous Victims	?	?	?	?	?	?	?
A History of the Israeli-Palestinian Conflict	?	?	?	?	?	?	?
A History of Israel	?	?	?	?	?	?	?
The Israel-Arab Reader	?	?	?	?	?	?	?

Note:
a Is there any mention of the Jewish dominance in other lands?

The survey finds the book was the most popular college-level textbook on the history of the Israel-Palestine question; the book is adopted widely in all six countries of the survey; in 97 syllabi in the United States, 17 in Canada, 16 in the UK, 6 in Australia, 4 in New Zealand and 3 in Ireland; altogether in 143 syllabi, in many cases as the main textbook of the course. The information provided by Google Scholar also suggests that the book has been cited frequently, in 395 cases, by other books or academic articles. The parts of the book examined in detail are:

- Preface
- Prologue: The Arab-Israeli Conflict in Historical Perspective: The Middle East and Palestine to 1517
- Chapter 1: Ottoman Society, Palestine, and the Origins of Zionism, 1516–1914
- Epilogue
- Chronology

Other parts of the book are left out of the examination as they do not deal with the history of the pre-Zionist era. The index of the book is used, at the final stage, to find any relevant matter that might have been missed during the earlier parts of the examination, or left out from the examination for the reason just mentioned.

Analysis

The main body of the relevant historiography of the pre-Zionist era appeared in two constitutive sections in the opening of the book: in the Prologue and in the first chapter. The Prologue, which is designed to cover 'the Arab-Israeli Conflict in Historical Perspective', is composed of three relevant parts:

- 'Ancient Israel and Palestine to the Coming of Islam'
- 'The Arabs and the Spread of Islam'
- 'The Chronology'

'Ancient Israel and Palestine to the Coming of Islam' is where the main historiography of the book about the pre-Zionist era of Israel is offered. This section starts with a noticeable statement: 'The past twenty years have seen a revolution in scholarship on ancient Israel' (Smith 2013: 2). It then mentions the main claims of the Zionist historiography about ancient Israel. The author comments: 'Recent scholarship, based on extensive archaeological excavations, has challenged many of these assumptions' (Smith 2013: 2). The writer recognizes, in this section, some major challenges that question the historicity of Zionist historiography and discount the biblical stories of a unified Jewish kingdom under David and Solomon. At the same time, it suggests – according to 'mainstream scholars' – a 'brief emergence of a unified Jewish state in all of Palestine, founded by Israel, the kingdom in the north' (Smith 2013: 2). The author uses a language that places some distance, through different means, between himself and the Zionist historiography, by formulating phrases such as 'biblical tradition dates' and 'supposed ... kingships' (Smith 2013: 2). The Bible's position as a source of true history is discounted in the book's account. The last statement of the section, asserting this argument, stresses that archaeological evidence does not support the Zionist claims about ancient Israel:

> The archaeological evidence thus summarized verifies the existence of Jewish settlements in Palestine prior to the appearance of Saul and David but views them as local tribal chiefs with little regional influence. The same can be said for Solomon, and no trace of his palace or temple has been found. Their mythical attainments were developed in later versions of the Old Testament, most of them composed during the sixth and fifth centuries BCE.
> Smith 2013: 2

Another section of the book, 'Palestine Under Roman and Byzantine Rule', is important for its involvement with another Zionist historiographical element: the Jewish expulsion. This section, also, does not represent Zionist historiography with the Roman expulsion of the Jews at its centre. The distancing of the book from the Zionist history of the expulsion is, however, limited; on one side it stresses the opinion that 'many Jews remained in Palestine' after the Roman treatment of the Jewish rebellion (Smith 2013: 3). In this sense, it might reject the idea of mass expulsion of the Jews. But, at the same time, it offers alternative accounts that support some chunks of the Zionist related claims:

> Although many Jews remained in Palestine, they were concentrated in the Galilee and, as punishment for the rebellion, were forbidden to enter Jerusalem, now in ruins. Jews outside Palestine far outnumbered those within it. Jewish communities had sprung up in the Greco-Roman world prior to the Roman conquest, but their numbers were small compared with those that resulted from the dispersions following the failed rebellions of 66 and 132 CE. Nevertheless, Jews still considered Palestine to be Eretz Israel, the land promised them by God, and Jerusalem remained the focal point of their religious observances.
> Smith 2013: 3

This statement can mean, but not necessarily, that the Roman expulsion of Jews (the dispersion following the failed rebellions) is the main source of a rise in the Jewish population outside Palestine. Another part of this statement (Jews still considered Palestine to be Eretz Israel, the land promised them by God), can work, also, to support the Zionist claim that their presence outside Israel was provisional and that they still considered Israel as their home. In a later statement, the Romans are introduced as responsible, again, for making 'the remainder' of the Jewish population in Palestine leave the land: 'He (the Roman emperor) imposed harsh tax measures throughout the empire, their application in Palestine led to a significant decline in the Jewish population. By 300 CE, Jews made up one-half of the population in the Galilee and less than one-fourth in the rest of the region' (Smith 2013: 4).

The chronology at the end of the Epilogue is of considerable importance for an analysis of how the historical developments prior to the Ottoman control of the land are listed. The chronology starts with the Canaanite control of the land, and not the Jewish, as narrated frequently in Zionist historiography: 'Canaanites inhabit Palestine West of Jordan River, Coastal Lebanon, and southern Syria' (Smith 2013: 10). The next development is characterized by Jewish and, noticeably, Philistine settlement in the land: 'Philistines and Jews settle in Palestine region of Canaan' (Smith 2013: 10). A further significance of this chronology comes from the fact that, unlike the Zionist historiography of the era, the supposed establishment of a Jewish united kingdom is not highlighted. But the Jewish dispersion is endorsed and introduced as a result of the Roman actions: 'Bar Kokhba revolt against Romans, Roman retaliation results in dispersal of many Jews, ending Palestine's autonomy' (Smith 2013: 10).

Zionist historiography tends to consider Zionism as the crowning of Jewish efforts to return to the homeland and the final representative of the Jewish redemptionist efforts that started right after the expulsion and lasted for two thousand years of diaspora. Against this claim, the book considers Zionism a modern phenomenon different from the Jewish traditional attachment to Zion:

> Modern Zionism differed from the traditional Jewish yearning to return to Zion, Eretz Israel, in that religious Jews viewed the matter as one to be decided by God. Just as their exile reflected Yahweh's punishment of Jews for their transgressions of His Laws, so would their return indicate that He had granted them redemption, a redemption that many believed could occur only when the end of the world was at hand.
>
> Smith 2013: 26

Against this statement, 'the Jewish commitment to the idea of a return to Eretz Israel' is considered, in the book, as centuries' long reality that was a challenge to the assimilationist desire of Jews to be part of the French nation:

> The French Revolution of 1789 and its Declaration of the Rights of Man proclaimed the equality of all people as the basis for true citizenship. Jews were specifically offered the opportunity to assimilate as individuals into French society. Assimilation meant that Jews would presumably give up their commitment to retain their distinctiveness as a separate community adhering to Jewish laws and, with that, their commitment to the idea of a return to Eretz Israel, a hope that had bound them together for centuries.
>
> Smith 2013: 27

Furthermore, the Zionist historiography demonstrates more impact in this part; 'For Jews, Palestine was "Eretz Israel" the ancient land of Israel, the land they hoped to redeem as a modern Jewish state, a goal that was finally accomplished in 1948' (Smith 2013: 1). It is, of course, a Zionist claim that Jews, during their history, hoped to redeem the land as a modern Jewish state. It is similarly problematic to consider the establishment of Israel in 1948 as a goal that was hoped for by Jews throughout their history. This claim, as mentioned, is rejected later in the book, itself, when this hope is characterized as a 'traditional Jewish yearning to return to Zion' that 'viewed the matter as one to be decided by God' and not, in any case, a hope for establishing 'a modern Jewish state' (Smith 2013: 26).

The Zionist historiography makes tremendous efforts to sell religiously motivated migrations to the land, by few Jews, as instances of the redemptionist efforts to return 'home', and to establishing their own state. The book does not subscribe to these stories, saying: 'but during most of the century, the Jews who came to Palestine did so for their own religious motives. They were making their pilgrimage to the land of ancient Israel, many in order to die there' (Smith 2013: 24).

Unlike mainstream Zionist historiography, the book concedes a substantial place for an Arab history of the land. The second part of the book's first section, the Prologue, deals with this question; entitled 'The Arabs and the Spread of Islam'. This part presents how Muslims came to control the land in the seventh century, and how this development characterized the history of the land till the modern period. Muslim different treatments of the Jews, are also stressed in the book; 'Unlike the Byzantines, Muslim authorities did not interfere in doctrinal matters and allowed Jews to visit and inhabit Jerusalem' (Smith 2013: 7).

The whole of Chapter 1, 'Ottoman society, Palestine, and the Origins of Zionism', is designed to cover the remainder of the Arab history of the land from 1516 onwards. This chapter covers the land's history from 1516 to 1914 while the Ottomans controlled the land. This emphasis on the Arab history of the pre-Zionist era is not considered as a Zionist tendency. It is recalled that the Zionist historiography tends to ignore the Arab history of the land, and usually makes a 2,000-year jump, over the Arab history of the land, to succeed in this endeavour. The chapter has, also, other non-Zionist elements: it does not try to introduce the land of this time as a barren and empty land with a few strangers who lurk there waiting for its original owners to come and cultivate it. It demonstrates the lively social and economic life of the land prior to the arrival of Zionism. Neither does it support the Zionist claim of Palestine as a poor land that the Zionist settlers encountered when they came first: 'As these figures indicate a major expansion of Palestinian agricultural and industrial productivity occurred before Zionist colonization' (Smith 2013: 22). The book refers to the internal sources of economic prosperity in the land including in the fields of agriculture and pilgrimage. It also situates the Zionist contention of 'difference' (between pre-Zionist Palestine and its post-Zionist condition) in the land's prosperity in a reasonable context of the difference between traditional means of economy and the modern technology that was brought by Zionist settlers from the modern societies they came from in Europe, a phenomenon similar to what happened frequently in other European colonized lands (Smith 2013: 23–5).

The first chapter, also, deals with Palestinian nationalism and identity; unlike the Zionist historiography that uses nationalism as a tool to support the idea that a Jewish nationalism has been planted in a land free of nationalist identity in order to reject the idea of occupying the other's home to build one's own, it stresses the existence of Palestinian consciousness and their awareness of the land's boundaries, at least among the educated Palestinians: 'the new scholarship does suggest, however, that educated Palestinian Arabs considered themselves to live in Palestine, establishing an identity with a region defined by boundaries. This identification was not simply the result of their encounter with Jewish nationalism in the form of Zionism, as has often been assumed' (Smith 2013: 25).

The text does not disregard the application of a Western criterion of nationalism to determine a land's fate full of eastern characteristics of identity, but it, of course, discounts the value of such an approach. It also reveals how this idea is used in Zionist historiography to justify the Zionist claim to the land: 'Nationalism in the European sense was, however, part of Zionism and would be used to justify Zionist claims to Palestine, where a Jewish kingdom had existed two thousand years earlier' (Smith 2013: 26). The book's apparent approach to balancing the competing narratives leads, in some cases, to presenting contradictory statements with no formula to resolve the contradiction. In the concluding remarks of this chapter, for instance, the Zionist claim about Palestinian nationalism, as a phenomenon that emerged when Palestine encountered Zionism, can be identified: 'Among educated Muslims and Christians in Palestine, Zionism contributed to a growing sense of their common identity as Palestinians' (Smith 2013: 39). Another statement made in the book, about Palestinian national consciousness also does not correspond with the discussion presented earlier in this regard: 'Nevertheless, a predominantly Palestinian Arab population does not necessarily indicate the widespread existence of a Palestinian Arab national consciousness at this time' (Smith 2013: 25).

The book also deals, in this chapter, with the controversial matter of Arab immigrants to the land; the Zionist historiography, in line with the complementary lines of the Zionist mega narrative, tries to exaggerate the number of Arabs who might have migrated from the neighbouring lands to Palestine at the time when the Zionist settlers came to the land. But the book considers that as a limited factor: 'Arabs undoubtedly did migrate to Palestine or were settled by Ottoman officials there during this seventy-year period, but they probably comprised no more than 8 percent of the Arab population of Palestine in 1914' (Smith 2013: 25).

The chapter refers to the very different nature of the Jewish–Islamic relations in the land (in the pre-Zionist era) that were characterized by peaceful coexistence to the extent that each side took part in the religious ceremonies of the other; the Muslim Nebi Musa festival, celebrating the birth of Moses, is mentioned as one instance (Smith 2013: 39). The book can work, also, to clarify that these relations were interrupted by the Zionist movement. It is stated, in the opening of the Prologue, that 'Palestinian and other Arabs, Christian as well as Muslim, opposed this movement, not because of Jewish immigration per se, but because Jewish statehood would automatically deny political rights to Palestinian Arabs, as was made clear in the Balfour Declaration of 1917' (Smith 2013: 1). In this chapter, there is another non-Zionist approach when the Palestinian Jews are considered closer to Arabs than the Europeans who came to the land to materialize the Zionist project: 'Out of the approximately 85,000 Jews then in Palestine, 12,000 lived on the land. Most Palestinian Jews were in their dress and appearance not dissimilar from Arabs, part of a Middle Eastern society quite different from the vision imparted by the European Jews who now appeared' (Smith 2013: 33).

The chronology at the end of the book has elements that support the idea that the book does not follow a Zionist historiographical pattern; it starts with a Zionist contention of the 'Kingdom of Israel and Judah founded' (Smith 2013: Chronology). But no efforts are made, in this section, to install other main elements of the Zionist historiography; the united Jewish kingdom under David and Solomon, the Jewish dispersion, or any reference to their supposed attempts to return, for instance.

Summary of the Analysis

The book is not designed, I conclude, to advance a Zionist story of the pre-Zionist era: the Zionist history of ancient Israel is challenged in the book; the historicity of the Bible is discounted; the supposed Roman forceful expulsion is narrated in a different and milder wording; nothing serious about the supposed Jewish redemptionist efforts to return to the Holy Land is mentioned, and finally, the Arab history of the land is taken as a significant part of the land's history. The land before Zionism, in the book's account, is not an empty land that waits for the original owners, the Jews, to come back and make it prosper. At the same time, the dominance of Zionist mythology over the relevant literature is not regarded as a problem in understanding the history of the question. As a result, no real attempt is made to reveal the grave consequences of the Zionist influential narrative on how the history of the land is perceived. The book does not seek to free the history of the question from the Zionist mythology; it is regarded, alternatively, as a natural phenomenon that occurs under the influence of 'mainstream scholars'. The book, however, is successful in distancing itself from Zionist claims when it engages historiography but, at the same time, relies extensively on the Zionist histories for the provision of details. The accounts from both sides are offered in some cases, in an attempt, apparently, to create balance. This approach leads, sometimes, to contradictory accounts with no consideration of how this contradiction can be solved or how this contradiction in historical reports can relate to what really happened. As a result, the reader remains wondering which one represents the true history of the question. The book's account of the main elements of Israel's pre-Zionist history is mostly different from the Zionist history but is not, at the same time, very far from it, as demonstrated by this analysis, in various cases. The book, however, is a good example of a Western scholarly attempt to distance itself from the Zionist historiography, despite its incomplete achievements in doing so.

A Concise History of the Arab-Israeli Conflict

This book is co-authored by two scholars in the field, Ian J. Bickerton, from the University of New South Wales in Australia, and Carla L. Klausner from the University of Missouri-Kansas City in the United States. The first edition of the book was published by Prentice Hall in 1991. Three other editions have been produced in 1995, 1998 and 2001 before the book's title changes to *A History of the Arab-Israeli Conflict*. 'Concise' was removed from the title when the book grew in size from a 300-page monograph to a 448-page volume. The fifth edition and the sixth (2009) are published under the new title. The third edition of the book (1998, 335 pages) is taken for analysis in this study. This edition's contents are structured in eleven chapters that deal with the question's history in chronological order:

1. Palestine in the Nineteenth Century
2. Palestine During the Mandate
3. World War II, Jewish Displaced Persons, and Palestine
4. The UN, Israel Established, the First Arab-Israeli War
5. The Conflict Widens: Suez, 1956
6. The Turning Point: June 1967
7. Holy Days and Holy War: October 1973
8. The Search for Peace
9. Lebanon and the Intifada
10. Peace of the Brave
11. The Peace Progresses

More chapters are added to the volume in the later editions of the book, dealing with recent developments of the question including 'The Collapse of the Peace Process' and 'The Arab-Israeli Conflict in the Post 9/11 World'. These chapters are preceded by a preface and then an introduction, and are followed by a conclusion. The book is furnished with a noticeable number of charts, maps and tables that enhance its position as a common textbook. All chapters are equipped with relevant original documents and a suggested list for further reading. Some segments of the book, those relevant to the analysis in this study, are examined for the sake of this research, including the following ones:

- Preface
- Introduction
- Chapter 1: Palestine in the Nineteenth Century
- Conclusion

The index is used, in the final stage, to spot any relevant content that might have gone unnoticed through the earlier stages of the analysis. The survey demonstrated that the book is taken as a textbook in four countries of the survey: the United States (118 syllabi), Canada (8), the UK (5) and Australia (5). These results suggest that the book is adopted widely in the United States and Australia; indeed, it is the most adopted textbook, on the question's history, in American academia. But the overall ranking of the book introduces it as the second most adopted textbook in Western universities, having been adopted, altogether, in 136 academic courses. The citing figure of the book in Google Scholar, 146, is not high compared with other selected textbooks but is sufficient to introduce it as a main reference for relevant scholarly works.

The book does not say much about the way it treats the history of the question; it stresses, however, 'balance' and 'objectivity': 'we have attempted to achieve some balance and objectivity about a subject upon which most people feel it necessary to adopt a partisan point of view' (Bickerton and Klausner 1998: xvi). It recognizes that there are two histories on two sides of the question, introducing the book's approach as based on presenting both while confessing that this approach does not free it from subjectivity: 'Throughout the book, we have tried to present both sides of the issues, although we realize that even the selection of material to be included reveals some subjective judgment on our part' (Bickerton and Klausner 1998: xvi). There is a brief attempt in the book to reveal its main goal: 'The primary object of this book is to make the Arab-Israeli conflict more intelligible without the distortions that result from oversimplification' (Bickerton and Klausner 1998: 2). This statement might be too general to reveal something meaningful about the book's attitude. What has been added to this statement suggests some sort of 'claim equality' as a leading theme of the text: 'Both the Arabs and the Israelis are locked into the histories they have created for themselves – into the dreams of their pasts. Both also seek to set in our minds favorable cultural images and symbols of themselves and unfavorable ones of their opponents' (Bickerton and Klausner 1998: 2). This can also mean recognizing the fact that there is a pro-Israeli history, besides a pro-Palestinian one, and the necessity of keeping at a distance from both in the interest of grasping the truth.

Analysis

The book's treatment of the pre-Zionist history of the question, and of 'ancient Israel' in particular, is truly concise; no particular part is designed to cover the history of that time. Numerous references, however, are made in different parts of the book, especially in the Introduction and Chapter 1, which can provide a picture of that time for the reader. The Introduction is, in fact, the main place where this picture is depicted. One paragraph, more than any other segment of the book, offers the history of 'ancient Israel':

> Judaism has gone through several stages in its long history. The first stage could be said to be that described in the Hebrew Bible, consisting of the Torah, the books of the Prophets, and a collection of other writings such as Kings, Chronicles, Ruth, Esther, and the Song of Solomon. It tells of the Jews' search under Moses for the land promised them by God after their expulsion from Egypt (the Exodus) and describes the Kingdoms of David and Solomon. The boundaries of Solomon's kingdom, with Jerusalem as its capital, included the

areas called Judea and Samaria, and extreme religious and nationalistic groups today insist that these biblical and historical boundaries of Eretz Yisrael, or the Land of Israel, must remain under Jewish control.

Bickerton and Klausner 1998: 5

The main elements of the Zionist historiography of the ancient time – the (Jewish) kingdom of David and Solomon, Jerusalem as the capital of the Jewish kingdom, and the boundaries of the kingdom (that take in the whole of historical Palestine) – are incorporated in this narrative but the Hebrew Bible is introduced as the source of this story. What comes before and after this statement, however, has the power to introduce the story as a report of history, and not only as a religious tradition; the pre-narrative statement (that Judaism has gone through several stages in its long history) introduces the narrative as a report of history. This has been confirmed after the narrative again when boundaries of Eretz Yisrael are called not only 'biblical' but also 'historical'. The language of the book, however, appears more accommodating of pro-Israeli historiography, when the remaining part of the ancient history is at stake; when it is not conditioned by a particular source it is narrated as a true report of what happened:

> The northern part of the kingdom, or Samaria, was conquered by the Assyrians in 721 B.C.E. The Jews of the southern kingdom, or Judea, were exiled to Babylonia in 586 B.C.E. after the destruction of the First Temple built by Solomon in Jerusalem, which had become the center of Jewish worship until it was destroyed by the army of King Nebuchadnezzar.
>
> Bickerton and Klausner 1998: 5

The Jewish kingdoms of 'Samaria' and 'Judea' and their supposed fate are introduced in this part. A Jewish Autonomy is, also, suggested as the last chapter of Jewish ancient settlement in the land. The Roman expulsion of the Jews is suggested as the main factor responsible for the termination of Jewish control of the land; 'Restored to Palestine by the Persians, the Jews built a Second Temple in Jerusalem and lived autonomously under a succession of foreign rulers until 70 C.E. when the Romans destroyed the Second Temple and dispersed the Jews (the Diaspora)' (Bickerton and Klausner 1998: 5). The rest of the text reveals that the Zionist historiography did not leave its footprint just on the generalities of the book but on its details; 'One of the last strongholds to fall to the Romans was the hillside fortress known as Masada. The Israeli slogan "Masada shall never fall again" has come to symbolize Israel's determination to fight to the death to maintain its national sovereignty. It is thus significant that recruits of the Israel Armoured Corps swear their allegiance at Masada' (Bickerton and Klausner 1998: 6). The role of the Roman treatment of the Jews in the Jewish disappearance from the land has been discounted, however, in the next chapter of the book (Chapter 1):

> Most historians agree that Jews migrated from Palestine voluntarily long before the Christian epoch, forming merchant classes around the Mediterranean basin.

The destruction of the Second Temple by the Romans in the year 70 C.E. led to a considerable increase in the number of the Jewish Diaspora, as those Jews who lived outside Palestine were called, and they were gradually transformed into a mercantile class.

Bickerton and Klausner 1998: 21

There are other references to 'ancient Israel' in other parts of the book, usually when other matters are at stake, which reinforces the Zionist narrative of the era. The following is one example:

Jerusalem also occupies a special place for Muslims. Sura (or chapter) 17 of the Qur'an recounts a mystical night journey of Muhammad to Jerusalem, to a spot known today as the Temple Mount, the platform upon which Solomon's and later Herod's Temple once stood. From here, he ascended to heaven for a vision of Allah. The Western Wall, all that remains today of Herod's Temple, and the Muslim shrines known as the Dome of the Rock and the al-Aqsa Mosque on the Temple Mount are important symbols for Jews and Muslims, and Jerusalem is a focal point of the Arab Israeli conflict.

Bickerton and Klausner 1998: 7

The book articulates historical Palestine as a homeland for both Jews and Palestinian Arabs, but the definition it provides of homeland is influenced heavily by the Zionist narrative:

The most important aspect of landscape to the Jews and Arabs of Palestine is the concept of homeland and the meaning attached to this concept. Almost all concepts of homeland have included the notion that such a place is the center of the world and that it is of supreme value. A homeland is usually tied to a specific location spiritually; it is a place to consort and speak with the gods, and continuity with the location takes on a special meaning, with dislocation causing chaos. This was especially true of the ancient religions. We must also keep in mind that the value people attach to such concepts are historically as well as culturally derived. A homeland provides nourishment, permanency, reassurance, and an identification with the soil, and it provides historical ties of identity. Looked at in this way, we can quickly see that Palestine takes on special significance to the two groups who have been in such bitter conflict for almost a century.

Bickerton and Klausner 1998: 10–11

This idea of 'homeland' is reinforced in other statements of the book: 'There has been, and still exists, a very close link between the landscape and the pattern of settlement in Palestine. These patterns, reinforced by historical, cultural, and religious experiences, reflect fundamental attitudes that the inhabitants, both Arabs and Jews, hold about the region and their identification with it as place and homeland' (Bickerton and Klausner 1998: 14). Moreover, there are other cases of referring to the land as the Jews' homeland in the book: 'This aspiration tapped another trend among the traditionalist Jews of Eastern Europe – that of preserving Judaism and the Jewish tradition through the reestablishment of a religiously based Jewish culture located in the traditional Jewish homeland Eretz Yisrael' (Bickerton and Klausner 1998: 25).

The book takes the Jews as a people, a nation that has existed since ancient times. But the statements it makes on this matter are contradictory in some instances. There is one instance, at least, of distancing from such a Zionist claim: 'Although Jews consider themselves a people, as do the Arabs, Jews are not simply a nationality, are not a race, and are more than a religion. They are at once an ethnic group, a religious group, and a cultural group' (Bickerton and Klausner 1998: 4). The book forgets this position when granting Jews, clearly, the status of a people, in another part of the book: 'Judaism is unique in that it is a religion limited to one people ...' (Bickerton and Klausner 1998: 9). Furthermore, Jews are recognized in the book as a nation: 'The coming together of these two aspirations – one secular, the other religious – led to the birth of modern Zionism as a political ideology and organizational tool, and it contributed to the settlements that became the foundation of the economic, social, and cultural rebirth of the Jewish nation' (Bickerton and Klausner 1998: 25). Other relevant Zionist claims are also taken as history in the book; rejecting the idea of Jewish converts, thus providing a safe space for the introduction of all Jews of different colours and nationalities as one people, is confirmed in the book; 'Although in many respects Judaism and Islam are similar, important differences exist that lead to tension between the two religious groups. While Judaism is not a proselytizing religion, and does not seek converts ...' (Bickerton and Klausner 1998: 9). The book takes a clear Zionist approach to the history when considering the European Zionists who came to Palestine in the twentieth century and claimed the land, as the same Jews who supposedly lived in the land thousands of years ago. This idea is reinforced when the book blames Palestinians for their treatment of the Jewish settlers as outsiders: 'Jews are seen by Arabs as violent and cowardly, ignoring the ancient ties of the Jews to Palestine, the Arabs regard them as aliens, as outsiders, as interlopers who do not belong' (Bickerton and Klausner 1998: 5).

No particular section is designed in the book to report the main bulk of the land's history, a time period after Roman control of the land in the first century and before the arrival of Zionist immigrants in the twentieth one, a period of almost two millennia when Jews, except for a few, were absent in Palestine. The Zionist historiography, as mentioned earlier, tries to fill this self-constructed gap with the Jews' history in other places where they, supposedly, consider Palestine as their homeland, making efforts to return to it. The book accommodates this constructed gap but what it offers to fill it with, 'the redemptionist efforts,' is quite limited; 'The Jewish return to Jerusalem and to Zion (Mount Zion, which came to stand for the Holy City and the Holy Land) became a central part of Jewish ritual and ceremonial practice' (Bickerton and Klausner 1998: 6). Besides confirming the Jewish attachment to the land in this period of time and the prayer to return, it rejects the idea that Jews have taken practical steps to return to Palestine before Zionism could change their condition:

> Many Zionists have explained the increase in Jewish settlement in Palestine as a reflection of the growing appeal and strength of Zionism. The difficulty with this explanation is that, despite the deep feeling of attachment to the land of Israel, which is such a distinctive feature of Jewish self-identity, the simple reality is that Jews did not move to the land of Zion, a land they prayed to be delivered to three times a day. This is the paradox of Zionism. Only about 1 percent of the almost 3 million Jews who emigrated from Russia in the thirty-five years following 1880 went to Palestine, and very few emigrated from Western Europe.
>
> Bickerton and Klausner 1998: 27

This non-Zionist assertion does not lead the book to question the Zionist claim of a Jewish striving to return; the rest (of the statement) justifies it in fact: 'Zionism was not the answer to the "Jewish question" for the great majority of Jews. This is largely because Zionism was not seen as a solution to the traditional Jewish problems of economic, political, social, religious, and racial oppression in Europe' (Bickerton and Klausner 1998: 27). The book provides two other notions that support the idea that Jewish nationalism, i.e. Zionism, was not a modern invention, but a reality that governed Jewish history in the diaspora. The first notion is that of 'cultural' or 'religious' nationalism: 'Like Arab nationalism, Jewish nationalism remained a religious and cultural phenomenon until the nineteenth century, when the idea of creating a Jewish state in Eretz Yisrael assumed the character of a political ideology' (Bickerton and Klausner 1998: 19). In this notion, all the religious and cultural attention paid by the Jews of the diaspora to the Holy Land is interpreted as a political and national reality. 'Modern Zionism' is the second notion that introduces Zionism as a modern version of a traditional Jewish movement that existed long before Herzl, as a long-standing character of Jewish life in the diaspora. In this way, Jewish messianism is regarded as an earlier version of Zionism whereas Zionism is called secular messianism. Zionism, according to this book, has not invented a new ideology; it 'transformed the passive, quietistic, and pious hope of the Return to Zion into an effective social force' (Bickerton and Klausner 1998: 27).

Like many Zionist histories of the land, Palestine before the Zionists' arrival is portrayed very negatively as a poor and insecure land:

> Palestine had been a poor and neglected part of the Ottoman Empire. Over the previous two centuries, local governors had become independent of Ottoman control, had become corrupt, and had neglected their duties. The result was that there was considerable disorder and insecurity: public works had not been carried out; agriculture and trade had declined: and the majority of the population were impoverished and oppressed.
>
> Bickerton and Klausner 1998: 16

The book, at the same time, takes a non-Zionist turn while introducing improvements brought to the land by Ottoman Emperor, Sultan Abdul-Hamid II:

> During the second half of the nineteenth century, the Ottomans gradually reestablished central control, Bedouin attacks became less frequent, general security increased, oppression of the urban population diminished somewhat, and the European powers greatly expanded their involvement in Palestine, as in the rest of the Levant. As a result, the area's economy and the conditions of the inhabitants significantly improved. Under Sultan Abdul-Hamid II, who ruled the Ottoman Empire from 1876 to 1909, important changes took place in Palestine. Abdul-Hamid encouraged modernization in communications, education, and the military in order to strengthen his control. When he began his rule, Palestine had no railroad, hardly any carriage roads, and no developed port. There were few medical services, and disease and illiteracy were widespread. Within a few years of accession, new roads were opened. And European companies completed a railroad between Jerusalem and Jaffa in 1892 and another between Haifa and Deraa, Transjordan, in 1905.
>
> Bickerton and Klausner 1998: 16–18

The Zionist historiography needs to provide some background of Jewish authority / Jewish independence in Palestine; having no chance to mine these notions from the established history of the land, it employs the religious traditions of Judaism for such a purpose; in this enterprise, a Jewish sense of authority, in a tribal context or in any kind of autonomy under former kinds of political organization, is taken as an instance of Jewish political control of the land. This Zionist historiographical machine works in the opposite direction when the same land, but populated with Arab Palestinians, is at stake; there is a tremendous effort to portray Palestine, before Zionism, as a land free from any character of political power, a condition, according to Zionist history, that lasted for centuries before it was remedied by Zionist Jews. This book, like many other books in the field, has been influenced by this Zionist construction: 'Under Ottoman rule, which lasted four centuries (1516–1918), Palestine never formed a political administrative unit of its own' (Bickerton and Klausner 1998: 16). The Zionist historiography, for understandable reasons, deprives Palestine not only of any political administration/power but of any political identity as well. The idea of nationalism is used in Zionist histories for such a purpose. The Palestinians are introduced as a people free from nationalist feelings before encountering Zionism. This Zionist history is confirmed in the book; 'As a result of all the factors mentioned above, there was no strong impetus toward Palestinian nationalism among the Muslim Arabs during this period' (Bickerton and Klausner 1998: 19). According to this report, Palestinian nationalism is formed only later, and as a response to a genuine and stronger nationalism: 'As time passed, nationalist sentiment among Arabs, including those in Palestine, also grew as a response to the strong nationalist feelings of Jews toward Palestine, or Eretz Yisrael (the Land of Israel)' (Bickerton and Klausner 1998: 19).

Summary of the Analysis

The analysis of the book suggests the idea that it reproduces the bulk of Zionist history in relation to 'ancient Israel', the exile and the history of the Jews in the diaspora. The limited – and noticeable in some cases – distance placed between the book and Zionist historiography is acknowledged in the analysis. Having said that, the Zionist metanarrative of the land has been accepted, more or less, as factual history in this textbook. The book has been influenced by other Zionist narratives, including that on Jewish political independence outside Palestine; the book not only ignores these polities but rejects their existence:

> Judaism differs from both Islam and Christianity in one important respect however. Both Islam and Christianity were militarily and politically successful over the centuries, establishing empires or states in which their respective beliefs and principles were put into practice. Judaism had no such experience from the destruction of the Second Temple in 70 C.E. until the establishment of Israel in 1948.
>
> Bickerton and Klausner 1998: 9

The overall analysis of this book, however, does not produce the conclusion that it is a Zionist work, not because of the limited but significant reservations it makes when delivering the Zionist historiography, but because of the genuine sympathy it shows with the Palestinian rights to the land, a factor that is absent in Zionist histories. The book advances, in this way, some sort of 'claim equality'; it considers both Jews and the Palestinian Arabs as peoples with true links to the land: 'It is impossible to understand the depth of feeling on both sides without an awareness of the ecological or environmental relationship that exists between the Jews and Arabs who inhabit the region, as well as the historical and cultural ties that link the two peoples to the land' (Bickerton and Klausner 1998: 11). The book's enthusiasm to provide some sympathy with both sides of the conflict through establishing the claim equality to the land introduces some misleading problems, however; first of all, the difference between myth and fact is suppressed in this approach. No serious efforts are made to question the narratives provided by Zionist historiography, including those that have no convincing evidence in any established history of Palestine, such as narratives of ancient Israel or the Roman expulsion of the Jews. This is in fact at odds with what the book itself recommends to students of history:

> The distinction between the past and the present is an artificial one; there is only the present. But constructing and controlling 'the truth' about the past to justify one's actions in the present is an important function of all political activity, and one task of a student of history is to separate the rhetoric designed by both sides to create a usable, legitimizing, and heroic past from the reality of past events.
>
> Bickerton and Klausner 1998: 2

The declared necessity of separating the rhetoric from the reality of the past is undermined by the book's attempt to sympathize with, and accommodate both sides of the conflict. This approach proves more problematic, leading to serious mistakes, when advancing the claim equality. Introducing the conflict as the extension of a historical rivalry/battle between Jews and Arabs over the land, a struggle that has existed, according to the book, since biblical times, is one instance: 'Many see the Arab-Israeli conflict as the present-day extension of enmity that has existed since biblical times. The issues underlying the conflict strike at the heart of the identity of the peoples involved. In addition to being the contemporary expression of a historic territorial battle over Palestine between two traditional ethnic rivals, Jews and Arabs' (Bickerton and Klausner 1998: 1).

In this vein, religion is introduced as a reason for Jews and Arabs to oppose each other in Palestine, neglecting a millennium-long history of Jewish-Arab peaceful coexistence in the Holy Land. There is considerable emphasis on the religious aspect of the question; and on the 'differences between Islam and Judaism' as a prominent feature responsible for the conflict: 'A key question in both religions as far as the Arab-Israeli conflict is concerned is: What is the attitude of the religion to the outsider. Both religions are ambiguous and contradictory in relation to this question. They make positive and negative references to others and are both welcoming and exclusive' (Bickerton and Klausner 1998: 9).

The results of this analysis do not introduce the book as a history that is structured to advance a Zionist version of the Palestinian-Israeli conflict. But it introduces the book as a work that is influenced heavily by Zionist historiography. The book does not take a critical attitude toward Zionist historiography. It takes it for granted in many cases, defining a Jew for instance, according to the terms provided by one side, the Jewish side, and accepting this definition as a true representation of reality: 'The term Jew can be best applied to those who have a Jewish mother, or who call themselves Jews because of conversion to Judaism' (Bickerton and Klausner 1998: 4). The book, however, takes a critical position towards the role of the West in the question. 'Orientalism' and 'anti-Semitism' are introduced as two Western destructive ideologies that have influenced the conflict. Islam and Christianity are also blamed for what went wrong in this question but Zionism and Judaism are exempted from such critical treatment while reporting the pre-Zionist history of the Israel-Palestine question (Bickerton and Klausner 1998: 4).

Righteous Victims

This book is written by Israeli author, Benny Morris, a Professor of History at Ben-Gurion University in Israel, and published by numerous publishing companies including Vintage Books in New York. The first edition of the book, which covered the history of the conflict from 1881 to 1999, was published in 1999. The edition used for this study is the reprinted one that was published in 2001 with the inclusion of a new final chapter, and covers the history of the conflict to that year.

The textbook is a long volume, about 800 pages, which offers the history of the question in fourteen chapters; the last one deals with Barak's government: 'Ehud Barak's 19 Months'. Some portions of the book, those that are seen as relevant to the pre-Zionist era, are examined for the sake of this analysis; they include the following parts:

- Preface
- Chapter 1: 'Palestine on the Eve'
- Chapter 2: 'The Beginning of the Conflict: Jews and Arabs in Palestine, 1881–1914'
- Conclusions

The index is used, in the next phase, to find relevant parts in the book that might be missed in the earlier examinations. The textbook has widespread usage in academic courses; the survey that was conducted for this purpose suggests it as the third most adopted textbook in Western universities. It is one of two books, the other being *Palestine and the Arab-Israeli Conflict*, that are adopted in all six countries of the survey. The main difference between these two texts lies in the fact that, unlike Smith's book, this textbook is not used widely as the main textbook of the course. This survey demonstrates that it has been adopted, altogether, in 123 syllabi: 82 syllabi in the United States, 18 in the UK, 15 in Canada, 4 in Ireland, 2 in Australia and 2 in New Zealand. The Google Scholar citation figure also confirms its extensive impact in the academic arena where 459 is suggested as a number for citations of the book in other academic publications.

The book starts with a preface where some useful information about its perspective of the question's history is provided; the first statement introduces this history as an attempt to 'relate the entire story in an integrated fashion, covering Israel, the Palestinians, and the Arab states from the 1880s to the present' (Morris 2001: xiii). The next clarification indicates that the political and military aspects of the conflict, and not the economic and cultural ones, are being focused on in this historiography. It is also mentioned that little attention is given to the internal politics of the conflicting societies. The writer introduces his approach to the history as a rejection of the maxim that 'there is no foreign policy, only internal politics' (Morris 2001: xiii). The last clarification, mentioned in the Preface, spells out that the book's history is based on secondary sources, and does not constitute a work that is produced by analysis of original historical documents itself (Morris 2001: xiii).

Analysis

The textbook has its own way of treating the question; it is categorized as a version of historiography out of the traditional Zionist realm, representing a critical work, with, at the same time, the potential to reinforce Zionist mythology. Its Preface might shed some light on this matter: first of all, it considers all works produced to date in this field as biased historiography: 'Almost from the start the subject has been treated with emphatic partisanship by commentators and historians from both sides, as well as by foreign observers' (Morris 2001: xiii). The book regards this bias as a characteristic that comes from the question's nature, and one difficult or impossible to avoid: 'There is a built-in imbalance in scholarly treatments of the conflict; this study is no exception' (Morris 2001: xiv). This is not, of course, a typical Zionist position on the historiography produced on the question. In this line, this book, similar to other writings of Benny Morris, is full of critiques of the Zionist narratives that no classic Zionist history can dare to offer. Lots of accounts offered by the book challenge the classic Zionist history. The whole historical evidence that is used by the Zionist side to write the question's history is undermined in the book: 'By and large, the documents contained in them were written by Zionists, in a Zionist context and from the Zionist perspective. This has almost inevitably affected the historiography based on these documents' (Morris 2001: xiv). The Arab view of the question has found its way into his historiography in many cases. At the same time, the work tends to put the Zionist historiography, even criticized or challenged, in a relatively higher position, where its superiority over Arab history is not lost. This can be seen in the book's general arguments about the subject as well as in its treatment of particular cases: 'At the same time the Zionist side tends to be illuminated more thoroughly and with greater precision than the Arab side, and this applies to both political and military aspects' (Morris 2001: xiv). Another general statement in the book can reconfirm this as well: 'Though Jewish officials, generals, and politicians have often also been self-serving and subjective in their published recollections, and past generations of Zionist-Israeli historians have been less than objective, they have been substantially more accurate and informative than their Arab counterparts' (Morris 2001: xiv). For having such a tendency, the book, like other of Morris's writings, might be seen as a work that challenges the traditional Zionist claims as well as Arab alternative accounts at the same time in one way, and, in the next, favours the Zionist story over its Arab rival, usually through the conclusion. Having said that, however, this might not be the case in all matters raised in the book.

The Preface does not have any reference to the history of the pre-Zionist era; Chapter 1: 'Palestine on the Eve', is the main place where that history is offered. The book, in fact, has no independent segment to present such a history; it is very brief about ancient Israel for instance. This can come from the book's fundamental choice to limit its coverage to a period, 1881–2001, which is located out of the pre-Zionist era. It also can show some kind of distance from the standard Zionist historiography where the pre-Zionist era has a noticeable place in the overall history of the question; if so, such distance, as can be seen through the following analysis, is quite limited.

The main reference to ancient Israel is made in the opening of Chapter 1:

> Toward the end of the millennium [the second millennium BCE] the Hebrews, or Jews, invaded and settled the land, and for most of the next millennium constituted the majority of the population and governed the bulk of the country.

The core of the Jewish state (at one point there were two Jewish kingdoms) was
the hill country of Judea, Samaria, and Galilee.

Morris 2001: 4

This statement, although very brief, is powerful and clear enough to register the land as a property of the then Jews, considering them the majority of the population, where they, by establishing the Jewish state, governed the land for 'most of the millennium'. Although this account does not mention the details of the Zionist narrative, it contains the central story, which is the main base for the Jews' historical right to the land. No means of distance or academic reservation is made here that might offer the story as a contested claim, or a story that lacks enough evidence to be introduced as a historical fact. The second chapter, 'The Beginning of the Conflict', is started by a quotation that enforces this claim: ' "Who can challenge the rights of the Jews in Palestine? Good Lord, historically it is really your country," wrote Jerusalem Muslim dignitary Yusuf Diya al-Khalidi to Zadok Kahn, chief rabbi of France, on March 1, 1899' (Morris 2001: 37). Another quotation, this time by a Jew, is offered in the book that has the same function:

Vladimir (Ze'ev) Dubnow, one of the Biluim, wrote to his brother, the historian Simon Dubnow, in October 1882: 'The ultimate goal ... is, in time, to take over the Land of Israel and to restore to the Jews the political independence they have been deprived of for these two thousand years.... The Jews will yet arise and, arms in hand (if need be), declare that they are the masters of their ancient homeland.'

Morris 2001: 49

Such an assertion is confirmed in the Conclusion of the book where 'Palestine' is introduced as a land 'where the Jews had lived and ruled during the first millennium B.C.' (Morris 2001: 676). Somewhere else in the book, Palestinians are blamed for not recognizing this fact: 'The Palestinians, from the start, never really understood the Zionist claim to the land. They were not aware of or didn't care about the Jews' roots in the country' (Morris 2001: 678). With all this, the book is, almost, free from details provided by the Bible of ancient Israel; no Jewish king, Saul, David or Solomon, is mentioned in the book as such. One mention of Solomon is registered with clear distance: 'But no agreement was reached on the future of the walled Old City and, more particularly, the Temple Mount (Haram ash Sharif) area within it, containing the Dome of the Rock and the al-Aqsa Mosque as well as the (presumed) underground remains of King Solomon's and Zerubabel's (and Herod's) temples' (Morris 2001: 659). One exception (of that quality), at the same time, is identified where Solomon's ally is mentioned in the book: 'The four-brigade attack was called Operation Hiram, after the Lebanese king of Tyre who had been King Solomon's ally three millennia before' (Morris 2001: 245).

In Chapter 1, where the main statement about ancient Israel is made, as above, another Zionist claim, the Jewish expulsion, is passed on as a historical fact: 'The chapter of Jewish sovereignty ended when the Romans invaded and then put down two revolts, in A.D. 66–73 and 132–35, and exiled much of the Jewish population' (Morris 2001: 4). This assertion is reinforced through remarks made by a French high-ranking official:

> On June 4, 1917, the director general of the French Foreign Ministry, Jules Cambon, issued the declaration that was to serve as a precedent and basis for the more significant Balfour Declaration: 'You [Sokolow] ... consider that, circumstances permitting, and the independence of the Holy Places being safeguarded ... it would be a deed of justice and of reparation to assist, by the protection of the Allied Powers, in the renaissance of the Jewish nationality in that land from which the people of Israel were exiled so many centuries ago.'
> Morris 2001: 74

The next phase of the Zionist historiography, in the main Zionist story of the pre-Zionist era, entails the Jewish redemptionist efforts to return to their homeland. The book, unlike the way it deals with earlier Zionist myths where one paragraph, at least, is designed to lend credibility to Zionist historiography, has no such statement to articulate the 'Jewish redemptionist efforts' which constitute another pillar of the 'Jewish historical right' to the land. Another technique, however, is used here to make such Zionist claim reasonable: Zionism, being a movement to return to the 'homeland', is introduced, somehow, as a movement with old roots in the Jewish tradition: 'Zionism – the drive for the return of the Jews to, and sovereignty in, Eretz Yisrael – was rooted in age-old millenarian impulses and values of Jewish religious tradition' (Morris 2001: 14). Zionism is introduced, in the book, as a secularized version of a Jewish long-standing goal: 'The mid- and late-nineteenth century saw the rapid secularization of the millenarian-Zionist goal amid an increasingly secularized Jewish population' (Morris 2001: 14). For this reason, the Zionist idea is introduced as 'completely natural, fine and just' (Morris 2001: 37). According to the book, the idea of 'return' was the original core of the story, that has been bound to the religious tradition of the past and to the secular idea in the modern era when Zionism arose:

> The return to Zion was conceived as a social and political act that would remedy the Jews' abnormal existence as an oppressed minority in the Diaspora. But ever since the Jews' exile from the land at the start of the first millennium A.D., the idea or vision of a return had been closely bound up with the cosmic, messianic theme of collective redemption and salvation.
> Morris 2001: 14

Diaspora, in its Zionist meaning, is used in the book, in this regard, without any distance. Jews who joined the Zionist movement to transfer to Palestine are taken as the same Jews who, supposedly, were expelled from the land two thousand years earlier; a position that represents typical Zionist historiography of the case.

Another element of Zionist historiography, as mentioned earlier, is that of undermining the Arab history of the land. This long and established history is discounted through different ways in the book: first of all, there are some accounts that exhibit the land as a barren and inhabitable land; Chapter 1 begins with the topic 'The Land and the People'. The opening of this section is a statement by Mark Twain about the land, in 1867, and its negative characteristics:

> Of all the lands there are for dismal scenery, I think Palestine must be the prince. The hills are barren.... The valleys are unsightly deserts fringed with a feeble vegetation that has an expression about it of being sorrowful and despondent.... It is a hopeless, dreary, heartbroken land.... Palestine sits in sackcloth and ashes.... Over it broods the spell of a curse that has withered its fields and fettered its energies.... Nazareth is forlorn; ... Jericho accursed ... Jerusalem ... a pauper village.... Palestine is desolate and unlovely.
>
> Morris 2001: 3

This depiction is taken, with some distance, as a fact by the book: 'He may have been indulging in hyperbole, but then neither was Palestine, in the mid-nineteenth century, the "land of milk and honey" promised in the Bible' (Morris 2001: 3). Later in this chapter, when the book describes Palestine before the arrival of Zionism, Morris uses many statements to portray such an image of the land: 'Through the nineteenth century the population was plagued by diseases such as malaria, trachoma, dysentery, cholera, and typhoid fever. Water supplies were inadequate and frequently impure' (Morris 2001: 6). A number of elements such as drought, Ottoman high taxation, Bedouin banditry and health hazards are suggested to picture Palestine as an 'insecure and poor' land that was inhabited by a weak and primitive society: 'Agriculture was primitive, with little irrigation' (Morris 2001: 5). The picture provided in the book is not so radical, to support, blindly, the idea of 'the land without people' but it, of course, sympathizes with that. The book, in fact, refers to some positive points of nineteenth-century Palestine. More importantly, it considers, in Chapter 2, this idea held by the first Zionist settlers about Palestine as a misconception:

> Many First Aliyah immigrants believed that they were coming to a desolate, empty land and were surprised to find so many Arabs about. After all, they were returning to their Promised Land; no one had spoken of anyone else being there. There is one testimony by Yosef Chaim Brenner, the Second Aliyah's leading novelist, saying on this point: 'Before going to Palestine, the country, for some reason, appeared in my imagination as one city inhabited by non-religious Jews surrounded by many fields, all empty, empty, empty, waiting for more people to come and cultivate them.'
>
> Morris 2001: 42

Another testimony is used later in the book to describe the same situation:

> Ahad Ha'Am, the leading Eastern European Jewish essayist, opened many Jewish eyes when he wrote, in 1891, after a three-month visit to Palestine: 'We abroad are used to believing that Eretz Yisrael is now almost totally desolate, a desert that is not sowed but in truth this is not the case. Throughout the country it is difficult to find fields that are not sowed.... Only sand dunes and stony mountains... are not cultivated.'
>
> Morris 2001: 42

In relation to the Arab history of the land when Arab Palestinians dominated the land for more than a millennium, and formed its population and society, the book has no statement to articulate that. On the contrary, it uses a different historiography to discount this history, considering Arabs as only one of many people who controlled the land after the supposed Jewish expulsion: 'After successive invasions and counterinvasions by Persians, Arabs, Turks, Crusaders, Mongols, Mamelukes, and (again) Turks, the country – at the beginning of the nineteenth century, under imperial Ottoman rule – had a population of about 275,000 to 300,000 people, of whom 90 percent were Muslim Arabs, 7,000 to 10,000 Jews, and 20,000 to 30,000 Christian Arabs' (Morris 2001: 4).

The book acknowledges the Arab population, as an overwhelming majority in Palestine, as Morris stated in the last quotation. This fact, however, does not make the Zionist historiography register the land as having a Palestinian identity. The Zionist historiography, as mentioned earlier, borrows the Western idea of nationalism to claim this oriental land populated by Palestinians, who form every aspect of this Arab society. This borrowing allows the cancellation of a Palestinian right to govern the land of their own simply because they, unlike Jewish people, had no qualification to form a nation:

> Yet, despite the indisputable presence of Arab communities in most areas of the country, the Jews, down to the 1920s, were right on one level: They themselves were the only 'nation' or 'people' in the country: The Arabs simply did not exist as a Palestinian people – as another, competing nationalism. The small minority of politically conscious Arabs saw themselves as part of the wider 'Arab nation' or of the 'Greater Syria' polity.
>
> Morris 2001: 678

Palestinian nationalism, the book asserts, emerged sometime later, and mainly as a response to the Jewish nationalist movement: 'It was at this time [First World War and its aftermath], too, that a distinct Palestinian local patriotism or proto-nationalism began to emerge. This tendency or orientation – it hardly qualified as a movement – gradually groped its way forward, largely in reaction to the burgeoning Zionist presence' (Morris 2001: 34). This 'first come, first served' game, that introduces the Palestinians as being too late to form a nation is introduced as the main reason why Jews occupy the country: 'Zionism emerged about a quarter of a century earlier than Arab nationalism, a head start in political consciousness and organization that proved vital to the Jews' success and to the Palestinian Arabs' failure during the following decades of conflict' (Morris 2001: 26). The context of the Jewish right to the land is simple and straightforward in this history; the colonial domination of the Ottoman Empire collapsed in the First World War. In other parts of this colony, nationalist movements established their own countries. The process in Palestine encountered a specific problem where two nationalist movements emerged to fill the gap produced by Ottoman withdrawal; Jews, one of the two, succeeded because they were earlier to take the chance:

> The Ottoman Empire was no more. In the lands south of Turkey there emerged over the years, under French and British tutelage, the states of the Arabian Peninsula, Syria, Lebanon, Transjordan (from 1948 Jordan), and Iraq. And there emerged the problem of Palestine, where, under the umbrella of the British Mandate, two national movements, Arab and Jewish, vied for dominance and, eventually, statehood.
>
> Morris 2001: 32

A main point about Morris historiography of pre-Zionist history is that of how he treats Islam as a main contributor to the conflict; unlike many other historiographies, even Zionist ones, which consider the Christian/European treatment of the Jews as a main reason for the rise of Zionism, and for what happened subsequently in Israel-Palestine, this book highlights the role of Islam in these happenings; Islam, first of all, is introduced as an anti-Jewish religion: 'The Koran is full of anti-Jewish asides and references' (Morris 2001: 9). Islam is seen in this historiography as a religion with a fundamental problem about Judaism: 'From the beginning, Islam suffered from the natural jealousy of a successor or "child" toward the monotheistic parent religions from which it sprang, Judaism and Christianity' (Morris 2001: 9). The hostile attitude to Judaism, according to the book, is codified in Islamic regulations since the beginning: 'Muhammad's relations with the Jews, and subsequent Koranic attitudes, were eventually embodied in the treaty of submission to Muslim rule, or writ of protection, known as the *dhimma*, or Pact of 'Umar, extended by Muhammad's successor, the second caliph, 'Umar 'ibn al-Khaṭṭāb (634–44)' (Morris 2001: 9). Against all the facts about how Islam treated others, Christians and Jews, far better than other powerful religions treated minority faiths, it is introduced as a religion with deep xenophobia: 'The principle of equality – between believer and nonbeliever as between man and woman – is alien to Islam, and the Islamic world, normally in conflict with Dar al Harb in one region or another, has traditionally exhibited a deep xenophobia' (Morris 2001: 8–9). In this endeavour, the historical fact that equality between believer and non-believer, and between women and men, did not exist in that period of history, and the fact that this perception of equality comes from modern ideas that managed to govern human societies very recently, is ignored. Islam's 'evil' treatment of the Jews is introduced right in the opening of the section on 'Islam and the Jews': 'Islam generally, and the Ottoman Empire in particular, treated the Jews in its midst as second-class citizens' (Morris 2001: 8). The golden time the Jews experienced under Islam would bring no credit, according to the book, to Islam: 'During the Islamic High Middle Ages, c. A.D. 850–1250, Judaism and the Jews had flourished, and would later designate the period a "golden era" of Jewish history' (Morris 2001: 8). But their occasional (presumed) poverty under Islam is regarded as a 'result of discriminatory practices': 'Other restrictions had nothing to do with security and everything to do with religious and economic discrimination, and Jewish poverty in most of the Ottoman lands in the nineteenth and early twentieth centuries appears to have been, in some measure at least, the result of discriminatory practices' (Morris 2001: 10).

After making those general statements about Islam's treatment of Jews, that is characteristic of this textbook, the longest list ever (as far as I have explored in Israel-Palestine histories) of Islam's 'crimes' against Jews is delivered. In this historiography the whole history of Islam as a religion which tolerated Judaism far better than other religions, and the fact of the Islamic world being a refuge for Jews during the long Islamic history is granted no value or relevance: 'Nevertheless, in general the Jews under Islam seem to have fared better than the Christians – if only because the former, usually poor, often abject, always powerless, were a threat to no one' (Morris 2001: 10). The well-established Islamic tolerance of Jews is undermined repeatedly in the book:

> 'Contemptuous tolerance,' in the phrase of historian Elie Kedourie, came to be the attitude adopted by Muslim states toward their Jewish communities. This stance was generally mixed with a measure of hostility, especially in times of political crisis. Tolerance was then superseded by intolerance, which occasionally erupted into violence. Throughout, Muslims treated the *dhimmi*, and perhaps especially the Jews, as impure.
>
> Morris 2001: 9–10

Against all the evidence of Islamic tolerance of Jews in history, the underlying attitude of Islam is introduced in line with the writer's pessimistic style: 'But the underlying attitude, that Jews were infidels and opponents of Islam, and necessarily inferior in the eyes of God, prevailed throughout Muslim lands down the ages' (Morris 2001: 11).

In this way, the history of Jews in Islam, according to the book, has a foreseeable summary: 'throughout they [the Jews] suffered discrimination, humiliation, and a sense of insecurity. Occasionally they were subjected to persecution and violence' (Morris 2001: 8).

This Islamic position towards the Jews has influenced, according to the book, the Israel-Palestine question:

> The history and tradition of Muslim attitudes and behavior toward the Jews was to affect profoundly the unfolding of Turkish-Zionist and Arab-Zionist relations in Palestine. The view of the Jews as objects, unassertive and subservient, was to underlie to some degree both the initial weak, irresolute Ottoman and Arab

responses to the gradual Zionist influx into Palestine – Why bother, the Jews could achieve nothing anyway! – and the eventual aggressive reactions, including vandalism and murder – the Jews were accursed of God and meant only harm; their lives and property were therefore forfeit.

Morris 2001: 13

The book here is reporting the history of the Arabs' treatment of Jews in modern Palestine, which entails both soft and hard reactions; the soft treatment of the immigrant Jews before the Balfour Declaration, and the hard reaction of the Palestinians when they encountered the Jewish claim to their land. The book does not record any credit to Muslims for being that soft to Jews. It is taken, astonishingly, as evidence to regard Muslims as anti-Jewish. In this way, however Muslims treated Jews, soft or hard, both prove their anti-Jewish position (Morris 2001: 13). Islam, according to the book, is not only responsible for the aggression shown by Muslims in the conflict, but also for the aggression committed on the Jewish side: 'Muslim attitudes to some degree affected the Zionist colonists in Palestine. They drove the colonists, at least during the early decades of Zionism, toward occasional over-assertiveness and even aggressiveness in an effort to wipe out the traces of their traditional, and for them humiliating, image' (Morris 2001: 13). Later in the book Islam, again, is introduced as a main source of the Arab-Israeli conflict: 'Islam posited the inalienability of land conquered by Muslims. Such tracts became automatically part of the divinely sanctioned Dar al Islam' (Morris 2001: 39). This statement of the book is explaining why Arabs resist the establishment of a Jewish state in Palestine, no matter whose land is this.

Summary of the Analysis

As the analysis demonstrates, the book, although different from classic Zionist histories, can pass on all the main elements of the Zionist mythology of the pre-Zionist era as historical facts. The biblical stories of ancient Israel are not acknowledged, but what Zionist historiography tries to pass on, by numerous names, dates and events taken from the Bible, is accepted, in a wholesale fashion, without bothering to prove Solomon's power, for instance, or locating his palace. The exile of Jews, as another element of the Zionist historiography, is confirmed as a historical fact on several occasions in the book. Zionism is described, by the writer, not as a recent European phenomenon, but as a modern version of Jewish long-standing tradition to return to their homeland. It is also introduced as a genuine national movement that emerged in Palestine when it was free from a nationalistic character. The long Arab history of the land is discounted in an exceptional way; Arabs are placed beside others, like Persians and Mongols who invaded the land and controlled it for a while. This has been reinforced by introducing Islam and Islamic history as a key factor that contributed to creating the conflict between Arabs and Jews in Palestine. Furthermore, no traces of any analytical doubt or academic scepticism that might challenge these contested, if not fake, claims are located in the book.

A History of the Israeli-Palestinian Conflict

This book is written by Mark A. Tessler, Professor of Political Science at the University of Michigan. The book was first published in 1994 in the United States. The second edition of the book was published, under the Indiana series in Middle East Studies, in 2009 by Indiana University Press. Consisting of 1,018 pages, the book is a long volume that deals with all phases of the history of the question, but it is more detailed on the events of 1948 and afterwards. The book's contents are organized into six distinct parts, the last one on the Palestinian Intifada and the Oslo Peace Process. Some portions of the book's second edition, only those relevant to the analysis in this study, are examined for the sake of this research, including the following ones:

- Preface to the Second Edition
- Preface
- Part I: 'Jews and Arabs Before the Conflict: The Congruent Origins of Modern Zionism and Arab Nationalism'
- Part II: 'Emergence and History of the Conflict to 1948'

The index is used, in the final phase, to explore any relevant content that might have gone unnoticed through the earlier stages of the examination. The survey demonstrated that the book is taken as a textbook in many courses related to the history of the question but this is not the case in all six countries of the survey. It is adopted in only three countries of the survey; the United States (61 syllabi), the UK (19) and Canada (13). But the figure coming from the total number of adoptions (in related courses) introduces it as the fourth most adopted textbook, having been adopted, altogether, in ninety-three academic courses. The figure cited for the book in Google Scholar, 356, demonstrates, also, its position as a main reference for other scholarly works.

The book, in its Preface, and also, in the Preface to the Second Edition, reveals some significant points about its perspective to the history of the question; it stresses first the book's robust scientific orientation. The loyalty to the relevant principles of objectivity, accuracy and non-partisanship is made clear in several statements: 'my aim has been to maintain a stance of considered objectivity. I have tried to represent both sides fairly when fundamental issues are discussed' (Tessler 2009: xvii). The book is introduced, in this respect, as a work that does not advocate a specific conclusion; 'My goal is not to foster specific conclusions about central issues in the conflict but to provide a basis for understanding and evaluating the actions of both Israelis and Palestinians' (Tessler 2009: xvii). The book's main mission is described as providing the arguments of both sides leaving the conclusion to the reader: 'the volume strives for a nonpartisan point of view; it seeks to present both Palestinian and Israeli analyses and to enable readers to form their own conclusions about the persuasiveness of competing arguments' (Tessler 2009: xvii).

This book might seem to take up a substantial distance from its stated position, first, when it advocates 'an engaged and sympathetic understanding of the parties to the conflict', a particular approach that is described by the book as 'objectivity without detachment' (Tessler 2009: viii). Objectivity, accuracy or any other truth-oriented value might be undermined when providing sympathy with the parties (of the conflict) is a priority. Such a position also might pave the way for a historiographical strategy which is referred to in the relevant literature as 'equal claims'. This strategy of prior rejection of all conclusions for the sake of one, claim equality, might fall in contradiction with the stated aim of this history i.e. objectivity; it also has the power to regulate the history of the question in a certain way, and might suppress the objectivity and other truth-oriented objectives when they do not provide such a conclusion. The claim equality is articulated, more evidently, somewhere else in the book, when it is introduced, also, as a fact rooted in history: 'The present study rejects these tendencies and offers a different approach. It assumes that both Israeli Jews and Palestinian Arabs have legitimate and inalienable rights. These rights are rooted in the historical experience of each people' (Tessler 2009: xiv). The 'equal claim' principle is taken further when both sides are entitled to the same sum of respect or condemnation: 'Consistent with this approach, the book presupposes that the Israeli-Palestinian conflict is not a struggle between good and evil but rather a confrontation between two peoples who deserve recognition and respect, neither of whom has a monopoly on behavior that is either praiseworthy or condemnable' (Tessler 2009: xiv–xv). This position is described in the book as '"approach-approach" perspective' (Tessler 2009: xv). It is revealed in the book, however, that this perspective is taken, partly, for practical purposes: 'This approach to the Israeli-Palestinian conflict is advocated not only in the name of objectivity and historical accuracy but with a conviction that there is practical value to what might be called an "approach-approach" perspective' (Tessler 2009: xv).

In this vein, the book exhibits its eagerness to provide some sort of middle way solution to the question. The partition of Palestine is introduced as a legitimate solution to the question, consistent with the equal claim strategy. The powerful enthusiasm of the book for such a solution might make it incapable of recognizing the conflicting objectives of Zionism and Palestinian aspirations: 'It demonstrates what an accurate reading of history shows to have been the case all along, that there is nothing about the essence of Zionism or of Palestinian nationalism that makes it impossible even to conceive of a solution to the conflict' (Tessler 2009: xviii). This preferred solution is supported wholeheartedly in another statement, flavoured by some kind of offensive positions against those who oppose such a solution: 'The principles of territorial compromise and mutual recognition appear to be supported by a majority on both sides of the conflict. To be sure, on both sides there are also hard-liners and rejectionists, those who for ideological reasons oppose territorial compromise and recognition of their longstanding adversary' (Tessler 2009: xviii). The book displays its highest point of perspectival confidence when, against numerous facts on the ground, and all the facts about the contradictory ends of the opposing parties of the conflict, considers 'psychology' as the main essence of the Arab-Israeli conflict:

I thus remain convinced that one of the biggest obstacles to peace, and arguably the biggest obstacle of all, is psychological in character. Peace will be possible if, and almost certainly only if, each side and its supporters reject the view that the Israeli-Palestinian conflict is a struggle between good and evil, accept the legitimacy of the other side's aspirations, and conclude from the history reported in this book that neither party has a monopoly on behavior that is deserving either of respect or of condemnation.

Tessler 2009: ix

Analysis

The main body of the book starts with a section (Part I) on 'Jews and Arabs Before the Conflict'. Two key reasons are offered for providing this survey. The first one is a non-Zionist one; 'There are several reasons to begin a study of the Israeli-Palestinian conflict with a general survey of Jewish and Arab history. One is to dispel the common misconception that the current struggle in Palestine is an extension of an ancient blood feud, fueled by ethnic or religious antagonisms dating back hundreds of years. This view is not only inaccurate ...' (Tessler 2009: 1). The book stresses, in this section, the fact that Arab hostility towards the Jews is a post-Zionism phenomenon; 'Present-day issues must be approached with a recognition that neither the Arab-Israeli dispute in general nor the Israeli-Palestinian conflict in particular is based on or driven forward by primordial antagonisms, and that it has in fact been less than a century since Jews and Arabs began to view one another as enemies' (Tessler 2009: 1). Typical Zionist historians, in contrast, try, often, to detach Zionism from the mess it created in Arab–Jew relations.

The second reason is rather different; it is based on a contention that there is a substantial symmetry between Arab and Jewish histories: 'There is also a remarkable congruence between Jewish and Arab history, and herein resides yet another reason to examine the experience of each people prior to the conflict in Palestine. Indeed, this may be the most important reason of all in the long run' (Tessler 2009: 2). This argument can work, when developed in certain ways, to advocate claim equality. Several instances of such tendency are offered in the book. The following is one: 'Thus, during their respective classical periods, Jews and Arabs both possessed the elements of peoplehood and transformed themselves into viable political kingdoms, with the members of each polity united by respect for an authoritative legal system and by shared bonds of religion, culture, and civilization' (Tessler 2009: 3).

The textbook is relatively detailed when treating Jewish ancient history; almost all the different chapters of Jewish ancient triumph, according to the biblical stories, are offered as the true history of the land. This history starts with the first chapter when Moses, supposedly, led his people towards the Holy Land:

Biblical record and archaeological evidence indicate that the Jews conquered and began to settle the land of Canaan during the thirteenth century before the

Christian era (B.C.E.). Moses had given the Israelites political organization and led them out of Egypt, bringing them to the borders of the Promised Land. Then, under Joshua, they initiated a prolonged military campaign in which they gradually took control of the territory and made it their home.

Tessler 2009: 8

The book, here and later, tends to rely on the Bible as a source of factual history. There are a few cases of making some distance from the biblical stories but the book, as a whole, remains very close to a position known as 'maximalist' where the Bible is regarded as a source of factual truth about history. The first instance of such a distance came just after the above-mentioned statement:

Most contemporary scholars believe that it took the Jews many decades to establish hegemony over Eretz Yisrael, and that even after it was secured and occupied, Canaanite enclaves remained for some time. Despite accounts in the Book of Joshua which suggest that the land was conquered in a single campaign, planned in advance by Moses and later Joshua, other Biblical testimony is consistent with those archaeological indications suggesting a struggle that lasted as much as a century.

Tessler 2009: 8

As this case demonstrates, such seeming distance from one biblical story is grounded on other biblical accounts as reliable sources of historical truth. Generally speaking, the language of the book is quite confident about what happened thousands of years ago in ancient Israel, similar to what is presented, in this regard, by the holy books: 'In any event, by the twelfth century B.C.E., the period of Judges, the Jews were firmly established in ancient Palestine, and the area of their control included substantial tracts of territory on both sides of the Jordan River' (Tessler 2009: 8). This confidence allows Tessler to provide a detailed map (map 1.1 in the book) of the territories controlled by the Jews at that time. The book's history continues with later developments of Jewish ancient accomplishments: 'The Israelite political community developed steadily, marked by the growth of national consciousness and the emergence of national institutions and reaching its apogee during the period of monarchical rule under David and Solomon' (Tessler 2009: 8). David and Solomon are taken as true historical figures in the book, and their religious stories are presented as historical facts:

David, who ruled until 960 B.C.E., greatly expanded and strengthened the Israelite kingdom. He had initially established his capital in Hebron, in the region of his own tribe, Judah, but within a few years he captured Jerusalem from the Jebusites and made it the center of his growing empire. Soon the kingdom of the Jews stretched from the Red Sea in the south to what is today the southern part of Lebanon, and from the Mediterranean Sea in the east across the Jordan River to Ammon and Moab.

Tessler 2009: 8, 10

As in this case, the book is quite assertive about its knowledge of ancient time providing the exact time, place and even details of ancient developments including, for instance, girls who come from the ruling families in Solomon's time; 'sealing some of them through marriage to women from the ruling families of foreign states' (Tessler 2009: 10). It is noteworthy that nothing is found in the book that constitutes some kind of scientific distance from such religious stories, or giving some awareness that this might not represent what really happened that far in the past. The reader/student takes these religious stories as historical facts if he relies on this textbook for the question's history. The Jewish ancient achievements continue, according to the book, in Solomon's time:

> The kingdom continued to develop and remained united through the reign of Solomon, David's son, who presided over a period of comparative peace and governed the country until 930 B.C.E. Solomon's accomplishments included construction of the royal complex in Jerusalem, consisting of the palace and the Temple; expansion and fortification of many other cities; and creation of an integrated political system for governing the country's twelve administrative districts.
>
> Tessler 2009: 10

Till now, and before the conquest of ancient Israel by its neighbours, the book adds 'several centuries of independence' to the Zionist historiographical account. Confirming this 'fact' the book provides more 'precise' details of Jewish independence when describing the Babylonian invasion: 'for the first time in more than four hundred years the ancient Middle East was without an independent Hebrew state' (Tessler 2009: 11).

In line with providing the 'precise' details of ancient historical developments, the book shows no scientific reservation about the use of exact figures; 42,000, for instance, as the number of exiled Jews who were 'repatriated in an initial wave of immigration' to return to Palestine after Cyrus dealt with Babylon (Tessler 2009: 11). A firm date is, also, offered for the construction of the supposed second temple; 'the Temple in Jerusalem was rebuilt between 520 and 515 B.C.E.' (Tessler 2009: 11). The book is articulate in re-establishing Jewish independence by providing more 'facts' on ancient Israel. The first phase occurred at the time of Cyrus: 'Judea was granted the status of a semi-independent territory, with Jerusalem its capital and the laws of the Holy Torah its constitution, and Jewish leaders were permitted to exercise authority over all the inhabitants of Judea' (Tessler 2009: 12). This semi-independent condition was followed by later fully fledged independence, according to the book: 'in 142 B.C.E. the Seleucid king, Demitrius II, also recognized the independence of Judea. Thus was established the Second Jewish Commonwealth in Palestine' (Tessler 2009: 12). This supposed independence, according to the book, expands to cover all the lands conquered earlier by David and Solomon: 'The kingdom also grew stronger under the Hasmoneans, so that, with the growing disintegration of the Seleucid Empire, it was able to recapture Samaria and other parts of *Eretz Yisrael* lying outside

Judea. At its zenith, it controlled almost as much territory as had the kingdom of David and Solomon more than eight centuries earlier' (Tessler 2009: 12, original italics).

This way of dealing with ancient Israel that passes on, without scholarly reservation, some religious traditions of a holy book as scholastic facts is far from a fair and fine academic historiography. This way of dealing with ancient Israel misleads college students, those who read and rely on the textbook as a source of scientific history; those who should be able to recognize ideas from facts in history, those who should understand what really happened in the past; those who should understand the past through reliable evidence or sources, those who should be able to differentiate between a fact and a fiction, those who should learn how the past is distorted and misused for the sake of present; those who should know about Zionism interfere in understanding the past in Palestine for obvious ideological reasons; these students are left to believe that biblical stories of the past are true histories of the land, as Zionists wish. The religious stories of the 'Holy Bible' are reproduced and converted into scientific history in such textbooks.

It has been mentioned earlier in this book that the main source of these accounts are holy books; no other reliable textual source provides such a report of history. Archaeological evidence also has no power to transform these stories into established facts. Some of them refute such a possibility, indeed. Most events mentioned in ancient Israel in this textbook are located in a time so far from us and so close to the prehistoric era that no unbiased historian dares to report it as the true history of that time, let alone providing details with such assertion and precision. Biblical stories (of ancient time) or relevant archaeological evidence might provide the chance for historians to provide some ideas or theories about what happened at that time. It is a legitimate undertaking, accordingly, if a history reproduces all those details about ancient Israel, and makes readers aware, at the same time, that this report is based on a specific source, the Holy Bible for instance, and those details are not counted as established facts: it is but one report of that time. Introducing those ideas as established facts, in contrast, is an offence against the most respectable principle that a modern history is based on: keeping a scholarly distance from historical myth, and claiming a historical fact only if relevant documents and evidence allow that. Such treatment of history does not serve a scholarly historiography, it serves Zionism in our case, and provides a chance for this aggressive ideology to claim a land that belongs to others.

The Zionist image of the land is completed, in the book, when the Romans' intervention is introduced as the main reason responsible for interrupting 'the ancient Jewish independence': 'Thereafter, at least from the time of Moses, Canaan was the center of Jewish life until the Hebrews were driven into exile by the Romans in the first century' (Tessler 2009: 287).

The second part of the Zionist mythology, the forced expulsion of the Jews from Palestine, is represented as a historical fact on numerous occasions in the book but in contrast with the history provided on ancient Israel, it is not detailed. No separate paragraph elaborates, in fact, this part of Zionist historiography. The book's treatment of the question is quite brief: 'Further, the movement of the Jews into a period of exile and dispersion was sealed by the tragic consequences of revolts initiated by Bar Kochba and others in the second century' (Tessler 2009: 13). Other references to the Jewish expulsion are made when other subjects are under discussion: 'even after the people of Israel had been driven into exile and dispersed' (Tessler 2009: 7).

The next part of the Zionist mythology entails the diaspora time when, according to Zionist historiography, Jews continued to consider Palestine as their homeland, kept the hope to return to it, and made redemptionist efforts to realize that hope. The book has a lot in common with this Zionist historiography. The biggest service it might make to supporting the Zionist history of this time is the innovative construction of Zionism as a genuine Jewish movement that lasted the whole era of the diaspora, first in the form of classical/traditional Zionism and then through the fashion of modern Zionism. In this way, Zionism is introduced as a Jewish movement that arose right after the 'Jewish expulsion', and was sustained until modern times when it experienced a transformation into a modern form:

> Following destruction of the Second Jewish Commonwealth in Palestine and dispersion of the Jewish people, Jews reaffirmed their chosenness and continued to think of themselves as a political community. Moreover, these notions came together in the form of Zionism, not modern political Zionism but rather classical or traditional religious Zionism, in which Jews expressed their belief that God would in the future bring about an ingathering of the exiles and restore the children of Israel to the Promised Land.
>
> Tessler 2009: 16

The constructed concept of classical Zionism has the capacity to carry the main elements of the Zionist historiography of this era:

> Classical Zionism proclaimed the Jews' continuing and unbreakable tie to Palestine, to the territory they regarded as *Eretz Yisrael*. According to one scholar, 'Despite the loss of political independence and the dispersion of the Jewish people, the true home of the Jews remained Jerusalem and the Land of Israel; the idea of eventual return from the four corners of the earth was never abandoned.' Moreover, the notions of return and an ingathering of the exiles were visible and salient within the lives of Diaspora Jews. As summarized by one present-day analyst, perhaps with slight hyperbole,
>
>> Most aspects of Jewish life in the Diaspora were intimately linked with Palestine. Jewish rabbinical law favored the settler in the ancient homeland. Religious literature echoed with such sayings as: 'It is better to dwell in the deserts of Palestine than in palaces abroad,' 'Whoever lives in Palestine lives sinless,' and 'The air of Palestine makes one wise.' There was no distinction between the spiritual and the physical Palestine in the minds

of most Jews. Although separated from the Holy Land by thousands of miles, to most it seemed closer than the neighboring Christian communities, which were regarded with hostility and fear.

Tessler 2009: 16, original italics

There are other statements constructed or quoted by the book to support such Zionist ideas; 'Jews further expressed their faith in a return to the Holy Land on many ceremonial occasions' (Tessler 2009: 19). The book acknowledges the religious and messianic properties of classical Zionism: 'Also central to classical Zionism is the notion of the coming of the Messiah, an event that the faithful believe will bring with it the millennium and be the occasion for the restoration of Jewish national independence in the Holy Land' (Tessler 2009: 16). Meanwhile, messianic beliefs, being part of the Jewish religious tradition, are taken as evidence to support the existence of diaspora everlasting Zionism:

> As expressed by Silver, three factors underlie the Messianic beliefs of the Jewish people: 'the loss of national independence and the attendant deprivations, the will to live dominantly and triumphantly as a rehabilitated people in its national home, and the unfaltering faith in divine justice by whose eternal canons the national restoration was infallibly prescribed.' These are the dominant and recurring themes of classical Zionism and the elements from which its political significance is derived. They include a lamentation of the Jewish people's exile from Palestine and subsequent dispersion, an affirmation that the Jewish nation's unity of purpose and tie to the Holy Land nonetheless remains and cannot be destroyed, and a profession of the Jews' unshakable faith that a restoration of their kingdom in *Eretz Yisrael* is part of God's plan and will accompany the arrival of Messiah.
>
> Tessler 2009: 19, original italics

In this vein, not only is the messianic religious message distorted, as shown above, into a political and national manifestation but messianic practices are also taken in a way that supports the Zionist idea:

> Although Messianic activity of this sort [those related to the coming of Messiah] was episodic, and usually confined to the more pious or even mystic elements of the Jewish community, other manifestations of traditional Zionist conceptions were much more routinized and widespread. Practicing Jews prayed daily for the time when the world would be delivered from evil and the people of Israel would be returned to Jerusalem.
>
> Tessler 2009: 18

The book makes some distance, however, between itself and Zionist historiography, in this regard, when recognizing that traditional Zionism is inspired by Jewish messianic beliefs, and does not entail any actual call to return to Palestine; it confirms, indeed, the opposite:

> While this constellation of beliefs continued to shape Jewish identity and thought into the modem era, Jews for the most part considered themselves passive before God. Indeed, this element of passivity, or patient anticipation, is also central to the definition of classical Zionism. Their sense of community and emotional attachment to *Eretz Yisrael* remained intense, but most Jews nonetheless did not believe it was appropriate to initiate steps toward the reconstruction of their national home in Palestine. On the contrary, such action would indicate a loss of faith and the absence of a willingness to wait for the creator's plan to unfold in its own divinely ordained fashion, and this, as a consequence, would rupture the covenant between God and the Jewish people and make illogical and illegitimate any proclamation of Jewish nationhood or any assertion of a continuing tie between Diaspora Jewry and the Land of Israel.
>
> Tessler 2009: 19–20, original italics

The distance becomes wider when the book admits that nothing notable happened, in the course of 'diasporic history', to signify a redemptionist effort by Jews to return to Palestine:

> It is for this reason, notes a prominent Israeli scholar, that the Jews' link to Palestine, for all its emotional and religious ardor, 'did not change the praxis of Jewish life in the Diaspora ... the belief in the return to Zion never disappeared, but the historical record shows that on the whole Jews did not relate to the vision of the return in a more active way than most Christians viewed the Second Coming.'
>
> These classical Zionist conceptions provided little motivation for a Jewish return to Palestine. As explained, quite the opposite was in fact the case; it would have been heretical for Jews to arrogate unto themselves the work of God, to believe that they need not await the unfolding of the Divine plan but rather could take into their own hands the fulfillment of a destiny for which they considered themselves chosen by the Creator. Thus, although there was an unbroken Jewish presence in Palestine from the destruction of the Second Commonwealth until the modern era, and while there were also periods of renaissance among the Jews there, during the early years of Ottoman rule in the sixteenth century, for example, the number of Jews residing in the Holy Land after the second century never constituted more than a small proportion either of the country's overall population or of world Jewry. Similarly, although small numbers of Jews traveled to Palestine from the Diaspora throughout the ages, sometimes making visits and sometimes going to settle, most sought only personal spiritual fulfillment and had no thought of contributing to the realization of political or nationalist objectives.
>
> At the dawning of the modern age in the latter half of the eighteenth century, only 5,000 or so of the estimated 2.5 to 3 million Jews in the world resided in Palestine.
>
> Tessler 2009: 20

This statement might constitute the most non-Zionist statement in the book of pre-Zionism history where the Tessler rejects the Zionist claim that diaspora history witnessed continuous Jewish attempts to return to Palestine, introducing Zionism as the last and the only successful one. The book, however, employs messianic Zionism as a source to support Jewish nationhood:

> As the preceding makes clear, traditional religious Zionism is inextricably bound up with the Jews' definition of themselves as a nation. The Messianic idea expresses and brings together the political, religious, and spiritual destiny of the Jewish people, making the bonds of their peoplehood not only a shared recollection of their Divinely guided history as a nation in Palestine and the sociological content of the law they struggle to observe in their communities scattered throughout the Diaspora, but also a firmly held conviction that they will be gathered together in the future and thus united as they were in the past.
>
> Tessler 2009: 19

The book's position on Jewish nationhood might represent one of the most pro-Zionist ideas of the book, where it supports, fully, the Zionist historiographical claim of considering the religious community of Jews as a nation. There is a clear emphasis on this in Chapter 1, 'Jewish History and the Emergence of Modern Political Zionism':

> It is inadequate to describe the Jews as a religious group in the modern-day sense of the term. Like Muslims, they are more appropriately regarded as a national community of believers. The Jews' sense of peoplehood is extremely well developed, inextricably bound up with their collective historical experience, with the Land of Israel where they built their ancient kingdoms, and with the sociological and political content of their law.
>
> Tessler 2009: 7

This is taken a bit further in another statement of this section: 'Therefore, again, the Jews are more than a religious group. They are also a historically legitimated political community possessing many of the attributes associated with nationhood' (Tessler 2009: 8). The book emphasizes, exclusively, Jewish religious law as a source that entitles Jews to the status of a nation: 'Interwoven with this experience in nationhood and these ties to the land of Palestine is the role of Jewish law in defining the peoplehood of the Jews' (Tessler 2009: 13). The book appears extremely eager, in another statement, to use all available sources to justify Jewish nationhood, raising its claim to the point where Jews can be perceived as the first nation in history:

> Thus, coupled with their historical experience in *Eretz Yisrael*, the law of the Torah and the Talmud makes the Jews a people, indeed a nation, rather than a religious group. The concatenation of these communal bonds produces a solidarity that is akin to nationalism, even though it is legitimized by an

understanding of Divine as well as natural and historical right. As expressed in the context of the modern-day world by Moses Hess, a mid-nineteenth-century Zionist thinker, this communal solidarity has made the Jews from the beginning of their history a nation in the modern sense – indeed the first such nation.

Tessler 2009: 15–16, original italics

It should be mentioned, at the same time, that the book does not use racial reasoning to support the Zionist claim of Jewish peoplehood. A thorough search in the book demonstrates, also, that the Holy Land has not been introduced as the ancestral land of the Jewish people. In contrast, it has been introduced in several cases, on pages 72, 73, 402, 433 and 439, as the ancestral land of the Palestinians.

The book's treatment of the Arab history of the land is, relatively, far from the Zionist historiography in several ways. It does confirm the ancient roots of the Palestinian people in Palestine: 'The Palestinians are descendants of two ancient peoples, the Canaanites and the Philistines' (Tessler 2009: 69). It affirms further their long possession of the land when considering them as a political community: 'The Palestinians do possess a sense of political community built, in part, on bonds and experiences that make them unique, including centuries of life in their ancestral homeland, their particular response to currents of reform in the nineteenth century, and subsequent confrontations with Zionism and European imperialism' (Tessler 2009: 72). The book, at the same time, does not go particularly far to emancipate its view of the Palestinian people from the Zionist emphasis on a Western idea of nationalism as a determinative factor in recognizing them as a people who own the land: 'Nevertheless, important as are these latter considerations, they did not come together to create and define a sense of Palestinian peoplehood, or nationalism, until the beginning of the present century' (Tessler 2009: 72).

Palestinian nationalism, however, is recognized as not less valuable than that of other Arab nations: 'One is to foster recognition that the late development of Palestinian nationalism represents a pattern that is common in the Arab world and, as a consequence, that the right to self-determination proclaimed by Palestinians is no less valid than that put forward by the Arab inhabitants of other territorial units' (Tessler 2009: 73). The book goes further, viewing the case from a wider, global perspective, to give further credit to Palestinian nationalism: 'It is thus no less indigenous, authentic, and genuine than that of dozens of societies whose claims to self-determination and national independence are today accepted without reservation' (Tessler 2009: 73). The book makes clear that the stake Palestinians have in the land entitles them to rule their own destiny in Palestine: 'It may be added that even were this not the case, Palestinians would still possess the right to reside in and rule over their ancestral homeland, managing their own affairs in accordance with the evolving will and consciousness of the majority of their country's citizens' (Tessler 2009: 73). The book, in this section, gives another non-Zionist credit to the Arabs of the land – they did not take an antisemitic view of the Jews of the land: 'A review of Arab history from pre-Islamic times until the present makes clear that this is not the case. Just as the history of the Jewish people has been shaped by both its own internal dynamics and the wider sweep of world events, and even in Palestine did not include a confrontation with Arabs until a century ago ...' (Tessler 2009: 73).

The image of the land, before the arrival of the first Zionist settlers, is mostly the one that is advanced by Zionist historiography: 'Palestine was poorly governed and marked by a climate of broad insecurity, which contributed directly to its underdeveloped character' (Tessler 2009: 123). Palestine, according to the book, was a land of diseases: 'In addition, such diseases as cholera, smallpox, and malaria were widespread, with epidemics common' (Tessler 2009: 124). These serious problems, according to Zionist historiography made it a piece of land without (a sizeable number of) people. This Zionist view is reflected in the book:

> These conditions forced land out of cultivation and disrupted agriculture, making hunger a serious problem in many areas. Trade and commerce were also discouraged by the unsettled circumstances of the territory, further reinforcing the country's impoverishment. These obstacles to development help to explain the small size of Palestine's population, which was approximately 300,000 during the latter part of the eighteenth century, or even less according to some estimates.
> Tessler 2009: 124

The book, however, provides some non-Zionist comments on that situation. First of all, the condition is described as similar to that in many other regions: 'Shaping the character of early contact between Zionists and Arabs was the fact that in the nineteenth century Palestine was among the less-developed regions of the Arab world. The circumstances of the country were by no means unique; the problems it faced, while serious, did not differ greatly from those confronting many other regions' (Tessler 2009: 123). It also refers to some improvement in the land's condition that is not related to Zionist involvement: 'Further, economic and political conditions improved noticeably during the last decades of the century, in ways, moreover, that had little to do with the arrival of the first Zionist settlers' (Tessler 2009: 123). An Ottoman sultan is introduced as the man responsible for this development: 'The poverty, lawlessness, and chaos of life in Palestine began to decline under the reign of Abdul Hamid, the Ottoman sultan who ruled from 1876 until 1909' (Tessler 2009: 125). It is made clear that these developments improved the condition of Palestine before an active Zionist presence in the land: 'Under these conditions, the standard of living gradually improved and the indigenous population began to increase. There was even a small amount of Arab immigration from northern Syria' (Tessler 2009: 125). This is not in agreement with the Zionist historiographical tendency that portrays the land as an uninhabitable place where living conditions improved only when the Zionist settlers came in.

Summary of the Analysis

In general, the book – as articulated in its Preface – tends to sympathize with both sides of the conflict: Palestinians and Israelis. This tendency regulates the arguments and conclusions offered by the book. There are efforts, hence, to portray a better and more understandable image of the conflicting forces in the land. This view not only advances the equality claim but also rejects any possibility of oppressor–oppressed or occupier–occupied relations between the two sides of the question. The Palestinians' history would be the main loser when such relations are ignored. It is notable that this tendency helps in some cases to exhibit a more understandable picture of the Palestinian case as well. The book seems willing to do this job. What limits the book's achievement in this area is its reliance, as a history based on secondary sources, on Zionist works. The book acknowledges, however, that there are biased works on both sides and tries to create a distance: 'Not surprisingly, Zionist supporters tended to minimize the figure, while pro-Arab sources inflated its magnitude' (Tessler 2009: 177).

The main concluding point about this textbook is related to the essential elements of the Zionist historiography of the pre-Zionist era: the book publishes, with considerable detail, the Zionist history of ancient times. All the Zionist claims about the Jewish ancient achievements in Palestine are presented as historical facts. Nothing is found in the book to raise some sort of scientific scepticism about the myths or contested claims promoted by Zionist historiography. The second element of the Zionist historiography is taken as such when the book takes the myth of expulsion as true history. The book makes no special effort to support this idea but it, clearly, takes it for granted, although with brief treatment. This brevity would not prevent the reader from relying on this story. In the next stage, the diaspora redemptionist efforts, the book places some serious distance between itself and the standard Zionist historiography when it rejects such happenings in Jewish diaspora history. It also confirms that the Jewish tradition not only made no call for redemption in Palestine but made the opposite – to be far from Zion – by calling it a divine plan.

The book, however, supports the main Zionist claim of this era; that Jews thought of Palestine as their homeland and hoped to return to it. The book acknowledges the religious and messianic property of such an attachment but this attitude is considered, according to the book, as a historical manifestation of Jewish aspiration, of a people who lost their home and hoped to return. An innovative notion, classical Zionism, is offered in the book with a power to translate all that happened in the Jewish history of the post-expulsion as redemptionist efforts to return to the homeland while the book admits, elsewhere, that such efforts did not taken place in practice. This notion, and its definition, can help to justify related elements of the Zionist historiography, and can legitimize the related Zionist claim. In this regard, the book emphasizes strongly the peoplehood of the Jewish people but it refrains from using racial reasoning or arguments to support the existence of such a nation. There is considerable reliance on biblical narratives as the authoritative sources of history. The history in this book, generally, is influenced by religious tradition. One instance can be seen when the book refers to 'false messiahs'; 'Messianic speculation continued through the ages, there being many false messiahs and many occasions when Jewish mystics proclaimed the Day of Judgment' (Tessler 2009: 17). It is evident, without a kind of reliance on religious traditions, there is no way to determine the falsehood of such messianic efforts.

The Arab history of the land also reveals a mixed treatment of the question; the book, similar to other Zionist histories, does not stress the long history of Arabs in the land. There is nothing to make the reader aware that the Jewish history of the land is not in a position to compete with the Arab history of the land; the difference between these two is very close to the difference between myth and fact; most of factual history of the land is located in the Arab era. The book, at the same time, refers, very briefly, to the centuries of Arab history of the land. Palestine before the arrival of the first Zionists is portrayed as a barren and dangerous land with a small population, as it has been exhibited in the Zionist historiography but at the same time, it considers this situation as not very different from that in other Arab lands, a consideration that might reduce the strength of the Zionist argument for a claim to the land. It also confirms that there were improvements in the land's condition before the Zionist involvement. This might further weaken the Zionist argument. The Palestinians are introduced as a distinct community but not as a nation. Palestinian nationalism is introduced as a late phenomenon, compared to that of the Jews, but not less valuable than other nationalist movements in other Arab lands. The book's treatment of the Arab history of the land is different from the standard Zionist historiography that tends to reject or weaken the Palestinian claim on Palestine. Such treatment of the question's history provides some space, as the writer wishes, for both sides to have something in the land they 'historically' belong to.

A History of Israel

This book is written by an American writer, Howard Morley Sachar, and published in the United States by Alfred A. Knopf publishing house in New York. The book originally was the first volume of a two-volume book when it was published first in 1976. The second one, *A History of Israel: From the Aftermath of The Yom Kippur War*, was written in 1979 to cover the history from 1974 onwards. At the time of the survey the latest edition was the third (2007), which covers the whole subject until the Israeli invasion of Lebanon in 2006. The book is now a long one, comprising 1,296 pages. It is a common source of reference on the history of Israel. Figures provided in Google Scholar demonstrate that it has been cited by 473 articles and books. It is, also, a book recommended by pro-Israeli groups as an 'authoritative' reading on the history of Israel (Rozenman 2004). The survey showed that it had been adopted as a textbook in five of the six countries of the research area: the United States (66), the UK (10), Canada (6), Australia (4) and Ireland (1), all together in eighty-seven extracted syllabi. As a result, it ranked in this research as the fifth most adopted textbook in Western countries, in the area of the history of Israel.

The book has forty-one chapters; the first thirteen are investigated for the sake of this research. Chapter 14 and the succeeding chapters deal with Israel's history after the establishment of Israel in 1948. It seems unlikely that any major reference to the pre-Zionist history of the land occurs in these unexamined chapters. The examined chapters are:

1. The Rise of Jewish Nationalism
2. The Beginning of the Return
3. Herzl and the Rise of Political Zionism
4. The Growth of the Yishuv
5. The Balfour Declaration
6. The Establishment of the Mandate
7. Building the Jewish National Home
8. The Seeds of Arab-Jewish Confrontation
9. Britain Repudiates the Jewish National Home
10. Palestine in World War II
11. The Yishuv Repudiates the Mandate
12. The Birth of Israel
13. The War of Independence

Analysis

This book has chosen to deal with Israel's history from the rise of Zionism as its title reflects; there is not a separate chapter or even a full paragraph to represent Jewish history in antiquity. There are certain parts of its contents, however, that deal, explicitly or implicitly, with pre-Zionist history under other subjects. The first one is presented right in the first lines of the book when French Jews' encounter Napoleon, and how they responded to Napoleon's nationalist call, is reported; French Jews, one can learn from the book, held a meeting in Paris to formulate their answer to twelve questions asked by Napoleon. This meeting is called, in the book, 'a modern version of the council [Sanhedrin] that had issued and enforced the laws during the Jewish Commonwealth of antiquity. The ancient body plainly had languished following the destruction of Jewish statehood at the hands of the Romans' (Sachar 2007: 3). The book used the opportunity, here, to present some history about ancient Israel, mentioning the 'fact' that there was a 'Jewish statehood' in Palestine that lasted until it was 'destroyed by Romans'.

Later in the book, another statement is constructed to report Napoleon's demands of French Jews, in return for what had been provided for them by the new French government: 'He demanded specific assurances that rabbinical jurisdiction in Jewish civil and judicial affairs was a thing of the past, that the Jews had turned their backs forever on their separate nationhood, on their corporative status, and not least of all on their traditional hope for redemption in Palestine' (Sachar 2007: 3). This assertion works to support the historicity of the Zionist claim that Jews considered themselves, before the rise of Zionism, as a separate nation, when Napoleon, allegedly, asked them to leave this position. A hope – to return to Palestine – carried by this 'nation' is immediately introduced here as another fact that characterized Jews before the Napoleonic era. This report is continued with the French Jews' answers to the questions asked by Napoleon: that 'they "no longer formed a nation"; and that they had renounced forever their dream of collective exodus to the ancestral Land of Israel' (Sachar 2007: 4). This sentence 'No longer formed a nation' which is part of the Jewish answer to question

5 is taken as a basis for supporting the Zionist claim that there was a Jewish nation, and there was an original Jewish dream of collective 'exodus' to Palestine which is defined by the book as their 'ancestral land'.

The knowledge provided by Shlomo Sand in *The Invention of the Jewish People* about the history of Jewish nationalism and its emergence in the second half of the nineteenth century informs us that using the term 'nation' shall not imply a reference to its modern meaning when it is used here in 1807. It might be used to stress the fact that French Jews are part of the French nation and do not see themselves in any other way. This can be seen more clearly if the relevant questions are taken into consideration. The quoted Jewish statement was part of the Jews' answer to the fifth question. The fifth question is asked in the context of the fourth one:

4. In the Jews' eyes, are Frenchmen considered as brethren or as strangers?
5. In either case, what relations does their law prescribe for them toward Frenchmen who are not of their religion?

Graff 2003: 77

As can be seen here, the questions posed are not about how Jews see themselves but how they view other Frenchmen who are not Jewish. This idea is supported in an answer to the next question, question 6:

6. Do the Jews born in France, and treated by the laws as French citizens, acknowledge France as their country? Are they bound to defend it? Are they bound to obey its laws and to follow all the provisions of the Civil Code?

Graff 2003: 77–8

The Jewish answer is reported thus: 'The response went on to declare that the Jews were so bound up with their country that a French Jew would feel himself a stranger in England, among Jewish company, and vice versa. Judaism was thus merely a religious confession' (Graff 2003: 86). With all this, even if Sachar's claim is valid, and this Jewish meeting in Paris used the term 'nation' in its modern sense, it is quite clear that he, in the wake of this French case, jumps to establish an overall conclusion, without providing further evidence from other cases, about all Jews in different European and American countries considering them a 'nation' with an aspiration to return to the 'ancestral land', i.e. Palestine. Sachar articulates this in the conclusion of the account:

To protect what they had achieved in civic freedom, moreover, Western Jews, in the United States and Europe alike, tended to accept the emerging nineteenth-century consensus that loyalty to a national state was incompatible with pluralism in cultures. In increasing numbers, they dropped the traditional allusions to Zion in their ritual observances and spoke of the messianic age less in terms of return to the Land of Israel than of a miraculous 'end of days,' or of an era of 'universal brotherhood.'

Sachar 2007: 4

This statement works to establish, again, that 'returning to the Land of Israel' was a Jewish national aspiration. This is not a fact. It is recalled that this is a Zionist claim produced by Zionist writers in the nineteenth and twentieth centuries. The statement also provides a justification, at the same time, for the fact that nothing significant can be found in the modern history of the Jews, in the United States or Europe, which demonstrates the Jewish attachment to such an aspiration. The Jews dropped the idea, the writer claims, for the sake of modern national rights in Western countries.

The next story that serves the same purpose is that of the Russian Jews:

> Among the most cherished features of the Russian Jewish cultural heritage, surely, was the memory of the ancestral homeland, the lost and lamented Zion that was enshrined in the ceremony and folklore of virtually every believing Jew. The truth was that throughout all the centuries of Jewish dispersion until modern times, Zion, hardly less than the Deity, functioned as a binding integument of the Jewish religious and social experience.
>
> Sachar 2007: 5

Here in support of another Zionist claim, Zion (Palestine) is introduced as the 'ancestral homeland' of the Jewish people. In the next sentence, the dispersion of the Jewish people from this land is confirmed. Later in this historical report, the religious obsession of Jews with the Holy Land is contextualized in a nationalist aspiration: 'Rabbinic and midrashic literature, the prayer book, medieval literary treatises, all displayed a uniform preoccupation with the Holy Land. Poets, philosophers, mystics, liturgists in Spain, North Africa, and Europe traditionally vied with one another in expressing the yearning of the People of Israel for the ravished cradle of its nationhood' (Sachar 2007: 5).

The dispersion from the national home was confirmed in another statement (of the book): 'Jewish festivities and holidays – Passover, Chanukkah, Sukkot, Shavuot – all evoked and refined memories of the departed national hearth' (Sachar 2007: 5). In a later statement, the writer establishes that Russian Jews, also, wished for a time in the future when 'redemption of the sacred soil' is realized: 'In the manner, then, of other ethnic-religious Eastern communities – of the Greeks and Armenians, for example – Russian Jews continued to nourish the vision of a future apocalypse, the redemption of the sacred soil' (Sachar 2007: 5).

In this section the writer produces another significant statement: 'On the other hand, the Jews of the Pale resisted all attempts to "force the end." In the seventeenth and eighteenth centuries the excesses and perversions of a series of false messiahs had burned their fingers badly. Messianism was transformed, rather, into attendance upon a halcyonic era that alone would signal final redemption in the Land of Israel' (Sachar 2007: 5).

This statement has the capacity to support the Zionist claims in two ways: first, it again stresses and supports the claim that there was a Jewish aspiration for redemption in Palestine, although it has been resisted. At the same time, it can provide some justification for why there was no sign of an actual step to signify such an aspiration; burning by 'false messiahs' made them not to 'force the end'.

The opening section, 'The Link with the Land', of Chapter 2, is the main place that Sachar supports Zionist historiography about the pre-Zionist era, including that related to 'ancient Israel'. The section starts with a report of some Jewish families in Peki'in, a village near Safed, that can 'demonstrate' – according to the book – the Jewish presence in the land from the ancient time: 'But authentic they are, these little Arabized Jews, the embodiment of a physical Jewish connection with Palestine that never quite expired' (Sachar 2007: 18). Here a claim by a few Jews about their continuous settlement on the land for more than two thousand years is taken as an evidence for the Zionist contention that the 'Jewish connection with Palestine never expired'. A statement is presented after that supports the historicity of the expulsion; 'The Romans may have laid the entire nation waste between A.D. 70 and 135, slaughtering as many as 600,000 Jews, and carrying off half that number in bondage. Yet even in the wake of this monumental dispersion, a few thousand Jews somehow remained on in the country' (Sachar 2007: 18). This presence also provides a context in a national sense, framing the settlement of a few Jews on the land as a 'remnant' of an ancient nation that has been expelled from the land.

In line with another Zionist myth these Jews who lived, supposedly, about two thousand years in an Arab community and spoke Arabic are not considered Arabs. Another term, 'Arabized' is constructed to put some difference between them and other Arab inhabitants of the land; Muslim and Christians for instance. This story is also a place where the destruction of the second Temple is presented as a fact while an old synagogue in the village is described: 'It is an ancient structure. We are informed that the two carved stones in its walls once belonged to the original Temple of Jerusalem, destroyed by the Romans more than 1,900 years before' (Sachar 2007: 18). 'We are informed' can mean that this is an ancient structure according to what is said on this matter in the village but the writer's business is producing a 'fact' when dealing with the 'Temple of Jerusalem' where an exact time for its destruction is also provided. The existence of this temple and where it was located is established in another statement; 'There, abutting the Haram el-Sharif complex of mosques, was the venerated Jewish Western Wall (often called the "Wailing Wall"), a remnant of the Hebrew Temple of antiquity' (Sachar 2007: 173). Other Zionist claims about Israel's antiquity such as Jerusalem being an 'ancient capital' of the Jewish state (Sachar 2007: 22, 23), and the existence of a Jewish kingdom under King David (Sachar 2007: 20) are passed on as history in this section. However, the main function of this section in supporting the Zionist mythology is the one which is constructed to establish the myth of continuous Jewish 'redemptionist efforts' to return to the homeland. Few migrations of a few Jews, similar to those that happened in almost all lands in which Jews lived, are taken for establishing two thousand years of Jewish efforts 'to return to the ancestral soil'.

A number of justifications are provided, also, to justify why, against all these efforts, the Jewish population was so limited on the land before the rise of Zionism.

In this regard not only contested stories are taken as facts but also kinds of factual statements are made that no fair historian can dare to provide for a time that far away: 'During the three and a half centuries of Roman dominion after the first century A.D., not a single Jew had been permitted to set foot in the ravaged capital' (Sachar 2007: 20). Many different reasons are provided, including the crusaders' involvement in Palestine, Ottoman treatment of the Jews and even an earthquake, to justify how all these redemptionist efforts have not resulted in increasing Jewish population in Palestine (Sachar 2007: 20).

There are other cases of advocating Zionist history in other parts of the book. The following statements by the writer represent some of them:

- Chapter 2 of the book, titled 'The Beginning of the Return'
- 'As early as 1894, Chaim Nachman Bialik, the greatest of the Hebrew poets, captured the anguish of a people deprived of its soil' (Sachar 2007: 74)
- 'How far, then, had the return to Zion materialized?' (Sachar 2007: 88)
- 'It was the anniversary of Chanukkah, commemorating the Maccabean triumph that had liberated ancient Palestine and opened a renewed era of Jewish national glory' (Sachar 2007: 113)
- 'There were other advantages, too, well beyond the emotional compensation of returning to the soil' (Sachar 2007: 150).

These cases can support, in one way or another, Zionist mythology about the history of the question. In this way, they work like the Zionist terminology that is used in Zionist reports of history. This terminology is constructed on the basis of Zionist stories and is loaded with Zionist claims. Using them without raising awareness of its covert claims can reinforce the Zionist myth, and mislead the students of history. It is noteworthy that nothing can be found in the book to make such awareness possible or to challenge the historicity of these loaded terms. There is no sign of creating some distance when these proprietary terms are used, including applying quotation marks. As a result, they can be taken easily as facts of history while some of them are contested claims. Many others come from a pure religious tradition or national myth, and not from an authoritative source of history. Some of these terms are mentioned earlier. A non-exhaustive list of these terms which are used frequently in the book is made here:

- Jewish ancestral land, or ancestral soil
- return, or return to Zion
- the ancient capital
- Jewish National Home
- Jewish soil
- the exodus (of German Jews for instance)
- exile
- Aliyah
- Diaspora
- redemption, or land of redemption

- Yishuv
- expulsion

In this area, the Jewish history of the land, the book avails itself of even tiny opportunities, if not inventing them, to portray this history as the real and principal history of the land. There is no reference, whatsoever, to inform the readers that this history concerns a time that is so far, thousands of years ago, that history, in a scientific sense, has only a limited chance to confirm what really happened then. There is no awareness, as well, that in practice there is not enough historical evidence to support the ancient Zionist stories.

The Arab history of the land, in comparison, is located in a very different part of history. It happened in times close to our time and to our eyes. It, also, lasted more than one thousand years. This part of the land's history is documented in many trustworthy sources of history. The situation is so different in this part of history where one can dare to argue that the whole history of the land, in its accurate and scientific sense, is Arab. There might not be many places in the world with such clear history. However, all this clear and established history is ignored in the Zionist historiography.

One clear example can be seen in this book: no real reference, whatsoever, was made to such history. In contrast, all opportunities are taken to undermine this history. There is a section in Chapter 8, in fact, that formulates a main thrust of this endeavour titled 'The Arabs of Palestine'. Without any mention of the long Arab history in the land, the book starts with an interesting statement: 'As late as 1882 the Arab population of Palestine barely reached 260,000. Yet by 1914 this number had doubled, and by 1920 it had reached 600,000. Under the mandate the figure grew even more dramatically, climbing to 840,000 by 1931, and representing 81 percent of the country's inhabitants' (Sachar 2007: 167). This statement can work to give some clear messages about the Arab history of the land: The Arab population of the land was so limited: 'It barely reached …'. The phrase 'as late as 1882' can mean that it was probably less in an earlier time. This statement works to deflect from the fact that Palestine's population was fully Arab when the Zionist settlers first entered the land. This 'unpleasant' fact is explained, in the book, through a sudden growth that happened for different reasons including the Arab migration from other countries; 'It was not all natural increase. During those twenty-four years approximately 100,000 Arabs entered the country from neighboring lands' (Sachar 2007: 167).

Palestine was, completely, an Arab land. Different strategies are used, in the book, to undermine this fact. First of all, Arab Jews are excluded from the Arab population when Christian Arabs are included regularly. Arab Jews who happened to oppose the Zionist project when it entered Palestine, however, are placed in another category, that of Jews, that regards them, wrongly, as part of the European Zionists. A different strategy is used by the writer in the quoted passage to show that the Arab population rate, 81 per cent, is a figure that was reached after an increase in the Arab population, misleading the readers on the fact that Palestine was fully Arab before the Zionist settlement.

The efforts to discount the Arab demographic reality in the land are reinforced by another statement:

> As a Marxist, Borochov did not justify the choice of Palestine along romantic, nationalistic lines. Rather, he argued that Palestine was a site dictated exclusively by 'stychic' (automatic, ineluctable) factors. In other nations, he explained, the absorptive capacity for immigration was limited. What was needed was a land in which Jews could freely enter all branches of the economy, where Jewish workers could participate in basic industries and agriculture. The land must be semiagricultural and thinly populated. Such a country, in fact, was Palestine, for Palestine alone was lacking in a national tradition of its own, in attraction for European immigrants, or in significant cultural and political development.
> Sachar 2007: 70

The Zionist claim to Palestine did need a construction that undermines not only the livelihood in the populated Palestinian land, but also offers a gap, a vacuum, in national tradition and institutions as the above passage manages to provide. The whole history of the land as a heartland of the Arab population is ignored in this construction. The only valid principle for accepting the fact that there are a people who live in the land they own, is the Western idea of nationalism, that Palestine lacked; 'Perhaps the Zionists were not altogether culpable in failing to take Arab nationalism seriously. The phenomenon barely existed before 1908' (Sachar 2007: 164). In other parts of the book, the land, before Zionism, is introduced as a dry, fruitless and diseased land that was characterized by poverty, disease, bandits and backwardness: 'The Moslem Arabs – the majority – were much more backward' (Sachar 2007: 167).

Summary of the Analysis

The analysis of the book, elaborated here, demonstrates that this textbook passes on the Zionist mega narrative as fact; it confirms that there was an ancient Jewish statehood; that this was destroyed by the Romans, who expelled the Jews of the land, except a few thousand, to their diaspora; that aspiration to Jewish nationhood, and also a hope for redemption in Palestine, as a national home, continued to live all the time after their expulsion from Palestine; that Palestine is the ancestral homeland of the Jews; that Jerusalem was the ancient capital of the Jewish state; that there was a Jewish kingdom under King David; that there were two thousand years of 'redemptionist efforts' to return to the homeland. All this history, constituting the main elements of the Zionist historiography of the pre-Zionist era, is represented as factual history; nothing is found in the related statements that demonstrate some kind of distancing from these Zionist claims, or raising any awareness that this story might not reflect what really happened; that this is one version of history or a contested claim. The strategy that governs passing this account on as factual history, in this book, is not, mainly, a direct one. The book commonly produces this history through statements that are directed at stating something else. The main elements of the Zionist historiography, presented in this book, are taken for granted when something else is apparently at stake. Some Zionist claims are, also, naturalized, in the book, through the sympathetic use of Zionist terminology; 'Jewish ancestral homeland' for instance.

In contrast to how the book treats the Jewish 'mythistory' of the land, the long Arab history of the land that is supported by many solid facts is ignored. No clear reference to lifetime Arab settlement in the land has been made; there are also attempts in the book to undermine it. Palestine, before the arrival of the Zionist settlers, is displayed as dry and diseased land, with a tiny population, far from civilization or national aspiration.

The Israel-Arab Reader

This book, edited by Walter Laqueur and Barry Rubin, was first published in 1969 by Citadel Press in the United States. Its latest edition at the time of the survey, the seventh, is examined for this textbook analysis. The citation figure of the book in Google Scholar, 305, also introduces the book as a popular reference used by other writers in the field. The book's popularity in scholarly circles was confirmed by the results of the survey; it had been adopted, altogether, in seventy-eight syllabi in four countries of the survey: the United States (60), Canada (9), the UK (7) and New Zealand (2). These results position the book as the sixth most adopted textbook in Western academia to teach the history of Israel.

The entire book is merely a collection of relevant documents that are organized in chronological order, from early Zionism in 1882 to the Annapolis Conference in 2007. There is no place for actual historiography in this book even to cover some common properties of a textbook such as 'Introduction' or 'Conclusion'. Very little is written by the editors of the book to narrate the Israel-Palestine history; a few lines are added in some cases to introduce a produced document. As a result, no real historiography can be found in its exact sense. This leaves not much chance of examining how the history of the question is written.

The book is, also, too short in clarifying how these documents are selected: why some documents are included and why others are excluded; how they are translated (in case of translation); how they are produced in the book, in full or in part; and if in part, what the governing principle was for excluding some parts of the document. A possible bias might lie here that could be a theme for a text analysis through other methods, those which focus on these aspects and not just on historical narrative. The book's scarceness of clarification on these points, however, does not promote its status as an unbiased textbook. The book is short, as well, on providing the proper references for the documents produced. From the close to 190 documents produced in this book, only forty-six have references. These references are too short, in many cases, to provide enough information about the source of the documents. In one case, in the first footnote, only the translator's name is mentioned (Laqueur and Rubin 2008: 10).

In view of the lack of historiography per se, even in the Introduction and Conclusion, the book cannot be subjected to historical narrative analysis, and it is therefore omitted from the final results.

From the standpoint of the research's textbook analysis, one point might be made: the book opens with a document that was published, according to the book, by a Jewish group, the Bilu Group, in Constantinople in 1882. This manifesto, as it is called in the book, has many elements of Zionist mythology about the pre-Zionist era:

> To our brothers and sisters in Exile!
>   'If I help not myself, who will help me?'
>   Nearly two thousand years have elapsed since, in an evil hour, after a heroic struggle, the glory of our Temple vanished in fire and our kings and chieftains changed their crowns and diadems for the chains of exile. We lost our country where dwelt our beloved sires. Into the Exile we took with us, of all our glories, only a spark of the fire by which our Temple, the abode of our Great One, was engirdled, and this little spark kept us alive while the towers of our enemies crumbled into dust, and this spark leapt into celestial flame and shed light on the heroes of our race and inspired them to endure the horrors of the dance of death and the tortures of the *autos-da-fé*. And this spark is again kindling and will shine for us, a true pillar of fire going before us on the road to Zion, while behind us is a pillar of cloud, the pillar of oppression threatening to destroy us. Sleepest thou, O our nation? . . .
>   WE WANT:
>   1. A home in our country. It was given us by the mercy of God; it is ours as registered in the archives of history . . .
>   We hope that the interests of our glorious nation will rouse the national spirit in rich and powerful men, and that everyone, rich or poor, will give his best labours to the holy cause.
>   Greetings, dear brothers and sisters!
>   HEAR, O ISRAEL! The Lord our God, the Lord is one, and our land Zion is our one hope.
>   GOD be with us!
>   THE PIONEERS OF BILU
>
> Laqueur and Rubin 2008: 3–4

The next document, 'Theodor Herzl: The Jewish State (1896)', a statement by Theodor Herzl, can reinforce the points made by the first document: 'The idea which I have developed in this pamphlet is a very old one: it is the restoration of the Jewish State' (Laqueur and Rubin 2008: 4).

Against this start with documents that contain a number of Zionist elements about the history of the question, there is no document, in this section on the early phase of the conflict, that works as a source of information about the facts of the Arab history of the land. It is, also, evident that this book is recommended by some pro-Israeli bodies, such as CAMERA, as an authoritative reference:

> The Israel-Arab Reader is a thorough and up-to-date guide to the continuing crisis in the Middle East. It covers the full spectrum of the Israel-Arab conflict

– from the earliest days, through the wars and peacemaking efforts, up to the Israel-PLO and Israel-Jordan peace accords. This comprehensive reference includes speeches, letters, articles, and reports dealing with all the major topics of interest in the area from all of the relevant political parties and world leaders.

'Suggested Book List', n.d.

Concluding Remarks

In this chapter, all selected textbooks are analysed, one by one, and the detailed results of this analysis, historical narrative analysis, have been offered in the preceding pages. Early in the chapter, before the detailed analysis began, Table 5.1 demonstrated the main targets of this analysis, its questions, and its possible answers. Now, after the analysis, Table 5.2 sets out the results.

Two Testimonies that Support the Results of the Analysis

There are two testimonies, from academic examinations, that can support the results of my textbook analysis. The first one comes from Israel: as mentioned in the Postscript, a research report titled 'A Critical Survey of Textbooks on the Arab-Israeli and Israeli-Palestinian Conflict', and published by Moshe Dayan Center for Middle Eastern and African Studies in Tel Aviv University (Mueller and Rabi 2017). This research project did a similar job and analysed college-level textbooks on the Israel-Palestine question that are adopted most, for teaching, in the anglophone universities. Four textbooks, from the five I have analysed in this chapter (i.e. excluding *The Arab-Israel Reader*), were examined in that project. The results of this investigation, which were conducted by a team of research assistants in the Moshe Dayan Centre for Middle Eastern and African Studies, led by Uzi Rabi (the director of the centre) and Dr Chelsi Mueller, confirms certain findings of my textbook analysis; in relation to Smith's textbook, *Palestine and the Arab-Israeli Conflict*, the Israeli analysis recognize the book's considerable distance from pro-Israeli history and describe it as a work that put 'greater preference for the Palestinian narrative of events' (Mueller and Rabi 2017: 49). The report adds: 'The author's preference for the Palestinian narrative is most noticeable in the shorter surveys and synopses, such as those given in the preface, prologue and epilogue' (Mueller and Rabi 2017: 50). These parts of the book are the main areas that have been analysed in my research. In this regard, the report criticizes the textbook's treatment of ancient Israel: 'Unnamed scholars who claim that Saul, David and Solomon never existed and that Solomon's temple is a myth are given a spotlight. Smith's narrative of the ancient Israelites most closely resembles the Palestinian narrative, which relies heavily on "temple denial" as a means of asserting exclusive claims to Jerusalem and the land of Israel/Palestine' (Mueller and Rabi 2017: 50).

Table 5.2 The results of the textbook analysis[a]

Textbook title	How selected textbooks treat the 'main elements of Zionist historiography'						
	History of the land starts with …	Ancient Israel	How Jews disappeared in Palestine?	Jewish redemptionist efforts to return	Position on Jewish ethnos	Arab history of the land	Jewish polity in other lands[b]
Palestine and the Arab-Israeli Conflict	Canaanites	Questions it by two comments: 1. Challenging the Bible's historicity and 2. Archaeological findings	Expulsion and Roman policy	Challenges the idea	One people: a nation	Takes into account but not as principal	No mention
A Concise History of the Arab-Israeli Conflict	Jews	Takes for granted	Mass expulsion but many left the land before	Yes but no actual step was taken	One people: a nation	Ignores but does not suppress	Deny
Righteous Victims	Jews	Takes for granted	Mass expulsion	Takes for granted	One people: a nation	Suppresses	No mention
A History of the Israeli-Palestinian Conflict	Jews	Takes for granted	Mass expulsion	Yes but no actual step was taken	One people: a nation	Takes into account but not as principal	No mention
A History of Israel	Jews	Takes for granted	Mass expulsion	Takes for granted	One people: a nation	Suppresses	No mention
The Israel-Arab Reader	This book has been exempted from the historical narrative analysis because of the nature of its content. See the preceding section for a fuller explanation.						

Notes:

a This table is designed to show an overall picture of the results of the textbook analysis that was applied to the selected textbooks. Accuracy may be somewhat compromised for the sake of simplicity and brevity, so please refer to the text for a fuller representation of the results of the analysis.

This Israeli report adds an important point about the significance of this undertaking: 'In the absence of knowledge about the Jewish connection to Jerusalem and the land of Israel since time immemorial, it is impossible to understand why the modern Zionist movement focused its attention on this small geographical territory' (Mueller and Rabi 2017: 50–1). The report, in its conclusion, does not recommend using this textbook in the related courses, but if used, should be accompanied with a pro-Israeli one: 'As such, the textbook, if used in a course on the conflict, would need to be supplemented with readings that convey Israeli views on the conflict (including mainstream views) in order to provide students with the full picture' (Mueller and Rabi 2017: 56).

The project results' in relation to another analysed textbook, *Righteous Victims*, are also in agreement with this study's findings; the project classifies the textbook as a pro-Israeli history:

> It can be said that the narrative in *Righteous Victims* is Israel centric. The author uses English and Hebrew sources (and Israeli archives) but not Arabic sources (xiii). Chapters are arranged according to milestones in Israeli history rather than shared history and make use of terminology that is exclusively Israeli, i.e. "The Six Day War." Geography is sometimes described in Hebraic terms, i.e. Judea and Samaria.
>
> Mueller and Rabi 2017: 38

The project's conclusion about the textbook's treatment of ancient Israel is, also, very similar to mine, if not the same:

> As noted, brief overviews of the relevant ancient and medieval history are given as part of the first chapter, 'Palestine on the Eve.' Morris gives a very brief, two paragraph summary of the Jewish presence in the region in ancient and medieval times (although he anachronistically calls the land Palestine even while describing its composition 3,000 years ago). His summary is brief enough to establish that Jews had an ancient presence and period of sovereignty in the land without delving into controversial historical and archaeological debates about the topic.
>
> Mueller and Rabi 2017: 39

The report should be given academic credit for its unbiased attempt to make readers aware of the book's pro-Israeli bias: 'Readers should be aware that this book represents an Israeli history of the conflict.... A good supplement to this book or object of comparison would be a book or article that draws upon Arabic sources to present the traditional Palestinian narrative' (Mueller and Rabi 2017: 42–3).

Concerning another analysed textbook, *A [Concise] History of the Arab-Israeli Conflict*, the report supports that this work, also, takes a pro-Israeli stance: 'There are indications that this text favours an Israeli narrative of the conflict, albeit a leftist and critical, Israeli narrative' (Mueller and Rabi 2017: 22). There are other assertions in the report that confirms this idea about the book; 'Furthermore, the authors seem to rely, to a greater extent, on Israeli views of events in constructing their story' (Mueller and Rabi 2017: 23). The report brings some instances of evidence to support this idea; 'the Palestinian narrative is given disproportionately less space in terms of description than the Zionist/Israeli narrative' (Mueller and Rabi 2017: 20). There are other instances of the biased treatment of the question, the report mentions. One is related to book's treatment of Sabra and Shatilla; 'Bickerton and Klausner's narrative does not delve into the issue of Ariel Sharon's degree of complicity for the Sabra and Shatilla massacre of Palestinians by Maronite militiamen, though it mentions that he was forced to resign as Defence Minister. In fact, the story of Sabra and Shatilla is summed up in a mere two sentences and referred to as a "tragedy" rather than a "massacre"' (Mueller and Rabi 2017: 22). The report can bring other instances to support its idea of the book: 'Another indication of affinity with an Israeli narrative is the way that the War of 1967 is termed the "Six Day War," as it is referred to by Israelis (167, 169, 206). Hebrew concepts, terms and proper nouns, such as names of parties and organizations are introduced and used more frequently than Arabic terms' (Mueller and Rabi 2017: 22–3).

Another popular textbook, *A History of the Israeli-Palestinian Conflict*, has also been analysed in this Moshe Dayan Centre project. This analysis has, also, noted the particular position that book takes to treat the question: 'In his [Tessler's] preface he states that his objectives for the second edition, as with the first, are to provide a book that "seeks not only to present a balanced and accurate history of the Israeli--Palestinian conflict," but also "to encourage a sympathetic understanding of the parties involved" (viii). In our assessment, this was a goal that the textbook achieved' (Mueller and Rabi 2017: 57). This analysis, also, confirms that such treatment poses some problems for the history, but this report stresses the problem from an Israeli perspective:

> While there may be an advantage in 'leveling the playing field,' before examining the causes of hostilities that erupted in the twentieth century, presenting disconnected historical events in a 'congruent' fashion can also create some historiographical problems. For example, in order to present both people groups as having ancient ties to the land of Palestine, Tessler adopts as fact, the 'Arab Canaanite' narrative (69). While it has been prevalent in Palestinian nationalist folklore since the 1920s, and has been utilized in Arab nationalist historiography since the 1950s, the narrative itself is based on theory, namely the Winckler-Caetani 'Semitic Wave Theory'. The theory, which posits that all the Semites have prehistoric origins in the Arabian Peninsula, has been accepted and expounded by Arab historians, and apparently also by Tessler, as an undisputed scientific truth.
>
> Mueller and Rabi 2017: 58–9

The first testimony, which has just been dealt with, came later than my original PhD thesis on the subject, and analysed the same textbooks, except one, in which

I have analysed in my textbook analysis. The second testimony, an academic article in *The History Teacher* – published by the Society for History Education – came much earlier than mine, in 2001, but I failed to locate it then when I was searching for the relevant literature. This article, 'Ancient Israel in Western Civ Textbooks', is written by Jack Cargill who used to teach introductory courses, called once 'Western Civilization' to undergraduate university students. This analysis of Western college textbooks does not involve examining textbooks that I have examined, and does not deal with the history of the Israel-Palestine question as a whole. However, it deals with a relevant topic: how Western college-level textbooks treat 'Ancient Israel'. The results of this analysis can support the idea that Western textbooks, in general, take the biblical story (of ancient Israel) for granted, and consider it, without any serious academic scepticism, as the true history of the land – the same conclusion of my analysis about the topic.

This innovative investigation elaborates how a major development in the relevant scholarship i.e. a paradigm shift from 'a literalist and fundamentalist reading of the history of ancient Israel as told in the Hebrew Bible' to an evidence based history of the era – that took place in recent decades – are ignored in the relevant college-level textbooks:

> one would never know from reading most of these textbooks' accounts that, in the viewpoint of a substantial group of scholars, during the last two or three decades of the twentieth century a virtual 'paradigm shift' in the treatment of the Hebrew Bible's relationship to the history of Israel has been occurring, one that involves a far more basic rejection of traditional interpretations than the essentially text-critical approach of commentators such as Morton Smith.
>
> Cargill 2001: 300

The article, which examined sixteen college-level textbooks, offers some details and instances that support such assertion; 'the biblical "conquest of Canaan" by Hebrews coming from outside seems to be generally accepted by the textbooks' authors' (Cargill 2001: 306). 'None of the texts even mentions scholars' suggestions that the "united monarchy" itself might be fictional' (Cargill 2001: 307). This textbook analysis criticizes Western college textbooks, adopted to teach undergraduate students in Western countries, for their unsophisticated and ill-informed dealing with the question: 'Nor does any of the textbooks surveyed discuss the Bible in primarily literary terms (only Cannistraro and Noble list any work by Alter among their recommended readings, for example). They all treat the Bible as a historical source, and my criticism relates to their generally unsophisticated and seemingly ill-informed ways of doing this' (Cargill 2001: 317).

Based on the results of this analysis, the best textbook – from the author's perspective – is Spielvogel's textbook, *Western Civilization* (2000). In Cargill's own words:

> Spielvogel is on the whole more consistent with the findings and observations of recent scholarship on ancient Israel than any of the other textbooks surveyed.

> The Hebrews' nomadic period, their descent from Abraham whose origins were in Mesopotamia, their sojourn and enslavement in Egypt, Moses and the exodus, the wilderness wanderings, their entry into Canaan, division into twelve tribes, and conflict with the Philistines – all are presented by Spielvogel only as 'a tradition concerning their origins and history that was eventually written down as part of the Hebrew Bible....' With 'according to tradition' and '[a]ccording to the biblical account' further inserted within the summary to reiterate the point that only tradition (not history) is being reported (33a–b). This summary of tradition is followed immediately (33b) by these observations: 'Many scholars today doubt that the early books of the Hebrew Bible reflect the true history of the early Israelites. They argue that the early books of the Bible, written centuries after the events described, preserve only what the Israelites came to believe about themselves and that recently discovered archaeological evidence often contradicts the details of the biblical account. Some of these scholars have even argued that the Israelites were not nomadic invaders but indigenous peoples of the Palestinian hill country'.
>
> Cargill 2001: 312

Cargill considers textbooks' treatment of the question as a bad scholarship in his conclusion:

> I am certainly not insisting that authors of Western Civilization texts for university classes should agree with the suggestions made about ancient Israel in recent decades by scholars such as those whom I have cited. What I am saying is that it is bad scholarship, and bad pedagogy, simply to ignore an important body of recent work, offering adult students a literalist-leaning account that is by scholarly standards probably twenty years out of date. At the very least, textbook authors should include more critical scholars' works and some minimalist works in their recommended readings, so that students would have a chance to confront such arguments on their own.
>
> Cargill 2001: 315

Cargill, in his analysis of Western college textbooks, also, pays attention to the authorship question: 'It is very rare to find in the texts surveyed any books listed that are written by any of the so-called "biblical minimalists"; their works mentioned specifically in my discussion here (text and notes) constitute the complete list of such citations within all the textbooks surveyed' (Cargill 2001: 314).

The next chapter, Chapter 6, is focused on the subject from an authorship perspective.

Chapter 6

WHO NARRATES THE HISTORY?

The way selected textbooks treat the history of the Israel-Palestine question has been analysed in the last chapter, Chapter 5, by means of historical narrative analysis. That analysis allowed an investigation, the aim of which is to answer the 'how' part of the main question of this thesis: how do Western college-level textbooks treat the history of the Israel-Palestine question? This was through an exploration of the structure of the selected histories. There is an emphasis in this analysis on the role of historians, whose decisions are seminal in determining the main structure of a constructed history; the point made in 'Methodology', in the Introduction (p. XXX), should be borne in mind:

> It is argued that the meaning of the 'facts' produced in a certain history is dependent on how they are placed in an overall story. The rhetoric is considered ineffective if not reinforced by a structure to support it. It is revealed that such structure comes from the main ideological positions that historians take towards history. There is an emphasis, in this methodology, on the role historians play in constructing historical knowledge.

Historical narrative analysis is influenced by an observation that promotes a shift from 'great stories' to 'great story tellers' (Vanhulle 2009).

From this perspective, historians are considered to be primarily responsible for the history produced. They constitute the immediate context of constructed knowledge, where wider contexts such as the social and the national are located, and they can be a relevant answer to 'why' part of the main question of this study: why do Western textbooks treat the Israel-Palestine question in that way?

The role historians play in determining historical knowledge is not stressed only in this methodology; it has been acknowledged and discussed in the broader literature on history; the matter is reflected in textbooks designed to address the key questions of the discipline. *History and Historians* is an instance. Its author, Mark T. Gilderhus, trying to clarify his point, gives an example about the historian's role: 'Lock ten of them in a room (or a cell) with the same bodies of evidence, and they would in all likelihood arrive at ten divergent judgments' (Gilderhus 1987: 82). He mentions some forms of identification such as class, race and religion, as main factors that contribute to how historians write history (Gilderhus 1987: 82).

This general idea develops when a deeper awareness of the roles played by historians is provided. This has been recorded in two different fields of academic history: theoretical and empirical studies. On the theoretical level, when epistemological matters are a concern, the matter has been discussed in the (critical) philosophy of history. Historiography, as a subdiscipline, became, also, a main site for the related discussions. This happened when the scholarly interest in the idea of 'narrative' and how this has been formed took place. Nowadays, new fields of academic endeavour such as memory studies are engaged in this discussion as well.

Mink and White are introduced as pioneer scholars who provided a considerable source for the study of historians and their loyalties, in the question of producing history (Roberts 2001: Introduction). They found this factor more important than historical evidence and facts. They emphasize the idea that the historian imposes his ideological beliefs on the facts (Topolsky 1998: 12). White, in his remarkable contribution to the field, *Metahistory*, elaborates his idea about how this is possible, and how a historian actually does this, introducing 'emplotment' as a main method used in this endeavour (White 2014). According to him, the historian does not just explore the historical matters but makes them. This is possible, according to White, by:

- arranging events in a certain order
- answering questions: what happened? when? how? why?
- deciding which events in the chronicle to include and exclude
- stressing some events and subordinating others (Rea 2015; White 2014: 6).

In empirical studies, some areas of history are acknowledged as those that provide plenty of evidence about how historians produce histories that comply with their identity or advance their goals. National histories are regarded as clear instances. Historians, when producing national history of their own nationality, use the outcomes of archaeology and ancient history as a tool to advance a mythical national history that provides an advantageous place for their nation in the history (Berger and Lorenz 2010). The real scope of such fabrication and its grave consequences has not been fully recognized but there are some scholarly works that touch upon this important matter; *The Use and Abuse of History: Or How the Past Is Taught to Children* is a book designed to produce some instances of such biases in various regions of the world (Ferro 2003). Another book, *Writing National Histories: Western Europe Since 1800* investigates the role of national historians who produce histories in Italy, Germany and France in advancing national ideologies, and how they use history against their political rivals including socialist, communist and Catholic internationalism (Berger, Donovan and Passmore 1999). A book has been edited by Stefan Berger and Chris Lorenz, *Nationalizing the Past: Historians as Nation Builders in Modern Europe*, that analyses and compares the national histories produced by professional historians of different European nationalities in the modern era. This analysis can demonstrate the extent to which these histories produce opposing accounts, and introduces their producers, historians, as myth makers who produce such histories for the sake of their national ideology (Berger and Lorenz 2010).

There are other scholarly works that make some valuable contributions to the related discussion: *The History and Narrative Reader* (2001), edited by Geoffrey Roberts, is one main instance that looks at the subject through the study of narrative. 'The Structure of Historical Narratives and the Teaching of History' is another instance. In this chapter, Jeretz Topolsky provides a useful analysis of narrative and its three-layer structure:

1. the surface of informing (logical and grammatical) layer;
2. the persuasive or rhetorical layer and
3. the theoretical-ideological or controlling (steering) layer

Topolsky 1998: 12

The third level is considered, in this analysis, as the main place where a historian's mind, with its ideas and goals, conscious and unconscious, informs the historical narrative, and appropriates it accordingly (Topolsky 1998: 18–19). The main elements of the historian's mind that intervene in such a process are introduced as follows:

1. the preliminary knowledge (factual and theoretical) in the light of which the historian is studying and conceptualizing the past;
2. the linguistic conventions shared by the historian which create a preliminary prism which (metaphorically) breaks up the light of the past into the set of words, notions, expressions, etc.;
3. the fundamental myths present in the cultural 'environment' of the historian which influence his or her thinking and imagination as a sui generis pressure guiding his or her work;
4. the theoretical and quasi-theoretical (i.e. spontaneous) conceptions about the world and man;
5. the metaphors in their epistemological function. i.e. a linguistic and at the same time extra-linguistic vehicle for myths, quasi-theories and theories; and
6. the ideology (understood in a more or less coherent way) represented by the author of the text.

Jeretz Topolsky 1998: 19

These elements are regarded as different lenses that mediate between a historian and the object of his study. The historian can see only what is allowed to pass through these lenses. This medium controls what a historian sees, understands and, ultimately, writes (Topolsky 1998: 19).

This crucial role that historians play in the production of history is emphasized, by others, particularly in relation to histories produced on the Israel-Palestine question: 'It hardly takes a regional expert to perceive that the way the "story" of the Arab-Israeli conflict is told depends on the perspective of the storyteller' (Isacoff 2005: 71).

This chapter views the question from this perspective. For this purpose, all producers of the selected textbooks, writers and editors, are subjected to analysis, to determine their background in relation to the subject matter of the knowledge they produce on the Israel-Palestine question. The eight historians chosen for this analysis are all those who wrote or edited the six selected textbooks. An investigation is conducted, the aim of which is to gain some insight into the ideological positions of these historians from their works, interviews, autobiographies, acknowledgements, CVs and so on, all from open source materials which should shed some light on their background. The following part of the chapter is devoted to the results of this investigation; the historians are dealt with in surname order.

Ian Bickerton

Ian James Bickerton is co-author with Klausner of *A Concise History of the Arab-Israeli Conflict*. He was born in Perth, Western Australia. Bickerton completed his undergraduate degree in history there before he moved to the United States for post-graduate studies, receiving his MA from Kansas State University, and his PhD from the Claremont Graduate School, in California. He later joined the University of New South Wales to teach in the School of History. Bickerton taught a number of courses mainly on the history of the Arab-Israeli conflict, the history of the modern United States, and the history of US foreign relations. He also lectured in several US universities including the University of California Santa Barbara and the University of Missouri at Kansas City. Apart from Australia and the United States, he has had some teaching experience in the United Kingdom, in other European countries and in Israel ('Ian J. Bickerton' n.d.).

Bickerton has numerous publications on the Arab-Israeli conflict and other Middle Eastern questions, including:

- *The Arab-Israeli Conflict: A Guide for the Perplexed*
- *The Arab-Israeli Conflict: A History*
- *Historiography of The Arab-Israeli Conflict: Contested Spaces*
- *Forty-Three Days: The Gulf War*

He is considered a prominent expert in Middle Eastern studies, and has contributed to a number of entries on Middle Eastern matters in world-class encyclopaedias and professional dictionaries, including:

- *Encyclopaedia Britannica*
- *Dictionary of American Foreign Policy*
- *SBS World Guide*

Bickerton, in his recent book, *The Arab-Israeli Conflict: A History*, acknowledging the reader's expectation to be given information about the writer's background, provides some material on this topic. He mentions his educational environment, where he was educated in a pro-Israeli environment:

> As a teenager I recall thinking with pride, like most Australians, how important the Australian prime minister, Sir Robert Menzies, must have been as he sailed out of Australia in 1956 to 'sort out' the 'Suez crisis' although, again, I had little idea of Israel's role in that abortive Anglo-French-Israeli venture to force President Nasser to 'disgorge' the Suez Canal. As a graduate student in California, I do remember the 1967 war, however. Like most, I was amazed at Israel's quick and overwhelming success in that short war.
>
> Bickerton 2009: 17

He considers his background as coming from 'Irish Catholicism', and does not hide his 'serious reservations' about it (Bickerton 2009: 19). No record of a critical report of his views on the Israel-Palestine question has been found in pro-Israeli academia monitors, including Campus Watch and CAMERA.

Carla Klausner

Carla L. Klausner, co-author with Bickerton of an analysed textbook, *A Concise History of the Arab-Israeli Conflict*, is an American academic. She completed her degrees in different American universities: History at Barnard College in 1958, MA in Middle East Studies in Radcliffe College in 1960, and PhD in History and Middle East Studies at Harvard University in 1963.

After graduation, she joined the University of Missouri-Kansas City as a faculty member and became director of the Judaic Studies programme in this university. As a professor of history, she taught various courses in the field of Middle East history, History of Islam, Arabs, Jews and Ottomans ('Department of History: Carla L. Klausner' n.d.). Her main monographs, two in fact, are co-authored with others:

- *From Destruction to Rebirth: The Holocaust and the State of Israel* with Dr Joseph Schultz, New York: University Press of America, 1978
- *A Concise History of the Arab-Israeli Conflict*, with Ian J. Bickerton, New York: Prentice Hall, first published in 1991

She is active outside academia as well. Gatherings of the Jewish community in Kansas are a main platform for her activities. She teaches frequently in the Rabbi Morris B. Margolies Center of Adult Studies in Congregation Beth Shalom. The 'Three Affairs' series is one instance. Klausner spoke in this programme, besides two other speakers, a rabbi and an assistant rabbi, on a topic titled 'The Damascus Affair'. The Congregation introduced these three speakers, in the relevant announcement, as 'three of the best teachers that Congregation Beth Shalom has to offer' ('The Scroll' 2009). Another case of such service is a joint presentation with Rabbi Scott White on 'The Arab Spring and What It Means to Israel' ('The Scroll' 2011). Carla Klausner is mentioned and thanked repeatedly in 'The Scroll', the Congregation periodical, for her contributions. Her name is also mentioned in the periodical as a 'Minyan Participant' who has attended the 'minyanim on a regular basis' ('The Scroll' 2008). Her relatives, including her mother, Rose Levine, and her husband, Tiberius Klausner, take part in the Congregation's activities as well ('Tiberius Klausner' 2014). She also co-authored with Joseph P. Schultz an article titled 'Rabbi Simon Glazer and the Quest for Jewish Community in Kansas City, 1920–1923'. In this article, a leading Zionist rabbi in Kansas, Rabbi Simon Glazer, is commended for his achievements in developing an organization for the Jewish community in the city, and for improving cooperation among Jewish Orthodox congregations. One notable achievement mentioned in the article is his campaign to have the US Congress support of the Zionist movement to colonize Palestine as a homeland for Jews: 'Rabbi Glazer's almost one-man campaign had resulted in the most formal possible American commitment in favor of a Jewish homeland in Palestine, and the congressional resolution, the first time Congress had been actually involved in support of the Zionist enterprise, is eloquent testimony to his vision, commitment, political acumen, and persuasiveness' (Schultz and Klausner 1983: 24–5).

Beth Shalom, a conservative Congregation, is based in Kansas City. It is a main centre for the Jewish community in the city and holds events to support Israel. A joint programme with Ohev Sholom Congregation on 'Media Bias Against Israel: What We Can Do About It' is one instance ('The Scroll' 2011). It also contributes to celebrating Israeli Independence Day and Israeli Memorial Day where the Congregation 'assemble gift packages for soldiers in the Israel Defence Forces' ('The Scroll' 2014).

There is other information which reveal Klausner's ideology in relation to the Israel-Palestine question: she was a member of a pro-Israeli society, Scholars for Peace in the Middle East (Klausner 2013). She has made many trips to Israel; her husband describes this as how 'We always ended up in Israel'. She has stayed in Israel several times; she stayed there with her family for six months in one visit. Her daughters went to Israeli kindergarten and Kita Aleph to learn Hebrew. Their father, in an interview, expressed his joy over their Israeli accent. He came back to the United States but admitted in an interview: 'I would have loved to stay in Israel'. He mentions job considerations as a reason for their return to the United States (Klausner 2013).

There are other links to Israel in her family. Her husband, Tiberius (Tibor) Klausner, was a member of a Zionist underground organization (Klausner 2013). He is introduced in a book, titled *From the Heart: Life Before and After the Holocaust* published by 'The Midwest Center for Holocaust Education' as one of '52 Kansas City Holocaust survivors and war refugees who began their lives in homelands far away, who saw their lives unalterably changed by the Holocaust, and who rebuilt their lives in America' (Midwest Center for Holocaust Education and the Kansas City Star 2001). In a message to local Jewish children on the Holocaust, which is published in the Midwest Center's website, Tiberius Klausner calls them to support

Israel: 'My message for you, our future generation, is to preserve your Jewish heritage and be proud of your Jewishness. When I was studying in Paris, they never let me forget I was a foreigner and a Jew. How do you change that? How do you change antisemitism? You must continue to learn about Judaism, practice it, live by its values, pray, and hope. And you have to support Israel' ('Tiberius Klausner' 2014). Tibor's immediate family, parents and brothers, are Israeli. His younger brother served in the Israeli army and participated in four Israeli wars (Klausner 2013).

Walter Laqueur

Walter Laqueur, co-editor with Rubin of *The Israel-Arab Reader: A Documentary History of the Middle East Conflict*, was born into a Jewish family. His parents are reported as victims of the Holocaust, and Walter himself is regarded as a 'survivor'. He moved to Israel in 1938 and studied at the Hebrew University of Jerusalem. In Israel, he joined a kibbutz and worked as an agricultural labourer for many years before he moved to Jerusalem to work as a political journalist. He was engaged in reporting the important developments of the Zionist movement in Palestine before 1948 and afterwards. He had personal relationships with many Zionist leaders including Chaim Weizmann, David Ben-Gurion, Moshe Sharett, Golda Meir and Yitzhak Rabin ('Biography' n.d.).

He later joined academia, teaching in Tel Aviv University as a visiting professor from 1972 till 1982. He has also taught in many high-ranking universities including Harvard, the University of Chicago and Johns Hopkins University in the United States. He has written and edited a number of monographs on the Israel-Palestine question, including:

- *A History of Zionism: From the French Revolution to the Establishment of the State of Israel*
- *The Changing Face of Anti-Semitism: From Ancient Times to the Present Day*

He has also published an autobiography titled *Thursday's Child Has Far to Go: A Memoir of the Journeying Years* (Laqueur 1992). This title changed later to *Best of Times, Worst of Times: Memoirs of a Political Education* (Laqueur 2009). A large part of his activities in the Zionist movement and his ideas about Israel are recorded in this book. He moved to the United States in 1953 but his children and grandchildren have remained in Israel ('Biography' n.d.).

The pro-Israeli organization, CAMERA, recommends Laqueur's book (*The Israel-Arab Reader*) in its programme, Adopt a Library, as a 'reliable' source of knowledge on the Israel-Palestine question:

> The Israel-Arab Reader is a thorough and up-to-date guide to the continuing crisis in the Middle East. It covers the full spectrum of the Israel-Arab conflict from the earliest days, through the wars and peacemaking efforts, up to the

Israel-PLO and Israel-Jordan peace accords. This comprehensive reference includes speeches, letters, articles, and reports dealing with all the major interests in the area from all of the relevant political parties and world leaders.

'Suggested Book List' n.d.

Benny Morris

Benny Morris, an Israeli historian, is the author of *Righteous Victims: A History of the Zionist-Arab Conflict*, which has been analysed in this research. He was born in Israel, in a kibbutz (Ein HaHoresh), to Jewish parents who migrated from the UK to Israel. His father, Ya'akov Morris, was an Israeli diplomat. Benny Morris served in the Israeli army and participated in the 1967 war. He was wounded in 1969 in an exchange of fire with Egyptian troops in the occupied Sinai near the Suez Canal. He completed his undergraduate studies in History at the Hebrew University of Jerusalem, and his PhD at the University of Cambridge. After graduation, he joined the Middle East Studies department of Ben-Gurion University of the Negev in southern Israel, where he subsequently became Professor of History (Wilson 2007; Slater 2012; 'Professor Benny Morris Biography' n.d.). He has written extensively on the history of the Israel-Palestine question, including:

- *1948: A History of the First Arab-Israeli War*
- *The Birth of the Palestinian Refugee Problem, 1947–1949*
- *One State, Two States: Resolving the Israel/Palestine Conflict*

In some circles, he is regarded as a post-Zionist or 'new' historian who challenged the Zionist myths. But he regards himself as a Zionist (Shavit 2004). His strong Zionist tendency has led him, arguably, to justify the ethnic cleansing of Arabs in 1948, and to wish for the expulsion of more Palestinians by Zionists (Abunimah 2004). The acknowledgements in his book, *Righteous Victims*, demonstrate that all the funds he received to complete this book are from Israeli sources except one contribution from the French Embassy in Israel (Morris 2001: xi); the archives he consulted to write the book are all Israeli, including the Israel State Archives, the Central Zionist Archives and the Israel Defense Forces (IDF) Archive (Morris 2001: xii). Furthermore, in the acknowledgements in *Righteous Victims*, all the people he thanks for their support are Israelis; there are a few from the United States or the UK but no one is Arab (Morris 2001: xi). He is known as a historian who uses and relies on Israeli sources, and not Arab ones.

Barry Rubin

Barry Rubin, an Israeli academic, is co-editor with Laqueur of *The Israel-Arab Reader: A Documentary History of the Middle East Conflict*. He was born in the United States, and completed his PhD at the Georgetown University in Washington,

DC. After graduation, he taught in many Israeli and American universities. For almost two decades, he was the director of the Global Research in International Affairs (GLORIA) at the Interdisciplinary Center Herzliya in Israel. He worked for the *Jerusalem Post* as a columnist for a long time. The Middle East and terrorism were his areas of expertise. He served as an editor on a number of specialized journals including the *Middle East Review of International Affairs* (MERIA), and the *Turkish Studies Journal* (Solomon 2014; Haaretz 2014). Rubin was a hardworking writer who authored and edited many books and articles, including:

- *Israel: An Introduction*
- *The Arab States and the Palestine Conflict* (Contemporary Issues in the Middle East series)
- *Revolution Until Victory? The Politics and History of the PLO* (Selection of the History Book Club)

His personal blog, *The Rubin Report* (http://rubinreports.blogspot.com), is a main source for his writings. Rubin is considered as a 'strenuous defender of Jews, Israel, and US interests' (Solomon 2014). In relation to a solution for the Israel-Palestinian conflict, he advocated the idea that 'Jews should defend themselves' (Solomon 2014). He was critical of the West for its shortcomings in supporting Israel. He has written about his ancestry, mentioning some members of his family as victims of the Holocaust. He was very passionate about the Zionist idea of the Jewish state. He wrote in this regard: 'For 2000 years my ancestors dreamed of returning to their homeland and reestablishing their sovereignty. I have had the privilege of living that dream. How amazing is that?' (Solomon 2014)

Howard Sachar

Howard Morley Sachar, an American historian, is the author of *A History of Israel: From the Rise of Zionism to Our Time*. He was born in St. Louis, Missouri, in the United States into a Jewish family, and studied in that country. He completed his undergraduate education at Swarthmore and received his PhD from Harvard. Sachar is based in Washington, DC as Charles E. Smith Professor of History Emeritus at George Washington University. He is known as an expert on Middle East affairs, and lectures in many American universities in this field. He also acts as a consultant in this area for many governmental bodies in the United States. Sachar has testified before the Foreign Affairs Committee in the US Congress. He has contributed to training programmes for US diplomats. Sachar has edited a 39-volume history of the question, *The Rise of Israel: A Documentary History* (Sachar 2007: 1271). He is the author of many articles and fourteen books in the field including:

- *The Course of Modern Jewish History* (1958)
- *Diaspora* (1985)

- *Aliyah* (1961)
- *Egypt and Israel* (1981)

He has strong links with Israel, Jews and pro-Israeli circles, and he lived in Israel for many years, worked on a kibbutz and founded the Jacob Hiatt Institute in Jerusalem, one of the first academic centres for American students to visit and study in Israel. He secured funds from the US State Department, in 1965 to found this institute, and served as its director for several years. He has also taught in Israeli universities: the Hebrew University and Tel Aviv University. Two National Jewish Book Awards have been granted to him. Sachar, also, was awarded an honorary degree of Doctor of Humane Letters from the Hebrew Union College – Jewish Institute of Religion in 1996 (Fuchs 2009; Sachar 2007: 1271). He is a member of the advisory council of J Street, a pro-Israeli lobby in the United States ('Advisory Council' n.d.).

Sachar's father, Abram (Abe) Leon Sachar, was also a leading Zionist figure: he was one of the founders of the B'nai B'rith Hillel Foundation. He acted as the director of the Illinois sector, and then as national director of this pro-Israeli Foundation (1933 to 1947). Abram Sachar was active in supporting Israel, and a close friend of its first prime minister, David Ben-Gurion ('Abram L. Sachar' n.d.).

There are other links in his family to Israel: his daughter and grandchildren live there. When he visited Israel after his graduate studies, and engaged in founding the Jacob Hiatt Institute, he described his mission thus: 'I was so infatuated with the land and the people and [I had a personal] resolve to get Jewish people closer to it' (Fuchs 2009).

Charles Smith

Charles Duryea Smith is an American academic who wrote *Palestine and the Arab-Israeli Conflict*. He completed his studies in the field of History and the Middle East Studies at US universities: his undergraduate degree was from Williams College, his MA from Harvard and his PhD from the University of Michigan. He has taught in various American universities including San Diego State University, Wayne State University, University of Virginia, George Mason University, the Virginia Military Institute and the Virginia Commonwealth University. He joined the University of Arizona, School of Middle Eastern & North African Studies, as a Professor Emeritus of Middle East History. He has had teaching experience both in Israel and in Arab countries; in Israel, he worked in the Institute for Advanced Study at the Hebrew University of Jerusalem. In Egypt, he was president of the American Research Centre ('Charles D. Smith' n.d.).

Smith has authored a number of publications on Middle East history in general, and on the Israel-Palestine question in particular:

- *The Modern Middle East and North Africa: A History in Documents* (co-authored with Julia Clancy-Smith)

- 'The United States and the 1967 War' in *The 1967 Arab-Israeli War: Origins and Consequences*
- 'The Arab-Israeli Conflict' in *International Relations of the Middle East*

In 2012 he received, from the Middle East Studies Association of North America (MESA), a Mentor Award for his efforts 'in advising and guiding students at the graduate and undergraduate levels'. In 2013, his co-authored book *The Modern Middle East and North Africa: A History in Documents* was accredited, by MESA, as 'the best book on undergraduate education' ('Charles D. Smith' n.d.).

There have been some occasions on which Smith has been attacked by pro-Israeli activists for statements he made about the Israel-Palestine question; one instance is recorded by the pro-Israeli monitoring body, Campus Watch which published a report, under 'Middle East Studies in the News' titled 'On-Campus Panels Attack Israel (Again) [incl. Charles Smith, Leila Hudson, Asher Kaufman]'. The report is written by Shlomo Aronson, a professor from the American-Israeli Cooperative Enterprise. In this report, Smith is described as a 'self styled "expert" on the Arab-Israeli conflict and the Palestinian issue, who is known for missing command of both Hebrew and Arabic' (Aronson 2009). The report contains a letter, from 'an outraged listener', on what went wrong in this panel. The letter, supposedly, states: 'Professor Smith left no question regarding his stance on the recent conflict. His presentation began by arguing, somewhat correctly, that Israel was responsible for the birth of Hamas. However, he continued to tell falsehoods and half-truths, culminating in a justification for Hamas' actions' (Aronson 2009). The letter criticizes Smith for another statement: 'He also made mention that the breakdown of the 2000 Camp David talks was, despite all accounts from individuals present at those negotiations, the fault of the Israeli leadership. He even went as far as to say, "Clinton, Dennis Ross, and [Ehud] Barak all lied about what happened there"' (Aronson 2009).

There are other cases of criticism of Smith from a pro-Israeli stance. One can be seen on a website called 'Rate my Professor'. A student, allegedly, makes another point in this regard: 'I took this class expecting an interesting account on Israeli-Arab relations, but instead I stepped into an anti-Semitic smear fest. Professor Smith is insensitive to the Holocaust and the aftermath of it. There are several issues that he just doesn't get. This class is a way over the top bias toward the Arab end of the spectrum' ('Rate My Professors' n.d.). In another case, Huffington Post Monitor, a pro-Israeli monitoring website, published a report titled 'Charles Smith Predicts the Future (and Israel's Demise)'. The report starts with: 'The latest red meat for the Huffington Post Jew haters is Charles Smith's article about "Israel's fateful hour". In it, this American academic takes the bold, courageous stance of ... criticizing Israeli settlements. Smith leads off with predictions about where the settlements will take Israel in the future, predictions that as usual don't make any sense' ('Charles Smith Predicts the Future' 2012). The report continues with another notable statement: 'Smith then quotes more from a book he read, repeats himself about Israel's imminent demise because of the settlements, describes Netanyahu as "messianic", and accuses Israel of acting like Bar Kochba, the Jewish revolt leader famous for committing suicide rather than surrendering to the Romans' ('Charles Smith Predicts the Future' 2012).

In 2004 Smith acted as a commentator for a panel on the Israeli attack on the USS *Liberty* at a conference held by the US State Department. He made a mild critique of the Israeli attack; in relation to Israel's claim that *Liberty* was mistaken for an Egyptian ship, Smith stressed that Israel should have recognized the identity of the American vessel. He concluded that 'If they didn't know, they didn't try hard enough to find out' (UA News Services 2004).

Mark Tessler

Mark Tessler, an American academic, is the author of *A History of the Israeli-Palestinian Conflict*. He completed his education in the United States, and received his PhD from Northwestern University in political science. He also had chances to study in Israel and in Arab countries; Tessler studied at the University of Tunis and received a Certificate of North African Sociology (1964–5). He also studied at the Hebrew University of Jerusalem in Israel (1961–2). Tessler served in this university as a research associate in political science in 1982. He stayed in Israel for more than three years. He served as a research associate at the University of Tunis (1972–3) as well. His knowledge of relevant languages includes 'good (though rusty) Hebrew' and 'some Arabic' ('Vita' 2020; the 2014 version of the vita, no longer available, omitted the qualification on the Hebrew). Tessler is considered to be one of the very few American scholars who has studied and lived in both the Arab world and Israel ('Mark A. Tessler' 2015).

Tessler has taught in various American universities as a professor of political science: the University of Wisconsin-Milwaukee, the University of Arizona and the University of Michigan. He has taught a number of courses including Politics and International Relations of the Middle East and North Africa, the Arab-Israeli Conflict, and Literature and Politics in North Africa. He has been appointed to numerous academic posts including:

- Director of the Centre for International Studies, 1991–9 (University of Wisconsin-Milwaukee)
- Director of the Centre for Middle Eastern Studies, 1999–2001 (University of Arizona)
- Director of the International Institute, 2005–10 (University of Michigan)

Tessler has also occupied some national positions in the area of Israel-Palestine studies. He served the Association for Israel Studies on the board of directors from 1985, then as vice president (1987–9) and as president (1989–91). He has been a member of the editorial board of the association's journal, *Israel Studies*. Tessler has also been a member of the steering committee of the Palestinian American Research Centre (mentioned in the 2014 Vita only). He has researched and written extensively on the Middle East and the Israel-Palestine question:

- *Israel, Egypt, and the Palestinians: From Camp David to Intifada* (co-authored with Ann Lesch)
- *Democracy, War, and Peace in the Middle East* (as co-editor)
- *Area Studies and Social Science: Strategies for Understanding Middle East Politics* (editor)

A History of the Israeli-Palestinian Conflict attained national honour, and was named by the *New York Times* as a 'Notable Book of 1994' ('Vita' 2020). The American Institute for Maghreb Studies (AIMS) awards a prize to students in Maghrib studies, that is called the Mark Tessler AIMS Graduate Student Prize Award for what is described as being 'in honor of his enduring interest in the Maghreb and his sustained efforts to develop graduate students prepared to work in the field' ('AIMS Newsletter' 2009).

Campus Watch published an article, under 'Middle East Studies in the News', titled 'The Clash over Middle East Studies'. This article was written by Jennifer Jacobson, and published originally in the *Chronicle of Higher Education*, reports a discussion on the subject. In this discussion, Martin Kramer, a well-known pro-Israeli activist and writer, charges Middle East professors with discouraging scholarly work on terrorism and Islamic fundamentalism. Tessler, an attendee at this discussion, opposed Kramer's claim by mentioning some book titles published by Indiana University Press including *Islamic Activism*. He concludes his response to the Kramer charges: 'The notion that [these centers] are not doing their job and that they're soft on terrorism and anti-Israel that is just not the case in my experience' (Jacobson 2004).

In another report published by the pro-Israeli organization, CAMERA, written to critique a radio series, 'A Middle East History', presented under a radio programme, *The World*, Tessler is criticized:

> The PRI series relies heavily on interviews with historian Mark Tessler from the University of Michigan, hardly an impartial scholar. A review of his 1994 book, *A History of the Israeli-Palestinian Conflict*, pointed to Tessler's selective citations of documentary sources, misleading quotes, one-sided reporting of facts and events, biased choice of language, and even the use of a fabricated quotation attributed to Israel's then military chief of staff, Yitzchak Rabin. The review concluded that Tessler's work presents only the version of events most damaging to Israel, doing 'so much to promote myth and so little to advance the truth' (*Midstream Magazine*, May–June 1999). The same can be said to sum up *The World*'s special series on the history of the Middle East.
>
> Hollander 2002

The Results of the Context Analysis

The second analysis of this study (context analysis) i.e. analysing some information – that has just been provided in this chapter – about the background of the authors of the selected textbooks reveals some remarkable results:

- Most writers or editors of the selected textbooks come from a particular national background; they are either American or Israeli, or both: Klausner, Smith and Tessler are American; Morris and Rubin are Israeli; Laqueur and Sachar have, probably, both citizenships. Laqueur was an Israeli citizen who moved to the United States, and Sachar was an American citizen who moved to Israel. The only exception is Bickerton; he is an Australian national. He, however, has strong links with the United States; he received his PhD in the United States, and taught in American universities for a long time. His selected textbook is also co-authored with a Jewish American writer. None of the writers or editors of these dominant textbooks come from a Palestinian or Arab background.
- Most producers of the analysed textbooks come from a particular educational environment; they are educated in the United States or Israel or both; there are two who received part of their higher education in other countries; Bickerton did his undergraduate work in Australia, and Morris received his PhD in the UK. The information provided suggests that none of them received any part of their education in a Arab country. The only exception is Tessler, who studied for one year in Tunis.
- The information provided about the languages that writers can use suggests that six of them (Klausner, Laqueur, Morris, Rubin, Sachar and Tessler) have good Hebrew. In contrast, there are only two or three (Tessler, Smith and Klausner) who have 'some Arabic'. This fact can reveal how Arab and Israeli sources are being treated differently while writing the selected histories on the Israel-Palestine question.
- All historians come from a particular religious background; they are either Jewish or Christians; six historians, from eight, come from a Jewish background including Klausner, Laqueur, Morris, Rubin, Tessler and Sachar. Bickerton introduces Irish Catholicism as his background. No evidence was found that introduces Smith as Jew. He probably comes from a Christian background. There is certainly not anyone who comes from a Muslim background. There is evidence that introduces all Jewish historians of the study, except one (Tessler), as having some record of supporting Zionist ideas and/or Israel. The non-Jewish historians of this study (two in total) had a greater link with Israel, compared to their link with Arab countries; they have a noticeable record, as has been detailed in this chapter, of living, studying and teaching in Israel.
- Two textbooks, those written by Smith and Tessler, that showed comparatively more sympathy with the Palestinian side (based on the results of the textbook analysis in the last chapter) come from authors who have had relatively more links with the Arab world. They both have some Arabic (language). They both had some experience of studying or teaching in Arab countries. They both were attacked by pro-Israeli watch bodies for their ideas on Palestine. Moreover, an interesting story links these two to each other and also to the Palestinian side; according to Tessler, they both spent most of 1982 in Jerusalem:

Charles Smith with a visiting Hebrew University appointment and me working for an independent research organization. The spring of 1982 saw an intense and broad Palestinian mini-intifada. I think this persuaded each of us to write a book about Israel-Palestine when we got home. Much of Carl's prior work was on Egypt and I had been working on North Africa. I had just finished a series of articles on politics in Morocco for the research organization that sponsored me in Jerusalem. But the 1982 Palestinian uprising grabbed our attention and motivated each of us to contribute what we could to an understanding of the Israel-Palestine conflict.

from an email interaction with Dr Mark Tessler on 8 July 2021

Table 6.1 The results of the context analysis[a]

Author	Nationality	Religion	Higher education	Language[b]	Ideology[c]
Bickerton	Australian	Christian	Australia, United States	No Arabic? No Hebrew?	Teaching in Israel
Klausner	American	Jewish	United States	Hebrew Some Arabic?	Pro-Israeli
Laqueur	Israeli/American	Jewish	Israel	Hebrew	Pro-Israeli
Morris	Israeli	Jewish	Israel/UK	Hebrew	Pro-Israeli
Rubin	Israeli	Jewish	United States	Hebrew	Pro-Israeli
Sachar	Israeli/American	Jewish	United States	Hebrew	Pro-Israeli
Smith	American	Christian	United States	Some Arabic Some Hebrew?	Teaching in Israel
Tessler	American	Jewish	United States	Hebrew Some Arabic	Lived in Israel

Notes:

a This table is designed to show an overall picture of the results of the context analysis that was applied to the eight historians. Accuracy might be compromised for the sake of simplicity and brevity, so please refer to the text for a fuller representation of the results of the analysis.

b The knowledge of the historians of the language of the conflicting sides of the question: Hebrew and Arabic.

c How historians are related, ideologically, to Zionism and Israel.

Conclusion

WHAT WENT WRONG IN WESTERN TEXTBOOKS?

It is already well established, through the relevant literature, that the Western role was crucial in founding the Jewish state and also in its successful survival. Much research has been done on the subjects of military support, financial assistance, media control, diaspora lobbying and so on, in relation to Western support of Israel. One area that has been surprisingly neglected is that of education, especially higher education. While there has been some work done on school textbooks, there has been no significant investigation into college textbooks, and yet this area can arguably be seen as much more important, since it is in colleges and universities that knowledge on any subject is produced. School textbooks just formulate this knowledge at a simpler level. Academic knowledge is trusted as authoritative and accurate. In fact, it assumes the status of truth about a subject. It is for this reason that an investigation into what college textbooks offer about Israel-Palestine is a timely and necessary enterprise.

The purpose of this research, therefore, is to analyse academic knowledge on the Israel-Palestine question in Western academia. This subject is important for more than one reason:

1. It can contribute to advancing a more inclusive notion about the idea of Western support of Israel, and its real dimensions, by highlighting another area of (presumed) Western pro-Israeli bias.
2. It addresses a question that can reveal relevant points about the causes of such a tendency in Western policy. This case is related to the influential role that knowledge plays in social and political affairs in Western democracies.
3. Western knowledge on the question is important not only for its impact on Western societies; it can occupy a governing position, like many other bodies of knowledge that come from the West, across a worldwide spectrum. This capacity to inform a much wider audience in the world makes its impact important on a global scale.
4. Knowledge occupies an important and respectable place in the West, and is considered the main reason for Western progress and development that characterize the region as a different and prominent part of the world. This achievement is introduced as an outcome of successful efforts to detach

knowledge from political and religious influences. Any possibility of undermining this fundamental quality in Western societies can be a serious matter of investigation.

The knowledge produced in the West on the Israel-Palestine question can be found in almost all the human sciences and disciplines. As covering all of them would be outside the scope of a single piece of research, history has been selected as the academic discipline that is more apt for this analysis. This choice is informed by the idea that the history of the Israel-Palestine question is a principal academic field where pro-Israeli activities can be observed. History, according to the pro-Israelis, gives the Jewish people a right to the land and in this sense, is a main source of the arguments and evidence presented in defence of Zionist's occupation of historical Palestine.

The first methodological question of the research emerges when access to knowledge of the history of the Israel-Palestine question is at stake: is there any site where this knowledge can be accessed? The literature suggests textbooks, encyclopaedia articles and journal articles as the main sources of knowledge (Myers 1991). Textbooks are introduced, at the same time, as a resource with a governing position. This was the main reason for calling textbook knowledge an official or dominant form of knowledge (Davis 2006: xiii).

The second methodological question of the research is related to textbooks that can represent Western knowledge on the question's history. The history of the Israel-Palestine question is taught in many courses across Western universities. Many books are introduced in these courses as the main source of relevant knowledge. An extensive survey was conducted for this study, to find the most frequently adopted textbooks that are used in anglophone Western universities to teach the history of the question. This survey allowed the formation of a list of the most commonly used textbooks in Western academia – six of which, the leading ones, are selected for the main analysis of this study. Chapter 3 is devoted to the relevant evidence and arguments that support the selected textbooks' status as truly representative of Western knowledge in this area. The following list reflects the results, exhibiting a textbook's position:

1. *Palestine and the Arab-Israeli Conflict: A History with Documents*, Charles D. Smith
2. *A Concise History of the Arab-Israeli Conflict*, Ian J. Bickerton and Carla L. Klausner
3. *Righteous Victims: A History of the Zionist-Arab Conflict*, Benny Morris
4. *A History of the Israeli-Palestinian Conflict*, Mark A. Tessler
5. *A History of Israel: From the Rise of Zionism to Our Time*, Howard M. Sachar
6. *The Israel-Arab Reader: A Documentary History of the Middle East Conflict*, Walter Laqueur and Barry Rubin

In advance of the main analysis of the study, that of textbook analysis, the related literature is reviewed; all works (forty-seven titles in total) which analyse the textbook treatment of the question, in Western countries, are studied for the sake of this research. Many of them deal only partly or indirectly with the question, through more general topics such as the Middle East or the Arabs.

The results of the studies identified in the literature review introduce bias as a main problem; two studies support the idea that textbooks are suffering from an anti-Israeli bias (Tobin and Ybarra 2008; Bard 1993), while others support, more or less, the opposite. This review suggests that history textbooks are deconstructed through different critical methods. Historical narrative analysis, the method applied for the main analysis in this research, focuses on the textbook (or history) as a whole rather than on its parts. The stress, in this analysis, has moved away from the portrayal of distinct historical 'facts' to how the whole history is presented, or how the mega narrative is structured. It engages with the central structure of the narrative. It is assumed that such a structure comes from the main ideological positions that historians take towards history. This structure can convey the principal message of the constructed history and refers to the main reason a given history is written for. With this method in the centre of the analysis, identifying a pro-Israeli structure in the relevant histories was the next task.

A model of a pro-Israeli structure of the history of the question is recognized in the relevant literature:

- It has a certain beginning where the history of the land starts with the Jews' presence in the land, ignoring others who possessed the land before them, or alongside their presence.
- The supposed Jewish time of possession of the land, that of ancient Israel, is constructed as the principal history of the land: it is narrated, also, in a way to provide the essentials of a perceived Jewish state; such as 'Jewish people', 'Jewish kingdom' and 'Jewish independence'.
- This 'glorious Jewish time' has a certain ending; the forced mass expulsion of the Jews from the land by the Romans, is articulated as the ending of the 'Jewish state', and the main event responsible for the absence of the Jews in the land for the last two millennia.
- It undermines any major Jewish collective experience in other lands except those that function as a reminder of the 'Jewish displacement'. In this way, thousands of years of the presence of Jewish communities in other lands – for instance, Iran and Iraq – are discounted. Jewish achievements in establishing states outside the Holy Land, such as the Himyarite kingdom and the kingdom of Adiabene, and even an empire, the Khazarian Empire, are seen as outside the main frame of Jewish historical experience.
- The main bulk of the land's history, the last two thousand years, that constitutes the most documented history of the land is not taken as a significant period in its history; the main history of this time, according to Zionist historiography, is located outside Palestine where Jews lived, who supposedly regarded Palestine as their homeland; their history is summarized simply as their efforts to keep the link with the motherland, their hope to return to it, and their striving to realize that hope.

Accordingly, the land's history is structured in such a way that it starts with the Jews, and ends with them, and leaves no space in between, in the land's thousands of years of history that might be filled by others' history. This structure secures a history-long Jewishness of the land, providing a safe historiographical place for the Jews where they are not bothered by others' presence, history and rights. In addition, all Jews of different nationalities and races in all times are taken as one: one ethnos and one nation. Accordingly, when a Jew migrates to Israel, from any part of the world, of any race and colour, with any nationality, they are regarded as the same Jew in ancestry as those who, supposedly, were forced to leave the Holy Land some two thousand years ago.

With a model of a pro-Israeli structure of the question's history at hand, all selected histories of the Israel-Palestine question have been put under extensive investigation, through historical narrative analysis, to identify the central structure of these histories in relation to the pro-Israeli model. One selected textbook, *The Arab-Israeli Reader*, is examined briefly but exempted from the textbook analysis. The entire book is merely a collection of relevant documents. There is no place for actual historiography in this book, even to cover some common properties of a textbook such as 'Introduction' or 'Conclusion'. Very little is written by the editors of the book, Walter Laqueur and Barry Rubin, to narrate the Israel-Palestine history; a few lines are added in some cases to introduce the document. As a result, no real historiography can be found in its exact sense. This leaves not much chance of examining how the history of the question is narrated. For that reason, the results of the main analysis come from the examination of the other five textbooks.

The textbook analysis supports the conclusion that all analysed textbooks have, more or less, a pro-Israeli structure; significant differences, however, exist. All histories of the land start with the Jewish people. *Palestine and the Arab-Israeli Conflict* is the only exception that starts this history with the Canaanites (Smith 2013: 10). This textbook is the only one that also challenges the pro-Israeli narratives of ancient Israel. It mentions the results of archaeological discoveries in the Holy Land that do not provide evidence to support the biblical stories of ancient Israel (Smith 2013: 2). Other textbooks do not question the main elements of the Zionist historiography of this time such as the Jewish people, the Jewish kingdom and Jewish independence. Some of them, *Righteous Victims* for instance, deal with this aspect of the question very briefly (Morris 2001: 4), while others, such as Tessler's textbook, support this history with extensive detail (Tessler 2009: 8–12).

Western academia makes a convincing claim about its detachment from the church that provided the modern knowledge with a chance to emancipate and flourish on an unprecedented scale. This state of affairs is very hard to see in the case of the history of ancient Israel. As revealed earlier, all leading textbooks of the field, except one, take what the Bible offers, in this regard, as true representation of historical reality while there is a noticeable absence of access to scientific evidence. Academic scholars, in this case, look like religious fundamentalists who regard the Bible literally as truth just because it is biblical. No need to repeat here that the history of ancient Israel is based, heavily if not exclusively, on biblical traditions.

What historians have, other than Bible statements, has not enough power to introduce that history as a true story of what really happened in that course of history. This claim to truth, hence, cannot be regarded as a scientific claim, it is a fundamentalist one – similar to those that are offered in the church, and not in the modern academia.

The third element of the Zionist historiography – the forced expulsion of the Jews – is accepted as a historical fact in all textbooks. Varying degrees of confirmation, however, is exercised. *Palestine and the Arab-Israeli Conflict* is the only account that does not support, openly, a mass expulsion of Jews by the Romans but it confirms, at the same time, the general idea of expulsion, and that Jews left the Holy Land because of Roman policy (Smith 2013: 3–4). Others do not challenge this story: one textbook, *A Concise History of the Arab-Israeli Conflict*, however, presents the idea that many Jews left the land voluntarily, before the expulsion (Bickerton and Klausner 1998: 21).

In relation to another element of Zionist historiography – the Jews' link, outside Palestine, with Palestine as a homeland and their redemptionist efforts to return – textbooks are, more or less, sympathetic. Again, *Palestine and the Arab-Israeli Conflict* is the only one that shows a very limited sympathy with this Zionist account, providing the idea that the religious traditions expressed by Jews in the pre-Zionist era about a final gathering in Zion are different from the Zionist ideas about the return to Palestine as a national home (Smith 2013: 26). In contrast, Morris considers Zionism a modern version of the old Jewish yearning to return to their home in Palestine (Morris 2001: 14). Sachar makes more efforts, relatively, to support this Zionist idea (Sachar 2007: Ch. 2). Others, Tessler and Bickerton and Klausner, provide some arguments to support the idea, mentioning, at the same time, that no actual step had been taken by Jews in this almost 2,000-year period to make that 'return' happen (Tessler 2009: 19–20; Bickerton and Klausner 1998: 27).

The selected textbooks demonstrate different treatments when the Arab history of the land is at stake; Sachar and Morris not only ignore the significance of the Arab history of the land but make clear efforts to suppress it. Smith and Tessler, on the other hand, take the Arab history of the land into consideration. Bickerton and Klausner ignore the history but make no obvious effort to downgrade it. All of them, at the same time, do not take the Arab history of the land as its principal history.

There are, also, other cases of accepting pro-Israeli elements: all textbooks support the Zionist idea of regarding Jews as one people, and as a nation. All of them regard the European Jews, from different nationalities, as the same Jews who, supposedly, were expelled from the land, two thousand years ago. All of them ignore Jewish links to other lands, and their achievements in establishing independent states outside Palestine. *A Concise History of the Arab-Israeli Conflict* rejects such a possibility (Bickerton and Klausner 1998: 9). None of the textbooks analysed in this research views the pro-Israeli structure of the dominant histories of the question as a real problem to understanding the Israel-Palestine question.

The overall results of this analysis introduce *Palestine and the Arab-Israeli Conflict* as the only textbook that entertained considerable reservations about some main elements of the Zionist narrative, and that has not, uncritically, accepted a pro-Israeli structure of the history. All others failed to do so. Two different classes, at the same time, are identified in this category: the textbooks written by Sachar and Morris reproduced all the main elements of the Zionist account without distancing themselves from them; the other two (Bickerton and Klausner, Tessler), however, managed to show some distance between their own position and that of the pro-Israeli narrative in some cases. As a result, these two textbooks are not regarded as histories that were developed to advance the Zionist version of history, but as histories that have been influenced by that history.

Four arguments, in general, can support the idea that the knowledge in the analysed textbooks is biased; the first one is based directly on the results of the main analysis of this research. All histories analysed, except one, have a pro-Israeli structure. This structure is a common character of all Zionist historiographies of the question. It is rooted in fundamental Zionist documents including Israel's Declaration of Independence, as elaborated in Chapter 4.

The second argument is related to another aspect of the identified structure i.e. its origin. This structure / mega story is invented by Zionist historians in the nineteenth and twentieth centuries. It is a recent phenomenon, with no precedent in history, and historical sources of the pre-Zionist era. It was constructed when the Zionist movement needed such a construction to advance its ideology (Sand 2008b).

The first of these arguments is based on an answer to the question of how a Zionist history of the Israel-Palestine matter is narrated. The second is based on a different question: when has such history been narrated, and by whom. Answers given necessitate a scholarly sensitivity to the political motivations responsible for such narratives, and their grave consequences for the Zionist historiography of the question. The third argument is therefore that all selected histories are found free of such sensitivity. Uncritical acceptance of the Zionist narratives, in such circumstances, is far from an objective historiography.

The fourth argument that supports the biased character of Western knowledge on the question is related to the historical and scientific value of the Zionist historiographical elements. There are serious problems, as revealed by critical historians, Israelis and others, that severely undermine the historicity of the Zionist accounts. The main elements of the Zionist history, including those that are related to ancient Israel, the forced expulsion of the Jews and their redemptionist efforts to return, suffer from such problems. There is not enough evidence to introduce them as historical facts; this has been elaborated in Chapter 4. There is evidence, in fact, that refutes such theories. It is not expected that an unbiased history would represent these claims as historical facts. An unbiased history makes enough effort to differentiate between myth and fact, and to place what can be categorized as not strictly either, in its right position. The way the history of the question is presented in the selected textbooks is quite different; Zionist historical elements, that are invented and advanced for ideological reasons, are reported as

Table C.1 How theories of the history are treated in Western textbooks

Textbook title	The main elements of the Zionist historiography		
	'Ancient Israel' is a:	Forced expulsion of the Jews from the land (by the Romans) is a:	'Jewish redemptionist efforts to return' is a:
Palestine and the Arab-Israeli Conflict	Theory	Fact (but Roman policy was influential as well)	Theory
A Concise History of the Arab-Israeli Conflict	Fact	Fact (but many left the land before)	Fact (but no actual step was taken)
Righteous Victims	Fact (as a whole but not in its details)	Fact	Fact
A History of the Israeli-Palestinian Conflict	Fact	Fact	Fact (but no actual step was taken)
A History of Israel	Fact	Fact	Fact

the true history of the question. Nothing serious is mentioned to reflect the real scientific value of these accounts and their problems. The only real exception is *Palestine and the Arab-Israeli Conflict*, written by Charles Smith. Table C.1 summarizes, simplifies and illustrates this argument and its components.

At odds with the documented bias of the selected textbooks, they make evident efforts to market their work as objective and unbiased products. For such purpose, they frequently stress that both the Israeli and Palestinian sides and their arguments are taken into (equal) consideration in narrating the related history. All the selected textbooks except *A History of Israel* offered such assertions in the book's opening section, the preface or introduction. Bickerton and Klausner presented their own statement in the preface of the book: 'We have attempted to achieve some balance and objectivity about a subject upon which most people feel it necessary to adopt a partisan point of view. Throughout the book, we have tried to present both sides of the issues, although we realize that even the selection of material to be included reveals some subjective judgment on our part' (Bickerton and Klausner 1998: xvi). Benny Morris made a similar claim in the preface to his textbook as well:

> I have tried to compensate by using relevant Arab materials to the extent that they were accessible, and by ferreting out the 'Arab side' or 'perspective' as manifested in documentation in Zionist-Israeli and Western archives (for example, by using intelligence documents reporting on thinking and activities from the Arab side) and writings. In doing so, I have attempted to approach the subject as objectively as possible, to bring reason and fairness to my reconstructions of the past.
>
> Morris 2001: xiv

Laqueur and Rubin, the editors of *The Israel-Arab Reader* made such a claim in brief in the introduction of their textbook: 'For four decades, *The Israel-Arab Reader* has tried to document these developments as objectively as possible' (Laqueur and Rubin 2008: xiv). Tessler, especially, is detailed in describing the 'unbiased' character of his textbook: 'This book seeks not only to provide an objective history of the Israeli-Palestinian conflict but also to encourage an engaged and sympathetic understanding of the parties to this continuing dispute. The aim of this approach may be described as objectivity without detachment' (Tessler 2009: xiv). This claim has been emphasized again in the book: 'Second, and consistent with this perspective, the book seeks not only to present a balanced and accurate history of the Israel-Palestinian conflict, it also strives to encourage a sympathetic understanding of the parties involved' (Tessler 2009: xiii). Tessler made enormous efforts to stress the objectivity of his work and its fair representation of both sides: 'Beyond this, however, my aim has been to maintain a stance of considered objectivity. I have tried to represent both sides fairly when fundamental issues are discussed' (Tessler 2009: xvii). He claims further that no conclusion is advanced by the book; it is left to the readers to make their own: 'the volume strives for a nonpartisan point of view; it seeks to present both Palestinian and Israeli analyses and to enable readers to form their own conclusions about the persuasiveness of competing arguments' (Tessler 2009: xvii). This is stressed again in the opening of the book: 'My goal is not to foster specific conclusions about central issues in the conflict but to provide a basis for understanding and evaluating the actions of both Israelis and Palestinians' (Tessler 2009: xvii).

It is quite illuminating that the most humble claim about the book's unbiased character and its capacity for true representation of both sides is made by the least biased book of the survey, *Palestine and the Arab-Israeli Conflict*: 'From its inception, this book has given equal emphasis to the modern histories of both Palestine and Israel, beginning with extended treatment of the nineteenth century, the critical era of World War I, and the period of British mandatory rule down to 1947 as points of departure for the era since Israel's independence' (Smith 2013: vi). Nothing else is identified in this book as a claim to some kind of impartiality. The pattern demonstrated in the other selected textbooks, laying emphasis on objectivity when the book is biased, and stressing fair representation of both sides while the book is pro-Israeli, leads to the conclusion that such claims are not only untrue but also misleading. It also suggests the idea that such emphasis might be made deliberately, in some cases, to sell a pro-Israeli product as a non-partisan and reliable source of related knowledge.

Further analysis of the selected textbooks, from the perspective of the authors' background, supports the results of the textbook analysis in this academic investigation. The second analysis went further, to ascertain the context of the texts produced, to provide some knowledge about why the selected histories are constructed in that particular way. The authors, historians, have been chosen as the most influential factors in the social context of textbook authorship, for their significant role in how college-level textbooks are written; they are the main authority that determines textbook contents (Squire 1960: 1416). This second analysis has delivered a conclusion that pro-Israeli textbooks are written by historians who come from a pro-Israeli background. This is evident in two pro-Israeli textbooks of this study i.e. those by Sachar and Morris, both from a pro-Israeli Jewish background. Other textbooks, which showed less pro-Israeli bias, originate from different backgrounds.

This analysis offers other significant results: almost all the writers or editors of the six selected textbooks come from a certain national background; they are American or Israeli, or both: Klausner, Smith and Tessler are American; Morris and Rubin are Israeli; Laqueur and Sachar have, probably, both citizenships. The only exception is Bickerton, an Australian historian. None of them come from a Palestinian or Arab national background.

All producers of the popular textbooks come from a certain academic environment; they are educated in the United States or Israel or both; there are only two who received part of their higher education in other countries, i.e. in Australia and the UK. None of them received any major part of their education in a Middle Eastern or Arab country. The language used, in the relevant studies, can be seen as another source of bias: six of the historians (Klausner, Laqueur, Morris, Rubin, Sachar and Tessler) have good Hebrew. In contrast, there are only two or three (Tessler, Smith and Klausner) who have 'some Arabic' ('Vita' 2020). All historians come from a particular religious background; either Jewish or Christian; six historians, from eight, come from a Jewish background including Klausner, Laqueur, Morris, Rubin, Tessler and Sachar. There is no one who comes from a different religious background. The related evidence introduces all Jewish historians of the study except one as having some record of supporting Zionist ideas and/or Israel. The non-Jewish historians of this study, two in total, do not have such a background, but they still have a greater link with Israel, compared to their link with Arab countries.

The main analyses of this study – textbook and context – have been conducted to provide some answers to the questions of 'how' and 'why' that drove the research: 'how do Western college-level textbooks treat the history of the Israel-Palestine question and why do they treat the question in that way?' The results of the textbook analysis support the claim that the textbook knowledge on the question is mainly pro-Israeli in bias. In relation to the question 'why', the analysis offers the 'Jewish pro-Israeli producer' as the main factor that can explain that bias in the produced histories. Another factor is identified in this analysis as well: the relevant knowledge has been produced in a particular, American or Israeli, national and educational environment. One needs to take into consideration the US position as the most pro-Israeli country in the world, to grasp the real dimensions of the social, national and educational environments that govern the production of these textbooks. It is equally significant to take into account the fact that there is no place in that context for the views of the other side, the Arabs, or even the views of less pro-Israeli countries in the West as influences on the related processes. This thesis supports the idea that the mainstream knowledge in Western academia, on the history of the Israel-Palestine question, is produced under the jurisdiction of an Israeli-American context.

Table C.2 The main questions of the thesis and its answers

No.	Question	Analysis	Answer
1	How do Western college-level textbooks treat the history of the Israel-Palestine question?	Textbook analysis	The textbook knowledge on the question is mainly pro-Israeli in bias
2	Why do they treat the question in that way?	Context analysis	1. Jewish pro-Israeli producer 2. American/Israeli environment of the textbook production

The findings of this study can open a discussion about the grave implications that such a state of affairs can have at the practical level: knowledge itself can be regarded as the first victim. Western knowledge is credited with being objective and dispassionate when compared with other bodies of knowledge in the world. The results of this study might undermine this idea; it is quite politicized when it comes to Israel. This problem cannot be discounted as an unavoidable social bias that no one, and no society, can escape; it is involved in undermining a fundamental quality of Western knowledge, that Western knowledge flourished when the fundamentalist religious ideas about the world were abandoned by scholars who replaced them with a scientific and objective method of producing knowledge. This tradition is still powerful in the West and governs its academia. The results of this study demonstrate that Western knowledge, when it comes to the Israel-Palestine question, is influenced heavily by the fundamental ideas of the biblical stories. These stories, in the history of the question, are taken as scientific facts as shown in the analysis.

Education is another area of practical consequences for the results of this research. Textbooks are taken, in this study, to represent academic knowledge but they can represent education as well. Textbooks' position as a central player in education is confirmed repeatedly. The dominant role of textbooks in education and their power to represent education as a whole, which is discussed in Chapter 1, can reveal the fact that the consequences of a pro-Israeli textbook can be serious. Textbooks determine what knowledge students receive about the Israel-Palestine question. This, in turn, can exhibit the influential power of certain powerful elites, textbook authors, to regulate the knowledge of the question. Here scientific knowledge and governing standards of teaching history, where differentiating idea from fact is articulated as a main objective, can be undermined by political and ideological motivations: 'There are some objectives assumed for teaching history such as: knowledge and facts, understanding, and critical thinking to realize the difference between fact and idea' (Blishen 1969).

Textbook knowledge not only influences students; it has a wider impact on society as a whole. This case constitutes the third level of the practical consequences of biased knowledge. Textbook knowledge has a profound impact on social beliefs and ideas. Historical knowledge, compared with other bodies of knowledge, has a particular power, enabling it to play a central role in society; presenting the past through history contributes significantly to controlling the present and shaping the future (Foster and Crawford 2006: 6). What people receive and believe as the past is able to produce huge social energy; it can make people die for a cause or kill for it (Foster and Crawford 2006: 6). Public opinion is formed and informed by knowledge. Public opinion is translated into public policy in democracies. Holsti (1962) makes a valuable contribution in this field through his idea of the 'belief system'. This system determines, he argues, how leaders make decisions and develop a policy, foreign policy for instance. According to Brockway, Holsti's idea has a clear meaning for the Middle East:

> In a democracy, leaders must be responsive to the views of their constituents and thus, leaders' belief systems are linked with those of the public. For example: if the people of the United States believe that inhabitants of the Middle East are terrorists, the people will support policies within the U.S. that reflect that, and they will be unlikely to support aid and policies friendly towards the Middle East. Even enlightened leaders will have to respond to these demands or face electoral defeat. Thus the belief systems of ordinary people are crucial to understand.
>
> Brockway 2007: 4

Holsti elaborates how this national state is related to international conflicts: 'The relationship of national images to international conflict is clear: decision-makers act upon their definition of the situation and their images of states – others as well as their own. These images are in turn dependent upon the decision-makers' belief system. And these may or may not be accurate representations of "reality"' (Holsti 1962). He concludes that for resolving conflicts it is necessary to correct the erroneous image of others. This theory can explain how biased knowledge on the Israel-Palestine question can form biased and erroneous public opinion. This biased public opinion, in turn, will influence Western policy towards the question.

The findings of this research suggest some implications on the theoretical level as well; how the impact of biased knowledge works in education and in the wider social realm, public opinion, has just been mentioned: it influences Western policy towards the Israel-Palestine question. As a result, this case of biased Western treatment, the biased knowledge, has the capacity to work as an explanatory factor for the whole problem as well; it might explain why the West supports Israel. This enables the present study to offer, while not discussing it, a theory in this regard: biased knowledge is the main reason, or one of the most important reasons, for the support of Israel by Western countries.

Another theoretical implication of the results of this research is related to Western knowledge. This study suggests that mainstream knowledge on the question in Western academia is biased. This might be attributed to a general problem in history, as an academic discipline, and the social sciences, where all historical narratives in general and national histories, in particular, are considered biased from one perspective. But it might refer, also, to a bigger and particular problem. Western knowledge on the Israel-Palestine question might represent an exception, an exceptional level of bias in Western academia. This study has not been conducted to assess this hypothesis. Such assessment is left to those who are familiar with other areas of bias in Western knowledge including national, racial and gender bias, to those who can compare different existing levels of bias in the West. This study suggests, at the same time, that such a theory about a particular and exceptional bias in this area of Western knowledge can be taken into consideration. One finding of this study, the fundamentalist nature of the relevant knowledge on Israel-Palestine history, where fundamental accounts, at odds with the governing values of Western science, are taken as factual statements, can support such a theory.

The last theoretical implication of this research can enforce the previous point, i.e. the exceptional nature of the Western scholarly treatment of Israel. This point is related to the general notion of the relationship between the history produced and the historians – the producers (Gilderhus 1987: 82). The findings of this study support the idea that historians produce histories that are in agreement with their background. Pro-Israeli historians, in this case, produced pro-Israeli histories. This conclusion supports the historical notion of the relationship between history and historians. There are, however, relevant considerations that limit such support. These considerations introduce the pro-Israeli historians as exceptional historians and not normal ones. There are reasons for such an assertion; first of all, pro-Israeli historians are aware that without a historical justification of the Zionist involvement in Palestine the whole Zionist project in the Holy Land and legitimacy of Israel is in danger. Israel might constitute the only case in the international community whose legitimacy faces such a grave challenge. Second, they undoubtedly are aware that without effective Western support Israel is not able to survive. Again, this is not a common reality in the world. There are governments, here and there, that might not survive without Western support but in Israel's case this survival is related to the very existence of a Jewish state. The third reason is related to the image that pro-Israeli scholars carry about the Jewish question and the outside world. Zionism was born out of the idea that the outside world is hostile to Jews, and Jews need a refuge of their own to survive. They take the Holocaust as evidence that there is a powerful tendency in the world at large to annihilate the Jews as a people. They consider, accordingly, the existing resistance to the occupation of Palestine, as efforts by antisemite forces to destroy this sole refuge of the Jewish people. It is understandable why, with such an image in mind, they promote the version of history that they do. The case, for them, is one of life and death. Consequently, they might use whatever is at hand to advance a history that guarantees the survival of this 'sole refuge'. These considerations, hence, might differentiate them from other/normal historians. Normal historians produce bias when they are engaged in writing national histories, for instance. It is hard, at the same time, to perceive that their background provides such extraordinary motivations for writing self-history in this particular way.

REFERENCES

Abraham, M. (2014), *Out of Bounds: Academic Freedom and the Question of Palestine*, New York: Bloomsbury.

'Abram L. Sachar' (n.d.), Brandeis University. Available online: https://web.archive.org/web/20150907015546/http://lts.brandeis.edu/research/archives-speccoll/findingguides/archives/presidents/sacharpersonal.html (accessed 23 April 2015).

Abunimah, A. (2004), 'Moral Decay and Benny Morris', The Electronic Intifada, 24 January 2004. Available online: https://electronicintifada.net/content/moral-decay-and-benny-morris/4963 (accessed 15 August 2021).

'Advisory Council' (n.d.), J Street. Available online: https://jstreet.org/supporters/advisory-council (accessed 23 April 2015).

'AIMS Newsletter' (2009), American Institute for Maghrib Studies, Spring–Summer 2009. Available online: https://web.archive.org/web/20160416093702/http://aimsnorthafrica.org/publications/archive/2009_01_spring_summer.pdf.

Airasian, P.W. (1994), 'Classroom Assessment', in T. Husén and T.N. Postlethwaite (eds), *The International Encyclopedia of Education Volume 2*, 793, 2nd edn, Oxford: Pergamon.

Al-Bataineh, A.T. (1998), 'The Development of a Content Analysis Instrument for Analyzing College-Level Textbooks Used in the United States to Teach about the Middle East', EdD diss., Illinois State University, Normal, IL. Available online: https://search.proquest.com/docview/304438854/ (accessed 15 August 2021).

Allin, D.H. and S. Simon (2003), 'The Moral Psychology of Us Support for Israel', *Survival*, 45 (3): 123–44.

Al-Qazzaz, A. (1978), *The Arab World: A Handbook for Teachers*, Albany, CA: NAJDA (Women Concerned About the Middle East).

Al-Qazzaz, A. (2002), 'The Image of Arab and Islam in Introduction to Sociology College Textbooks in the United States', *Digest of Middle East Studies*, 11 (2): 34–56.

Aronson, S. (2009), 'On-Campus Panels Attack Israel (Again) [incl. Charles Smith, Leila Hudson, Asher Kaufman]', Campus Watch, 11 February. Available online: https://www.campus-watch.org/article/id/6889 (accessed 15 August 2021).

Bain, K.R. (1979), *The March to Zion: United States Policy and the Founding of Israel*, College Station, TX: Texas A & M University Press.

Bamberger, R. (1992), 'The Austrian Institute for Textbook Research', in H. Bourdillon (ed.), *History and Social Studies – Methodologies of Textbook Analysis: Report of the Educational Research Workshop Held in Braunschweig (Germany), 11–19 September 1990*, 115–19, Lisse, NL: Swets & Zeitlinger.

Bard, M. (1993), 'Rewriting History in Textbooks', Jewish Virtual Library, The American-Israeli Cooperative Enterprise (AICE), Chevy Chase, MD. Available online: https://www.jewishvirtuallibrary.org/pub/texts.html (accessed 15 August 2021).

Bard, M.G. and D. Pipes (1997), 'How Special Is the U.S.–Israel Relationship?', *Middle East Quarterly*, 4 (2): 41–8.

Barlow, E. (1995), 'Middle East Facts and Fictions', *Journal of the International Institute*, 2 (2). Available online: https://quod.lib.umich.edu/j/jii/4750978.0002.207?view=text;rgn=main (accessed 15 August 2021).

Ben-Zvi, A. (1993), *The United States and Israel: The Limits of the Special Relationship*, New York: Columbia University Press.

Bercuson, D.J. (1985), *Canada and the Birth of Israel: A Study in Canadian Foreign Policy*, Toronto: University of Toronto Press.

Berger, S. and C. Lorenz, eds (2010), *Nationalizing the Past: Historians as Nation Builders in Modern Europe*, New York: Palgrave Macmillan.

Berger, S., M. Donovan and K. Passmore, eds (1999), *Writing National Histories: Western Europe Since 1800*, London: Routledge.

Bickerton, I.J. (2009), *The Arab-Israeli Conflict: A History*, London: Reaktion Books.

Bickerton, I.J. and C.L. Klausner (1998), *A Concise History of the Arab-Israeli Conflict*, 3rd edn, Upper Saddle River, NJ: Prentice Hall.

'Biography' (n.d.), Official Site of Walter Laqueur. Formerly available at: www.laqueur.net (accessed 22 January 2015).

Blishen, E. (1969), 'History, Teaching Of', in *Blond's Encyclopaedia of Education*, London: Blond Educational.

Bloor, M. and F. Wood (2006), *Keywords in Qualitative Methods: A Vocabulary of Research Concepts*, London: Sage.

Borhani, S.H. (2015), 'Palestine Studies in Western Academia: Shifting a Paradigm?', *Iranian Review of Foreign Affairs*, 5 (4): 119–50. Available online: https://www.academia.edu/29671654/Palestine_Studies_in_Western_Academia_Shifting_a_Paradigm?auto=download (accessed 15 August 2021).

Boyer, M.A., N.F. Hudson and M.J. Butler (2013), *Global Politics: Engaging a Complex World*, New York: McGraw-Hill.

Brockway, E.M. (2007), 'The Portrayal of the Middle East in Secondary School U.S. Textbooks', MPA diss., Bowling Green State University, Bowling Green, OH. Available online: http://rave.ohiolink.edu/etdc/view?acc%5Fnum=bgsu1174677061 (accessed 15 August 2021).

Buckingham, B.R. (1960), 'Textbooks', in C.W. Harris (ed.), *Encyclopedia of Educational Research*, 3rd edn, 1517–25, New York: Macmillan.

Cargill, J. (2001), 'Ancient Israel in Western Civ Textbooks', *History Teacher*, 34 (3): 297–326.

Carlson, T. (2009), 'The Trouble With Textbooks', Fox News, 3 September. Available online: https://web.archive.org/web/20130402070634/http://www.foxnews.com/opinion/2009/09/03/tucker-carlson-textbooks/ (accessed 15 October 2013).

Chandler, M. (2020), 'Pearson to Update GCSE History Textbook After "Anti-Israel" Claims', *The Bookseller*, 20 January. Available online: https://www.thebookseller.com/news/pearson-update-gcse-middle-east-textbook-after-anti-israel-claims-1169456 (accessed 15 August 2021).

'Charles D. Smith' (n.d.), School of Middle Eastern & North African Studies, University of Arizona, Tucson, AZ. Available online: https://menas.arizona.edu/people/charles-d-smith (accessed 4 December 2014).

'Charles Smith Predicts the Future' (2012), *Huffington Post Monitor*, 29 June. Formerly available at: http://hpmonitor.blogspot.com/2012/06/charles-smith-predicts-future-and.html.

Chomsky, N. (1999), *Fateful Triangle: The United States, Israel and the Palestinians*, updated edn, London: Pluto Press.

Cohen, D.J. (2005), 'By the Book: Assessing the Place of Textbooks in U.S. Survey Courses', *The Journal of American History*, 91 (4): 1405–15.

Cronin, D. (2011), *Europe's Alliance with Israel: Aiding the Occupation*, London: Pluto Press.

Davis, O.L. Jr (2006), 'Preface', in S.J. Foster and K.A. Crawford (eds), *What Shall We Tell the Children? International Perspectives on School History Textbooks*, xi–xiv, Greenwich, CT: Information Age.

'Department of History: Carla L. Klausner' (n.d.), University of Missouri-Kansas City. Available online: https://web.archive.org/web/20141110031339/http://cas.umkc.edu/history/faculty/klausner.asp (accessed 2 December 2014).

Dixon, M.M.A. (2007), *Textbook on International Law*, 6th edn, Oxford: Oxford University Press.

Dorliae, A.T. (1998), 'United States Global Studies Textbooks' Treatment of Foreign Countries: A Comparative Study of World Regions and Countries Marked by Socio-Economic Differences', PhD diss., State University of New York, Buffalo, NY. Available online: https://search.proquest.com/docview/304470674/ (accessed 15 August 2021).

Edmunds, D.R. (2020), 'British History Textbook Withdrawn over Anti-Israeli Bias', *Jerusalem Post*, 28 April. Available online: https://www.jpost.com/diaspora/antisemitism/british-history-textbook-withdrawn-over-anti-israeli-bias-626234 (accessed 15 August 2021).

Eichner, I. (2018), 'Anti-Semitic Caricature Removed from Belgian Textbook', Ynetnews, 31 May. Available online: https://www.ynetnews.com/articles/0,7340,L-5275625,00.html (accessed 15 August 2021).

Farrell, J.P. and S.P. Heyneman (1994), 'Textbook Development in Developing Nations, Planning For', in T. Husén and T.N. Postlethwaite (eds), *The International Encyclopedia of Education, Volume 11*, 2nd edn, 6360–6, Oxford: Pergamon.

Feldman, L.G. (1984), *The Special Relationship Between West Germany and Israel*, Boston, MA: Allen & Unwin.

Ferro, M. (2003), *The Use and Abuse of History: Or How the Past is Taught to Children*, Routledge Classics, Abingdon: Routledge.

Foster, S. (2006), 'Whose History? Portrayal of Immigrant Groups in U.S. History Textbooks, 1800–Present', in S.J. Foster and K.A. Crawford (eds), *What Shall We Tell the Children? International Perspectives on School History Textbooks*, 155–78, Greenwich, CT: Information Age.

Foster, S. and K. Crawford (2006), *What Shall We Tell the Children? International Perspectives on School History Textbooks*, Greenwich, CT: Information Age.

Franzosi, R.P. (2004), 'Content Analysis', in M.A. Hardy and A. Bryman (eds), *Handbook of Data Analysis*, 547–66, London: Sage.

Franzosi, R., ed. (2008), *Content Analysis*, Sage Benchmarks in Social Research Methods, London: Sage.

Fuchs, S. (2009), 'All in the Family: Dr. Howard Sachar and the Jacob Hiatt Institute', *The Brandeis Hoot*, 11 September, Brandeis University, Waltham, MA. Available online: http://www.thebrandeishoot.com/articles/6474 (accessed 15 August 2021).

Gerstenfeld, M. (2007), *Academics Against Israel and the Jews*, Jerusalem: Center for Public Affairs.

Gies-Chumney, M. (2009), 'Exclusive: Review: "The Trouble with Textbooks –Distorting History and Religion"', Family Security Matters, 8 October. Available online: https://web.archive.org/web/20141127180937/http://www.familysecuritymatters.org/publications/id.4471/pub_detail.asp (accessed 15 October 2013).

Gilderhus, M.T. (1987), *History and Historians: A Historiographical Introduction*, Upper Saddle River, NJ: Prentice-Hall.

Gilman, B.A., ed. (2000), *The Treatment of Israel by the United Nations: Hearing Before the Committee on International Relations, House of Representatives*, Serial No. 106-53, Darby, PA: Diane Publishing.

Goodlad, J.I. (1979), *Curriculum Inquiry: The Study of Curriculum Practice*, New York: McGraw-Hill.

Graff, G. (2003), *Separation of Church and State: Dina De-Malkhuta Dina in Jewish Law, 1750-1848*, Tuscaloosa, AL: University of Alabama Press.

Griswold, W.J. (1975), *The Image of the Middle East in Secondary School Textbooks*, New York: Middle East Studies Association of North America.

Gvosdev, N.K. (2006), '[Reviews] *Holy Fire: The Battle for Christ's Tomb*. By Victoria Clark. San Francisco, Calif.: Macadam/Cage, 2005. 294 pp. $28.50 and *Standing with Israel: Why Christians Support the Jewish State*. By David Brog. Lake Mary, Fla.: Front Line, 2006. 285 pp. $15.99', *Journal of Church and State*, 48 (3): 691-3.

Haaretz (2014), 'Barry Rubin, Israeli Columnist and Professor, Dies Aged 64', *Haaretz*, 3 February. Available online: https://www.haaretz.com/jewish/.premium-barry-rubin-dies-at-64-1.5318344 (accessed 15 August 2021).

Hamilton, D. (1990), 'What Is a Textbook?' *Paradigm*, 3: 5-8.

Hardy, M.A. and A. Bryman, eds (2004), *Handbook of Data Analysis*, London: Sage.

Hartnett, A. (1982), *The Social Sciences in Educational Studies: A Selective Guide to the Literature*, London: Heinemann Educational.

Hilal, S. and S.A.M. Rizvi (2008), 'The Syllabus Based Web Content Extractor (SBWCE)', *Communications of the IIMA* 8 (1). Available online: https://scholarworks.lib.csusb.edu/ciima/vol8/iss1/2/ (accessed 15 August 2021).

Hollander, R. (2002), 'The World's Version of Mideast History', CAMERA (Committee for Accuracy in Middle East Reporting and Analysis), 1 July. Available online: https://www.camera.org/index.asp?x_context=6&x_article=258 (accessed 15 August 2021).

Holsti, O.R. (1962), 'The Belief System and National Images: A Case Study', *Journal of Conflict Resolution*, 6 (3): 244-52.

Husain, M.E. (2010), 'Academic Freedom: Costs, Consequences, and Resistance', EdD diss., University of California, Davis. Available online: https://search.proquest.com/pqdtft/docview/757228035/ (accessed 15 August 2021).

Husén, T. and T.N. Postlethwaite, eds (1994), *The International Encyclopedia of Education*, 2nd edn, Oxford: Pergamon.

'Ian J. Bickerton' (n.d.), Amazon author page. Available online: https://www.amazon.com/Ian-J.-Bickerton/e/B001ITX086 (accessed 22 April 2015).

IMRA (2011), 'Jewish Civil Rights Group Warns Hundreds of University Presidents Over Anti-Israel Hate on American College Campuses', Independent Media Review Analysis, 8 September. Available online: http://www.imra.org.il/story.php?id=53638 (accessed 8 September 2021).

Isacoff, J.B. (2005), 'Writing the Arab-Israeli Conflict: Historical Bias and the Use of History in Political Science', *Perspectives on Politics*, 3 (1): 71-88.

Jackson, P.W., ed. (1992), *Handbook of Research on Curriculum: A Project of the American Educational Research Association*, New York: Macmillan.

Jacobs, D. (1981), 'Teaching the Arab World: Evaluating Textbooks', *The Social Studies*, 72 (4): 150-3.

Jacobson, J. (2004), 'The Clash Over Middle East Studies', *Chronicle of Higher Education*, 6 February. Available online: https://chronicle.com/article/The-Clash-Over-Middle-East/12144/ (accessed 15 August 2021).

Jaschik, S. (2016), 'Textbook Destroyed', Inside Higher Ed, 8 March. Available online: https://www.insidehighered.com/news/2016/03/08/mcgraw-hill-education-withdraws-textbook-maps-viewed-anti-israel (accessed 15 August 2021).

JNS (2020), 'UK School Textbook Removed from Sale, Asks if Israel Was Responsible for 9/11 Attacks', *The Algemeiner*, 23 February. Available online: https://www.algemeiner.com/2020/02/23/uk-school-textbook-removed-from-sale-asks-if-israel-was-responsible-for-9-11-attacks/ (accessed 15 August 2021).

JTA (2015), 'Israeli Embassy Slams "Outrageous" Dutch Textbook' *The Times of Israel*, 27 May. Available online: https://www.timesofisrael.com/israeli-embassy-slams-outrageous-dutch-textbook/ (accessed 15 August 2021).

Kermani, N. (2006), 'Israel's Clenched Fist', *Süddeutsche Zeitung*, 7 August [in German]. Available online: http://www.signandsight.com/features/900.html (accessed 15 August 2021).

Klausner, T. (2013), 'Tiberius Klausner Interview, 22 November 1999', Midwest Center for Holocaust Education, Overland Park, KS. Available online: https://web.archive.org/web/20151009203705/http://mchekc.org/admin/wp-content/uploads/2014/09/KlausnerTiborTranscript.pdf (accessed 15 August 2021).

Klausner, T. (2014), 'Tiberius Klausner', The Midwest Center for Holocaust Education, Overland Park, KS. Available online: https://web.archive.org/web/20151016134820/http://mchekc.org/admin/wp-content/uploads/2014/02/KlausnerTiberiusLetter.pdf (accessed 15 August 2021).

Knopf-Newman, M.J. (2011), *The Politics of Teaching Palestine to Americans: Addressing Pedagogical Strategies*, New York: Palgrave Macmillan.

Kousha, K. and M. Thelwall (2008), 'Assessing the Impact of Disciplinary Research on Teaching: An Automatic Analysis of Online Syllabuses', *Journal of the American Society for Information Science and Technology*, 59 (13): 2060–9.

Kuhn, T.S. (1970), *The Structure of Scientific Revolutions*, 2nd edn, Chicago: University of Chicago Press.

Laqueur, W. (1992), *Thursday's Child Has Far to Go: A Memoir of the Journeying Years*, New York: Charles Scribner's Sons.

Laqueur, W. (2009), *Best of Times, Worst of Times: Memoirs of a Political Education*, Waltham, MA: Brandeis.

Laqueur, W. and B. Rubin, eds (2008), *The Israel-Arab Reader: A Documentary History of the Middle East Conflict*, 7th edn, New York: Penguin.

Leahey, C.R. (2007), 'Hegemony and History: A Critical Analysis of How High School History Textbooks Depict Key Events of the Vietnam War', Ded diss., State University of New York, Binghamton, NY. Available online: https://www.proquest.com/openview/07104b3667ce913f28f5e667399574ce/1.pdf?pq-origsite=gscholar&cbl=18750 (accessed 15 August 2021).

Leeke, J. (2005), 'A Novel Reading: Literature and Pedagogy in Modern Middle East History Courses in Canada and the United States', MA diss., McGill University, Montreal. Available online: https://escholarship.mcgill.ca/concern/theses/4t64gn45n (accessed 15 August 2021).

Lewan, K.M. (1975), 'How West Germany Helped to Build Israel', *Journal of Palestine Studies*, 4 (4): 41–64.

Lewis, B. (1993), *Islam and the West*, New York: Oxford University Press.

'Mark A. Tessler' (2015), SourceWatch, Center for Media and Democracy, Madison, WI, 23 April. Available online: https://www.sourcewatch.org/index.php?title=Mark_A._Tessler (accessed 15 August 2021).

McCulloch, G. (2004), *Documentary Research in Education, History and the Social Sciences*, London: RoutledgeFalmer.

McCulloch, G. and D. Crook, eds (2008), *The Routledge International Encyclopedia of Education*, Abingdon: Routledge.

Mearsheimer, J.J. and S.M. Walt (2008), *The Israel Lobby and U.S. Foreign Policy*, London: Penguin.

Mendes, P. (2009), 'The Australian Left's Support for the Creation of the State of Israel, 1947–48', *Labour History*, 97: 137–48.

Merkley, P.C. (2004), *American Presidents, Religion, and Israel: The Heirs of Cyrus*, Westport, CT: Praeger.

Meymand, P. (2019), 'Beyond "Through the Looking Glass" Borders: A Content Analysis of North Africa/Southwest Asia in College-level World Regional Geography Textbooks', PhD thesis, University of Wisconsin-Milwaukee. Available online: https://dc.uwm.edu/etd/2102/ (accessed 26 August 2021).

Michael, I. (1990), 'Aspects of Textbook Research', *Paradigm*, 2: 5.

Midwest Center for Holocaust Education and The Kansas City Star (2001), *From the Heart: Life Before and After the Holocaust – A Mosaic of Memories*, Kansas City, MO: Kansas City Star Books and the Midwest Center for Holocaust Education.

Miller, Y.A. (2015), 'Educating to Hate', Aish.Com, 30 May. Available online: https://www.aish.com/jw/mo/Educating-to-Hate.html (accessed 15 August 2021).

Mirkovic, M. and K. Crawford (2003), 'Teaching History in Serbian and English Secondary Schools: A Cross-Cultural Analysis of Textbooks', *International Journal of Historical Learning, Teaching and Research*, 3 (2): 91–105.

Morgan, H. (2002), 'The Portrayal of the Middle East in School Textbooks from 1880 to the Present', EdD, Rutgers, The State University of New Jersey, New Brunswick, NJ. Available online: https://search.proquest.com/docview/305555329/ (accessed 15 August 2021).

Morris, B. (2001), *Righteous Victims: A History of the Zionist-Arab Conflict, 1881–2001*, reprint edn, New York: Vintage.

Mueller, C. and U. Rabi (2017), 'A Critical Survey of Textbooks on the Arab-Israeli and Israeli-Palestinian Conflict', Working Paper no. 1, Tel Aviv: Moshe Dayan Center for Middle Eastern and African Studies. Available online: https://dayan.org/content/critical-survey-textbooks-arab-israeli-and-israeli-palestinian-conflict (accessed 8 September 2021).

Mulhall, J.W. (1995), *America and the Founding of Israel: An Investigation of the Morality of America's Role*, Los Angeles: Deshon Press.

Myers, G. (1991), 'Textbooks and the Sociology of Scientific Knowledge', *Paradigm*, 6. Available online: https://web.archive.org/web/20110817020104/faculty.ed.uiuc.edu/westbury/paradigm/myers2.html (accessed 31 August 2021).

Nicholls, J. (2003), 'Methods in School Textbook Research', *International Journal of Historical Learning, Teaching and Research*, 3 (2): 11–26.

Olson, D.R. (1989), 'On the Language and Authority of Textbooks', in S. de Castell, A. Luke and C. Luke (eds), *Language, Authority and Criticism: Readings on the School Textbook*, 233–44, London: Falmer.

Organski, A.F.K. (1990), *The $36 Billion Bargain: Strategy and Politics in U.S. Assistance to Israel*, New York: Columbia University Press.

Pappé, I. (1988), *Britain and the Arab-Israeli Conflict, 1948–51*, Basingstoke: Macmillan.

Pearcy, M. (2011), ' "We Have Never Known What Death Was Before": A Just War Doctrine Critique of U.S. History Textbooks', PhD diss., University of South Florida,

Tampa, FL. Available online: https://search.proquest.com/pqdtft/docview/876177339/ (accessed 15 August 2021).

Perry, G. (1975), 'Treatment of the Middle East in American High School Textbooks', *Journal of Palestine Studies*, 4 (3): 46–58.

Petras, J. (2006), *The Power of Israel in the United States*, Atlanta, GA: Clarity Press.

Porat, D. (2006), 'Reconstructing the Past, Constructing the Future in Israeli Textbooks', in S.J. Foster and K.A. Crawford (eds), *What Shall We Tell the Children? International Perspectives on School History Textbooks*, 195–210, Greenwich, CT: Information Age.

'Professor Benny Morris Biography' (n.d.), Torah in Motion. Available online: https://web.archive.org/web/20210301055138/https://www.torahinmotion.org/users/professor-benny-morris (accessed 22 April 2015).

'Rate My Professors' (n.d.). Formerly available at: http://www.ratemyprofessors.com/ShowRatings.jsp?tid=485345 (accessed 23 April 2015).

Rea, T. and J. Wright (1997), *The Arab-Israeli Conflict*, Oxford: Oxford University Press.

Rea, V. (2015), 'Online Review of White's "Metahistory": How Historians "Make" History', Lehigh University. Available online: https://web.archive.org/web/20151218022958/http://www.lehigh.edu/~ineng/syll/syll-metahistory.html (accessed 15 August 2021).

Reich, B. (1984), *The United States and Israel: Influence in the Special Relationship*, New York: Praeger.

Roberts, G., ed. (2001), *The History and Narrative Reader*, London: Routledge.

Rock, M. (1996), 'The Arab-Israeli Conflict as Depicted in Children's and Young Adult Non-Fiction Literature', MA diss., Queens College, The City University of New York. Available online: https://eric.ed.gov/?q=source%3a%22Social+Studies+and+the+Young+Learner&ff1=pubDissertations%2fTheses+-+Masters+Theses&pg=4&id=ED407942 (accessed 15 August 2021).

Rogers, R., ed. (2004), *An Introduction to Critical Discourse Analysis in Education*, Mahwah, NJ: Lawrence Erlbaum.

Romanowski, M.H. (1993), 'The Ethical Treatment of the Japanese-American Internment Camps: A Content Analysis of Secondary American History Textbooks', PhD, Miami University, Oxford, OH. Available online: https://search.proquest.com/docview/304071091/ (accessed 15 August 2021).

Roth, A.I. (2009), 'Reassurance: A Strategic Basis of US Support for Israel', *International Studies Perspectives*, 10 (4): 378–93.

Rozenman, E. (2004), ' "One Land, Two People," and Dozens of Errors', CAMERA (Committee for Accuracy in Middle East Reporting and Analysis), 1 September. Available online: https://www.camera.org/index.asp?x_context=55&x_article=813 (accessed 15 August 2021).

Sachar, H.M. (2007), *A History of Israel: From the Rise of Zionism to Our Time*, 3rd edn, New York: Alfred A. Knopf.

Sadker, D. and M. Sadker (1994), 'Sex Equity: Assumptions and Strategies', in T. Husén and T.N. Postlethwaite (eds), *The International Encyclopedia of Education, Volume 9*, 5441–5, 2nd edn, Oxford: Pergamon.

Said, E.W. and C. Hitchens, eds (2001), *Blaming the Victims: Spurious Scholarship and the Palestinian Question*, London: Verso.

Sand, S. (2008a), 'Shattering a "National Mythology" ', interview by O. Ilani, *Haaretz*, 21 March. Available online: https://www.haaretz.com/general/shattering-a-national-mythology-1.242015 (accessed 15 August 2021).

Sand, S. (2008b), 'Israel Deliberately Forgets Its History', *Le Monde Diplomatique*, September. Available online: https://mondediplo.com/2008/09/07israel (accessed 15 August 2021).

Sand, S. (2009), *The Invention of the Jewish People*, London: Verso.

Schultz, J.P. and C.L. Klausner (1983), 'Rabbi Simon Glazer and the Quest for Jewish Community in Kansas City, 1920–1923', *American Jewish Archives*, 35 (1): 13–26.

Serrie, J. (2013), 'Textbook Case of Bias? Parents Say School Reader Is Biased vs. Israel', Fox News, 27 April. Available online: https://www.foxnews.com/us/textbook-case-of-bias-parents-say-school-reader-is-biased-vs-israel (accessed 15 August 2021).

Shaheen, J.G. (2009), *Reel Bad Arabs: How Hollywood Vilifies a People*, Northampton, MA: Olive Branch Press.

Shavit, A. (2004), 'Survival of the Fittest? An Interview with Benny Morris', *LOGOS*, 3 (3), Winter 2004. Available online: http://www.logosjournal.com/morris.htm (accessed 15 August 2021).

Slater, R. (2012), 'An Evolving Historian', *The Jerusalem Post*, 26 December. Available online: https://www.jpost.com/Jerusalem-Report/Jewish-World/An-evolving-historian (accessed 15 August 2021).

Smith, A.L. (2011), 'How Have Descriptions of the Arab-Israeli Conflict Changed in High School U.S. History Textbooks Since the 1950s?' Med diss., Cedarville University, Cedarville, OH. Available online: https://www.semanticscholar.org/paper/How-Have-Descriptions-of-the-Arab-Israeli-Conflict-Smith/3e746231b23dded8401484e9cfae3f344ae52af3 (accessed 15 August 2021).

Smith, C.D. (2013), *Palestine and the Arab-Israeli Conflict: A History with Documents*, 8th edn, Basingstoke: Palgrave Macmillan.

Solomon, A.B. (2014), ' "Jerusalem Post" Columnist Barry Rubin Dies', *Jerusalem Post*, 3 February. Available online: https://www.jpost.com/National-News/Jerusalem-Post-columnist-Barry-Rubin-dies-340192 (accessed 15 August 2021).

Sosniak, L.A. (1994), 'Textbooks', in T. Husén and T.N. Postlethwaite (eds), *The International Encyclopedia of Education, Volume 3*, 1420–2, 2nd edn, Oxford: Pergamon.

Squire, J.R. (1994), 'Textbook Publishing', in T. Husén and T.N. Postlethwaite (eds), *The International Encyclopedia of Education, Volume 3*, 1414–20, 2nd edn, Oxford: Pergamon.

Stephens, E. (2006), *US Policy Toward Israel: The Role of Political Culture in Defining the 'Special Relationship'*, Brighton: Sussex Academic.

Stephens, E.L. (2004), 'United States Policy Towards Israel: The Politics, Sociology, Economics and Strategy of Commitment', PhD thesis, University of London.

'Suggested Book List' (n.d.), CAMERA (Committee for Accuracy in Middle East Reporting and Analysis). Available online: https://web.archive.org/web/20150716185341/http://www.camera.org/index.asp?x_context=2&x_article=704 (accessed 22 April 2015).

Tessler, M. (2009), *A History of the Israeli-Palestinian Conflict*, Bloomington: Indiana University Press.

'The Scroll' (2008), Congregation Beth Shalom, November. Formerly available at: http://www.bethshalomkc.org/media/Archive_Scroll/2008/Nov-08.pdf (accessed 15 August 2021).

'The Scroll' (2009), Congregation Beth Shalom, September. Formerly available at: http://www.bethshalomkc.org/media/Archive_Scroll/2009/Sept-09.pdf (accessed 15 August 2021).

'The Scroll' (2011), Congregation Beth Shalom, September. Formerly available at: http://www.bethshalomkc.org/media/Archive_Scroll/2011/Sept-%2011.pdf (accessed 15 August 2021).

'The Scroll' (2014), Congregation Beth Shalom, April. https://www.bethshalomkc.org/wp-content/uploads/2019/08/April-2014.pdf (accessed 15 August 2021).

'Tiberius Klausner' (2014), The Midwest Center for Holocaust Education, Overland Park, KS. Available online: https://web.archive.org/web/20151009212012/http://mchekc.org/admin/wp-content/uploads/2014/09/KlausnerTiborFTHProfile.pdf (accessed 15 August 2021).

Tobin, G.A. and D.R. Ybarra (2008), *The Trouble with Textbooks: Distorting History and Religion*, Lanham, MD: Lexington Books.

Topolsky, J. (1998), 'The Structure of Historical Narratives and the Teaching of History', in J.F. Voss and M. Carretero (eds), *International Review of History Education, Vol. 2: Learning and Reasoning in History*, 9–22, Abingdon: RoutledgeFalmer.

UA News Services (2004), 'Charles Smith on State Department Panel on 1967 'Liberty' Incident', University of Arizona, 16 January. Available online: https://uanews.org/story/charles-smith-state-department-panel-1967-liberty-incident (accessed 15 August 2021).

Van de Ven, S.E.K. (1990), 'State Adoption Policies, Publishing Practices, and Authorship: The Production of Middle East Chapters in World History Textbooks', EdD diss., Harvard University, Cambridge, MA. Available online: https://search.proquest.com/docview/303827527/ (accessed 15 August 2021).

Vanhulle, B. (2009), 'The Path of History: Narrative Analysis of History Textbooks: A Case Study of Belgian History Textbooks (1945–2004)', *History of Education*, 38 (2): 263–82.

Venezky, R.L. (1992), 'Textbook in School and Society', in P.W. Jackson (ed.), *Handbook of Research on Curriculum*, 436–62, New York: Macmillan.

'Vita' (2020), University of Michigan, August. Available online: https://cps.isr.umich.edu/wp-content/uploads/2020/06/Mark-Tessler-vita-April-2020.pdf (accessed 29 August 2021).

Walls, M. (2010), 'Framing the Israel/Palestine Conflict in Swedish History School Textbooks', PhD diss., University of Gothenburg, Göteborg, Sweden. Available online: https://gupea.ub.gu.se/bitstream/2077/23789/1/gupea_2077_23789_1.pdf (accessed 26 August 2021).

Walls, M. (2011), 'How the Israel-Palestinian Conflict Is Framed in Swedish History School Textbooks Voice', Dissident Voice, 3 March. Available online: https://dissidentvoice.org/2011/03/how-the-israel-palestinian-conflict-is-framed-in-swedish-history-school-textbooks/ (accessed 15 August 2021).

Weinbrenner, P. (1992), 'Methodologies of Textbook Analysis Used to Date', in H. Bourdillon (ed.), *History and Social Studies – Methodologies of Textbook Analysis: Report of the Educational Research Workshop Held in Braunschweig (Germany), 11–19 September 1990*, 21–34, Lisse, NL: Swets & Zeitlinger.

White, H.V. (2014), *Metahistory: The Historical Imagination in Nineteenth-Century Europe*, 40th anniversary edn, Baltimore, MD: Johns Hopkins University Press.

'Widely Adopted History Textbooks' (n.d.), American Textbook Council. Available online: https://historytextbooks.net/adopted.htm (accessed 13 February 2013).

Wills, M.(H.)F. (1992), 'A Computer-Assisted Content Analysis of the Treatment of Religion during the Colonial Period of American History in College Level United States History Textbooks', EdD diss., University of Arkansas, Fayetteville, AR. Available online: https://search.proquest.com/pqdtft/docview/303977092 (accessed 15 August 2021).

Wilson, S. (2007), 'Israel Revisited', *Washington Post*, 11 March. Available online: https://www.washingtonpost.com/wp-dyn/content/article/2007/03/10/AR2007031001496.html (accessed 15 August 2021).

Wiseman, A. (2014), 'Representations of Islam and Arab Societies in Western Secondary Textbooks', *Digest of Middle East Studies*, 23 (2): 312–44.

Woodward, A. (1994), 'Textbooks', in T. Husén and T.N. Postlethwaite (eds), *The International Encyclopedia of Education, Volume 11*, 6366, 2nd edn, Oxford: Pergamon.

Young, M.F.D. (1971), *Knowledge and Control*, London: Collier Macmillan.

INDEX

1948 Arab-Israeli War 27, 29, 35, 37, 38, 40, 42, 43, 88, 137, 158, 194
  see also al-Nakba
1967 Arab-Israeli War 19, 27, 30, 38, 39, 41, 140, 184, 191, 194
  see also Six Day War
1973 Arab-Israeli War 19, 27, 33, 41, 140
4th International Conference of the Global Forum for Combating Antisemitism xxiii

A Concise History of the Arab-Israeli Conflict (Bickerton and Klausner) 54, 140–8, 191, 204, 207
  see also *A History of the Arab-Israeli Conflict*
A Critical Survey of Textbooks on The Arab-Israeli and Israeli-Palestinian Conflict xvii
A History of the Arab-Israeli Conflict (Bickerton and Klausner) xvi, xvii, 140
A History of Israel, see Sachar, Howard
A History of the Israeli-Palestinian Conflict, see Tessler, Mark
A History of Modern Palestine: One Land, Two Peoples, see Pappé
A Novel Reading: Literature and Pedagogy in Modern Middle East History Courses 31
Abdul-Hamid II 146, 169
Abraham (prophet) 4, 128, 186
Abraham, Matthew xxii
  Out of Bounds: Academic Freedom and the Question of Palestine xxii
Academic Friends of Israel xxv
Adiabene 122, 123, 205
Afghanistan 32
AIPAC xxv
al-Aqsa Mosque 143, 151

Al-Bataineh, Adel Tawfig 25, 30
al-Khalidi, Yusuf Diya 151
al-Nakba 35
  see also 1948 Arab-Israeli War
Al-Qazzaz, Ayad 25, 28
Alfred A. Knopf publishing house 171
Aliyah 123, 153, 176
Allah 143
alternative knowledge xxii, xxiii, xxiv, xxv
Amazon 15, 48
American xxii, xxiii, xxv, 3, 11, 13, 19, 25, 26, 27, 28, 29, 30, 31, 32, 33, 40, 41, 42, 43, 44, 45, 50, 51, 127, 132, 141, 171, 173, 190, 191, 192, 195, 196, 197, 198, 199, 200, 211, 212
  American Academy of Religion 51
  American Institute for Maghreb Studies 199
  American Jewish Committee 25, 44
  American Political Science Association 51
  American Research Centre 196
  American Textbook Council 3, 33
  American textbooks xxii, 13, 26, 27, 28, 29, 30, 31, 40, 41, 42, 43, 45
  American University in Cairo 50
  American-Israeli Cooperative Enterprise xxv, 42, 197
Ammon 161
Amnesty International xx
ancient Hebrews 4
Ancient Israel 16, 35, 36, 128, 131, 134, 135, 137, 139, 141, 143, 147, 150, 151, 157, 161, 162, 163, 172, 175, 181, 183, 185, 186, 205, 206, 208
ancient Israelites 26, 181
Andalusia 127
  see also Spain
anglophone 16, 17, 50, 53, 181, 204
Annapolis Conference 179

Anti-Defamation League xxv
anti-Israel xxii, xxiv, 26, 42, 45
anti-Israeli bias xxii, 25, 42, 43, 205
anti-Semitism xxiv, 37, 148, 193
    anti-Semites xxiv
    anti-Semitic xxi, xxiii, xxvi, 45, 168
apartheid 15
Apple, Michael 13, 14
Arab Spring 82, 192
Arab World and Islamic Resources 45
Arabian Peninsula 155, 184
Arabic (language) xv, xx, 175, 183, 184, 197, 198, 200, 211
    Arabic country 38
    Arabic novel 31
Arab-Israeli Conflict as Depicted in Children's and Young Adult Non-Fiction Literature 30
Arafat, Yasir 41
Armenians 174
Aronson, Shlomo 102, 197
Ashkenazie Jews 29
Association for Israel Studies xv, 198
Assyrians 142
Australia 24, 50, 54, 134, 140, 149, 171, 190, 191, 200, 211
    Australian universities 54

Babylonia 127, 142
Baghdad 127
Balfour 30, 35, 36, 41, 131, 139, 152, 157, 172
Bar Kochba (and Bar Kokhba) 136 164, 197
Barak, Ehud 149, 197
Bard, Mitchell 42, 43
    Rewriting History in Textbooks 42
Barlow, Elizabeth 30
    Evaluation of Secondary-level Textbooks for Coverage of Middle East and North Afrtica 29
Barnard College 191
Bedouin 146, 153
Begin, Menachem 41
Belgian textbook xx
belief system 11, 32, 213
Ben-Gurion, David 41, 193, 196
Ben-Gurion University 148, 194
Beth Shalom (Congregation) 191, 192

Bialik, Chaim Nachman 176
Bible 7, 122, 124, 126, 128, 135, 139, 151, 153, 157, 161, 163, 185, 186, 206, 207
    maximalist (Bible studies) 161
    minimalist (Bible studies) 186
    see also Hebrew Bible
Bickerton, Ian xvi, xvii, 140, 184, 190–1, 200, 204, 207, 208, 209, 211
    Forty-Three Days: The Gulf War 190
    Historiography of The Arab-Israeli Conflict: Contested Spaces 190
    The Arab-Israeli Conflict: A Guide for the Perplexed 190
    The Arab-Israeli Conflict: A History 190
Bilu (Group) 180
Biluim 151
Blackwell's (publishing house) 51
Blaming the Victims: Spurious Scholarship and the Palestinian Question 42
Bloomsbury (publishing house) xxii
B'nai B'rith Hillel Foundation xxv, 196
Borochov, Ber 178
Bourdieu, Pierre 12
Brenner, Yosef Chaim 153
Bresheeth, Haim xv
British xix, xxi, 13, 37, 41, 58, 125, 155, 210
    British (history) textbook xxi
    British mandate 41, 155; *see also* Mandate
    British universities 54, 58
Brockway, Elizabeth Marie 33, 213
    The Portrayal of The Middle East in Secondary School U.S. Textbooks 32
Buckingham, B.R. 8
Bunton, Martin xvi
    The Palestinian-Israeli Conflict: A Very Short Introduction xvi
Byzantine 135

California 20, 190, 191
Cambon, Jules 152
CAMERA xxv, 180, 191, 193, 199
Camp David 41, 197
Campus Watch xxv, 191, 197, 199
Canaan 4, 35, 136, 160, 163, 185, 186
    Canaanites 136, 168, 206
Canada 24, 50, 54, 134, 140, 149, 158, 171, 179
    Canadian universities 51, 54, 65

Cargill, Jack 185, 186
Caspian Sea 122, 123
Catholic 13, 188
Cedarville University 41
Central Zionist Archives 194
Chanukkah 174, 176
Chomsky, Noam xxii
Christian xv, 125, 138, 142, 154, 155, 161, 165, 177, 200, 211
    Christianity 44, 147, 148, 155
Chronicle of Higher Education 199
Citadel Press 179
City University of New York 30
civilization of the book 9, 10
Claremont Graduate School 190
Cleveland, William 32
    A History of the Modern Middle East 32
Clinton, Bill 197
Cold War 15, 94
Collier, David xxi, xxvi
Conflict in the Middle East: 1945–95 xxi
Congregation Beth Shalom 191
Constantinople 180
Council on Islamic Education 44, 45
Councils for Social Studies, Geography, and World History 31
counter attack xxiii
Crusaders 154, 176
curriculum 24, 7, 9, 12
Cyrus (King) 162

Dar al Harb 155
Dar al Islam 157
David (King) 41, 124, 128, 134, 135, 139, 141, 142, 151, 161, 162, 163, 175, 178, 181
David Project xxv
Declaration of Independence (Israel) 122, 125, 208
Demitrius II (King) 162
democracy 10, 33, 213
Denmark 53
Deraa 146
Dhimma (and dhimmi) 155, 156
Diaspora (Jewish) 36, 142, 143, 152, 164, 166, 167, 176
Dissident Voice (online newsletter) 40
District of Columbia 28
Dome of the Rock 143, 151

Dubnow, Vladimir 151
Durkheim, Emile 12
Dutch textbook xx

Eastern Europe 15, 126, 127, 144, 154
Education Media and Publishing Group Limited 13
educational systems 8, 13, 16, 19
educationalists 12, 24
Egypt 27, 30, 38, 128, 141, 161, 186, 196, 201
    Egyptian 38, 194, 198
Ein HaHoresh 194
Einstein, Albert 15
Emile 15
encyclopedia articles 4, 14, 204
Engage xxv
England 173
English 5, 7, 50, 53, 183
English as a Second Language xxi
Eretz Yisrael 4, 142, 144, 145, 146, 152, 154, 161, 162, 164, 165, 166, 167
European Centre for Palestine Studies xv
Exodus (and exodus) 128, 141, 172, 173, 176, 186

Fairfax County 28
Finkelstein, Norman xxii, 124
Finland 53
First Temple 142
First World War 154, 155, 210
forced expulsion (of Jews) 121, 131, 163, 207, 208
    see also mass expulsion
former Yugoslavia 15
Foucault, Michel 13
Fox News 43
French 5, 12, 13, 136, 152, 155, 172, 173, 191, 194
    French Revolution 136
From the Heart: Life Before and After the Holocaust 192

Galilee 135, 136, 151
Gaza 38
GCSE xxi, xxii, 125
Gelvin xvi
    The Israel-Palestine Conflict: One Hundred Years of War xvi

George Mason University 196
George Washington University 195
Georgetown University 194
Germany 15, 123, 188
    German 5, 123, 176
Gerstenfeld, Manfred xxiv
Gilderhus, Mark 187
    History and Historians 187
Glazer, Simon 192
Global Politics: Engaging a Complex World xx
Global Research in International Affairs 195
Golestan 7
Google 17, 15, 31, 48, 50, 51, 52, 134, 141, 149, 158
Google Scholar xvii, 15, 48, 134, 141, 149, 158, 171, 179
Graetz, Heinrich 123, 124, 126
Greeks 174

Ha'Am, Ahad 154
Haifa 124, 146
Hamas 197
Haram el-Sharif (and Haram ash Sharif) 151, 175
Harvard 28, 191, 193, 195, 196
Hasmoneans 162
Hebrew Bible 141, 142
    books of the Prophets 141
    Chronicles 141
    Esther 141
    Kings 141
    Ruth 141
    Song of Solomon 141
    Torah 141, 162, 167
    see also Old Testament
Hebrew Union College 196
Hebrew University of Jerusalem 193, 194, 196, 198
Hebrews 150, 163, 185, 186
Hebron 161
Herod's Temple 143
Herzl, Theodor 37, 145, 172, 180
Hess, Moses 168
Himyarite (and Himyarites) 122, 123, 205
historical narrative analysis xxvi, 3, 5, 18, 25, 131, 180, 181, 187, 206
history textbook xvii, xxi, xxv, 10–11, 12

History Workplace xxi
Hitchens, Christopher 42
Hodder Education xxi
Holocaust (and holocaust) 35, 36, 37, 38, 39, 42, 45, 131, 192, 193, 195, 197, 214
Holsti, O.R. 32, 33, 213
holy book 10, 163
Holy Land 30, 35, 121, 122, 124, 125, 127, 139, 144, 145, 148, 160, 165, 166, 168, 174, 205, 206, 207, 214
HTML 52
Huffington Post Monitor 197

Indiana State University 26
Indiana University Press 158, 199
Institute for Curriculum 44
Institute for Jewish and Community Research xxii, 25, 43
Interdisciplinary Center Herzliya 195
international law 1, 38
Intifada 39, 140, 158
Introduction (of the book) 1–6
    Limitations of the Study 4–5
    Method Used 3
    Methodology 2–3
    Selecting the Sample 3–4
    Structure of the Book 5–6
Iran 29, 122, 205
    Iranians 28
Iran-Iraq war 29
Iraq 28, 32, 122, 155, 205
Ireland 50, 54, 134, 149, 171
    Irish universities 54, 75
Islam 28, 32, 44, 134, 144, 147, 148, 155, 156, 157, 191
    Islamic 42, 44, 138, 155, 156, 157, 168, 199
    Islamism xxiv
IsraCampus xxv
Israel Academia Monitor xxv
Israel Armoured Corps 142
Israel Campus Roundtable xxv
Israel Defense Forces Archive 194
Israel on Campus Coalition xxv
Israel State Archives 194
Israel Studies 102, 198
Israeli curriculum 12

Israel-Jordan peace accords 194
Italy 188

J Street 196
Jacob Hiatt Institute 196
Jacobs, Deborah 28
Jacobson, Jennifer 199
Jaffa 146
Jericho 153
Jerusalem xxi, 35, 36, 121, 127, 135, 137, 141, 142, 143, 144, 146, 151, 153, 161, 162, 164, 165, 175, 178, 181, 183, 196, 200, 201
Jerusalem Post 195
Jewish Diaspora 143
Jewish dispersion 122, 136, 139, 174
Jewish ethnos 121, 126
Jewish State 1, 43, 45, 121, 123, 124, 128, 134, 137, 145, 151, 157, 175, 178, 180, 195, 203, 205, 214
Jewish Virtual Library 42, 51
Johns Hopkins University 193
Jordan 45, 136, 155, 161, 181
Jordan River 136, 161
Joshua (King) 161
journal articles 4, 14, 49, 50, 204
Journal of Palestine Studies 26
Judaism 37, 44, 123, 126, 141, 142, 144, 146, 147, 148, 155, 156, 173, 193
Judea 35, 125, 142, 151, 162, 163, 183

Kansas State University 190
Kedourie, Elie 156
Khalidi, Rashid xvi
  The Hundred Years' War on Palestine: A History of Settler Colonialism and Resistance xvi
Khazarian (and Khazars) 122, 123, 126, 205
Klausner, Carla xvi, 140, 184, 190, 191–3, 200, 204, 207, 208, 209, 211
  From Destruction to Rebirth: The Holocaust and the State of Israel 191
Klausner, Tiberius 192
Koran 155
  see also Qur'an
Kramer, Martin 199
Kuhn, Thomas 14

Laqueur, Walter xv, xvii, 179, 193–4, 200, 204, 206, 210, 211
  A History of Zionism: From the French Revolution to the Establishment of the State of Israel 193
  Best of Times, Worst of Times: Memoirs of a Political Education 193
  The Changing Face of Anti-Semitism: From Ancient Times to the Present Day 193
  Thursday's Child Has Far to Go: A Memoir of the Journeying Years 193
Lebanon 41, 136, 140, 155, 161, 171
Leeke, Jane 32
Levant 146

Maccabean 176
Mamelukes 154
Mandate 140, 172, 177
  see also British mandate
map of Palestine xix
Maronite 184
Maryland 28
Masada 142
Masalha, Nur-eldeen 35
mass expulsion (of Jews) 125, 129, 135, 205, 207
  see also forced expulsion
McGraw-Hill xx, 13
Mediterranean 125, 127, 142
  Mediterranean Sea 161
Meir, Golda 41, 193
Menzies, Robert 191
Mesopotamia 186
Messiah 127, 165
  Messianic 152, 165, 167, 170, 173, 197
  Messianism 174
Metahistory 188
Methods of Textbook Analysis 16–18
  Process-oriented textbook analysis 16
  Product-oriented textbook analysis 16
  Reception-oriented textbook analysis 16
Meymand, Parisa 25
Microsoft Word 52
Middle Ages 36, 156
Middle East Outreach Council 30
Middle East Review of International Affairs 195

Middle East Studies Association 27, 30, 197
Midwest Center for Holocaust Education 192
Mississippi 10
Missouri 140, 190, 191, 195
MIT 51
Moab 161
modern Israel 35, 37, 121, 131
Mongols 154, 157
Montgomery County 28
Morgan, Hani 31
   The Portrayal of the Middle East in School Textbooks from 1880 to the Present 31
Morris, Benny xv, xvi, 148, 154, 155, 183, 194, 200, 204, 207, 208, 209, 211
   1948: A History of the First Arab-Israeli War 194
   One State, Two States: Resolving the Israel/Palestine Conflict 194
   Righteous Victims 16, 54, 148–57, 183, 194, 204, 206
   The Birth of the Palestinian Refugee Problem, 1947–1949 194
Morris, Ya'akov 194
Moses (Prophet) 138, 141, 160, 161, 163, 186
Moshe Dayan Center for Middle Eastern and African Studies xvi, xvii, 181
Moslem (and Moslems/Muslims) 19, 27, 28, 137, 138, 143, 156, 157, 167, 178
Mossad xxiv
Mueller, Chelsi xvii, 181, 183
Muhammad (Prophet) 143, 155
mythistory, *see* Sand, Shlomo

Napoleon 172
Nasser, Gamal Abdel 27, 41, 191
National Association of Arab Americans 28
national histories 11, 188, 213, 214
   writing national histories 188
national identity 11, 121, 122
Nationalizing the Past: Historians as Nation Builders in Modern Europe 188
natural sciences 15
Nazareth 80, 153

Nebi Musa festival 138
Nebuchadnezzar 142
Negev 194
Netanyahu, Benjamin 197
New York 148, 171, 191
New York Times 199
New Zealand 24, 50, 54, 134, 149, 179
   New Zealand universities 54, 73
Newton, Isaac 15
NGO 39
nomads 36
Noordhoff (publishing house) xxi
North Africa 30, 122, 126, 174, 198, 201
Northwestern University 198
Norway 53
Nunan, David 31

official knowledge 13, 14
Ohev Sholom Congregation 192
Old Testament 127, 135
   see also Hebrew Bible
online syllabi 5, 49, 50, 52, 53, 54
OPEC 33
Orientalism 148
Oslo Peace Process 158
Ottoman xix, xx, 136, 137, 138, 146, 153, 154, 156, 166, 176
   Ottoman Empire 145, 146, 155
   Ottoman sultan 169
   Ottomans 137, 146, 191

Palestine and the Arab-Israeli Conflict, see Smith, Charles
Palestinian American Research Centre 198
Palestinian refugee 27, 40
Palme, Olaf 40
Pappé, Ilan xvi, xxiii, 53, 55, 124
   A History of Modern Palestine: One Land, Two Peoples xvi, 53
   The Israel/Palestine Question: A Reader 53
   The Making of the Arab-Israeli Conflict, 1947–51 53
Paris 172, 173, 193
Partition Plan 35
Passover 174
PDF 52, 68, 100
Peace Process 140

Pearson xxii, 13
Peki'in 175
Perry, Glenn 26
   Treatment of the Middle East in American High School Textbooks 26
Persians 142, 154, 157
Persson, Göran 40
Perth 190
PhD 5, 16, 19, 28, 31, 33, 35, 46, 184, 190, 191, 194, 195, 196, 198, 200
Philistines 136, 168, 186
PLO 29, 181, 194
Post 9/11 41, 140
post-Zionist 137, 194
power/knowledge 34
Prentice Hall 29, 140, 191
pre-Zionist era xx, 123, 127, 128, 131, 134, 138, 139, 149, 150, 152, 170, 175, 178, 180, 207, 208
Promised Land 153, 161, 164

qualitative (method) 16, 17, 18, 24, 33, 41
quantitative (method) 16, 24, 41
Qur'an (and Quran) 7, 143
   see also Koran

Rabi, Uzi xvii, 181, 183
Rabin, Yitzhak 41, 193, 199
Radcliffe College 191
Red Sea 161
Righteous Victims, *see* Morris, Benny
Rock, Marlene 30
Roman xx, 125, 131, 135, 136, 139, 142, 144, 147, 176, 207
Romans 36, 121, 124, 125, 126, 129, 135, 136, 142, 143, 152, 163, 172, 175, 178, 198, 205, 207
Ross, Dennis 197
Rousseau, Jean-Jacques 15
Rubin, Barry xv, 179, 193, 194–5, 200, 204, 206, 210, 211
   Israel: An Introduction 195
   Revolution Until Victory? The Politics and History of the PLO 195
   The Arab States and the Palestine Conflict 195
Rubin Report 195
Russian Jews 174

Sabra 184
Sachar, Abram Leon 196
Sachar, Howard 171, 173, 175, 195–6, 200, 204, 207, 208, 211
   A History of Israel 54, 102, 171–9, 195, 204, 209
   Egypt and Israel 196
   The Course of Modern Jewish History 195
Sadat, Anwar 41
Safed 175
Said, Edward xxii, 42
Samaria 142, 151, 162, 183
San Diego State University 196
San Francisco xxii, 25, 43, 218
Sand, Shlomo 36, 123, 124, 125, 126, 127, 128, 173
   mythhistory 132, 179
   The Invention of the Jewish People 124–8, 173
Saul (King) 135, 151, 181
Sa'adi 7
Scholars for Peace in the Middle East xxv, 192
schoolbook 7
Schultz, Joseph 191, 192
Second Temple 142, 143, 147
Second World War 15, 34, 140, 172
Seleucid 162
Semites 184
Sephardic Jews 29
Shakespeare 7
Sharett, Moshe 193
Sharon, Ariel 184
Shatilla 184
Shavuot 174
Shuker, Edwin xxi
Sinai 38, 194
Six Day War 27, 41, 183, 184
   see also 1967 Arab-Israeli War
Smith, Andrea L. 19
Smith, Charles xv, xvi, xvii, 132, 149, 181, 196–8, 200, 201, 204, 207, 209, 211
   Palestine and the Arab-Israeli Conflict xvi, 17, 54, 132–9, 149, 181, 204, 206, 207, 208, 209, 210
   'The Arab-Israeli Conflict' in *International Relations of the Middle East* 197

The Modern Middle East and North Africa: A History in Documents 196
'The United States and the 1967 War' in *The 1967 Arab-Israeli War: Origins and Consequences* 197
Smith, Morton 185
social sciences/studies 10, 15, 20, 28, 49, 213
Society for History Education 185
Solomon (King) 124, 128, 134, 135, 139, 141, 142, 143, 151, 157, 161, 162, 163, 181, 195
South Africa 15
Spain 127, 174
   see also Andalusia
Stand with Us xxv
Students for Academic Freedom xxv
Suez 41, 140
   Suez Canal 41, 191, 194
   Suez crisis 191
Sukkot 174
Sura 143
Susser, Asher xvii
Sweden 19, 34, 53
   Swedish 34, 35, 36, 39, 40
Switzerland 53
Syllabi 5
syllabus 9, 31, 32, 48, 50, 51, 52, 53, 57
Syllabus Design: Language Teaching: A Scheme for Teacher Education 31
Syllabus Finder 50, 51
symbolic capital 12
synagogue 175
syntax 17
Syria 136, 154, 155, 169

Teaching the Arab World 20, 28
Tel Aviv University xvi, xvii, 181, 193, 196
Temple Mount 143, 151
Temple of Jerusalem 175
Tennessee xxi
Tessler, Mark xv, xvi, xvii, 158, 167, 184, 198–9, 200, 201, 204, 206, 207, 208, 210, 211
   A History of the Israeli-Palestinian Conflict 16, 54, 158–71, 184, 199, 204

Area Studies and Social Science: Strategies for Understanding Middle East Politics 199
Democracy, War, and Peace in the Middle East 199
Israel, Egypt, and the Palestinians: From Camp David to Intifada 199
textbook (theory of) 7–15
   textbook (education's contribution) 12–13
   textbook as knowledge 14–15
   textbook (power's contribution) 11–12
   textbook production 13–14
   textbook (the significance) 9–10
   textbook (what is it?) 7–9
textbook analysis xviii, xxvi, 5, 15, 16, 17, 18, 24, 30, 32, 33, 42, 45, 46, 50, 131, 132, 133, 179, 180, 181, 185, 200, 204, 206, 210, 211
textbook analysis (methods of) 16–18
   comparative analysis 24
   content analysis 18, 17, 24, 25, 31, 41
   discourse analysis 17, 24
   latent analysis 17
   latitudinal 16, 18
   longitudinal 16
   narrative analysis 18, 131, 187, 205
   semiotic Analysis 17
textbook knowledge xxvi, 12, 34, 41, 47, 52, 204, 211, 212
textbook production 13
The Arab World 28
The Arab-Israeli Conflict 62, 66, 125, 140
The Board of Deputies of British Jewry xxi
The Cultural Landscape: An Introduction to Human Geography xxi
The Development of a Content Analysis Instrument for Analysing College-Level Textbooks Used in the United States to Teach About the Middle East 30
The History and Narrative Reader 189
The History Teacher 185
The Israel-Arab Reader xvii, 179–81, 193, 194, 204, 210
The Middle East: Conflict, Crisis and Change 1917–2012 xxi
The Netherlands xxi, 53

The Palestinian-Israeli Conflict, see Bunton, Martin
The Politics of Teaching Palestine to Americans 40
The Portrayal of the Middle East in School Textbooks from 1880 to the Present, see Morgan, Hani
The Structure of Historical Narratives and the Teaching of History 189
The Trouble with Textbooks: Distorting History and Religion xxii, 43
The Use and Abuse of History 188
Thursday's Child Has Far to Go, see Laqueur, Walter
Tobin, Gary xxii, 9, 12, 13, 43, 44, 45
Topolsky, Jeretz 189
Transjordan 146, 155
Traweek, Sharon 14
Treatment of the Middle East in American High School Textbooks, see Perry, Glenn
Turkish Studies Journal 195
Turks 28, 154
Turner, Caroline xxi
Twain, Mark 153
Tyre 151

UK Lawyers for Israel xxi
Umar ʿibn al-Khattāb 155
    Pact of ʿUmar 155
Understanding History: Britain in the Wider World, Roman Times-Present xxi
UNESCO 31
United Kingdom/UK 13, 50, 51, 54, 134, 140, 149, 158, 171, 179, 190, 194, 200, 211
United Nations 2, 27, 45
United States xv, xix, xxii, xxiii, xxiv, xxv, 10, 13, 15, 19, 24, 25, 26, 27, 30, 33, 40, 41, 48, 50, 51, 54, 127, 132, 134, 140, 149, 158, 171, 173, 174, 179, 190, 192, 193, 194, 195, 196, 198, 200, 211, 213
    US Declaration of Independence 15
    US universities 54, 76, 190, 196
    USS Liberty 198
University of Arizona 132, 196, 198
University of California, Davis xxiii

University of California, Santa Barbara 190
University of Cambridge 194
University of Chicago 193
University of Exeter xv, xxiii
University of Gothenburg 33
University of Michigan 158, 196, 198, 199
University of Missouri, Kansas City 140, 190, 191
University of New South Wales 140, 190
University of Tunis 198
University of Virginia 196
University of Wisconsin-Milwaukee 198

Valorebooks 48
Van de Ven, Susan Elizabeth Kerr 16, 19, 28
Vintage Books 148
Virginia 28
Virginia Commonwealth University 196
Virginia Military Institute 196

Wailing Wall 175
    see also Western Wall
Walls, Michael 19, 34, 35, 36, 37, 38, 39, 40
    Framing Conflict and War in Lower Secondary School Books: Israel and Palestine 34
    Framing the Israel/ Palestine Conflict in Swedish History School Textbooks 33
Washington 28, 194, 195
Wayne State University 196
Web of Knowledge 48
Weizmann, Chaim 193
West Bank xx, 38, 39
Western academia xxii, xxiii, xxvii, 2, 6, 50, 132, 179, 203, 204, 206, 211, 213, 214
Western Civilization 185, 186
Western countries xxii, 1, 2, 24, 25, 42, 47, 48, 50, 51, 53, 54, 55, 57, 171, 174, 185, 205, 213
Western democracies, 2, 203
Western societies 2, 203, 204
Western universities 25, 5, 47, 50, 141, 149, 204

Western Wall 143, 175
  see also Wailing Wall
White, H.V. 188
White, Scott (Rabbi) 192
White Paper 37
Widely Adopted History Textbooks 3
Widely Adopted Textbooks 33
Williams, Raymond 13
Williams College 196
Women Concerned about the Middle East 28

Yahweh 136
Ybarra, Dennis R. xxii, 43
Yiddish 127
Yishuv 88, 172, 177

Zadok Kahn 151
Zerubabel's temple 151
Zion 121, 127, 136, 137, 144, 145, 152, 166, 170, 173, 174, 176, 180, 207
Zionist terrorism 45

Printed in Great Britain
by Amazon